CW00661198

Advising
Ultra-Affluent Clients
and Family Offices

Founded in 1807, John Wiley & Sons is the oldest independent publishing company in the United States. With offices in North America, Europe, Australia, and Asia, Wiley is globally committed to developing and marketing print and electronic products and services for our customers' professional and personal knowledge and understanding.

The Wiley Finance series contains books written specifically for finance and investment professionals as well as sophisticated individual investors and their financial advisers. Book topics range from portfolio management to e-commerce, risk management, financial engineering, valuation, and financial instrument analysis, as well as much more.

For a list of available titles, visit our web site at www.WileyFinance.com.

Advising Ultra-Affluent Clients and Family Offices

MICHAEL M. POMPIAN

WILEY

John Wiley & Sons, Inc.

Published by John Wiley & Sons, Inc., Hoboken, New Jersey.
Published simultaneously in Canada.

For general information on our other products and services or for technical support, please contact our Customer Care Department within the United States at (800) 762-2974, outside the United States at (317) 572-3993 or fax (317) 572-4002.

Wiley also publishes its books in a variety of electronic formats. Some content that appears in print may not be available in electronic books. For more information about Wiley products, visit our web site at www.wiley.com.

Library of Congress Cataloging-in-Publication Data:

Pompian, Michael M., 1963–
  Advising ultra-affluent clients and family offices / Michael M. Pompian.
     p. cm.
  Includes bibliographical references and index.
  ISBN 978-0-470-28231-1 (cloth)
  1. Rich people. 2. Investments–Decision making. I. Title.
  HT635.P66 2009
  305.5′234–dc22

                                                      2008051561

Printed in the United States of America

10 9 8 7 6 5 4 3 2 1

*To all professional advisers
who make a difference in the lives of their clients*

Contents

Foreword   xiii

Preface   xv

Acknowledgments   xvii

PART ONE

Introduction to Advising Ultra-Affluent Clients and Family Offices   1

CHAPTER 1
Who Are the Ultra-Affluent?   3

Defining the Ultra-Affluent   5
Quantifying Ultra-Affluence Among Total Global Wealth   10
Looking to the Future   11
A World of Opportunities for Advisers   17

CHAPTER 2
Understanding the Mindset of the Ultra-Affluent Client   19

Why Advising the Ultra-Affluent is Different   20
What Ultra-Affluent Clients Value in an Adviser   23
Building Relationships by Asking Questions and
    Listening to the Answers   29
Matching Client with Adviser   32
Consultant Questionnaire   33
Conclusion   37

CHAPTER 3
Wealth Attitudes, Aspirations, and Investor Behavior of
Ultra-Affluent Clients   39

Family Aspirations   40
Wealth Attitudes of Ultra-Affluent Clients   42

Where Psychology Meets Finance   47
Investor Biases   48
Conclusion   60

CHAPTER 4
Noninvestment Best Practices   **61**

The Challenges Associated with Wealth   61
Guidelines for Sustaining Multigenerational Wealth   63
Conclusion   71

PART TWO
Investment Strategies for Ultra-Affluent Clients and Family Offices   **73**

CHAPTER 5
Practices of the Best Investment Organizations   **75**

Differences between Endowments and Private Investors   76
Investment Committees   77
Investment Policy Statements   82
Key Considerations for Portfolio Oversight   88
Conclusion   93

CHAPTER 6
**Asset Allocation Considerations for Ultra-Affluent Clients
and Family Offices**   **95**

What Is Asset Allocation?   96
The Importance of Assumptions in the Asset Allocation
    Selection Process   97
The Importance of Asset Allocation   99
Considerations in Asset Allocation for Individual Investors 100

CHAPTER 7
Domestic and International Equity   **111**

Introduction to U.S. and International Equity Securities   112
The Five-Step Equity Strategy Process   115

CHAPTER 8
Domestic and International Bonds   **135**

Introduction to Bonds   137
Descriptions of Bond Asset Classes   141

CHAPTER 9
Private Equity **159**

What Is Private Equity and How Does It Work? 162
Three Primary Types of Private Equity Investments 166
Creating a Customized Private Equity Program 172

CHAPTER 10
Hedge Funds **179**

What Is a Hedge Fund? 180
Hedge Fund Investing by UACs and Family Offices 185
A History of Hedge Funds 187
The Legal Environment of Hedge Funds 189
Hedge Fund Strategies 191
Manager Selection 202

CHAPTER 11
Real Assets **203**

The Portfolio Benefits of Real Assets 204
Real Estate: A Long-Term Inflation Hedge 205
Natural Resources 210

PART THREE

**Multigenerational Considerations for Ultra-Affluent
Clients and Family Offices** **223**

CHAPTER 12
Selecting an Adviser **225**

Trust: The Key Ingredient 226
How UACs Select an Adviser 228
Questions for Prospective Advisers 234
Conclusion 237

CHAPTER 13
Selecting a Custodian and Investment Vehicle Structure **239**

Custodial Services 239
Investment Vehicle Structure 250
Conclusion 257

CHAPTER 14
Considerations for Creating a Family Office   **259**

What is a Family Office?   261
Challenges of Wealth   262
Practical Reasons to Create a Family Office   264
Challenges of Running a Family Office   265
Services Provided by a Family Office   267
Administrative Considerations for Establishing a
   Family Office   268
Considerations for Establishing a Private Trust Company   274
Conclusion   277

CHAPTER 15
Wealth Transfer Planning   **279**

Estate Planning Basics   282
Conclusion   295

PART FOUR
Special Topics for Ultra-Affluent Clients and Family Offices   **297**

CHAPTER 16
Concentrated Equity Risk Management   **299**

What Constitutes a Concentrated Equity Position?   300
Concentrated Stock Risk Minimization Strategies   304
Conclusion   315

CHAPTER 17
Family Governance   **317**

Generational Division   318
Family Governance: An Essential Part of Successful
   Wealth Transfer   319
The Incredible Family   320
Policies   326
Stages of Development   327
Conclusion   328

CHAPTER 18
Risk Management and Asset Protection   **331**

Family Office Risk Management   332

Individual Family Member Risk Management 337
Legal Asset Protection 341
Conclusion 344

CHAPTER 19
Philanthropy **345**

Philanthropic Strategy Development through Asking
Questions 347
Mission Statement 348
Implementation of Philanthropic Strategy 349
Philanthropic Investing 352
Best Practices of Giving Large Gifts to Colleges and
Universities 355
Appendix: The Next Generation: Redefining the
Philanthropic Landscape 358

CHAPTER 20
Multigenerational Asset Allocation Strategies **367**

Different Asset Allocations for Different Generations 369
Single Allocation for an Entire Family 370
Customized Asset Allocation by Generation or Family Unit 371
Asset Allocation Targeting 374
The Behavioral Finance Approach to Asset Allocation 374
Conclusion 375

Notes **377**

Index **387**

Foreword

The global financial system is suffering from historic stress and the cracks are showing. This period of time will be marked as the tipping point for the wealth management industry even though the actual trend has been quietly forming for years.

At the center of the trend is a reevaluation of trust and a desire on the part of clients to understand the essential nature of their financial service providers—and to specifically understand the provider's core competencies and how they fit into the client's overall wealth management program. In addition to this new awareness of the business models of financial service providers, is recognition of the interplay between trust, incentives, and economic behavior.

I have worked with ultra-affluent clients and family offices for many years, first as an adviser for the last seven years as the Managing Partner of a private association of family offices, and recently as the founder of a technology platform for wealth management content. Through these experiences, I have had the great luxury of seeing a sort-of collective consciousness of ultra-affluent families and their advisors. Family offices in particular, due to their unique makeup—essentially serving as private investment holding companies—are often leading indicators of future trends. Due to their financial resources, access to top advisers, and ability to take action quickly, family offices can lead the way towards activities that become more broadly adopted by clients and financial service providers at all levels of the wealth spectrum.

And one of the most powerful trends underway within the family office and ultra-affluent market is the separation of advice from recordkeeping and investment products. In the standard approach, clients are offered a bundled solution whereby their wealth manager (or private bank, broker, investment adviser, etc.) offers consolidated recordkeeping and custody, advice, and proprietary investment products—or in some cases, investment products from outside partners where revenue sharing is common.

Now the wealthiest clients obtain advice from independent advisers and consultants who help assemble best-in-class investment products from a global spectrum of providers, and then aggregate and track results through dedicated master custodians. Thus, successful advisors to ultra-affluent families not only need demonstrated domain expertise, but a transparent business model, and a willingness and ability to cooperate with multiple external advisers and providers.

Advising Ultra-Affluent Clients and Family Offices is the first comprehensive guidebook that succinctly lays out the separate components or building blocks for structuring a sophisticated wealth management solution. But just as important as assembling the right financial components, is understanding the human side of the equation. This is why Michael Pompian provides such a unique perspective in *Advising Ultra-Affluent Clients and Family Offices*. Michael is the rare financial writer who is at once a wealth management practitioner at the top of the industry he writes about, as well as a researcher and writer on human economic behavior. The subject of his first book, *Behavioral Finance and Wealth Management*, is evidence of Michael's deep understanding of the human factors that greatly influence financial outcomes.

Essentially all ultra-affluent clients are trying to ensure three things: long term growth of capital with limited volatility, predictable cash flows from interest, dividends, rents, royalties, and capital gains, and minimal friction from taxes, fees, and losses. The wealth holder also wants to understand what they own, how they are doing, and what they should be doing in the future—essentially requiring a balance sheet, income statements, and strategic plan—they also want this information and advice *integrated and in real time*. So planning, investing, and measuring become a continuous process. This is very hard to do. Michael Pompian articulates a clear and insightful roadmap which outlines the process, components, and human factors needed to create a sustainable world-class wealth management program—both advisers and wealth owners would be wise follow Michael's lead.

STEPHEN MARTIROS
Managing Partner, CCC Alliance
Founder, Summitas

Preface

Despite the downdraft in the markets that began in 2008, an explosion in wealth has occurred in the last 25 years. Many ultra-affluent individuals and family offices need significant help preserving and growing their wealth. Entrepreneurs are often very good at creating wealth, but they are often not as skillful or interested in managing their wealth. Moreover, much of the wealth in the world will change hands over the next 25 years from more experienced family members to newer generations that may not be as focused on wealth management as those generations that created it. Thus, there is a significant opportunity to advise ultra-affluent clients (UACs) and family offices now and well into the future. I have a personal stake in this: I am an adviser to UACs and family offices myself, having been in the financial advisory business going on two decades.

I review in this book key topics that are crucial to building the skills necessary to effectively advising UACs, especially soft issues such as family dynamics, philanthropy, and family governance. What advisers to this client segment need to realize is that these soft issues are taking an equal and sometimes greater place in some cases than investments in the work that advisers do with their clients. This is especially true with third- and fourth-generation family members; at this stage, investing in human capital (i.e., investing in the development and wellbeing of family members) is often more critical to the long-term health of the family than making great financial investments. Wealth preservation across multiple generations is a question, therefore, of productive human behavior. If proper development of family members is not done, wealthy families can succumb to the dreaded "shirtsleeves to shirtsleeves in three generations" curse. At the same time, and especially in the current environment, advisers to UACs also need to have solid investment knowledge, and there are a number of chapters dedicated to investments such as real assets, hedge funds, and private equity that UACs are broadly investing in.

There are four parts to the book. Part One begins with an introduction to advising UACs. This includes a discussion of what is considered ultra-affluent and understanding the mindset of UACs—their attitudes, aspirations, and investor behavior. In Part Two, I discuss investment strategies for UAC, which covers best practices of the top investment organizations and a review of many of the alternative investments that UACs invest in. Part Three delves in to key aspects of advising multigenerational families, including selecting an adviser, considerations for creating a family office, and selecting an investment vehicle structure. Part Four covers special topics in advising UACs that include wealth transfer, family governance, equity risk management, asset protection, creating a philanthropic strategy, and developing a multigenerational asset allocation strategy. A common theme running throughout the book is the idea that UAC advisors need not be expert in all areas of wealth management. You simply cannot do it all yourself. Bringing in experts to help you in critical areas, as I have done in many places in this book, is critical for success once you have uncovered an issue that goes beyond your level of knowledge or area of expertise.

You will notice that there is little in the book about taxes. Although taxes are a critical subject when it comes to advising UACs, there are entire books devoted to this subject that advisers should read and keep handy. I recommend Doug Rogers's book, *Tax-Aware Investment Management: The Essential Guide,* published by Bloomberg. Another subject not covered in the book is transitioning from a business-oriented family to a financial family. On this subject, I recommend a piece published by Family Office Exchange in Chicago titled *Managing Family Wealth Separately from the Family Business.* Please feel free to email me with any comments or questions: mpompian@haifc.com.

Acknowledgments

I would like to acknowledge all the people who made this book possible. The list is long, so I hope to not leave anyone out. First, I thank my clients, whom I have the pleasure and responsibility to serve every day. They have been the source of the thinking behind many parts of this volume, and without the experience I have gained in serving them, it would not have been possible to write the book. Second, I would like to thank all my colleagues at Hammond Associates who help me to serve our private wealth clients and especially those who helped review the book. The firm contributed greatly with investment research and keen topical insights; there are simply too many people to thank at the firm to single anyone out. I also thank all of the investment managers with whom we work. Special thanks to Hedge Fund Research, Campden Research in London, and Pertrac for their invaluable help in providing data and researching investment themes for the book.

I would also like to thank all these great people: John Benevides, David Lincoln, and Angel Webb at Family Office Exchange (FOX); Charlotte Beyer at the Institute for Private Investors; Stephen Martiros at CCC Alliance and Summitas; Raffi Amit at the Wharton Global Family Alliance; Lisa Gray at Graymatter Strategies who contributed to Chapters 3 and 18; David Zell and Joel Shapiro at Timbervest who contributed to Chapter 11; Jean Brunel at Brunel Associates who provided key advice and guidance; Paul Perez at Northern Trust for his review of the entire manuscript; Joe Grunfeld at Merrill Lynch/Bank of America for his key insights; Brad Fisher at Springcreek Advisors who contributed to Chapter 19; Michael Lynch et al. at Twenty-First Securities who contributed to Chapter 16; Marcy Hall at Hub International who contributed to Chapter 18; and Dan Rubin at Moses & Singer who contributed to Chapter 18.

In addition, there are people at numerous firms across the country who have helped elevate the investment consulting industry as a whole and challenged me to be a better advisor. These firms include Cambridge Associates, Greycourt, CTC Consulting, and many more. I thank members of the New York Society of Security Analysts (NYSSA) and the CFA Institute who have been invaluable friends and colleagues in my career. I also thank conference organizers such as NMS Management, Financial Research Associates (FRA), and Opal, who have worked to provide venues for idea exchanges in the ultra-affluent and family office space.

Last but not least, I thank my family for supporting me in my endeavors; much of what I do day in and day out is with them in mind.

Advising Ultra-Affluent Clients and Family Offices

Introduction to Advising Ultra-Affluent Clients and Family Offices

CHAPTER 1

Who Are the Ultra-Affluent?

I don't believe in a law to prevent a man from getting rich;
it would do more harm than good.

—Abraham Lincoln

Despite the downdraft in the financial markets that began in 2008, which has dealt a blow to the portfolios of many ultra-affluent clients, an explosion in wealth has occurred in the world in the last 25 years. Global equity markets have performed exceptionally well since the recession of the early 1980s, albeit with periods of volatility like the one we have seen recently, and that performance has created large numbers of ultra-affluent individuals and families across the globe. In addition, a flood of money into private equity over that time has created valuable new companies and helped existing companies grow to become even more valuable. For advisers, this activity has created a wide and vast pool of potential clients who need help on a variety of fronts. What an exciting time to be in the financial advisory business.

Seldom is opportunity without challenge. The complexities of managing wealth have never been greater. Advisers to wealthy families have had to improve their skills in order to serve their clients. Family members who are involved in managing their wealth have needed to educate themselves on topics that go well beyond investment management. There are multiple layers of activities to manage simultaneously. Ultra-affluent clients and family offices are now acting like institutions, starting with governance policies that guide the activities of the family. Figure 1.1 shows the integrated complexities advisers and families alike face.

If an adviser considers himself qualified to advise ultra-affluent clients (hereafter UACs), he needs to have a deep and broad skill set. As you will learn throughout this book, managing wealth is about developing a

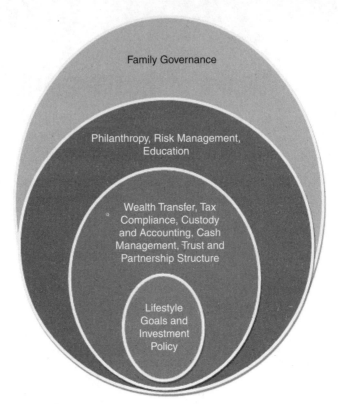

FIGURE 1.1   Multilayered Complexities of Managing Wealth

process, and only those advisers who understand both key investment and noninvestment issues—and know that they can't do it all themselves—will succeed. Advisers with the skill sets to manage vast wealth *properly* and without conflicts will be the advisers of choice in the future. But fret not! This chapter is intended to get you fired up! If you are reading this book, you are preparing yourself to serve clients in a dynamic segment of the financial services industry. Serving ultra-affluent clients and family offices is a fantastic business opportunity with lots of upside potential.

Many financial families, particularly those not involved in running a business day-to-day, are becoming more sophisticated in their understanding of investment and noninvestment issues, and are fostering new attitudes and perspectives that challenge advisers to be at their best. These clients from around the world are in command of the language they need so they can decipher complex wealth management concepts. This is partly driven by the proliferation of financial and nonfinancial news, data, and analyses available. This information is provided not only by public news agencies but also through UAC networking groups, by fund managers, and by sophisticated legal and tax professionals who target UACs directly. In the process of selling services to potential clients, they also provide education about sophisticated strategies. The result is that ultra-affluent clients are sometimes better informed than the people who pretend to have the skills to advise them! Clearly, this is not a good situation to be in if you are holding yourself out as an adviser to UACs.

Advising ultra-affluent clients is about much more than getting an extra 20 basis points return on a portfolio or creating the most efficient estate plan. It's equally—or potentially even more—about soft issues such as family governance and philanthropy. These issues are taking an equal footing with investment issues for today's UACs. Advisers with the ability to bring the client a wide array of resources that serve the wide variety of needs will be successful. This book can help not only advisers wishing to take their advisory practice to the next level, but also UACs wishing to broaden their knowledge of key issues they face when managing their own wealth and dealing with the advisers who serve them. Before we jump into advisory topics, it's important that we define what we mean by a UAC. There are a number of ways to potentially define this type of client, and we need to have a common understanding of the types of clients that can benefit from the broad range of topics I cover in this book.

DEFINING THE ULTRA-AFFLUENT

If you ask 20 advisers of wealthy clients how they define ultra-affluent, you will likely get 20 different answers to the question. For the purpose of this book, however, it is important that we put some parameters around what we are to consider *ultra-affluent* as distinguished from *mass-affluent,* or what I call *intermediate-affluent*. There are numerous factors that could be considered to define ultra-affluent, which I discuss in the next section. But first, let's establish a baseline definition.

In researching various definitions of ultra-affluent, I found that PricewaterhouseCoopers's (PWC) categorization of affluent investors is as good as any that I've seen; it will be modified somewhat, however, for our purposes. Figure 1.2 shows five categories of affluent individuals, along with three definitions that are used throughout the book. The five PWC categories are: Affluent ($100,000 to $500,000); Wealthy ($500,000 to $1 million) High Net Worth ($1 million to $5 million); Very High Net Worth ($5 million to $50 million) and Ultra High Net Worth ($50 million and more).[1] Although I

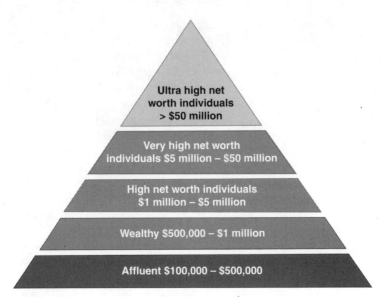

FIGURE 1.2   Categories of Affluent Investors
Source: PricewaterhouseCoopers.

do think this is an excellent breakdown, I prefer to further simplify these categories into these three: mass-affluent (MA), intermediate-affluent (IA), and ultra-affluent (UA). MA describes individuals with $100,000 to $5 million; IA, $5 million to $50 million; and UA, $50 million and more. As a general rule, for the purpose of this book, I regard a client with $50 million and more to be UA. But that definition may dip below $50 million for some conceptual applications and rise above $50 million for others. Regarding family offices, and the levels of wealth associated with them, please see Chapter 14.

You may be asking, "Why $50 million?" There are numerous factors that could be considered to define ultra-affluent. Three key factors are discussed next: complexity of needs, investment access, and service model.

Complexity of Needs

Perhaps the most intuitive definition of ultra-affluent has to do with the complexity of the needs of the client rather than an absolute dollar amount. UACs have complicated lives, and advisers who work with these types of clients must be aware of a vast array of issues, many of which are serviced by specialists (internal or external to the advisers' firms) such as CPAs, attorneys, philanthropy advisers, and so on. Figure 1.3 shows the complex needs of the UAC.

FIGURE 1.3 Needs of Ultra-Affluent Clients

Needs such as tax compliance, philanthropy, and investments, among others, are typically handled by a team of professionals. These professionals must work together, either across different firms or within the same firm, to service the client. MA or IA clients may not need or be willing to pay for services that are demanded by UACs—but some IA clients may have these complex needs while other UACs may not. Table 1.1 shows the types of services demanded by UACs compared to those that may be demanded by MA and IA clients.

Investment Access

In my daily work providing investment consulting services to UACs and family offices, my definition of ultra-affluence is actually higher than $50 million. I consider UACs to be those who have $100 million or more. Because the primary service my firm offers is investment advice, this definition has more to do with the type of investment program the client can undertake than an absolute wealth level or the complexity of the family's needs. For example, when considering alternative investments generally, and hedge funds, private equity, and private real assets in particular, I consider a client to be UA if she has the ability to directly invest in these funds or through the highest quality fund of funds. Naturally, this dollar amount is open to a significant amount

TABLE 1.1 Services Demanded across the Spectrum of Affluent Clients

Type of Service	Mass-Affluent	Intermediate-Affluent	Ultra-Affluent
Investment Advice Providers	Self-directed, brokerage, banks and financial planners	Private banks and multifamily offices (MFOs)	Investment consultants, multi- and single-family offices (SFOs)
Philanthropy	None or commingled vehicle	Commingled or family foundation	Professional philanthropy
Tax Preparation	Self or CPA	CPA or integrated with investment provider	MFO, SFO, or sophisticated CPA firm
Investment Access	Modest	Good	Great
Life Insurance	Local agent or broker	Higher-end provider integrated with estate plan	Intergenerational insurance planning by many specialists
Estate Planning	Local attorney	Regional or national firm	Integrated insurance, investments and tax plan by many specialists
Lifestyle/Concierge Services	None	Modest	Extensive

of debate. Yes, there are some investors who have $50 million or $75 million and are well-connected enough in the investment world that accessing the best managers at lower minimums is not an issue. And yes, there are some who might argue that $100 million is too low because the best managers in the world require a minimum of $5 million—and how could a proper portfolio be created with one or more managers taking up five percent of the total portfolio? In my experience, creating an outstanding portfolio of alternative and traditional managers is certainly doable with $100 million.*

Nonetheless, investors with $25 million to $50 million have substantial buying power and could in some circles be considered UA.

---

*It should also be noted that clients of my firm have the ability to invest in volume, as we gain access to top managers at reduced minimums by placing large sums with the managers we work with. Any client with $100 million has the ability to hire a consulting firm like mine.

Service Model

As already mentioned, UACs have more complex needs than MA clients. They must, therefore, be serviced differently. Generally speaking, as wealth level increases, the complexity of needs increases. As an MA client passes through the stages of the investor life cycle, he or she can usually be serviced by the same firm or even the same individual adviser throughout all of these stages. For example, as a client moves from the initial phases of accumulation, to managing wealth, to wealth planning, to wealth transfer, a single source such as a full-service private bank may be sufficient.

As clients move into intermediate wealth, they may find commercial family offices to be their best options. A commercial family office is usually a large investment firm that offers a high level of personal assistance and a wide offering of services such as financial, estate and tax planning, asset allocation, and manager selection. It may offer its own products, however, and may not provide some services of the traditional family office like bill paying, financial reporting, and tax compliance. The UAC with $50 million or more typically has needs beyond what can be delivered by a full-service private banking firm or commercial family office. Figure 1.4 shows the complexity of needs as wealth level increases.

A multifamily office (MFO) or single-family office (SFO) is generally the best option for UACs. The MFO and SFO typically provide objective advice (that is, they only receive fees from clients and not from investment managers) and can service all of the intergenerational needs I have already

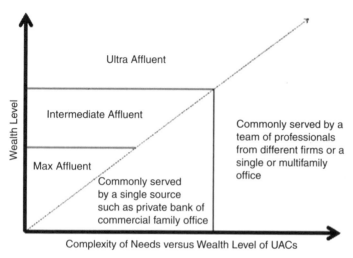

FIGURE 1.4 Complexity of Needs versus Wealth Level of UACs

touched on. I review in great detail later in the book the services that a family office offers and what level of wealth is appropriate for creating a family office. For now, I have established a baseline definition of the UAC: A $50 million client with complex, intergenerational wealth management needs. So now that you have this definition, I can turn to some numbers and trends involving UACs. As you will see, the UA market is growing, and those advisers who can service these clients are positioned well for the future.

QUANTIFYING ULTRA-AFFLUENCE AMONG TOTAL GLOBAL WEALTH

Although the number of UACs in the world is debatable, one thing is clear: the number is growing. Sources of information about the number of UACs are limited because there is no central database of ultra-wealthy households like there is for other classes of investors such as colleges, foundations, or pension funds. There is one widely accepted source, however, from which we can get some idea of the number of UACs worldwide: the annual Capgemini/Merrill Lynch survey. Although this survey is focused mainly on MA clients with five million dollars or less in net worth, there is a good amount of analysis done on UACs. The cutoff for UA in this survey is $30 million. Granted, this number is smaller than the $50 million figure I am using, but you can still gain some good insight into UAC trends from these data.

Figure 1.5 shows the number of Capgemini/Merrill Lynch–defined Ultra-High Net Worth (UHNW) individuals in the world. In the 2006 survey, the latest information at the time this book was written, the number of UNHW individuals, or people with net assets of at least $30 million, was 94,970 worldwide. This number had risen by 11.3 percent since 2005 and the group's aggregate wealth increased 16.8 percent to $13.1 trillion. Of these individuals, nearly 50 percent are in North America—and although the survey doesn't break down the numbers by country, it may fairly be concluded that the vast majority of the 40,000 or more North American UACs are in the United States.[2] Are you surprised by that number? Consider this: Even if all 40,000 of those families had only $30 million each, that's an aggregate amount of $1.2 trillion, which is approximately the gross domestic product of Spain![3]

Perhaps the most exciting part of the financial advisory business at the upper end of the wealth scale is the sheer volume of clients that are available to be serviced—not only now but into the future.

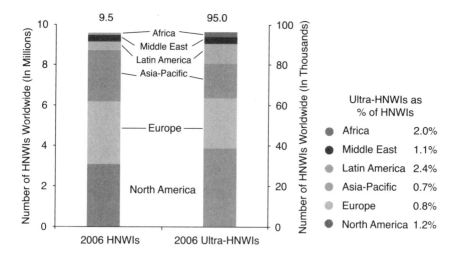

Note: Ultra-HNWI is defined as an individual with more than US$30 million in financial assets

FIGURE 1.5   Number of Ultra-Affluent Clients Worldwide as of 2006
Source: © 2007, Merrill Lynch and Capgemini. All rights reserved.

LOOKING TO THE FUTURE

There are several macroeconomic trends in place that point to a robust market for those who serve UACs globally, both in developed markets and developing countries. I next discuss two major trends: wealth accumulation in developing countries, and aging business ownership in developed countries.

Wealth Accumulation in Developing Markets

Wealth creation is moving beyond developed markets and slowly but surely seeping into developing markets. This trend is expected to increase rapidly as we move into the twenty-first century. Jeremy Siegel, of the Wharton School of Business, estimates that by 2050 developing countries should account for 75 percent of the world's gross domestic product (GDP), up from 25 percent today. "The population of India and China, among the countries with the fastest economic growth, will be eight times that of the U.S. Those huge populations will make the products that the U.S. will stop producing, and consume those that the U.S. will continue to provide."[4]

This growth in developing countries will fuel a boom in wealth creation. Developing countries today are creating large numbers of millionaires and UA individuals at a much faster rate than developed countries. Although the number of UACs worldwide is dominated by North America (especially the United States) and Europe, nearly 40 percent of UACs are outside these two geographies.[5] In Figure 1.5, Capgemini shows the percentages of UACs in 2007. Note that the developing countries had much higher growth rates of UACs compared to the United States and Europe.

Asia and the BRIC Countries   As shown in Figure 1.6, the number of millionaires in the world jumped significantly between 2004 and 2006, led by growth in emerging markets like Brazil, Russia, India, and China (BRIC). The BRIC nations are playing increasingly important roles in the global economy, as demonstrated by the 53 percent increase in the MSCI's BRIC Index in 2006. Two of these four countries made their way onto the list of the 10 fastest-growing High Net Worth Individual (HNWI) populations in 2006.[6] GDP in China, for example, has grown by an average of about nine percent per year for the past decade.[7] China's HNWI population grew by almost eight percent in 2006.[8] Singapore and India are seeing high growth in the number of millionaires as well. Japan, despite being home to the second-largest HNWI population in the world, has showed sluggish growth for many years; wealth is not being dramatically created there.[9]

Russia's market capitalization has accelerated since the beginning of 2000, on the heels of IPOs and the liberalization of the country's banking sector.[10] Shares of Russian banks have led the way to wealth creation. Brazil's commodity-based economy has also created significant wealth. In 2006, the total number of HNWIs in Brazil increased by 10.1 percent. India continued its strong expansion, with real GDP growth of 8.8 percent in 2006, and a HNWI population increase of 20.5 percent in 2006.[11]

Latin America, the Middle East, and Africa   Latin America continues to add to its HNWI population, with Argentina, Brazil, Peru, and Chile leading the way. Real GDP is healthy, reflecting China's growing demand for local commodities as well as its mounting foreign direct investments in the region. Latin America's HNWI population is growing faster than the global average; in 2006, it expanded by 10.2 percent, up from 9.7 percent in 2005.

The Middle East benefits from high oil prices and developed nations' heavy dependence on fossil fuels, creating staggering amounts of wealth. The Gulf Cooperation Council (GCC) countries (Bahrain, Kuwait, Oman,

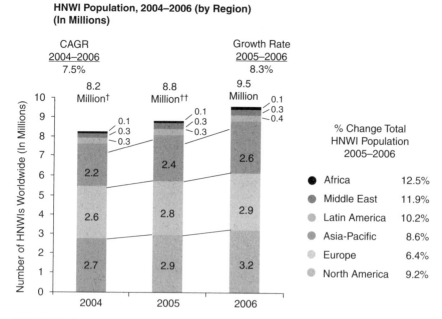

FIGURE 1.6 Growth Trends among Global High Net Worth Individuals
Source: © 2007, Merrill Lynch and Capgemini. All rights reserved.

Qatar, Saudi Arabia, and the United Arab Emirates) continue to drive wealth creation throughout the region.[12] The following excerpt, taken from the Capgemini/Merrill Lynch Global Wealth Report, discusses Africa and Latin America.

> On the back of high commodity prices worldwide, Africa's real GDP rose 5.1 percent in 2006. This surge in turn led to increased interest in foreign direct investment, particularly in the mining and exploration sectors. Much of this interest has centered on South Africa and its gold-mining activities. China has been an active player in Africa, as in Latin America, investing heavily in various sectors and showing particular interest in mining.[13] Taken together, these factors bolstered the continent's HNWI population, helping it grow by 12.5 percent in 2006, and increasing its wealth by 14.0 percent.[14]

For those advisers with a global scope, there are ample business opportunities. Figure 1.7 summarizes growth in HNWI populations.

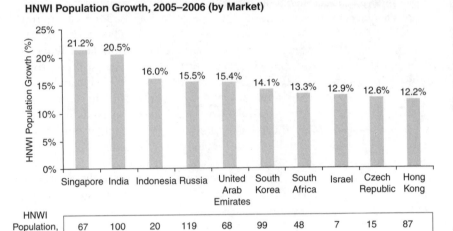

FIGURE 1.7 Highest Growth Rates in HNWI Population Globally

Source: © 2007, Merrill Lynch and Capgemini. All rights reserved.

Business Transition in Developed Markets

During the next two decades, trillions of dollars in wealth in established private businesses are expected to change hands and become liquid in the developed world, particularly in the United States and Europe. With the number of private businesses at an all-time high and an increase in the number of aging business owners that are either passing away or planning to retire, a surplus of businesses will be up for sale or transition in the United States and Europe in the upcoming years. The implication of this trend is that the need for UA advisers will increase significantly in the coming years because the number of UACs is likely to double or even triple by 2020. Those advisers, who can adequately prepare themselves on both domestic and international fronts, will have a very strong business opportunity to capitalize on in the future.

United States Given current trends, the demand for UA advisers will remain very strong in the United States. Why? Steady growth in private business in the United States over the past several decades is going to have a significant impact on the amount of private business wealth available to be transferred or sold in the next decade. Most of the private businesses started in the 1980s and early 1990s are owned by people 50 years old and older.[15] Just as the Baby Boomer demographic bulge threatens the solvency of the Social Security system as boomers approach retirement, the private business owner demographic bulge will seriously strain and possibly overwhelm the available supply of buyers and the support infrastructure for business transition and transactions as these owners approach retirement. Some industry observers have dubbed this activity the *Business Transition Tidal Wave*.[16]

More than four out of five U.S. family businesses are still controlled by their founders, and the coming wave of change will likely catch many business owners and their families off guard because they have not taken the time or made the effort to put ownership succession plans in place.[17] According to the Family Firm Institute, about 40 percent of family businesses expected the leadership of their companies to change by 2008; well over half of family businesses expect a leadership change by 2013.[18] This activity presents abundant opportunities for those in the right position to become trusted advisers by helping to bring resources to this problem. Ownership succession planning is the one subject that the family or the family's professional advisers should be thinking about.

As of 2007, the number of established private businesses in the United States was about 12 million, with an estimated value of $10 trillion. Not only has the number of private companies significantly increased, but the rate at which private business owners are transferring or selling their companies has increased as well. In 2001, 50,000 business owners in the United States planned to retire, while in 2005, 350,000 business owners planned to retire.[19] As shown in Figure 1.8, nearly 60 percent of business owners are 55 years or older and 30 percent of business owners are 65 years or older.

After a private business is created and has experienced a period of growth and success, the next natural stage in the business cycle is the transfer of ownership. When business owners retire, they face four possible courses: usually one third will sell the business to an external buyer, one third will sell the business to a family member, and one third will either sell the business to current employees or close the business.[20] This means that over two thirds of businesses will have new owners, either within the family or not.

For the purpose of this analysis, I am assuming that over the next 10 years, 25 percent of owners aged 55 to 65 will relinquish ownership and that 75 percent will do the same among owners aged 66 and older. With the estimates of CEO age, transition assumptions, and the prediction that two thirds of businesses will have new owners, we can roughly calculate that approximately $1.5 trillion dollars will change hands in the next 10 years due to current business owners currently aged 55 to 65. With regard to business owners aged 65 and older, approximately $2.25 trillion will change hands in the next 10 years. This totals $3.75 trillion that is estimated to be changing hands in the United States during the next 10 years. This estimation is generally consistent with some long-run forecasts on private business transition made by various researchers. The Austin Family Business program

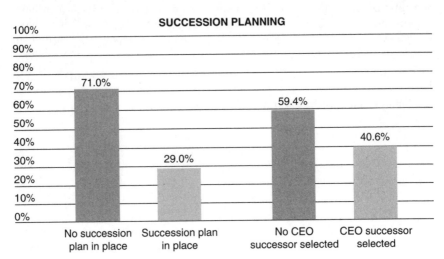

AGE OF MAJORITY SHAREHOLDER	
18 to 34	1.2%
35 to 44	8.9%
45 to 54	31.3%
55 to 64	28.5%
Older than 65	30.1%
Total	100%

FIGURE 1.8 Trends in Succession Plans for Private Family Businesses
Source: © Laird Norton Tyee Family Business Survey, 2007.

estimated in 1999 that $4.8 trillion of net worth will be transferred in the United States by 2020 and by 2040, $10.4 trillion will be transferred. By 2052, $41 trillion will be transferred.[21]

Europe Europe is also providing robust opportunities for UA advisers. In fact, a number of U.S.-based multifamily offices have recently announced plans for expansion in Europe.[22] The reasons for this opportunity in Europe are similar to those in the U.S. For example, the European Commission has reported two recent trends concerning European private businesses that point to accelerated business transitions in the next decade. First, entrepreneurs are more often relinquishing their ownership rights before the typical retirement age so they may enjoy those years earlier. Second, entrepreneurs are attempting to diversify their life experiences by staying with one venture for shorter periods of time, rather than staying in the same enterprise for their entire careers.[23]

TABLE 1.2 Estimated Value of Business Transition by 2017

Country	Value of Private Business (50% is private) – (GDP/2)	Percent that Will Transition	Value of Transition
Italy	$900 billion	40	$360 billion
Austria	$155 billion	23	$36 billion
United Kingdom	$1.2 trillion	33	$396 billion
France	$1.1 trillion	33 (approx)	$363 billion
Sweden	$185 billion	33 (approx)	$61 billion
Germany	$1.5 trillion	33 (approx)	$495 billion
Total			$1.4 trillion

Source: European Commission, *Transfer of Businesses—Continuity through a New Beginning,* MAP 2002 Project, Final Report, 2006.

In Europe, family businesses account for 55 to 65 percent of the Gross National Product and 70 percent of employment.[24] Expectations of ownership transfer over the next 10 years are increasing. In 2002, it was estimated that 610,000 small- and medium-sized companies in Europe would change ownership every year.[25] By 2006, the estimate increased to 690,000 ownership transfers.[26] These data imply that over 10 years, up to 6.9 million enterprises, representing one third of all European entrepreneurs, will be transferred or sold to new owners.[27]

Ownership transfer in Europe can be broken down into individual countries. Forty percent of all Italian companies, 23 percent of all Austrian companies, and one-third of all companies in the United Kingdom are expected to change hands in the next 10 years. Six hundred thousand French companies and 45,000 to 50,000 Swedish companies will transfer ownership in the next decade. In Germany, 354,000 companies' owners are expected to withdraw in the next five years.[28] In these countries alone, approximately $1.4 trillion will be transferred in the next 10 years as calculated in Table 1.2.

A WORLD OF OPPORTUNITIES FOR ADVISERS

Successful succession requires clear strategic planning. Although a massive ownership transfer is expected to occur, many business owners have not begun to prepare. In the United States, fewer than half of the owners who plan to retire in the next five years have selected successors. For those expecting to retire in the next 6 to 11 years, fewer than one third have selected successors.[29] A similar situation exists in Europe. One and a half million European owners plan to retire in the next decade, but many have not selected successors.[30]

One effect of this phenomenon will be the increase in demand for professionals with transition experience and wealth management expertise. Ownership transfer requires accountants, lawyers, valuation advisers, and insurance professionals. With these transitions comes liquid wealth—and with liquid wealth comes significant demand for investment advisers to manage this wealth. Although all professionals will profit from the increased demand, if the supply of these professionals is too low, their resources will be stretched and the quality of their work could potentially deteriorate. We need to prepare for the coming onslaught! With the Baby Boomers in the United States transitioning into retirement and the large European population aging, the next decade will be a turning point in the amount of private business wealth that will be transferred or sold.

CHAPTER 2

Understanding the Mindset of the Ultra-Affluent Client

The real source of wealth and capital in this new era is not material things ... it is the human mind, the human spirit, the human imagination, and our faith in the future.

—Steve Forbes

In my experience working with UACs, I have found that many clients know exactly what they are looking for from their advisers. This situation makes for a superb working relationship because each party knows their role. For example, some clients prefer to be the "CEO" of the portfolio and the adviser's job is to provide information and recommendations to make the best decisions. In other cases, some clients want to defer key decisions to their adviser—both parties know this and so the relationship works. Some clients, however, seek characteristics in their advisers that may not necessarily be in their best long-term interest. For instance, some UACs prefer to hire advisers who agree with all their decisions. For example, a client may insist that his adviser recommend a list of active equity managers as opposed to passive index funds. Upon hearing this, the adviser, knowing his role, proceeds to extol the virtues of active management even if the adviser believes that passive investing is better for the client based on the long-term investment horizon of the client. Often these same clients cannot accept the inevitable periods of underperformance that accompany the decision to use active equity managers, and may even blame their advisers for such a poor investment decision.

Still other clients prefer meek or even passive advisers. For instance, these advisers allow their clients to control the timing and selection of investments, even if their clients have no proven ability to make successful investment decisions. But these same clients can delay making investment decisions because they fear buying in at the wrong time, or make investment decisions for the wrong reasons—for example, investing with a manager because the two belong to the same country club or share the same circle of friends (one can look to the Madoff scandal that broke in 2008 to see the potential failures of not having a strong hand guiding the advisory process).

The key to a successful working relationship with UACs is to advise them by striking a balance between two key elements—flexibility and conviction. UAC advisers need to be flexible enough to adapt to the style of the client and their expectations, while at the same time have conviction in their beliefs about what is in the best long-term interest of the client. Understanding the mindset of the UAC is essential to being able to strike this balance, which we will explore in this chapter.

WHY ADVISING THE ULTRA-AFFLUENT IS DIFFERENT

UACs enjoy high-touch services, sophisticated planning, and access to the best investment managers available. Perhaps not so surprisingly, they have gotten used to such a high level of service that an adviser who offers plain-vanilla wealth management services (basic financial planning and traditional investments such as stocks, bonds, and cash) will find that she is not properly equipped. Many UACs, particularly those who are not involved in the day-to-day activities of operating a business, are much more knowledgeable than they used to be about sophisticated financial concepts and will not tolerate incoherent or opaque discussions. Differentiation among advisers is becoming more and more difficult and these challenges are demanding that traditional wealth advisers figure out new ways to add value in new and distinct ways. Before we discuss how advisers who desire to serve UACs should develop their approach, we need to discuss what many advisers serving MA and IA clients are doing that will not work for the UAC. I've made a few observations from working for an independent consulting firm serving UACs after having worked in several mass affluent firms. In short, this is what you should *not* do when advising the ultra-affluent.

Avoid Opaqueness

A common technique employed by some large wealth management firms serving mass-affluent clients is to give the client the impression that there are no fees associated with an account or part of an account. For example, in many individually managed bond accounts (i.e., municipal, government, or corporate) there are low or no account-level management fees. Unless the client looks carefully, he will not notice that the manager or broker actually takes a spread when buying or selling a bond or buys at the highest price (lowest yield) of the day. Because these spread fees often don't show up on the client statement, the client can get the impression that there are no fees, and some advisers choose not to delve in to the details of how this works. UACs are wise to this trick and they will not permit this or any other type of breach of transparency about their fees.

Don't Be Conflicted

Many mass-affluent firms offer a variety of investment choices to their clients through what they call an *open architecture* platform. However, open architecture is not exactly open in that many distributors of products (i.e., banks and brokerages) get paid by mutual fund and other investment management companies to sell their products. Distributors often place the highest-profit-margin products in front of the customer whenever they can. In addition to selling high-margin, nonproprietary products, many distributors also recommend a healthy portion of their own proprietary products to clients. The best advisers steer clear of these conflicts by not accepting money from anyone except the client, period. This way, the interests of the client are aligned with the interests of the adviser. The one exception to this rule is offering a pooled investment access vehicle (i.e., a fund of funds) of certain specialized investments such as hedge funds or private equity that are inaccessible to small clients, or offering convenience in the form of an investment vehicle with only one document to sign for multiple managers.

Maintain Relationship Consistency

Many large financial services organizations suffer from an ongoing disease: turnover-itis. This happens where there is a high turnover of employees involved in relationship management (also known as RMs). This may occur because an RM gets fed up with being a salesperson, gets a better offer elsewhere, relocates, or takes a different job in the organization. The key problem with RM turnover is that just as the client gets used to a relationship manager, the RM moves on to a different role and the client needs to get involved with a new person all over again. The UAC has little patience for this type of turmoil. Consistency of relationship is essential. UACs are hiring for the long run.

Leave the Transaction Model in the Past

Some mass-affluent firms choose a transaction model for doing business. That is, their financial advisers get paid on the basis of doing investment transactions (e.g., trades) with their clients, such as trading bonds or selling products with high commissions. Although this method worked well for decades throughout the twentieth century, it is inherently flawed because asset allocation, the primary driver of investment returns, is often ignored. Progressive firms, which encourage their advisers to adopt a consultative, asset allocation-based approach, are the firms whose advisers will be successful at serving UACs.

Make Sure You Are Right for the Job

A number of firms that serve mass-affluent clients, who haven't yet figured out the right service model, have the wrong people doing the wrong jobs while servicing the client relationship. For example, in certain firms the person who manages the client's money also serves as the RM. Paradoxically, the traits that make people good money managers often make them poor RMs because they are not thinking about serving the client, but about what is happening in the capital markets (which is what they should be thinking about when managing money!). A good relationship management system is one in which the RM remains with a client throughout the overall wealth management process and maintains knowledge of the client's holistic needs. At the same time, a team of specialists in such areas as estate planning, trust management, taxes, and so on support the relationship manager's efforts. UACs will not tolerate a skill set mismatch in their relationship managers.

Don't Think You Can Do It All

Very few firms at any level of client wealth excel in all areas of wealth management and can truly deliver a comprehensive in-house solution that is free from conflicts of interest. Yet, some firms position themselves as being capable of providing so-called best-of-breed services in all areas versus the alternative method of outsourcing these services to highly specialized people. UACs expect that the best advisers will rely on specialists, the best providers for whatever service is needed, rather than maintaining less-than-excellent service providers in-house.

Offer Top Quality Alternative Investments

Some firms claim to have top quality alternative investment access or capabilities when in reality their product selections are mediocre. One clear example of undifferentiated product capabilities is in the hedge fund of funds arena. In general, hedge funds that are on the platforms of large wire-house or bank product platforms have an inherent problem in their business. Mass-affluent investors, those investing $100,000 in a hedge fund product, often need liquidity. When these investors redeem, hedge fund of funds managers must go to their underlying managers for that liquidity. The problem is that the fund of fund managers will turn first to the managers that offer the best liquidity terms, rather than rebalancing across the entire portfolio of funds. Also, in general, the best hedge funds are turning away money rather than trying to raise assets in $100,000 increments. UACs will not take up with a firm that offers "me too" alternative investment products.

I cover in the next section best practices of working with UACs that are rooted in actual research from interviews with UACs.

WHAT ULTRA-AFFLUENT CLIENTS VALUE IN AN ADVISER

Now that we have an understanding of what we *shouldn't* do, let's talk about what we *should;* that is, what UACs value in an adviser. A good source of information on this subject is a survey done by the Institute for Private Investors (IPI) in the fall of 2004. IPI surveyed 78 of their 366 member investors (over 75 percent of IPI's members have greater than $50 million in assets under management) about what they value most in advisers. Figure 2.1 shows the results.

In short, UACs are turning to advisers who possess what I call the Four C's: Candor, Competence, Customization, and Comprehensiveness. Before I review each of them for you, a point of clarification is needed. A recent study of 500 mass-affluent clients done by the Wharton School at the University of Pennsylvania and State Street Global Advisors in June of 2006 showed that *trust* was the most important quality in a financial adviser—identical to the IPI's highest ranking quality. (Forty-eight percent had portfolios of less than $500,000, 20 percent had $500,000 to $999,000, 20 percent had $1 million to $5 million, and 6 percent had over $5 million.)[1]

It therefore follows by extension that many of the characteristics that UACs value in their advisers would naturally be valued by mass-affluent clients. It's not critically important to distinguish between what UACs value from what mass-affluent clients value. What is important is to (a) know that

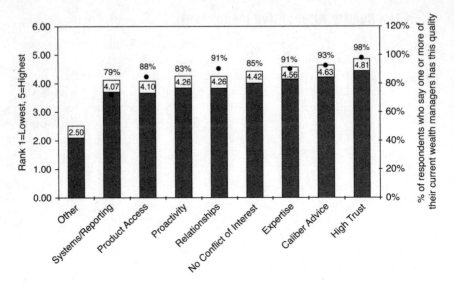

FIGURE 2.1   Qualities that are most important in a wealth manager
Source: "Wealth Management: Is it that simple?" (Spring 2004 Survey). Institute for Private Investors, New York, NY. www.memberlink.net.

the characteristics in Figure 2.1 were taken from actual UACs (so we can be sure that the characteristics presented are, in fact, what UACs value), and (b) know the order in which UACs rank these characteristics.

Candor

As my one and only diversion of this kind in the book, I mention here a line from a movie that can be applied to an important point in advising UACs. If you have seen the movie *Jerry Maguire,* you may remember the scene in which Jerry (played by Tom Cruise) comes into the house of his girlfriend, Dorothy (Renee Zellweger), after a night out on the town. He is forced to speak to Dorothy's sister, Laurel (Bonnie Hunt), while waiting for Dorothy to appear. The dialogue goes something like this:

Jerry: I'm Jerry Maguire.
Laurel: You seem just the way I pictured you. I'm her disapproving sister, Laurel.
Jerry: Honesty. Thank you.[2] (with that characteristic Tom Cruise grin)

If you haven't seen the movie, you may not get the impact of the message, but the point is that candor, true forthrightness, is essential to advising UACs and is generally lacking in the typical client-adviser relationship. The good news is that Jerry's reaction to Laurel's candor is the reaction you are likely to get from your UACs when you tell them all the fees they will have to pay for your investment advice and money management. Above all else, what clients cherish most about their great advisory relationships is straightforward advice. Most surveys of UACs put this at the top of the list. You can have the best products in the business, but if you hide your fees or embellish your track record or your credentials, you are no better than the proverbial used car salesman across town trying to make a buck instead of building a great relationship with a client. Honesty is what UACs want. They can live with disappointing results, mistakes, delays in getting things done—temporarily—but what they cannot accept is lack of transparency at any level.

Perhaps the best application of the issue of candor is the challenge of being a fiduciary and avoiding conflicts of interest. While many institutional consulting areas such as pension, endowment, and foundations management are accustomed to their advisers signing on as fiduciaries, families with large pools of assets are increasingly turning to advisers who agree to be fiduciaries on their accounts as well. For those with questions on fiduciary standards, the Foundation for Fiduciary Studies publishes a book called *Prudent Practices for Investment Advisors*. Fiduciaries, by statute, are obligated to put their clients' interests first and make every effort to steer clear of potential conflicts of interest.

In addition to being a fiduciary, an adviser who has an independent ownership structure and avoids affiliation with other providers such as brokers, custodians, or fund managers, will be the adviser that UACs turn to. These advisers pride themselves on the fact that their only source of revenue is the fees paid by their clients. The fact that they do not accept payment in any form from any other source, directly or indirectly, will garner the confidence of UACs. Doing business this way helps to ensure that the advisers' interests are aligned with those of their clients. Freedom from conflicts of interest has become increasingly important in the investment advisory business, where consulting services are often offered as an adjunct business to brokerage operations, asset custody, or investment management.

Customization

Historically, large wealth management firms such as banks and brokers have had a difficult time offering the type of customized solutions that are demanded by UACs. There are a number of key reasons for this. First, large firms have traditionally been driven by product or product-based service offerings. This approach often does not permit the adviser selling the products to have a holistic (asset allocation) basis for delivering his or her advice. Second, advisers at large firms typically have heavy client loads. It is common for an adviser at a firm serving MA clients to have 100 or more clients. This client load does not permit the adviser the amount of time necessary to serve the customized needs of UACs. Third, large firms employ the services of specialists who do estate planning, banking, credit, and so on, but these people are often extremely overloaded, may be less than adequately trained, and generally are of marginal value to a UAC who has complex, demanding needs. Table 2.1 summarizes the differences between the MA/IA business model compared to the UA business model.

Conversely, advisers in SFOs or MFOs who take a more client-focused, needs-based approach, offer objective solutions, and can assemble a team of specialists that can take the time necessary to serve the client will be best equipped to serve UACs. Service quality and satisfying client needs are vital to attracting and retaining UACs. Taking a needs-based approach allows firms to better identify drivers of client satisfaction, leading to client retention and acquisition. Furthermore, these needs have to be continuously monitored because they inevitably change over the course of time. Understanding client needs in a static state will not cut it. Leading wealth management advisers are addressing these issues by moving toward a more dynamic service delivery methodology that assesses client needs using a more customized and iterative approach.

TABLE 2.1 Customization Characteristics

	Mass/Intermediate Affluent Client Business Model	UAC Business model
Service Provider	Brokerage or bank	Multi- or Single-Family Office
Client Segmentation	Based on assets under management	Based on client needs
Product Approach	Sell product to meet discrete needs	Determine solution and then find objective solution
Adviser/Client Ratio	Often 1 to 50 or 100	Often 1 to 10 or fewer
Specialists	Often in-house with lack of time to provide in-depth advice	Often outsourced with ample time to give excellent advice

Competence

UACs expect, demand, and deserve top quality talent. When they call you to ask for something and you're not there to answer the phone, they want you to call back immediately, if not sooner. When they have client meetings with their advisers, they don't want a dramatic reading of the last quarter's activities. They want proactive, thoughtful advice. And yes, when they call, they expect a senior relationship manager to return the call, not a junior associate. But what they want most of all is a knowledgeable, competent person advising them. Just as there are unqualified advisers serving MA and IA clients, there are those who serve UACs who are not qualified to do so. But what all UAC advisers need to know is that they can't be expected to do it all or know it all. Delegating critical tasks to those more qualified than they are is not only acceptable but expected. Figure 2.2 shows various fields of expertise compiled by Charlotte Beyer's organization, the Institute for Private Investors. Can any one person be expected to excel in all of these categories?

So, advisers to UACs need to know how to get information by asking questions that probe deeply into areas that they know enough to have an

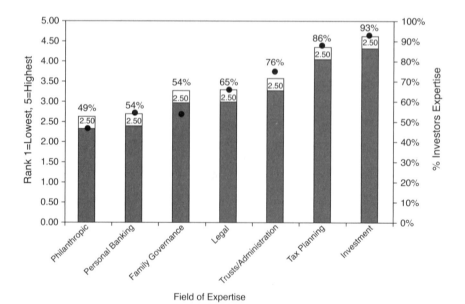

FIGURE 2.2 Fields of Expertise among UAC Advisers
Source: "Wealth Management: Is it that simple?" (Spring 2004 Survey). Institute for Private Investors, New York, NY. www.memberlink.net.

TABLE 2.2   Areas with which UAC Advisers Must Be Familiar

Investments	Family Issues	Intergenerational
Economics	Family governance	Estate planning
Investment policy	Family meetings	Philanthropy
Asset allocation	Concierge services	Selection of trustees
Manager selection	Financial education	Succession planning
Performance analysis	Mentoring	Strategic planning
Tax strategies	Conflict resolution	Family values transfer
Investment vehicle	Teamwork and	Mission statement
structure	communication	development

intelligent conversation about. At the same time, they must know their limits and be able to bring in a specialist when they have reached the boundaries of their knowledge. Table 2.2 shows areas with which UA advisers need to familiarize themselves.

All UAC advisers must have a basic foundation of knowledge. And frankly, this knowledge usually comes from experience with real UACs dealing with real issues. In one client meeting, you may need to be competent in discussing best practices in designing an investment vehicle structure, while in the next you may need to run a family meeting where the family members are not getting along and need cohesion. At the next, you may need to know the Sharpe ratio of the client's portfolio. In all of these examples, you may need to bring in an expert if some subject is too deep for you. But that's all right. Bringing in an expert does the important thing: *It solves the problem!* Call the best CPA you know and tell her about the fact that your clients need to restructure their investment vehicle structure because it's too complex to make effective investment decisions. Call the best family counseling person you know and invite him to speak to the family member best positioned to introduce positive change to the family cohesion issues. And bring your chief investment officer to your next meeting. *You* will be the hero at the end of the day.

Comprehensiveness

Although it is inherently related to competence, comprehensiveness is its own category. Not only to do you need to be knowledgeable and competent in a wide variety of subject areas, but you also need to put all of the pieces together for the benefit of the client, addressing both investments and noninvestment solutions. Clients need a comprehensive investment plan that meets the family's investment objectives as well as a comprehensive family plan that solves key family issues and meets intergenerational needs. This requirement for comprehensive solutions is driving the popularity of SFOs and MFOs.

Comprehensive Investment Solutions   More and more families are relying on independent investment consultants to provide comprehensive investment solutions. Free from the previously mentioned conflicts of interest, these consultants advise clients on investment policy statement development, asset allocation selection(s) (intergenerational, trust, foundations, etc.), manager selection (including access to top managers), and performance measurement. UACs also need investor education for family members. And overarching it all, they want responsive service. Good investment consultants can deliver on this promise. Why should a UAC want this? What college endowments have taught us is that following a well-drafted investment policy, adherence to an asset allocation, and regular rebalancing discipline are the greatest contributors to long-term investment success. Investment consultants can be instrumental in achieving these goals. But many clients want their investment objective tied to their family objectives. This is where comprehensive noninvestment solutions come in.

Comprehensive Family Services   Perhaps the best thing about the family office concept is that it offers comprehensive services that can be customized to match the family's needs. For example, a family office might offer a full spectrum of noninvestment services—accounting, estate planning, family counseling, life insurance, trust services, bill paying, record keeping, family governance, and so on—while at the same time integrating investments into these processes. UACs want their advisers to create a comprehensive solution that pulls these disparate areas together into a smooth-running operation. For example, they want their estate plan integrated with their insurance plan, which is integrated with their philanthropic plan, which is integrated with their tax plan. And all of these plans need to be integrated with their investments.

Now that we have reviewed the Four C's, let's turn our attention to the ways in which advisers can build great relationships with their clients.

BUILDING RELATIONSHIPS BY ASKING QUESTIONS AND LISTENING TO THE ANSWERS

Most advisers, in their quest to close a deal or sell a product (usually at the beginning of a relationship, the most critical time) do most of the talking and infrequently ask any meaningful questions. The only listening that is done is listening for little bits of information that they can use to help them make a preordained solution (product) fit the client. Advising UACs correctly requires the exact opposite approach. Asking key questions and listening carefully to the responses shows great advisory skill. I discuss both of these areas in the next two sections.

Ask Questions

Establishing close relationships with clients is what advising UACs is all about. By definition, a close relationship involves a complete understanding of the needs and expectations of the other party involved. How can you expect to have a close relationship with someone if you do all the talking? Your job as a UAC adviser is to ask questions that uncover the client's deepest beliefs regarding wealth. Only then will you know your clients well enough to provide them with the full range of appropriate, value-added solutions.

For those of you who are reading this and thinking: "Oh, asking questions isn't that important—making the sale is what's important!" keep in mind that there is an important rule, Rule 2310 of the National Association of Securities Dealers that requires all advisers' recommendations for clients be "appropriate for their situation."[3] If you don't ask questions to get to know your client, you should do it to be in compliance. In recommending investments to a client, an adviser needs to have reasonable grounds for believing that the recommendation is suitable on the basis of knowledge gained in the process of understanding the client's financial situation, tax status, investment objectives, and other information that could reasonably be considered relevant to the investment decision-making process.

Beyond compliance, advisers should take the time to find out what makes the client tick. You need to think of yourself as a physician that needs all of the relevant information to make an accurate diagnosis. You need to go beyond dollars and cents and get to the feelings and emotions of your clients. One of the best questions I know of that can get you there is "What keeps you up at night?" Not only does it get at the general question of what is important to a client, but it also asks what worries the client the most. Sometimes, a client will answer, "Nothing, life is very good." Well, this answer isn't to be trusted. Everyone has something financial that keeps them up at night. Whether it's leaving too much to their children, or fees, or asset allocation, there is always something to be concerned about. The trick here is to continue probing for the real answer while maintaining decorum. There are some great add-on questions that work well in these situations.

You need to use them in variation so you don't give the impression that a cross-examination is taking place. They are:

- "What else should I know?"
- "Is there anything you want to add to that?"
- "Anything further to note?"
- "What else?"
- "Please tell me more."

Asking these types of questions is really the only way to get a complete representation of your client's financial picture. Advisers to UACs need to do this type of probing. There is no doubt that there may be uncomfortable moments during these questioning sessions, but you need to take the time and perhaps risk affronting your client to get inside her head. But it's worth it! You will create solid, long-lived relationships if you do.

Listen Up!

The UAC needs to know that his or her adviser is a listener. When you ask the questions you learned here, you actually need to listen to the answers. Even when you want to jump in and start talking, don't! Listen as if you were listening to your five-year-old tell you about his swimming lesson. Listening and trying to see things from the client's perspective will enable you to serve his fundamental needs. There are three levels of great listening: listening for facts, listening for feelings, and listening for values.

The first level, listening for facts, involves details you would normally ask about during a client profiling session. Facts are things such as income, tax status, asset allocation, and so forth. The next level is listening for feelings. Here, you are trying to understand how the client *feels* about the facts that were revealed. At this point, you need to listen without judgment. If a client says that she doesn't mind paying taxes because she made a lot of money over the years doing business with the federal government, you need to accept that sentiment and incorporate it into the plan, regardless of how ridiculous it may sound to you. Otherwise, the client may not fully reveal her true feelings. Listening for values is the last level of listening. To reach beyond facts and feelings, you need to find out what is really important to the client. Dig deep with questions like "How much is enough to leave to your children?" and beyond that, "What legacy do you want to leave?" By inquiring into why clients regard certain things to be important, you'll eventually uncover their deepest values.

Some of you might not be comfortable entering the great listening zone. But you should be aware that UACs expect listeners, not talkers.

The industry's best advisers master the art of great listening, which pays huge dividends over time by creating solid relationships with clients by managing wealth based on what matters most: feelings and values.

MATCHING CLIENT WITH ADVISER

In addition to listening to your client, advisers often need to listen to themselves—particularly when drawing conclusions about what a working relationship would be like with a given prospect. One of the most problematic situations that can occur in managing relationships with UACs (or any client for that matter) is the one in which after a period of time, it becomes clear that there is a mismatch in personality or temperament between the client and the adviser. In the quest to build business, advisers often accept any client willing to pay a reasonable fee. Even in the early stages of one's business, however, advisers are best served by attempting to understand what it's going to be like working with the prospects they meet. But how can this be done?

One of the most intuitive, practical and timeless methodologies for understanding the behavioral characteristics of private clients developed by Charlotte Beyer, founder of the Institute for Private Investors. In her 1992 article entitled "Understanding Private Client Characteristics," Beyer provides a framework for advisers to analyze the characteristics of their clients as shown in Figure 2.3.[4] On the x-axis is a continuum of control. Here, the adviser is attempting to ascertain how much control the prospect wishes to have over the advisory process. If you, the adviser, do not do well with clients who exert control over their advisers, then this client may not be right for you. On the y-axis is sophistication. Here, the adviser is judging how sophisticated the client is. If the client is not sophisticated, do you have the patience and aptitude to educate your client? If not, you may not be well suited for a given prospective client.

Putting these two axes together, the adviser can really get a sense of whether or not a certain client would be a good fit. For example, "the low sophistication, high control quadrant in the lower right panel is where many of the most frustrating clients fall—the family with one holding of low-cost stock. To quote one manager, "I have tried for five years to teach this family group the importance of diversification but with no success." I use this framework often when beginning the process of getting to know a prospective client. I try to imagine that I am interviewing the prospect as much as she is interviewing me. Naturally, I am the one interviewing for the job, but I do my best to try to match personalities with a prospective client. Thinking through what it would be like to work with a client, and vice-versa

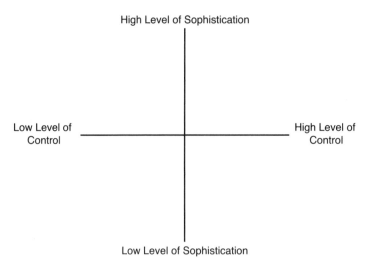

FIGURE 2.3 Quadrants of Control and Sophistication
Source: Charlotte B. Beyer, "Understanding Private
Client Characteristics."

for investors contemplating working with a certain adviser, is important and is often overlooked by both parties.

CONSULTANT QUESTIONNAIRE

Well-informed UACs have a clever way of assessing a potential provider of financial advice: the questionnaire. I thought it would be highly instructive to include one in this chapter so you can see what you will likely need to do to curry favor with the UAC. To be sure, no one has every base covered. But covering as many as possible will get you that much closer to acquiring UACs. This questionnaire is a compilation of several I have seen over the years.

1. Basic Firm Information
   A. Provide the name, address, telephone numbers, and e-mail address of the key contact for us at the firm.
   B. Please provide a brief history of the firm.
   C. What services does the firm offer?
   D. Has the firm been a party to any merger, sale, or acquisition? Are there any planned transactions?

E. Please list the firm's principals and their backgrounds.
F. Describe the ownership structure of the firm. Are there any unique aspects that encourage the retention of key personnel?
G. What is the management structure of the firm?
H. What are the firm's areas of recognized expertise?
I. Provide all office locations and headquarters.
J. How many employees does the firm employ?
K. How many clients does the firm serve?
 1. What are the clients' asset size ranges within these categories of clients:
  a. Institutional Tax-Exempt Clients (Endowments or Foundations, etc.)
  b. Private Wealth Families (with more than $50MM in assets)
  c. Other
L. Who are the firm's target clients?
M. What percentage of the firm's revenues is derived from investment consulting? If investment consulting is less than 80 percent, identify other sources of revenue.
N. Does the firm manage money? If so, please provide details.
O. Do you receive referral fees or referrals from money managers or other firms? If yes, please describe.
P. Legal Questions:
 1. Is the firm a Registered Investment Adviser? (If so, provide all Form ADVs.)
 2. Has the SEC or any other regulatory agency ever investigated the firm or a principal?
 3. What potential conflicts of interest does the firm have when recommending investment products to me, and will the firm disclose those conflicts?
 4. Has the firm been a party to litigation within the last five years? If yes, please provide the details.
 5. Are you required by law to always act in the client's best interests? Will you put that commitment in writing?
 6. Please provide a written record of any disciplinary history for the firm.
2. Investment Consulting
 A. Service Team
  1. Provide names and backgrounds of team members servicing our relationship.
  2. What are their roles?
  3. What are their particular areas of expertise?

    B. Provide the name of the contact person for administrative questions.

    C. How many consulting clients does the firm currently serve? Of these, how many are taxable investors? How many are family offices?

    D. What is the amount of assets under advisement? How much is taxable? Please provide a breakdown of how the assets are distributed between asset classes (stocks, bonds, hedge funds, private equity, real estate, etc.).

    E. Are taxable and tax-exempt clients assigned to different consultants?

    F. Discuss the firm's abilities and level of expertise pertaining to alternative investments.

    G. How do you prepare for a meeting with a client?

    H. What services do you offer throughout the month?

3. Investment Management Process

    A. How are the firm's capital markets projections derived? Please provide the firm's near-term and long-term asset class projections.

    B. What do you see as the toughest challenges facing investors over the next five years?

    C. Is the firm's asset allocation software developed in-house or externally? Please provide an example.

    D. Describe in detail the steps you take in preparing an asset allocation study. How long does it take to complete?

    E. Describe the firm's investment philosophy.

        1. Discuss the firm's philosophy on strategic versus tactical asset allocation.

        2. What are the most important aspects of this philosophy and how long has it been in place?

        3. Please describe the aspects of the firm's investment philosophy that differentiate it from similar firms.

    F. Investment performance history over the last 3, 5, and 10 years

        1. Break down the performance into asset classes and styles.

        2. Provide published tactical allocation changes over this period of time.

    G. Research Department

        1. Provide the organization chart for the firm's research department and indicate asset class responsibility among the staff.

        2. Provide bios on the firm's research staff.

    H. Current model asset allocation

        1. Discuss how you go about designing an asset allocation.

        2. Discuss details of an asset allocation plan with specific comments about style allocations within asset classes.

4. Money Manager Search and Monitoring
   A. Does the firm maintain a database of money management or-ganizations? If so, is the database compiled internally or pur-chased from an outside source? Please provide names of purchased databases.
   B. Please describe the firm's search process for manager selection.
   C. How many managers does the firm currently track?
   D. What guidelines does the firm use to terminate managers? How many have been removed from the firm's recommended list in the last two years?
   E. Is the investment of funds limited to those managers in the data-base?
   F. Are money managers required to pay fees for inclusion in the firm's database?
   G. Describe the firm's process of monitoring managers.
   H. How often do analysts talk to each money manager? How often do the firm's analysts speak with money managers, both in-house and on site?
   I. What type of reports or feedback does the firm provide to clients after meeting with a money manager?
   J. How do the firm's processes to evaluate and monitor traditional long-only managers, hedge funds, private equity, real estate, and other nontraditional asset classes differ?
5. Performance Measurement and Reporting
   A. Please describe the firm's performance reporting services. What is the frequency and timing of the firm's reports?
   B. Do you calculate performance in-house or do you use an outside service?
   C. Do you calculate investment performance after taxes and manage-ment fees?
   D. How do you create the benchmark for an account?
   E. Please provide a sample report that includes performance measure-ment and other portfolio analysis (sector breakdown, risk/return, attribution analysis).
   F. Please provide samples of client reports and routine information sent to clients.
6. Controls
   A. Describe the firm's internal portfolio control and review procedures used to assure that portfolios comply with the firm's organizational policies and client mandates.
   B. How is portfolio risk monitored and controlled?
   C. Is the firm AIMR compliant? At what level?

7. Fees and Fee Structure
   A. Please outline the firm's fee structure, including fixed and variable fees, and any performance-based fees. Please indicate all services you propose to provide and the associated fees.
   B. What is the term of the agreement?
   C. Do you receive referral fees from money managers or other firms? If yes, please explain.
   D. Does the firm receive any other form of compensation, including soft dollars? If so, what is the form of compensation?
8. References
   A. Please provide names and contact information of clients who have taxable portfolios similar in size to ours.
9. Technology
   A. Describe the technology structure. What software is used?
   B. Describe the level of integration with custodians. With which custodians do you work?

As you can see, this is an incredibly in-depth assessment process. UA families are not going to take the decision to hire a consultant lightly. They look at this decision as one that could be in place for decades. UAC advisers need to understand this and know that it takes many months to transition a client from one firm to another.

CONCLUSION

After reading this chapter, you should have a good understanding of the mindset of the class of UACs. Clearly, there are differences between serving UACs and serving MA and IA clients, and advisers need to tweak their service offerings. We now move to Chapter 3, which covers attitudes and investor behavior of UACs.

CHAPTER 3

Wealth Attitudes, Aspirations, and Investor Behavior of Ultra-Affluent Clients

No one inherits a meaningful life.
—Thayer Willis

Building upon the previous section about why advising UACs is different from advising MA or IA clients, this chapter is intended to guide you to the attitudes, aspirations, and behaviors that you will experience while working with UACs. UAC advisers need to be aware of some of the attitudes that their clients have toward money. Inheritors of money are especially complex to deal with, because they have had to live with the reality of money from birth: their parents were influenced by it, their childhood was influenced by it, and the rest of their lives will be influenced by it. In regard to aspirations, I review some of the things that UACs want their money to do for them outside of the notion of simply using money to make more money! After all, beyond the basic needs of life—food, clothing, and shelter—our money can do many other things. Understanding noninvestment issues is critical. I discuss at the end one of my favorite subjects, behavioral finance, and review some of the investor behaviors you are likely to encounter when dealing with UACs. What is interesting here is that wealth level has no bearing on the likelihood that you will see irrational investor behavior. I have worked with clients with $1 million and clients with hundreds of millions of dollars, and both client types display irrational behaviors.

Why are nonfinancial issues so important? UAC advisers need to realize first and foremost that noninvestment issues take an equal and sometimes higher priority to investing in regard to issues that dominate client meeting agendas. Put simply, UACs' primary goals are not usually to simply build more and more wealth. They are often trying to figure out how to preserve it (with modest growth) and determine what to do with it for the benefit of family members and other beneficiaries, such as charities. Furthermore, they are trying to do this without creating intrafamily squabbling, dysfunctional child development, or unhealthy family relationships. Family issues around such subjects as inheritance often dominate adviser-client conversations with questions like: What is an appropriate financial inheritance? What effect will this inheritance have on my children? When should I tell them about this inheritance? Should I let them give input on the structure or contents of their inheritance? To answer these questions, families need to have a set of guiding principles. Many have these principles, but have not taken the time write them down.

FAMILY ASPIRATIONS

Once a family understands that building wealth is not the primary driving force in life, they turn to what many UACs consider to be their most important goal: shaping children (and other family members) who grow up healthy and happy and will (hopefully) perpetuate the family. The first step in the process is for family members who are leaders to communicate to the rest of the family that their children need to live in the real world. As such, families need to realize that the highest aspiration they can have is to get their children to build identities of their own. Regardless of the chosen pursuit of the child, parents need to respect their child's decisions. There are three key traits that parents should raise their children to value: self-esteem, effective communication, and delayed gratification. If parents can foster these characteristics in their children, they will have a much better chance of attaining a harmonious, self-perpetuating family. I discuss these characteristics now.

Self-Esteem

Self-esteem is gained when children make decisions for themselves. They obtain a huge amount of satisfaction when they are successful in endeavors they undertake on their own initiative; and even if they are not successful, they get satisfaction out of knowing that they tried their best. The best thing a parent can do is to nurture individual skills that are unique to each child and encourage the development of these skills. When children have no responsibilities or have too much done for them by servants or other domestic workers, they have no opportunity to acquire the skills necessary to independence. In addition, if parents are unduly harsh with their children for small mistakes or don't offer praise when it is deserved, children are subject to low self-esteem. Above all, children need to make decisions on their own and learn from the bad decisions they make. If parents or other people make all the decisions for a child, she never gains the knowledge necessary to make effective decisions. Kids need to do for themselves from an early age, and this should continue as they get older. Assigning tasks around the house, such as emptying the wastebaskets or helping to prepare meals, aids in fostering a can-do attitude in children. All of this adds up to self-esteem.

Effective Communication

Perhaps the greatest skill a child can develop is the ability to communicate effectively with his or her family and with people in general. Children who can clearly express their desires, opinions, feelings, and thoughts are prized members of the family and contribute to the human capital of the family. Likewise, parents need to be effective communicators. Children learn much from their parents; if a parent is a poor communicator, then the child is likely to be a poor communicator, and vice versa. But communication doesn't always involve dictating edicts to children. Just because parents have all the power in the family relationship doesn't mean that they should do all the talking. Parents also need to be able to listen to their children. Listening to our children (just as we should listen to our clients) validates them and makes them feel important. This is obviously not limited to parent-child relationships; everyone wants to be listened to, including you!

The manner in which parents communicate with their children is nearly as important as what is actually being said. Body language, tone of voice, and approach to conversations are critical. Such attitudinal indicators are part of our generational makeup. A family who understands its unique generational maze can open a door of communication through which children's (inheritors') dreams may be discovered and subsequently fostered to regenerate the family wealth.[1] Children respond to nurturing conversations and are repelled by shouting or overbearing parenting. A great way to foster communication is to have regular family meetings. This gives family members the opportunity to express feelings and openly communicate. It also encourages participation in all aspects of the family's life by the next generations, participation which Gray says is key to any family's wealth management success.

Delayed Gratification

One of the things I try to instill in my own children is the concept of delayed gratification. Imagine how difficult it is for a child who gets everything he wants, just by asking, to practice delayed gratification. How many times have you seen overindulged children on the street or in a store and thought, "What a spoiled brat!"? In my view, spoiling children is one of the worst things a parent can do. At the extreme, self-indulgent children can turn to higher and higher forms of gratification which can manifest as credit card debt, drug abuse, or worse. UA parents need to take every opportunity to make their kids appreciate what they have and to earn material goods. Parents often give presents because it makes *them* feel good. The wealthy should avoid this practice, as it often does more harm than good. A highly effective way for kids to appreciate what they have is to have them do volunteer work, especially for the poor, so that they can understand the value of what they have. This may help them to think twice before engaging in self-indulgent behavior.

Strategies for Overcoming Wealth Attitudes

What we have done here is get readers familiar with some of these issues and what you may be up against as a UAC adviser when beginning to work with a new client. If you are in a position of trust and feel comfortable advising your clients in this area, there are several ways in which you can help your clients develop a positive attitude toward their wealth.

1. Ask your client to write down what money means to him.
2. Ask your client to assess whether he believes that money has caused him to be dysfunctional in his interpersonal relationships, and if so, how.
3. Ask your client if he feels controlled by money or in control of his ability to deal with money. If it is the former, ask why and brainstorm about ways to deal with this issue.
4. Ask your client if he is constantly focused on money. Ask if issues such as health, children, hobbies, community, religion or spirituality, or other nonfinancial issues are relevant. Doing this will get the client thinking and possibly seeing the error of his ways.

The best thing you can do is be available to your client when the time arises to discuss these issues.

WEALTH ATTITUDES OF ULTRA-AFFLUENT CLIENTS

Wealth can have powerful effects, both positive and negative, on human beings. People who create wealth can have very different attitudes toward wealth from those who inherit wealth. I have seen many first-generation wealth creators, with hundreds of millions of dollars in the bank, live in the same houses that they raised their kids in (usually a modest three- or four-bedroom home) and drive the same cars they drove 10 years ago. I have also seen inheritors of the same amount of wealth build huge mansions and drive incredibly expensive sports cars. Understanding this difference in wealth attitude is crucial because if it is not carefully managed, wealth can dissipate from one generation to the next.

There is a phrase that is commonly used in UA circles that describes the phenomenon of later generations spending money unwisely that was inherited from previous generations: Shirtsleeves to shirtsleeves in three generations. This is an intercultural phenomenon, not just a Western civilization tendency. The most enlightened UACs have terrific attitudes toward their wealth, while others do not. Some UACs focus primarily on the financial aspects of wealth, while others focus on human capital. There is no right or wrong here. As we all know, our family upbringing and personal experiences, along with religious, political, and social experiences, help shape who we are. How do these attitudes and experiences influence the way UACs make decisions about their wealth? Lisa Gray, founder of family wealth consultancy graymatter Strategies, LLC, states that not only are they influential, they are woven within each generation's unique fabric of perspectives. Our generational lenses are permanently imprinted upon us during our formative years.[2] They shape our particular view of the world, serving as an automatic frame of reference which colors our decision making processes throughout our lifetime.*,[3] Gray says these perspectives, in turn, shape the dynamics of the family. Family dynamics influence the way family members interact with each other, specifically in the way they communicate and their ability to establish trust with each other. When large sums of money overlay the factors that influence our attitudes and beliefs, negative results are a possibility.

In her book, *Generational Wealth Management: A Guide for Fostering Global Family Wealth*, Gray says that different generational perspectives within a family serve as a foundation for biases and misperceptions of family members' goals and desires. Each generation has its own way of thinking about family life, gender roles, investing, wealth management, and the future. Figure 3.1 illustrates how such misperceptions can lead advisors as well

---

*Karl Mannheim states these first impressions of the world formed between ages 14 and 17 (generational biases) create a predisposition for "a certain characteristic mode of thought and experience and a characteristic type of historically relevant action.... Even if the rest of one's life consisted of one long process of negation and destruction of the natural world view acquired in youth, the determining influence of these early impressions would still be predominant."

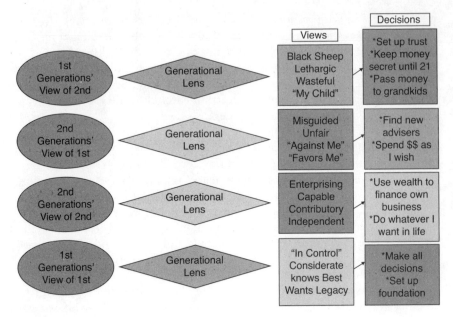

FIGURE 3.1   How Generational Biases Affect Wealth Management Decisions
Source: © 2009, graymatter Strategies, LLC. All rights reserved.

as family leadership to make assumptions about a family's wealth management goals which may or may not be aligned with the family's authentic needs. Each layer of wealth management decisions builds upon the other based on each generation's views of the others' attitudes and goals, making it difficult for the family to make cohesive decisions about its wealth. This contributes significantly to the successful fulfillment of the "Shirtsleeves to shirtsleeves" proverb.

It is prudent for UAC advisers to get a sense of some of the attitudes that can be destructive to a family's financial and social wellbeing so they can be prepared to deal with them. The implications of these attitudes are far reaching. They not only influence the way families make wealth management decisions but they also have a direct effect upon a family's ability to form a successful governance system, a guiding set of principles designed to benefit all family members. Each of the following five sections is a brief introduction to the way wealth attitudes filter into and influence the decision-making processes (the governance structure) of families. An adviser who understands these attitudes can successfully guide a UAC family in fostering all forms of its wealth for generations to come.

Desire to Exert Control

Perhaps one of the more dangerous side effects of wealth accumulation is the desire to exert control over others, particularly children. Children who are brought up in highly affluent families are often pressured to achieve predetermined goals: attend certain schools, socialize with certain classes of people, and enter certain professions, such as those practiced by their parents. This can be highly destructive to family cohesion and the mental health of those upon whom this pressure is exerted. Children need to be treated as individuals and supported in their own abilities, interests, and goals. As children grow, they need to feel that they have the freedom to pursue their own dreams, socialize, and enter marriage with whomever they deem fit—in short, live their own lives on their own terms.

Absence of Love and Affection

Sadly, UA parents often neglect their family relationships, particularly with their children. They get caught up in their own lives with such activities as charitable endeavors, running a business, country club friendships, travel, and the myriad other pastimes that UACs pursue. Children often display resentment, and when this happens, parents often overcompensate by splurging and buying the children expensive gifts. Money, gifts, or other material goods effectively take the place of that which is so critical in life: love and affection. Parents fail so often to understand how much their children crave their approval. As a result, children grow up incapable of sustaining loving relationships because of a flawed belief that love is something to be purchased, not created or earned. Love is measured not in romantic dinners, flowers, walks on the beach, or extended conversations, but by material possessions. This phenomenon occurs not only with potential spouses but also with normal friendships, and can lead to extreme unhappiness and bitterness over the course of time.

Low Self-Esteem

A significant problem with generational wealth is that of low self-esteem. The issue here is that an inheritor of wealth has every possible need taken care of through a trust fund or other source, but doesn't feel worthy of receiving it because she hasn't earned the money. This can produce feelings of guilt and low self-esteem. This is why fostering the dreams of inheritors is so important. You don't want to have children thinking that people view them as weak or inferior simply because they inherited wealth.

Relationship Authority

People with money sometimes feel that they have more authority in their interpersonal relationships than those who don't. For example, suppose a woman with money marries a man without money. The man goes out to work every day, having grown up with a strong work ethic. The woman, lacking this work ethic, does not work, in part because she knows that she does not need to work because she has brought a disproportionate amount of money to the marriage. Despite the situation of the husband working every day to earn money, the wife may feel like she has more authority to make financial decisions. This situation could spark an argument:

Wife: I bought that new dress because it was half off.
Husband: But darling, you have seven new dresses that you haven't worn yet that you bought over the last twelve months.
Wife: I have the right to buy whatever I want, so don't tell me what to do!
Husband: What kind of example are you setting for our children?

And on and on. When people enter a marriage, no matter who brings what to the marriage, they need to make joint decisions to maintain the harmony of the family.

Affinity of Social Relationships

Wealthy people tend to gravitate toward their own kind—meaning other wealthy people. This is true for several reasons. If an affluent person befriends a middle- or low-income person, the lower-income earner may eventually experience feelings of envy or resentment. This does not make for a healthy friendship. Additionally, an inheritor with a low self-esteem wealth attitude will naturally feel comfortable in the company of another inheritor who can empathize with the situation. As a result, wealth can create problems in developing a wide variety of friendships, which is often what makes life interesting and fulfilling.

There are certainly more attitudes toward money that could be reviewed here that have to do with such areas as the need for power, sexual intimacy, religion, gender-role issues, and a host of others. A great resource in this area is a book by Lynne Twist called *The Soul of Money: Reclaiming the Wealth of Our Inner Resources* (Norton, 2003).

WHERE PSYCHOLOGY MEETS FINANCE

Behavioral finance, commonly defined as the application of psychology to finance, has become a very hot topic, generating new credence with the rupture of the tech-stock bubble in March of 2000. While the term is bandied about in books, magazine articles, and investment papers, many people lack a firm understanding of the concepts behind behavioral finance. In my previous book, titled *Behavioral Finance and Wealth Management*,[4] I break the topic down into two subtopics, behavioral finance micro and behavioral finance macro. Behavioral finance micro (BFMI) covers behaviors or biases of individual investors that distinguish them from the rational actors envisioned in classical economic theory. Behavioral finance macro (BFMA) detects and describes anomalies in the efficient market hypothesis that behavioral models explain. As wealth management practitioners and investors, our primary focus is BFMI, the study of individual investor behavior. Specifically, we want to identify relevant psychological biases and investigate their influence on asset allocation decisions, so that we can manage the effects of those biases on the investment process.

Wealth management practitioners have different ways of measuring the success of an advisory relationship, but every successful relationship shares a few fundamental characteristics:

1. The adviser understands the client's financial goals.
2. The adviser maintains a systematic (consistent) approach to advising the client.
3. The adviser delivers what the client expects.
4. The relationship benefits both client and adviser.

Understanding investor behavior can help you in all of these areas.

Formulating Financial Goals

Experienced financial advisers know that defining financial goals is critical to creating an appropriate investment program for the client. To best define financial goals, it is helpful to understand the psychology and emotions underlying the decisions to create the goals. The biases reviewed in this chapter suggest ways in which advisers can use behavioral finance to discern why investors are setting certain goals. Such insights equip the adviser to deepen the bond with the client, producing a better investment outcome and achieving a better advisory relationship.

Maintaining a Consistent Approach

Most successful advisers exercise a very consistent approach to delivering wealth management services. Incorporating the benefits of behavioral finance can become part of that discipline, and does not mandate large-scale changes in the adviser's methods. Behavioral finance adds professionalism and structure to the relationship, because advisers can diagnose irrational behaviors in the client profiling process, which precedes the delivery of any actual investment advice. Clients will appreciate the addition of this part of the process, and it will make the relationship more successful.

Delivering What the Client Expects

There is perhaps no aspect of the advisory relationship that could benefit more from behavioral finance than delivering on clients' expectations. Addressing these expectations is essential to a successful relationship; in many unfortunate instances, the adviser doesn't deliver what the client expects because the adviser doesn't understand the needs of the client. Behavioral finance provides a context in which the adviser can take a step back and attempt to really understand the client's motivations. Having gotten to the root of the client's expectations, the adviser is better equipped to help realize them.

Ensuring Mutual Benefits

There is no question that actions that result in happier, more satisfied clients will also improve the adviser's practice and work life. Incorporating insights from behavioral finance into the advisory relationship will enhance that relationship and lead to more fruitful results.

INVESTOR BIASES

It is well known by those in the individual investor advisory business that investment results are not the primary reason that a client seeks a new adviser. The number one reason that practitioners lose clients is that the clients do not feel as though their advisers understand, or attempt to understand, the clients' financial objectives. The primary benefit that behavioral finance offers is the ability to develop a strong bond between client and adviser. By getting inside the client's head and developing a comprehensive grasp of her motives and fears, the adviser can help the client to better understand why a portfolio is designed the way it is, and why it is the right portfolio for him—regardless of what happens from day to day in the markets.

In my previous book, *Behavioral Finance and Wealth Management,* I covered 20 of the most common biases that financial advisers are likely to encounter. I review these 20 biases briefly here and will include a description of each bias, a classification of whether it is cognitive (stemming from faulty reasoning) or emotional (stemming from impulses or feelings), and situational examples. The distinction between cognitive and emotional is an important one, because advisers will want to advise their clients differently based on which type of bias is being acted out.

Endowment Bias

Bias Type: Emotional   Endowment bias occurs when the value a person assigns to an object depends upon whether he possesses the object now and is faced with its loss, or does not possess the object and has the potential to obtain it. In short, if one loses an object that he owns, and the magnitude of loss is greater than the magnitude of the corresponding gain if the object was newly acquired, endowment bias is present. This behavior is inconsistent with rational economic theory, which says that a person's willingness to pay for an object should equal the person's willingness to dispose of the good or object for compensation.

Application: There are some practical examples that can demonstrate endowment bias. First, some investors may hold securities for extended periods so they can avoid transaction costs or taxes even if an investment no longer fits into the current investment plan. A second element of endowment bias that can lead to investment mistakes is familiarity. That is, if investors know from experience the characteristics of securities they already own, such as a portfolio of municipal bonds or a large equity position that pays a consistent dividend, then they may feel reluctant to transition into instruments that seem relatively unknown. Familiarity, effectively, has value. Finally, some investors who inherit securities may feel disloyal if they dispose of securities that had been owned by previous generations, particularly concentrated equity positions or real estate that may have created the family's wealth to begin with.

Loss Aversion Bias

Bias Type: Emotional   Loss-averse investors feel the pain of losses more than the pleasure of gains. A common rule of thumb that has emerged from behavioral finance research says that, on average, avoiding a loss is twice as powerful a motivator as the possibility of making a gain of equal magnitude. Loss aversion can prevent people from unloading unprofitable investments, even when they see little to no prospect of a turnaround. Research into a losing investment often reveals a company whose prospects don't forecast a rebound. Some industry veterans have coined a diagnosis, *get-even-itis*, to describe the behavior of investors who will not sell until they get even.

Application: Holding on to losing investments too long in the hope that they get back to break-even can result in serious negative consequences by depressing portfolio returns when investments stay in losing territory for extended periods. Loss aversion can also cause investors to sell winners too early, in fear that their profit will evaporate unless they sell. This behavior limits the growth potential of a portfolio, and can lead to too much trading, which has been shown to lower investment returns, not only due to commissions but also from poor trading decisions.

Status Quo Bias

Bias Type: Emotional Status quo bias predisposes those it affects, when facing an array of choice options, to elect whatever option keeps conditions the same. This is a very typical passive investor trait. People less readily abandon a condition when they tell themselves "things have always been this way," enabling themselves to avoid making a new decision.

Application: A common example of status quo bias is the investor who has been doing things a certain way for many years, and then hires a new financial adviser. The new adviser may propose practical changes that are grounded in solid asset allocation or other investment principles only to find that the investor takes only some or nearly none of the advice. It's not that the client doesn't need good advice—she does—but rather fears change or is simply unwilling to change the way things are being done because of an attachment to the status quo.

Regret Aversion Bias

Bias Type: Emotional People exhibiting regret aversion bias avoid taking decisive actions because they fear that, in hindsight, whatever course they select will prove less than optimal. These people hesitate most at moments that may actually merit aggressive behavior. Regret aversion causes investors to anticipate and fear the pain of regret that comes with incurring a loss or forfeiting a profit. The potential for financial injury isn't the only disincentive that these investors face; they also dread feeling responsible for their own misfortunes.

Application: Regret aversion can cause investors to be too conservative in their investment choices. Having suffered losses in the past (i.e., having felt the pain of a poor decision regarding a risky investment), many people shy away from making bold, new investment decisions, and accept only low-risk positions. This behavior can lead to long-term underperformance, and can jeopardize investment goals. Regret aversion can also cause investors to hold on to losing positions for too long. People don't like to admit that they're wrong, and will go to great lengths to avoid selling (i.e., confronting the reality of) a losing investment. This behavior, similar to loss aversion, can be hazardous to one's wealth.

Anchoring Bias

Bias Type: Cognitive   Investors who are subject to anchoring bias are influenced by purchase points or arbitrary price levels, and tend to cling to these numbers when facing questions like "Should I buy or sell this security?" This bias is connected to both loss aversion and status quo bias. Anchoring typically emerges when new information regarding a security is introduced. Rational investors treat new pieces of information objectively, and do not reflect on purchase prices or target prices in deciding how to act. Anchoring, however, causes investors to perceive new information through an essentially warped lens by taking into account the price at which the investment was acquired.

Application: One of the most common examples of anchoring bias occurs during implementation of a new asset allocation, usually with a new client. The client agrees to a new asset allocation, but won't move forward with implementing it because he or she has an irrational attachment to certain investments. For example, suppose a client comes to you with 30 percent of his or her portfolio in a single stock. Further suppose that the stock is down 25 percent from its high, which it reached 10 months ago ($75 a share versus $100 a share). For simplicity's sake, assume that taxes on the sale are not an issue. The client will frequently be resistant to meet the new allocation because he is anchored to the $100 price that was previously reached. The downside of this behavior is that the stock can easily fall further, highlighting the risk of holding a single stock.

Mental Accounting Bias

Bias Type: Cognitive   Mental accounting occurs when people treat various sums of money differently based on where these sums are mentally categorized or the nature of the money's intended use. Mental accounting, with its many manifestations, can cause a variety of problems for investors.

Perhaps the most notable example is the act of combining different assets whose performances do not correlate with each other, which is an important consideration for risk reduction that can be neglected. Some investors are risk averse, and like to segregate their assets into safe buckets. As a result, investment positions held without regard to correlations might offset one another in a portfolio context, creating suboptimal inefficiencies. This common, detrimental oversight stems from mental accounting.

Application: Some investors imagine that their investments occupy separate buckets, or accounts; these categories can include a college fund, a retirement fund, or next-generation money. If all of these assets are viewed as safe money, and not diversified across many asset classes, suboptimal returns are usually the result. Another display of mental accounting is irrationally distinguishing between returns derived from income and those derived from capital appreciation. Many people feel the need to preserve capital—that is, principal—and prefer to spend interest. Some investors, as a result, chase income streams, and can unwittingly erode principal in the process. Consider, for example, a high-yield (junk bond) fund, or a preferred stock that pays a high dividend yet, at times, can suffer a loss of principal because of interest rate fluctuations or credit problems. Mental accounting can make instruments like these appealing, but they may not benefit the investor in the long run.

Recency Bias

Bias Type: Cognitive   Recency bias is a predisposition that causes people to more prominently recall and emphasize recent events or observations. As many wealth managers know, recency bias ran rampant during the bull market period between 1995 and 1999. Many investors implicitly (and wrongly) presumed, as they have during other cyclical peaks, that the market would continue its enormous gains forever. In this context, investors need to be advised to follow fundamental investment principles and not focus only on recent performance.

Application: Some investors extrapolate patterns and make projections based on historical data samples that are too small. Investors who forecast future returns based on only a recent sample of prior returns are vulnerable to purchasing at price peaks. This behavior might cause one to enter an asset class at the wrong time, and end up experiencing losses. One of the most obvious and most pernicious manifestations of recency bias among investors pertains to their misuse of investment performance records for mutual and other types of funds. These investors do not pay heed to the cyclical nature of asset class returns and so, for them, funds that have performed spectacularly in the very recent past appear unduly attractive.

Hindsight Bias

Bias Type: Cognitive   Investors who lack independent thought on investments are susceptible to perceiving investment outcomes as if they are
predictable—even if they aren't. This behavior is precipitated by actual outcomes that are more readily grasped by the mind than the infinite array of
outcomes that could have but didn't materialize. Thus, some people underestimate the uncertainty preceding the event in question, and underrate the
outcomes that could have materialized, but did not. In sum, hindsight bias
leads some investors to exaggerate the quality of their foresight. A side effect
of this bias is that if someone actually believes her own fallacious conclusions, she may overestimate her risk tolerance in the future. Many investment
advisers have observed hindsight bias in practice. They watch clients fool
themselves into thinking that they could have predicted the outcome of some
financial gamble, but achieve this insight only after the fact.

Application: Perhaps the most obvious example of hindsight bias is the
response by investors to the behavior of the U.S. stock market between 1998
and 2002, when, initially, many viewed the market's performance as normal
(i.e., not symptomatic of a bubble), only to later say, "Wasn't it obvious?"
when the market melted down. Hindsight bias's biggest consequence is that
it gives investors a false sense of security when making investment decisions, and excessive risk-taking behavior can take hold. When an investment
appreciates, hindsight-biased investors tend to rewrite their own memories
to portray the positive developments as if they were predictable. This rationale can, over time, inspire excessive risk-taking, because hindsight-biased
investors begin to believe that they have superior predictive powers when in
fact they do not.

Framing Bias

Bias Type: Cognitive   Framing bias is the tendency of investors to respond
to various situations differently, based on the context in which a choice
is presented (framed). Investors often focus too restrictively on one or two
aspects of a situation, excluding other crucial considerations, which compro-
mises their decision-making effectiveness. For better or worse, an investor's
willingness to accept risk can be influenced by how scenarios are presented
to him.

Application: The use of risk tolerance questionnaires provides a good
example of framing bias. Depending upon how questions are asked, framing
bias can cause investors to communicate responses to questions about risk
tolerance that are either unduly conservative or aggressive. For example,
when questions are worded in the *gain* frame, then a risk-averse response is

more likely. When questions are worded in the *loss* frame, then risk-seeking behavior is the likely response. The optimistic or pessimistic manner in which an investment or asset allocation recommendation is framed can affect people's willingness or reluctance to invest. Optimistically worded questions are more likely to garner affirmative responses, and optimistically worded choices are more likely to be selected than pessimistically phrased alternatives. Framing contexts are often arbitrary and uncorrelated and therefore shouldn't affect investors' judgments, but they do.

Cognitive Dissonance Bias

Bias Type: Cognitive   In psychology, cognitions represent attitudes, emotions, beliefs, or values. When multiple cognitions intersect, and people attempt to harmonize these conflicts, cognitive dissonance can result. In short, people rationalize their decisions even when faced with facts that demonstrate that they made a less-than-optimal decision. People who attempt to achieve cognitive harmony are not always rational, and there are two important aspects of cognitive dissonance that pertain to decision-making. The first is selective perception. People suffering from selective perception register only information that appears to affirm a chosen course, producing a view of reality that is incomplete and inaccurate. The second aspect of cognitive dissonance is selective decision-making, which usually occurs when emotional commitment to an original decision is high. Selective decision-making rationalizes actions that enable a person to adhere to that course, even if the decision may not result in favorable economic outcomes. Many wealth management professionals note that clients often go to great lengths to justify prior investment decisions, especially losing ones.

Application: Investors who suffer from cognitive dissonance bias can be known to continue to invest in a security that they already own after it has gone down to confirm an earlier decision to invest in that security, without judging the new investment with objectivity and rationality. This is a common example of the phrase "throwing good money after bad." Cognitive dissonance can cause some investors to get caught up in herds of behavior. That is, some investors avoid information that counters an earlier decision (cognitive dissonance) until the point is reached that so much contrary information is released that investors herd together and cause a deluge of behavior that is counter to the original decision.

Ambiguity Aversion Bias

Bias Type: Cognitive   Ambiguity aversion is a difficult bias to explain; an example, therefore, works best. Suppose a researcher asks Mr. Jones for the probability of an ambiguous situation such as whether a certain sports team will win its upcoming game. The estimate given is a 60 percent likelihood that the team will win. Further suppose that the researcher presents Mr. Jones with a 50-50 slot machine, which offers no ambiguity, and then asks which bet is preferable. If Mr. Jones is ambiguity-averse, he will likely choose the slot machine, even if he feels confident about the team winning. Those who can handle ambiguous situations and are confident in the team's chances may choose to bet on the team.

Application: Translating this idea to the investment world, when investors feel skillful or knowledgeable, they may not be willing to stake claims on ambiguous investments like stocks, even those whose outcomes they believe they can predict on the basis of their own judgment. They may prefer to be in an investment they can understand, such as AAA bonds or cash, which both offer unambiguous outcomes; hence, the propensity to hold high cash balances. Ambiguity aversion also may restrict investors to their own national indexes because foreign indexes may appear to be ambiguous while the domestic index does not.

Conservatism Bias

Bias Type: Cognitive   Conservatism bias occurs when people cling to a prior view or forecast at the expense of acknowledging new information. These investors tend to cling tenaciously to a view or forecast because they are independent thinkers. Many wealth management practitioners have observed clients who are unable to rationally act on updated information regarding their investments because the clients are fixed upon prior beliefs.

Application: Those with conservatism bias behave too inflexibly when presented with new information. For example, assume an investor purchases a security based on the knowledge that the company is planning a forthcoming announcement regarding a new product. The company then announces that it has experienced problems bringing the product to market. The investor may cling to the initial, optimistic impression of the positive development by the company and may fail to take action on the negative announcement.

Availability Bias

Bias Type: Cognitive   Availability bias occurs when people estimate the probability of an outcome based on how prevalent or familiar that outcome is in their own lives. People exhibiting this bias perceive easily recalled possibilities as being more likely than those prospects that are harder to imagine or difficult to comprehend. In short, the availability bias underlies judgments about the likelihood or frequency of an occurrence, considering only available information, which results from the individual's biased assumptions—not necessarily complete, objective, or factual information.

Application: Some investors' investment decisions may be influenced by what they find while doing their own research. Consider the following example. Suppose an investor is asked to identify the best mutual fund company. Most would perform an Internet search and, most likely, find firms that engage in heavy advertising, such as Fidelity or Schwab. Investors subject to availability bias retrieve the memories of these companies most readily, and thereby may be influenced to pick funds from such companies, despite the situation that some of the best-performing funds advertise very little, if at all.

Representativeness Bias

Bias Type: Cognitive   Some investors try to relate new information to prior experiences because they trust their instincts. Representativeness bias, which is a mental shortcut, occurs as a result of a flawed perceptual framework that processes new information by incorporating insights gained from past experiences. The new information sometimes resembles, or is representative of, past knowledge, when in reality it is different. To make information easier to process, some investors project outcomes that resonate with their own preexisting ideas, even though these projections are not based on solid research.

Application: Some investors rely on stereotypes when making investment decisions. For example, one might view a particular new investment as a value stock because it resembles an earlier value stock that was a successful investment—even when the new investment is not a value stock at all. For example, let's say a high-flying biotech stock with scant earnings or assets drops 25 percent in value after a poor product development announcement. Some may believe that this situation is representative of a value stock because it is cheap; but biotech stocks have typically never had earnings while traditional value stocks have had earnings in the past but temporarily are underperforming.

Self-Attribution (Self-Serving) Bias

Bias Type: Cognitive   Self-attribution bias (or self-serving bias) refers to the tendency of individuals to ascribe their successes to innate characteristics, such as talent or foresight, while blaming failures on outside influences. Self-serving bias can actually be broken down into two constituent tendencies, or subsidiary biases. Self-enhancing bias occurs when people claim an irrational degree of credit for their successes. Self-protecting bias occurs when people deny responsibility for failure.

Application: Suppose an investor who is susceptible to self-attribution bias purchases an investment that goes up. The investor will believe that success is not due to random variables such as economic conditions or competitor failures, but to his or her investment savvy. This is classic self-enhancing bias. In contrast, when an investor purchases an investment and it goes down, then it was due to bad luck, bad management, or some other factor that was not the investor's fault, a clear example of self-protecting bias. The main disadvantage of this bias is that independent-minded investors who are proven right and never proven wrong may not learn from their investment mistakes and, therefore, engage in excessive risk-taking behavior.

Confirmation Bias

Bias Type: Cognitive　Confirmation bias occurs when people observe, overvalue, or actively seek out information that confirms their claims, while ignoring or devaluing evidence that might discount them. Individualist investors often have an all-too-natural ability to convince themselves of whatever it is that they want to believe. They attach undue emphasis to events that corroborate the outcomes they desire, and downplay whatever contrary evidence arises. Confirmation bias can be observed easily. Some investors fail to acknowledge anything negative about investments they've just made, even when there is substantial evidence to the contrary.

Application: There are two examples of confirmation bias that are useful to understand. First, confirmation bias can cause investors to seek out only that information that confirms their beliefs about an investment they have made, and not seek out information that may contradict those beliefs. This behavior can leave investors in the dark regarding, for example, the imminent decline of a stock. Second, confirmation bias can cause investors to continue to hold under-diversified portfolios. Many practitioners have seen clients become infatuated with certain investments. Such a client might accrue a large equity position over the course of years, which ultimately produces a lopsided portfolio. These clients do not want to hear anything negative about a favored investment, but rather single-mindedly seek confirmation that the position will pay off.

Overconfidence Bias

Bias Type: Cognitive　Overconfidence is best described as unwarranted faith in one's own opinions and abilities. Investor overconfidence manifests itself in investors' overestimation of the quality of their judgments. For example, having decided that an investment is a good idea, some investors become blind to the prospect of a loss; they are then surprised or disappointed if the investment performs poorly. This behavior is often recognized by financial advisers because aggressive clients reveal that they consider themselves smarter and better informed than they actually are about investments. Although this is principally a cognitive phenomenon, there are elements of emotion also at work. Some people simply believe, emotionally and irrationally, that they are superior decision makers. This often happens because aggressive clients are successful in other areas of life and believe that they will also be successful in their investment activities, which often will not be the case without significant guidance. The implication of this behavior is that investors may underestimate the risks in their portfolios by underdiversifying their portfolios or trading too much.

Application: Many overconfident investors claim above-average aptitudes for selecting stocks, but little evidence supports this belief. A study done by researchers Odean and Barber examined the 1991 to 1997 investment transactions of 35,000 households, all holding accounts at the same large discount brokerage firm. They showed that after trading costs (but before taxes), the average investor underperformed the market by approximately 2 percent per year because these investors held an unwarranted belief in their ability to assess the correct value of investment securities.[5] Many overconfident investors also believe they can pick mutual funds that will deliver superior future performance. The market-trailing performance of the average mutual fund is proof that most mutual fund clients also fail in this endeavor. Worse yet, investors tend to trade in and out of mutual funds at the worst possible times, suffering because they chase performance. From 1984 to 1995, the average stock mutual fund posted a yearly return of 12.3 percent (versus 15.4 percent for the S&P), while the average investor in a stock mutual fund earned 6.3 percent.[6]

Illusion of Control Bias

Bias Type: Cognitive The illusion of control bias occurs when people believe that they can control or, at least, influence investment outcomes when in fact they cannot. Some investors are used to being deeply in control of their business and personal life activities, and some irrationally believe they can control or influence the outcome of their investments as well. This is not to say that some people cannot have a positive effect on investment-related decisions, such as asset allocation or even fund selection. However, some people believe that they should dictate the process by regularly making changes in strategy or even in individual investments. Rational investors know that investing is a probabilistic endeavor and having a long-term diversified strategy is the best approach.

Application: Similar to overconfident investors, investors who are subject to illusion of control bias believe that the best way to manage an investment portfolio is to constantly adjust it. For example, trading-oriented investors, who accept high levels of risk, believe themselves to possess more control over the outcomes of their investments than they actually do because they are pulling the trigger and making each decision. Similar to the phenomenon of wanting to be in control of a pair of dice in a gambling setting, some investors need to believe that trading is a probabilistic endeavor. Unfortunately for these people, academic research has shown that excess trading results, in the end, in decreased returns.[7]

Self-Control Bias

Bias Type: Emotional   The self-control bias is a human behavioral tendency that causes us to consume today at the expense of saving for tomorrow. Some successful investors have created their wealth and want to take advantage of the fact that they have it. We have all seen plenty of people sabotage their own long-term objectives for temporary satisfaction. The primary concern for wealth management practitioners with regard to self-control bias is a client with high risk tolerance coupled with high spending desires. This behavior can be deleterious because retirement can arrive too quickly for investors who have not saved enough. Frequently, then, some investors incur inappropriate degrees of risk in their portfolios later in life in an effort to make up for lost time. This approach can aggravate the problem if they are investing in risky assets that may lose significant amounts of money.

Application: Self-control bias coupled with high risk tolerance can cause asset allocation imbalance problems. For example, suppose you have a client who prefers aggressive investments and has high current spending needs when suddenly the financial markets hit some severe turbulence. This client may be forced to sell solid long-term investments that have been priced down because of current market conditions just to meet current expenses. Selling at just the wrong time—when prices have dropped—just to maintain a lifestyle can cause serious long-term problems with a portfolio. Advisers who have these client types may need to constantly adjust the asset allocation because of these spending issues.

Optimism Bias

Bias Type: Emotional   Some investors are overly optimistic about the markets, the economy, and the potential for positive performance of the investments they make. Many overly optimistic investors believe that bad investments will not happen to them; they will only afflict others. Such oversights can damage portfolios, because people fail to mindfully acknowledge the potential for adverse consequences in the investment decisions they make.

Application: One of the most obvious examples of optimism bias involves the purchase of company stock by employees in their retirement plans. Risk tolerant employees who participate in 401(k) plans that offer employer stock funds often invest a good portion of their plan assets in company stock. Undue optimism on the part of employees, coupled with illusion of control bias, is a key driver of this phenomenon because it leads people to perceive their own firms as being exceptionally unlikely to suffer from economic misfortunes. Optimism bias can cause investors to potentially overload themselves with company stock by making them think that other companies are more likely to experience downturns than their own.

CONCLUSION

Throughout this chapter we have focused on the importance of nonfinancial issues. UAC advisers need to keep at the forefront of their mind that noninvestment issues take an equal or sometimes even higher priority to investment issues vis-à-vis issues that arise during client meetings. Remember: a UAC's primary goals are not usually to simply build more and more wealth. They are often trying to figure out how to preserve it and moreover determine what to do with it in regard to developing well-adjusted family members. Furthermore, they are trying to do this without creating intrafamily squabbling, dysfunctional child development, or unhealthy family relationships. Now that we have a solid understanding of who the UACs are, their mindset as clients, and their individual behavior, it is time to turn to how best to implement these ideas by examining some noninvestment best practices.

CHAPTER 4

Noninvestment Best Practices

[T]he parent who leaves his son enormous wealth generally
deadens the talents and energies of the son, and tempts him to lead
a less useful and less worthy life than he otherwise would.
                    —Andrew Carnegie, *The Gospel of Wealth*

THE CHALLENGES ASSOCIATED WITH WEALTH

Paradoxically, families with substantial wealth face significant challenges in
their lives. It's not just about country clubs, private schools, charity events,
and fancy vacations. Significant wealth requires careful oversight and stable
guidance; in the wrong hands, wealth can go wildly awry. A successful
transition of wealth from one generation to the next, particularly from the
second to the third, is rarely a question of proper financial asset management
(i.e., sustaining financial capital). Rather, it's about the development of
family members themselves. Throughout this chapter I refer to this notion as
sustaining *human capital*. Two challenges stand out and need to be addressed
if a family is to succeed in sustaining financial and human capital. I discuss
these challenges and unveil a comprehensive plan to address them.

Statistics Are Stacked Against Most Families

The first challenge that families face in their quest to successfully transition
financial capital from one generation to the next is simple statistics. The
odds of successfully transitioning wealth to subsequent generations are
stacked against most families. In their book, *Philanthropy, Heirs and Values*
(Robert D. Reed Publishers, 2005), Roy Williams and Vic Pressier demonstrate that 70 percent of estates fail in their transition into the hands of
heirs. The duo conducted a study of 3,250 families who transitioned wealth
and found that the oft-quoted paradigm of "shirtsleeves to shirtsleeves in

TABLE 4.1 International Phrases Illustrating Dissipation of
Intergenerational Wealth

Country	Quote	Translation
China	"Fu Bu Guo Dan Dai"	Wealth never survives three generations
Italy	"Dalle stalle, alle stalle"	From the stalls to the starts to the stalls
Spain	"Quien no lo tiene, lo hace, y quien lo tiene, lo deshace"	Those who don't have it, make it, and those who have it, lose it.
USA	Rags to riches to rags	

Source: Roy Williams and Vic Pressier, *Philanthropy, Heirs and Values* (Bandon, Ore.: Robert D. Reed Publishers, 2005).

three generations" is alive and well not only in the United States but across the world.[1] To make this point, I show here numerous phrases that refer to the intergenerational failure to retain or grow assets from many countries, which is summarized in Table 4.1.

What should be of keen interest to readers is that professional advisers from the legal, accounting, and investment professions are rarely to blame for this transition failure. The problem, according to Williams and Pressier, is that *assets* often successfully make the transition, but the *family members* often do not. And the reason that family members do not make a successful transition is completely explainable: Many families simply do not have a post-transition plan for the development of members of the family. The financial capital is what gets the most transition attention, rather than the human capital. Table 4.2 highlights the difference in successful versus unsuccessful estate transitions, according to Williams and Pressier.

TABLE 4.2 Comparison of Successful versus Unsuccessful Estate Transitions

Major Differences in Post-transition Outcomes	
Successful	**Unsuccessful**
Entire family (including heirs and spouses) had reached consensus on long-term mission for the family wealth, as well as the Strategy and Roles necessary to attain the mission.	Parents only (working with professional advisers) designated the estate transition, focusing on traditional elements taxation, preservation, and governance (control).
Heirs (and spouses) participated in defining their post-transition roles and responsibilities, and took responsibility to assume their roles.	Heirs discovered their responsibilities at the time of the estate transfer, with widely varying role experiences before that time. Spouses not involved.

Source: Roy Williams and Vic Pressier, *Philanthropy, Heirs and Values* (Bandon, Ore.: Robert D. Reed Publishers, 2005).

Wealth Can Have Detrimental Effects

The second challenge that families face is the potentially damaging effect that inheriting substantial wealth can have on family members. Andrew Carnegie's quote at the beginning of the chapter demonstrates this point. Bill Gates, founder of Microsoft, agrees, and explained his views on the subject at a news conference in New Delhi in 2002, as reported in *Tribune India*. "I don't think it's constructive to grow up having billions of dollars. The idea that I will take a sizeable portion of my fortune and have [my children] inherit that, I don't think that would be to society's benefit or to their benefit. Certainly I'll make sure they are taken care of in a sense that they can live a very comfortable life."[2] Families of substantial wealth need a plan to not only sustain wealth, but to do so in a way that ensures that the wealth has a positive impact on family members.

As may be evident, the answer to these challenges is not to hire a great investment adviser who can continue to earn bundles of money for the family (although it's a good idea to have one, nonetheless). Families need to establish a plan, administered by trusted advisers, that implements best practices not only with investments but also with its human capital, so that family members are capable of handling the responsibilities and challenges of wealth. Families need to focus on creating lasting emotional bonds through the generations. Some families do this by passing stories from one generation to the next that communicate the family's value system. This kind of activity assures that multigenerational relationships remain strong and family members know where they came from.

In my experience working with substantial families, I have seen that sustaining wealth is possible. There are naturally numerous examples of successful multigenerational wealth, but they don't get nearly as much press as those who are failing at the task. As a UAC adviser, you can add tremendous value to your clients' lives by advising them on nonfinancial issues. Keep in mind, however, that families are not corporations, in that they don't simply respond to edicts to begin behaving in a certain way or to adopt plans that you think they should adopt. Families evolve over time and accept advice that *they* think will work, which is not necessarily what you think will work. Be patient and flexible. The plan that I review here is not intended to be an all-or-nothing plan. If your clients can adopt even 50 percent of a plan like the one presented here, you are doing great.

GUIDELINES FOR SUSTAINING MULTIGENERATIONAL WEALTH

Although not entirely obvious, it should make sense that as a family moves from one generation to another, it has a need (and an incentive) to put

FIGURE 4.1   Phases of Wealth Sustainability

more structure in place to manage wealth. In the first generation, the focus is on wealth creation. Subsequent generations are the ones usually tasked with establishing a wealth sustainability plan, which usually involves more attention to human capital issues and less to financial capital issues. So, the game plan is really broken down into three phases: first generation, second and third generation, and then everyone else. Figure 4.1 summarizes the three phases of wealth sustainability and the key components of each. In Phase I, the first generation, the focus is on the creation of financial capital. In Phase II, the second and third generations, the focus is on financial capital preservation and education of human capital. In Phase III, the fourth generation, the focus is on growing and developing human capital.

Phase I: Creating Wealth and Building a Solid Financial Foundation for Future Generations

After investing every available ounce of blood, sweat, and tears into the creation of a successful enterprise, Mr. and Mrs. First Generation Wealth (hereinafter the FGWs) can't believe they actually made it. But wait ... have they? Not only have the FGWs had to endure threats from their business competitors, potential lawsuits, disgruntled employees, and the rest of the laundry list that could torpedo their legacy, they face another threat that they never considered—their kids! Many of us are familiar with the *Pritzker versus Pritzker* case in which a woman sued her father for a "fair share"— $6 billion—of the family wealth, and in the process helped divide one of America's most storied and wealthy families.[3] By working so hard, the FGWs neglect or don't have time to instill the kind of work ethic that made them successful in to their children, and they end up with children who consider family money not as a legacy inheritance or a supplement to their own wealth creation, but as their primary source of income.

What are the FGWs to do, then, to preserve their wealth for their children and grandchildren? The road to sustainable wealth starts in the first generation with a focus on creating a foundation for the family's financial capital that (hopefully) cannot be dissipated by subsequent generations. For UAC advisers, this means bringing in the best investment, tax, banking, insurance, and estate planning professionals that you can find to build a solid financial plan to transition wealth effectively. Put simply, without a solid platform of wealth from which subsequent generations can grow, there is little reason to think about other human capital activities.

Phase II: Financial Capital Preservation and Education of Human Capital

If by some good fortune, a family is in the 30 percent minority that successfully passes wealth to the second generation, some bleak statistics await them. According to the Family Firm Institute of Brookline, Massachusetts, 88 percent of families fail to pass wealth successfully to the third generation, and 97 percent fail by the fourth generation and beyond.[4] Why? Well, the second and third generations have something strong working against them: the laws of nature. Many of us are familiar with the concept of *mean reversion* in the investment world, whereby asset class values tend to move toward their long-term averages over time. The same concept can be applied to family wealth. For example, in Peter L. Bernstein's book, *Against the Gods: The Remarkable Story of Risk* (John Wiley, 1998), Bernstein talks about the power of mean reversion in reference to intergenerational wealth. "Change and motion from the outer limits toward the center are constant, inevitable, foreseeable ... the driving force is always toward the average, toward the restoration of normality.... It is at the root of all homilies like 'what goes up must come down,' 'pride goeth before a fall,' and 'from shirtsleeves to shirtsleeves in three generations.'"[5]

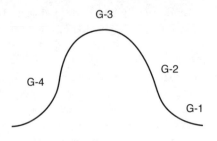

FIGURE 4.2 Hughes's Mean Reversion Concept of Intergenerational Wealth
Source: James E. Hughes, Family: The Compact Among Generations, page 199 © 2007 James E. Hughes. Published by Bloomberg Press. Used by permission.

One of the best ways I've seen to express the challenge faced by second-generation families in the context of mean reversion and wealth dissipation is the brilliant work of James Hughes Jr., a significant contributor to the knowledge base of UAC advisers through his books. In his most recent work, *Family: The Compact Among Generations* (Bloomberg, 2007), Hughes aptly points out the connection of mean reversion and family wealth by plotting four generations of a family on a normal distribution curve (see Figure 4.2). He notes that unless a family can reverse the forces of "normalcy" by the third generation, it will become "average." Hughes's bell curve illustration highlights the critical importance of the second generation: It must keep functioning somewhere on the right side of the bell curve if it is to have a future. "It does that by consistently helping to bring each new generation's dreams to life and second by teaching its members to become dynamic steward-conservators of the earlier generation's dreams. A family that has the foresight to see the risks of becoming average and can help its second generation to be generative by bringing its dreams to life—and using that same process, keep every generation as generative as the second—will stay in the sweet spot on the middle of the right tail of the curve, the spot where I believe long-term success in avoiding the proverb's prediction is achievable."[6]

So the point here is that the focus of the family begins to shift from building a financial foundation (which, incidentally, must be continuously maintained by professionals), to a focus on the development of family members. Both the financial foundation and the development of family members can best be achieved through the establishment of a family office, whether it is a single-family, multifamily, or commercial version. I also encourage all UA families to join information-exchange organizations such as the Family Office Exchange, the Institute for Private Investors, or the CCC Alliance to give them the information they need to address both financial and human capital needs. UAC advisers can play a vital role in this process by participating in both the financial and human capital development of the family at the second and third generation.

Phase III: Governing the Enterprise

By now, in the fourth generation, the family has experienced many of the rituals that normal life brings: death, divorce, illness, infighting, jealousy, you name it. Like any growing community of people, some ground rules need to be established that guide acceptable behavior. Think back to your early education when you learned about the 41 pilgrims who landed in Massachusetts on the Mayflower with no governing body to guide them. They commonly consented to the Mayflower Compact, a code that brought them together for the greater good of the colony they would form.[7] Family governance is no different: a group of people with a diverse membership who depend upon one another to achieve a common goal and who need rules and guidance to live by. Family governance, however, is a tricky area and of all the areas in which the UAC adviser is likely to provide insight, family governance may be the furthest afield. Simply put, there are but a few truly qualified specialists in the field that are expert in offering professional family governance advice. It is therefore critical that UAC advisers get to know these people and bring them into a situation when the timing is right. Given the need for specialists, this section provides a brief overview of family governance so you can familiarize yourself with key concepts.

An excellent resource for getting familiar with family governance is a primer on the subject put out by the National Center for Family Philanthropy aptly titled, "Family Governance: A Primer for Philanthropic Families." In the article, author Patricia Angus focuses on three crucial elements of family governance: principles, practices, and policies.[8] These three elements form a triangular structure: family principles top the triangle, the principles form the family policies, and the family practices are the working part and foundation of the system, as is shown in Figure 4.3. The system can either be informal and casual or have more formal structures and processes.

Family Principles   The family must discover its unique set of principles—its vision, mission, and values. These uniform principles must be shared and supported by the family, as they in turn affect the formation of the family's

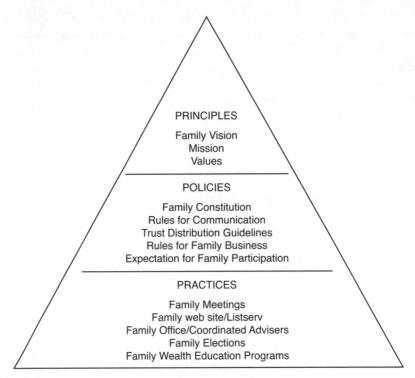

FIGURE 4.3   Three Elements of Family Governance
Source: Patricia Angus, *Family Governance: A Primer for Philanthropic Families* (Washington, D.C.: National Center for Family Philanthropy, 2004).

policies and practices. It is important when forming these principles that the personal aspirations of family members are set aside. The principles should also have certain characteristics: they should respect family member differences and be inspirational, yet realistic. Questions to be answered include:

- What are the family's shared values?
- What makes our family different from others?
- What is our common vision for the family and its future generations?
- What is our mission?

From the answers to these questions, a mission statement, vision statement, or a list of shared values can be developed. Family members need to remain flexible if this process is to be effective. For an example, see the list of shared values found in "Building on Your Best Hopes: From Vision to Action," from *Splendid Legacy: The Guide to Creating Your Family Foundation:*

> "Our family keeps in touch. We're on the phone and the Internet all the time with the grandparents, the parents. We help each other out with advice and support."
> "Our family takes our name very seriously. We have a lot of pride in our ancestors. We have a history, and we're proud of that history."
> "We care about our community and take part in community affairs."
> "We value diversity of opinion. Our family members represent a wide range of views."
> "Our family values education. Any time any family member graduates from anything, it's a big deal.

Policies   The policies that families put in place are the ground rules for communication and action about matters that are common to family members. An example of such a policy is a family constitution, which is a written document describing the vision, values, and guidelines regulating relationships within the family. Typical issues addressed in a constitution are the guidelines for the system of administration, trustee or director appointments, communication, lifestyle, family business and investments, the role of spouses, education, investment objectives, and philanthropy. These general guidelines help family members interact with one another, especially if they have differing personal views on the issues.

A terrific resource on the subject of family mission statements and family constitutions is the author Stephen Covey. He is an advocate of drafting these documents, and is one of the most frequently cited sources in this area. In his best-selling book, *The 7 Habits of Highly Effective Families* (St. Martin's Press, 1997), Covey proposes that families develop a family mission statement. Doing so can help with any number of issues that ail society, such as school shootings, work and family conflicts, marriage problems, or family dysfunction. Covey identifies through his work a change from a family-friendly to a family-hostile society in which families can no longer rely on the rest of civil society or on the government to support and reinforce family values.[9] He argues that in the past families could "successfully raise a family 'outside-in,' because society was an ally, a resource. People were surrounded by role models, examples, media reinforcement, and family-friendly laws and support systems that sustained marriage and helped create strong families."[10] Thus, even if there were family problems, these social institutions offered support. By contrast, in the last 30 to 50 years, "the trends in the wider society . . . have basically shifted from pro-family to anti-family."[11]

The family, he argues, is "the most important, fundamental organization in the world, the literal building block of society. ... No other institution can fulfill its essential purpose," and yet, "in most families members do not have a deep sense of shared vision around its essential meaning and purpose."[12]

Practices   Practices support the family principles and policies during day-to-day activities of family members. How the family interacts needs to be agreed upon through these practices. Some families hold scheduled meetings organized by advisers or family members. Others coordinate their activities and share information through a secure web site or listserv. A family office can also be used to administer the family's nonfinancial affairs, or the family can hire an independent consultant or adviser team. At the end of the day, it doesn't matter what form of communication the family chooses to use; it is just imperative that the chosen interactions best suit the specific family.

Stages of Development   In developing a family governance system, the family experiences three phases: chaos, coordination, and cohesion. In the first stage, chaos, the family responds to immediate needs and does not have a firm grasp on its long-term goals. Support structures are set up when the need appears, such as the writing of a will right before the first big family vacation or right after the birth of a couple's first child. Family members often act

TABLE 4.3   Phases of Development for a Family Governance System

Phase	Characteristics	Actions	Goals
Chaos	Uncoordinated, short-term focus Responds to immediate needs	Create basic estate plans Minimize transfer taxes	To sleep at night Cover emergencies
Coordination	Family sees big picture Family meetings Leaders emerge	Define family goals Begin tax planning and education	Create coordinated system Choose leaders Begin succession planning
Cohesion	Act in view of long-term goals Establish regular meetings	Choose family leaders Clarity between joint and individual needs	Sustainability Integration of family members

Source: Patricia Angus, *Family Governance: A Primer for Philanthropic Families* (Washington, D.C.: National Center for Family Philanthropy, 2004).

independently of the greater good of the family during this phase. The second stage of coordination usually begins when a major event occurs in the family that signals to family members that a more coordinated system is crucial to the family's continued existence. They no longer have a short-term focus in mind; they begin to develop their principles and policies and select their leaders and advisers. The last and most rarely reached stage is cohesion. The family operates under an integrated system, regularly communicates, and looks toward a sustainable future. Once this stage is attained, it is important that the family continues to act in ways that support the cohesive state.

Table 4.3, adapted from "Family Governance: A Primer for Philanthropic Families," summarizes the three phases of development of a family governance system.

CONCLUSION

No single system can be applied to every family, but for the governance system to be effective, the family principles, policies, and practices must be agreed upon and supported by a fostering environment. Certain elements, such as open communication, a respect for the rules and for family member uniqueness, a sense of community, and a clear distinction between the needs and wants of the group and of individuals, can help create this environment. Despite all of the obstacles to effectively governing a family, it is possible to achieve harmony.

Investment Strategies for Ultra-Affluent Clients and Family Offices

Practices of the Best
Investment Organizations

The trustees of an endowed institution are the guardians of the
future against the claims of the present. Their task is to preserve
equity among generations.
> —James Tobin, 1981 Nobel laureate, Sterling Professor of
> Economics, Yale University

As the director of private wealth investment consulting for the second-largest consultant to college endowments in the United States, I am in an excellent position to observe and apply some of the best investment management practices in the world to private families. Given their long-term outlook, sophisticated boards, and disciplined approach, college endowments are on the forefront of investment thinking and have given rise to the *endowment model* of investing. Although 2008 has presented some daunting challenges for even the most sophisticated of these endowment institutions—for example, the venerable Harvard University—I still believe this is the right way to approach managing an investment portfolio. It is imperative, however, that UAC advisers recognize the differences between institutions and humans. It is simply not enough to insist on an endowment approach for even the most sophisticated private wealth investor who believes intellectually in it but has unique psychological or practical needs. Furthermore, not all the practices presented here will work for every client. I suggest that you consider incorporating over the course of time what you believe will work best from what you learn here into your practice of advising UACs, rather than trying to take a dogmatic approach all at once. You may also wish to consider complementing the approach outlined here with the behavioral finance approach described in Chapter 20.

There are certain core concepts of the endowment model that we will cover here that families can adopt and implement for their benefit: investment committees (including establishing investment policy, using staff or consultants, and following guidelines for maintaining an effective committee) and using investment policy statements in practice. The last part of the chapter reviews some key considerations for oversight of a portfolio: asset allocation strategies, the use of contrarian strategies (i.e., leveraging a long-term investment horizon), and inflation protection. I begin by reviewing some key differences between endowments and private investors.

DIFFERENCES BETWEEN ENDOWMENTS AND PRIVATE INVESTORS

There are key differences between UACs and college endowments which present challenges to the UAC adviser. Perhaps the most obvious difference, but one not often given proper attention, is that with private investors, the adviser is dealing with *their* money. Meanwhile, consultants to endowments are dealing with trustees or investment committee members who help to oversee funds—but it's not *their* money. UAC advisers must remember that when applying an endowment-type approach with a potentially long time horizon, emotional responses especially to losses, often emerge. Additionally, families often lack the ability to instill discipline in their investment processes. I can provide several examples of how this can happen. For instance, families are often plagued by personality conflicts (read here: disagreements) that are rooted in family history or longstanding resentments that can affect beliefs about how funds should be managed (e.g., for the current generation or the next) or how money should pass from one generation to the next (quickly or slowly and with few or many restrictions). These disagreements can often make reaching consensus on both investment and noninvestment decisions difficult at best and impossible at worst.

Another example of impediments to discipline is that humans have emotional and/or cognitive biases (as we saw in Chapter 3) which can affect opinions about how money should be invested. For example, a family member may work for a hedge fund and because of this, the family invests in hedge funds in a higher percentage than may be prudent and may have a larger than appropriate position in the family member's fund. Another key difference is that college endowments often have fresh inflows of capital each year from new donations. Many UACs live entirely off of the earnings from their investment portfolio. Also, let's not forget taxes—college endowments don't pay any, which makes both asset class and manager selection and rebalancing much less tricky endeavors for them.

Advisers to UACs should realize that it takes many years for families to adopt processes that work for them. Generally, first generation wealth has little to no wealth management process in place because the wealth creator is not focused on managing wealth but creating it. As the second and third generations (and beyond) evolve, it is easier to apply the principles that you will learn in this chapter. Patience is critical. It may take years, but UAC advisers should strive to apply these practices to their clients over the course of time.

INVESTMENT COMMITTEES

One of the most effective weapons a college endowment (or a UAC and family office) can use in its quest to create a top performing investment portfolio is the establishment of an investment committee (IC). In the cases of Yale, Harvard, and other top endowments, the IC is highly effective in accomplishing its core tasks, which include but are not limited to:

1. Establishing, approving, and implementing investment policy
2. Hiring and maintaining the best possible team of internal staffers and/or consultants
3. General oversight of the investment (family) office

In addition, the IC can potentially add a layer of value by providing access to great investment managers and, perhaps most importantly, having the sophistication to make complex, leading-edge investment decisions that mainstream institutions simply do not. We will now review the core tasks of the investment committee as listed above.

Establishing Investment Policies

There are a number of key tasks that an investment committee will undertake to develop an investment policy. These are to establish:

1. An appropriate risk level for the portfolio.
2. A long-term performance target for the portfolio.
3. An asset allocation strategy designed to achieve the stated long-term performance target.
4. Selection criteria for asset classes and types of investments (including any preference for active or passive management) that will be used in the portfolio.
5. An appropriate time horizon for the portfolio.
6. The spending and liquidity needs of the portfolio.
7. Provisions for any unique requirements that need to be accounted for.

All of these items are captured in a formal written investment policy statement (IPS), a sample of which is reviewed in detail later in this chapter. In addition to these items captured in the IPS, the IC needs to carefully monitor the costs associated with implementing the portfolio, as fees and expenses can have a tremendous effect on long-term returns.

Hiring of Staff and Consultants

Another key responsibility of the IC is to recommend a management structure for oversight of the funds. The options for oversight are for the institution to engage an investment consultant, vest responsibility of investment decisions in a Chief Investment Officer (CIO), use both an investment consultant *and* a CIO, or outsource the job completely to an investment management company (although this tactic is reserved for only the largest endowments, such as Harvard and Princeton). In most of the largest endowments, the responsibility of being accountable for the results of the portfolio is vested in the CIO. Most investment professionals who are involved in endowment management agree that this type of oversight structure is most likely to produce excellent results (as does the Harvard and Princeton investment company model). The following sidebar "What is the Best Endowment Governance Structure?" shows what some of the top experts have to say.

WHAT IS THE BEST ENDOWMENT GOVERNANCE STRUCTURE?

"[Such a structure] shifts investment decision-making authority (but not ultimate responsibility) to a group of individuals that monitors investment and capital markets on a continuous basis and that has well-defined personal incentive (including ... pecuniary incentives) to deploy investment assets in a manner that comports fully with an institution's return objectives and time horizon."
—David Salem, founder and president of
The Investment Fund for Foundations

"The committee should address itself almost exclusively to formulating investment policy and to ensuring that policy is implemented properly. The committee shouldn't even meet with individual managers. ... Leading corporations and foundation funds in the industry today do tend to operate somewhat like the model recommended here."
—Gary Helms, former CIO at the University of Chicago

> *"Whenever economically possible, a great deal of responsibility and accountability should be delegated to full-time professional investment staff rather than borne by part-time, volunteer investment committee members, however well-qualified."*
>
> —Cambridge Associates
>
> *"More and more it is coming to be recognized that outstanding portfolio management can only be achieved by vesting the decision making responsibility in one excellent professional. The decision maker must have the authority, experience, and courage not only to make a "minority" decision but also to do it in the face of compelling opposing arguments from people with impressive credentials."*
>
> —Advisory Committee to the Ford Foundation
> in Managing Education Endowments
>
> Source: Jay A. Yoder, Endowment Management: A Practical Guide (Association of Governing Boards of Colleges and Universities, 1993), 50.

So how do we know that colleges are such good investors? Figure 5.1 summarizes 1- and 10-year returns of college endowments versus several benchmarks, as measured by the National Association of College and University Business Officers (NACUBO). For details on this annual survey, visit nacubo.org. As you can see, endowments have generally done very well, especially the largest ones.

Some may argue that there are other factors that account for investment success, such as access to investments and the sheer amount of funds being invested. But we must not underestimate the value of the Board-CIO model. The previously referenced book, *Endowment Management,* demonstrates the difference a senior investment professional can make. Jay Yoder and Tonya Dixon performed interviews at 97 colleges and universities that had 10-year investment returns for the period ending June 2002. They looked at whether there was a relationship between successful performance and employing a board along with a senior investment professional. (See Table 5.1.) Those schools in the top quintile (top 20 performers) had a median return of 9.8 percent while the bottom quintile (bottom 20 performers) showed a median return of 3.7 percent, a difference of 6.1 percent. Eighty percent of the best performers employed a CIO, while only 35 percent of the poor performers employed CIOs. Fifty-five percent of top performers had employed a CIO for more than five years, while only 15 percent of bottom performers had.[1] This is telling information as to the power of the Board-CIO structure.

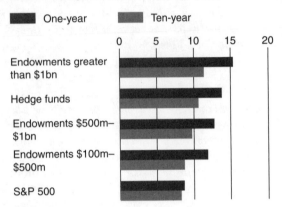

U.S. university endowments versus benchmarks
Returns ending June 30th, 2006, % per year

FIGURE 5.1 U.S. University Endowments versus Benchmarks
Source: National Association of College and University Business Offices; Hedge Fund Research, *The Economist*.

Guidelines for Maintaining the Effectiveness of the Investment Committee

For an investment committee to function properly, especially in the realm of a family office, guidelines should be established as to the following: size of the committee, tenure of members, composition of the membership of the committee, and meeting objectives. With regard to size of the committee,

TABLE 5.1 Comparison of Top and Bottom Quintile Performers

	Institutions with Top Quintile Performance	Institutions with Bottom Quintile Performance
Median 10-Year Return	9.8%	3.7%
Proportion of institutions with CIO position	80%	35%
Proportion of institutions where CIO has existed for more than five years	55%	15%

Source: Jay A. Yoder, *Endowment Management: A Practical Guide* (Association of Governing Boards of Colleges and Universities, 1993), 53.

experts in the field generally agree that smaller committees are more effective than larger ones. Colleges and universities generally have boards of about eight members, according to the latest data.[2] Families tend to prefer smaller boards as well. Generally, I recommend that a family's committee contain no more than six members. For support on this issue, I turn to a quote from Russell Olson, the former director of Pension Investments Worldwide at Eastman Kodak and author of *The Independent Fiduciary: Investing for Pension Funds and Endowment Funds* (Wiley, 1999): "I favor a smaller committee of members who will take their responsibility seriously and will attend meetings regularly. A committee of five might be optimal."[3]

Regarding member tenure, a comparison can be made with political office: the tenure of its members should be limited. Good committee guidelines ensure that those leaving the board transition out smoothly, while new members are welcomed in. Turnover of members is likely to attract new and qualified people, provide board members with fresh ideas, and safeguard the integrity of the board. On the subject of investment committee composition, diversity of thought is essential to the effectiveness of the committee. If a board is made up of all noninvestment-oriented members, disaster is around the corner. Similarly, if the board is made up entirely of investment-focused people, without representation from noninvestment focused members (such as philanthropy or social issues advisers), a dysfunctional situation could arise. Creating board composition guidelines may help to keep the board consistently at its best, for example, "The board shall consist of no more than six members and two of those members will be from the family. The other members will be investment professionals, with at least one being a board member of another family office."

Finally, with respect to committee meetings, the board should be clear on what it will attempt to accomplish at meetings. At a minimum, the committee should meet on a quarterly basis, and set dates and times well in advance so that members have ample time to review recent results of the fund. For the specifics to cover at each meeting, the committee should review the performance of the overall portfolio funds against an appropriate benchmark, and review the performance of each investment manager against the benchmark established for that manager. The committee should also review the compliance of the family's investments with all guidelines contained in the investment policy statement (see the next section), and of each of the family's investment managers with the specific guidelines created for that manager. The committee should review at least annually the allocation strategy of the portfolio to determine whether changes in that strategy are merited. Changes at the strategic asset allocation level are appropriate only if there has been a change in the family's return objectives, risk tolerance, or other special circumstances, or if the committee itself feels as if it should review the portfolio's asset allocation strategy, given a change in market dynamics or valuations.

INVESTMENT POLICY STATEMENTS

An investment policy statement memorializes the policies, strategies, and procedures that will be used in the management of an institution or family's investment portfolio. Although it normally is reviewed and revised annually, the investment policy statement should also be brought out in times of change or market turmoil so that the family can remember why they established their portfolio the way they did. Over time, the rationale for designing a portfolio a certain way can get hazy or, worse, forgotten. This is especially likely during periods of market turmoil, when the temptation to depart from long-term strategies is high. It is crucial that the family and those in positions of leadership of the portfolio not give in to this temptation. A review of the reasons why a long-term strategy was adopted to begin with can temper the urge to make unneeded short-term changes. The following is an abbreviated sample of an investment policy statement that can be used by either an endowment or a family.

In short, the statement of investment policy is set forth to:

1. Define the investment policies, guidelines and objectives of the Smith Family portfolio (the portfolio). Although the policies and objectives are intended to govern the investment activity, they are designed to be flexible enough to be practical.
2. Create a framework from which to evaluate performance and explore new opportunities to enhance the investment portfolio.
3. Provide guidance for, expectations of, and limitations on all parties bearing investment responsibilities for the portfolio.

The following is an example of an investment policy statement.

Investment Policies and Objectives
General Investment Philosophy

Investment Objective: The portfolio's primary investment objective is *long-term growth,* to be achieved by selecting the highest quality money management firms, both passive and active, consistent with the asset allocation targets set by the family in concert with its consultant.

Core Beliefs: The family has adopted a diversified approach to investing that relies on the philosophy that asset allocation explains the majority of investment returns.

General Investment Considerations

Volatility and Risk Tolerance: The risk tolerance of the portfolio is *moderate.* The portfolio will be designed to attempt to limit the risk consistent with the chosen policy asset allocation; it is understood, however, that risks will be taken to achieve the policy return objective.

Liquidity: The portfolio's liquidity will be consistent with the spending policy detailed here.

Time Horizon: The portfolio's time horizon is approximately 20 years.

Spending Policy: The estimated maximum spending amount from the portfolio is targeted to be 2 percent.

Taxes: Consideration must be given to the impact of taxes on returns when selecting investment managers and rebalancing the portfolio. It will be assumed that its members pay the highest marginal federal income tax rates when evaluating investments.

Unique Circumstances: The family has a concentrated equity position outside the diversified portfolio consisting of XYZ stock.

Long-Term Objectives   The investment objectives of the portfolio are based upon a 20-year investment horizon, which allows intermediate-term fluctuations to be viewed with appropriate perspective. While there cannot be complete assurance that the defined objectives will be realized, it is believed that the likelihood of their realization is enhanced by portfolio diversification. The portfolio will aim to achieve the long-term objective while maintaining acceptable risk levels. Appendix A provides the portfolio's asset allocation policy.

Active managers will be expected to provide returns greater than appropriate benchmarks, net of fees, while maintaining acceptable risk levels over moving 36-month periods. Index or passive managers will be expected to earn returns nearly identical to the appropriate benchmarks, before reasonable fees, with volatility comparable to the benchmark.

Total Return Policy   The family has adopted a total-return approach to calculating investment returns. The family recognizes that the portfolio's total return is composed of traditional income (interest and dividends) and realized and unrealized net capital gains.

Asset Allocation   Investment research has determined that a significant portion of a fund's investment behavior can be attributed to the asset classes and styles employed by the fund, and the weighting of each asset class and style. It is the responsibility of the family to select, with the advice of the consultant, the policy asset allocation that offers the highest probability of achieving the portfolio's investment objectives with the lowest amount of risk. The family, with guidance and recommendations from their consultant, shall review the asset mix on an ongoing basis and recommend revisions as necessary.

The policy asset allocation is based on a comprehensive asset allocation study completed by the consultant and reviewed in detail by the family. The policy asset allocation of the portfolio is designed to balance the overall structure of the investment program over the time horizon. However, several factors may affect the policy asset allocation, requiring an asset allocation review and possible rebalancing. These factors include:

- The family's assessment of the intermediate- or long-term outlook for different asset classes and styles.
- The consultant's assessment of the intermediate- or long-term outlook for different types of asset classes and styles.
- Divergence in the performance of the different asset classes and styles, and cash balances maintained above the asset allocation policy.

Portfolio Rebalancing   Since policy asset allocation is the most critical component of return, it is desirable to rebalance the portfolio periodically to minimize deviations from the policy asset allocation mix.

The portfolio should be rebalanced if any individual asset class allocation differs from policy by more than 20 percent of the target weight, with a minimum deviation threshold of 2 percent of the total portfolio value. For example, if the policy asset allocation for an asset class is 3 percent of the total portfolio, then the portfolio's actual allocation must be either below 1 percent or above 5 percent of the total portfolio before rebalancing is required. An actual allocation of 1.5 percent would have a deviation of 50 percent from the target weight but not meet the 2 percent minimum deviation threshold.

The consultant will make recommendations, however, for rebalancing, bearing in mind the cost basis and the incurred tax consequences, attempting to harvest any losses to offset taxable gains.

Hiring, Evaluation, and Termination of Money Managers

Hiring: Investment managers will be selected by carefully considering numerous factors to include: (list of factors).

Monitoring: The consultant will monitor all managers in the portfolio with regard to performance, tracking error, and conformance to style mandates. Managers will be measured versus peers and appropriate style benchmarks. Any sustained negative relative performance of one year should trigger an evaluation. Structural changes in the management firm may also elicit a manager evaluation.

Termination: Generally, the consultant uses comparisons against a benchmark portfolio and a peer universe of similarly managed portfolios to evaluate manager performance; no specific rules, however, are used to terminate managers. The family also has the ability to terminate any manager at will. Certainly, should any of the factors used to hire a manager be compromised, termination may follow. Structural changes within the investment management firm always initiate an in-depth evaluation.

Delegation of Responsibilities

The Family or Investment Committee

- Selecting investment managers and custodians.
- Setting investment policy guidelines.
- Approving investment objectives and performance measurement standards consistent with its financial needs.
- Approving the policy asset allocation and rebalancing strategies.
- Reviewing and evaluating investment results in the context of predetermined performance standards and implementing corrective action as needed.

Consultant: (*responsibilities of the consultant listed here*).
Investment Managers: (*responsibilities of the investment managers listed here*).
Custodian: (*responsibilities of the custodian listed here*).

Permissible Investments   The policy asset allocation of the portfolio is expected to include a wide range of asset classes, as displayed in Appendix A. The asset classes include:

- Domestic and International Public Equity.
- Domestic and International Fixed Income.
- Real Estate Investment Trusts.
- Nontraditional (alternative) assets.
  - Domestic or International Private Equity.
  - Domestic or International Hedge Funds.
- Real Assets.
  - Real Estate.

- Natural Resources and Commodities.
- Other Hard Assets.
- Cash Equivalents.

Investment Policies for Investment Managers   The following are performance goals and constraints placed on individual managers within specific asset classes:

- Index managers shall be terminated if performance or volatility significantly differs from that of the benchmark.
- Active managers may be terminated because of strategy changes, management turnover, poor long-term investment performance, or other material changes.

Alternative Investments   Alternative investment managers typically must have significant latitude in the strategies they employ and the leverage they introduce into a portfolio. As a result, it is generally not feasible to impose guidelines and restrictions on such managers. The family may instead choose to terminate a manager, subject to the liquidation policy, if they are dissatisfied with the manager or his strategy.

Other   *Securities Lending:* Investment managers may engage in securities lending, or the loan of the portfolio's securities in return for interest, to broker-dealers as a means of enhancing income.

Standards of Performance   The performance of the portfolio will be reviewed monthly and quarterly to ensure that it is achieving the investment objectives and the appropriateness of the investment policy for achieving these objectives. It is not expected that the investment policy will change frequently. In particular, short-term changes in the financial markets should not require an adjustment to the maximum commitment levels by asset class as set forth by this investment policy.

In consideration of the family's goals and objectives, several standards will be used to evaluate investment performance as opposed to a single measure. These standards reflect several aspects of investment performance, including the specific objectives and the market indexes used to measure the performance of individual managers. The specific basis for performance evaluation of active managers is as follows:

A. Each manager should exceed the passive standards or benchmarks for the style and type of management as established for each asset class.

B. Each manager is expected on a rolling three-year basis to perform in the top fiftieth percentile of the manager's peer group, as measured by an acceptable comparable professional performance measurement service that evaluates balanced, equity, and fixed-income managers as to style, risk, return, and responsibility who have like styles and requirements.

C. Investment performance of various classes of securities will be compared to unmanaged market indexes as follows:

1. Equity performance will be compared with nationally recognized equity indexes such as the S&P 500, the Russell 3000, or the Russell 2000. Equity performances will also be compared with a nationally recognized style index depending on the manager's orientation toward growth or value. Finally, equity performance will be compared to an appropriate peer group universe.

2. Fixed-income performance will be compared with nationally recognized bond indexes such as the Lehman Brothers Aggregate or Municipal Indexes or Government/Corporate Index. Fixed-income performance will also be compared to an appropriate peer group universe.

3. International equity managers or international pooled funds will be compared against a nationally recognized international equity index, such as the Morgan Stanley Capital International All Country World ex-US Index.

4. Real estate performance will be compared with the total return of the National Council of Real Estate Investment Fiduciaries Index (NCREIF) and the National Association of Real Estate Investment Trusts (NAREIT).

5. Private equity returns will be compared over the long term, 5–10 years, to the S&P 500 Index plus 5.0 percent and private real assets are compared to the CPI plus 5 percent.

6. Hedge fund performance will be compared to the Hedge Fund Research Fund of Funds (HFR FOF) equal weighted collection of fund of funds managers.

An evaluation of the investment manager's performance will be conducted quarterly to include not only measurement with respect to the standards described above, but also an overall qualitative evaluation of strategy during the quarter and the past year. However, specific quantitative measures, especially the more absolute oriented measures, will be considered of more importance over a full market cycle or a three- to five-year period, whichever occurs first.

Procedure for Revising Guidelines All investment policies and performance goals will be reviewed every six months or when deemed necessary.

To facilitate timely adjustments and rebalancing, the family may revise the policy asset allocation at any time.

Conflicts of Interest   All persons responsible for investment decisions, involved in the management of the portfolio, or consulting or providing any advice whatsoever to the family shall disclose in writing any relationships, beneficial ownership, or other material interests the person has or may reasonably be expected to have with respect to any investment issue under consideration. The family may require such persons to remove themselves from the decision-making process.

Appendix: Asset Allocation Policy

(Asset allocation policy listed here.)

This investment policy statement must be reviewed at least once a year and confirmed as appropriate or amended as necessary at that time.

KEY CONSIDERATIONS FOR PORTFOLIO OVERSIGHT

As most of you who are reading this book know, asset allocation is the process of deciding which asset classes will be included in the portfolio and the percentage that each asset class will have in same. As referenced in the investment policy statement offered here, several important studies have shown that asset allocation is the primary driver of investment returns.[4] The next chapter will delve deeply into this topic. For now, readers should know that the most important responsibility of UAC advisers is to recommend a sound asset allocation strategy for the family's portfolio. In doing so, she should consider modern portfolio theory's principles of diversification: investment returns have a direct relationship with the amount of risk (variability) that is assumed in the portfolio, and correlations across asset classes can serve to decrease the overall risk level for a given level of expected return. In making the asset allocation recommendations, the UAC adviser should identify and recommend one or several possible asset allocation strategies (also known as an asset allocation study) that produce the best possible expected return per unit of risk incurred. The adviser should then select from among the efficient asset allocation strategies that specific strategy that seems best to meet the return and income needs and the risk tolerance of the family.

Some investors and advisers like to use ranges of asset classes when selecting an asset allocation policy. For instance, for "U.S. Fixed Income" an allowable range is 10 to14 percent versus a hard target of 12 percent. An alternative method is to use rebalancing rules to guide asset class ranges as reviewed in the rebalancing section of the investment policy statement in the last section.

Many families have accumulated wealth by ignoring basic asset allocation principles; that is, by concentrating their investments in a single stock such as Johnson & Johnson or a single asset class such as real estate. Thus, there may be a temptation to do the same when it comes to investing what is intended to be a wealth preservation portfolio, concentrating in high risk asset strategies, which, depending upon one's ability to select managers, may be deleterious to one's wealth. I encourage all advisers to adopt modern portfolio theory's principles of diversification when working with UACs. In doing so, you can take comfort in the knowledge that the best universities in the world take the same approach.

Portfolio Monitoring

Just as is done in the endowment world, the performance of the family's portfolio should be reviewed on a quarterly basis by the CIO, the consultant, and the family. To properly complete this task, the portfolio should have a benchmark that reflects indexes associated with the asset classes contained in the portfolio with each index weighted in accordance with the target asset allocation. The family should be educated as to how investment results should be interpreted. That is, the family needs to know that short-term investment performance is random and may not adequately reflect the results of the portfolio that may be achieved over the long run (i.e., the portfolio as a whole will be expected to achieve its objectives over a complete market cycle). In addition to assessing investment performance, the family should review compliance with their investment policy statement, with special attention paid to their risk tolerance and tax situation.

One area of portfolio monitoring that causes confusion for many clients is that of private equity, which often calls for a separate report. The reason for this confusion is that clients and advisers alike often neglect to consider cash flows and timing when looking at private equity performance numbers. In the early years of a private equity investment, a fund will have low or even negative returns because of management fees and from underperforming investments whose values are adjusted to account for poor performance, or written down. In subsequent years, the sale of portfolio companies or IPOs results in cash or stock distributions to the limited partners. Over time, increasing proportions of a fund's performance reflect actual cash distributions received, rather than valuation estimates. The most widely used measure of private equity performance is the internal rate of return (IRR). The formula for IRR takes into account the timing of cash flows to and from the partnership and the length of time an investment has been held by the investor. Perhaps a better measure of performance is using a multiple of invested capital. This statistic measures the proceeds received from a fund plus the valuation of the remaining investments divided by the capital contributed to the fund. Table 5.2 provides an example of a private equity performance chart from CalPERS.

Contrarian Strategies (Long Time Horizon)

One of the key tenets of the endowment approach is that endowments invest in contrarian strategies. This can consist of investments that others have little or no familiarity with, such as African infrastructure, or asset classes that are severely out of favor. Either way, the fact that endowments have a long time horizon plays a critical role. In principle, their investment horizon is not measured in weeks, months, or years, but is interminable. In theory, each endowment has a single client, itself, that needs to extract whatever it deems necessary to keep the wheels of scholarship turning (there is no mandatory payout for college endowments as there is in the case of foundations and other non-profits—a fact that is under scrutiny right now by the U.S. government). Unlike pension funds, which have to match assets with liabilities, endowments can tolerate volatility, which permits them to make, and weather, contrarian bets. As shown in Figure 5.2, Harvard and Yale make extremely nontraditional bets.

As of June 2006, real assets were the largest category at Yale, accounting for nearly 28 percent of the school's portfolio. At Harvard, it was nearly 21 percent. Yale's allocation of 23 percent to absolute-return strategies was double its commitment to U.S. stocks. As might be expected at big research universities, this aggressive move away from traditional assets was rooted in academic research, suggesting that investors can earn a higher long-term rate of return with less risk by diversifying beyond the traditional mix of stocks and bonds. Both endowments avoided the downturn of U.S. markets after the tech bubble popped in 2000. Other asset categories helped compensate, as in the case of hedge funds, which were able to benefit from a market decline, and private equity, real estate, and commodities, which soared as interest rates dropped. The endowment approach is now being copied to varying degrees by nearly every major university and institutional endowment in the country.

Of course, there are differences between venerable institutions with billions to invest over perpetual time horizons and individuals whose resources

TABLE 5.2 Example of Private Equity Performance

	Capital Committed	Cash In	Cash Out	Cash Out & Remaining Value	Net IRR[1,2]	Investment Multiple
Total	$49,067.50	$29,554.30	$22,485.50	$42,423.50	14.50%	1.4×
1990 Vintage Year	125.3	121.9	295.3	295.9	15.8	2.4×
1991 Vintage Year	171.7	179.6	509.3	509.5	27.6	2.8×
1992 Vintage Year	160	156.6	340.2	341.9	20.6	2.2×
1993 Vintage Year	563	560	1,041.40	1,076.70	20	1.9×
1994 Vintage Year	1,507.60	1,416.90	2,326.30	2,437.30	14.7	1.7×
1995 Vintage Year	1,197.90	1,141.30	1,791.20	1,922.70	15.8	1.7×
1996 Vintage Year	1,155.90	1,133.70	1,458.30	1,533.40	9	1.4×
1997 Vintage Year	1,111.90	1,090.00	1,399.10	1,592.10	9.1	1.5×
1998 Vintage Year	2,216.70	2,175.70	2,561.60	3,050.60	8	1.4×
1999 Vintage Year	1,207.40	1,149.40	1,176.80	1,550.10	7.4	1.3×
2000 Vintage Year	3,977.90	3,647.70	2,986.70	4,979.60	9.2	1.4×
2001 Vintage Year	4,816.80	4,225.10	3,667.70	7,669.50	21.5	1.8×
2002 Vintage Year	1,092.60	958.6	766.5	1,551.00	24.8	1.6×
2003 Vintage Year	1,496.20	1,235.50	1,025.70	2,303.10	N/M	N/M
2004 Vintage Year	2,014.60	1,471.00	580.1	2,219.30	N/M	N/M
2005 Vintage Year	3,932.00	2,519.70	418.1	2,940.10	N/M	N/M
2006 Vintage Year	9,317.20	3,440.50	132.2	3,590.10	N/M	N/M
2007 Vintage Year	13,002.90	2,931.00	8.9	2,860.50	N/M	N/M

[1]Because of the long-term nature of investing in private equity, funds can produce low or negative returns in the early years of the partnership. In the first few years of the partnership, management fees are drawn from partner's capital and portfolio companies are held at cost, leading to an understatement of ultimate value.

[2]Due to numerous factors, including the lack of standardized valuation and reporting standards, the IRR information in this report may not reflect the expected returns of the partnerships. The IRRs contained in this report are calculated by CalPERS and have not been reviewed by the General Partners.

Source: http://www.calpers.ca.gov/index.jsp?bc=/investments/assets/equities/aim/private-equity-review/overview.xml.

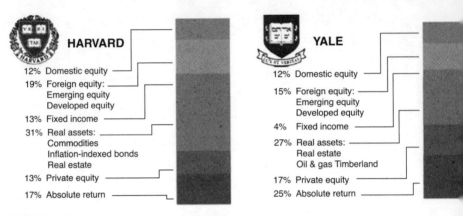

FIGURE 5.2 Harvard and Yale Asset Allocations
Source: Yale and Harvard 2006 Annual Reports.
Note: Totals more than 100 percent because Harvard uses leverage to improve returns.

and life spans are finite. Harvard's and Yale's superior performances are a function not just of wide diversification and a limitless time horizon, but also of the quality of their asset managers. Yale and Harvard are so large that they can select the best managers and provide the seed capital for top managers to launch new funds. Today, the top hedge, private equity, and venture capital funds are closed to new investors, and many others require enormous minimum investments or don't allow individual investors at all.

Inflation Protection

One of the most commonly overlooked areas of investing, which most endowments take very seriously, is the effect inflation has on a portfolio's purchasing power. UAC advisers need to be acutely aware that inflation protection is one of the most critical areas to address in portfolio oversight. In Figure 5.3, note the inflation changes from 1998 to 2008 of the Consumer Price Index. As we can see, inflation has risen significantly since 1998.

Even though 2009 will likely show some deflation in the global economy, the likely outcome of the U.S. and other governments' policy of money supply expansion to fight the global recession will be inflationary. Devoting a minimum of 15 percent to inflation protection assets is recommended. Please see Chapter 11 for ways to fight the effects of inflation.

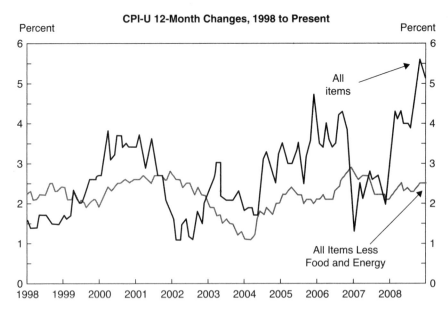

FIGURE 5.3   Consumer Price Index 1998–2008
Source: U.S. Department of Labor—Bureau of Labor Statistics,
http://www.bls.gov/cpi/cpid0809.pdf.

CONCLUSION

We reviewed in this chapter some of the key elements of the investment
practices of the best investment organizations. Many UACs are acting like
institutions; a term that some use to describe these people is *instividual*.
UAC advisers therefore need to be aware of the essential elements of institutional best investment practices and implement them with their UACs
whenever possible. I now move to asset allocation considerations—essential
knowledge for implementing a portfolio for UACs.

CHAPTER 6

Asset Allocation Considerations for Ultra-Affluent Clients and Family Offices

There are several important aspects of asset allocation: get your risk level correct, match it to your horizon, be diversified, be tax-efficient, and then get high alpha—but only after you've accomplished all those other things.
—Roger Ibbotson, Founder of Ibbotson Associates and
Yale University Professor of Finance

Nearly everyone involved in advising private clients on their investments knows or has heard that asset allocation is the most important decision an investor can make vis-à-vis long-term investment performance. After 2008, there may be some doubters out there. For the record, I firmly believe in asset allocation despite the fact that most asset classes have retreated en masse thereby virtually eliminating the benefits of diversification. This action is a result, in the view of North Trust Company's chief economist Paul Kasriel, of a *global margin call*. To his point, when a plethora of market participants needed liquidity all at once, indiscriminant selling caused everything to go down in tandem—and when this happened, even rational investors fled risky assets to seek the safety of U.S. treasury securities, exacerbating the problem. This "black swan" event is not a common occurrence, but it has happened in the past—with 2008 being an extreme example. I hope that only a trivial number of advisers choose to ignore the time-tested principles of asset allocation and think they are smart enough to pick a few hot investment managers (usually without regard to the efficiency of asset classes that the active managers participate in) that can outperform a well-diversified investment portfolio. These advisers end up either with very unhappy clients or, in the extreme, out of the business. So, if it is necessary to say again, asset allocation is the most important decision an investor makes when designing his investment portfolio—period.

Asset allocation is both a quantitative and a qualitative exercise. Because asset allocation is quantitative by nature—we talk about expected return, efficient frontier, percentages, and so on as inputs into the asset allocation selection process—there is a tendency for advisers to take a mostly, if not purely, quantitative approach. However, there is just as much art as there is science in selecting an appropriate asset allocation for your client. And when one factors in psychological biases, risk tolerance, multigenerational issues, and taxes, the asset allocation decision becomes even more subjective.

This chapter is intended to provide an overview of not only the importance of asset allocation, but also a primer on key issues that crop up when dealing with UACs with regard to asset allocation selection. The chapter is organized as follows: I first discuss why asset allocation is so important and review some of the academic research demonstrating how critical the asset allocation decision is, for nonbelievers or those who may need a refresher. I then discuss, without getting too technical, the importance of the assumptions that are used when modeling potential asset allocations for clients. At the end, I dig into some key considerations for UACs selecting asset allocations by looking at the inputs of an investment policy statement. Before moving to the importance of asset allocation, let's first define what we mean by *asset allocation*.

WHAT IS ASSET ALLOCATION?

In its simplest form, asset allocation is the process of determining how many and which asset classes will be included in a client's portfolio and the percentages that each class will represent. The right asset allocation for a client (i.e., which asset classes and in what amounts) will depend upon how well the allocation's characteristics and behavior match the client's objectives and constraints, which are typically captured in the investor's investment policy statement. Regardless of what level of risk a client is comfortable with, modern portfolio theory, which stresses diversification, tells us that our job as advisers is to obtain for our clients the best possible expected return for a given level of risk. The method used to attain this goal is to maximize the Sharpe ratio (return per unit of risk) for each portfolio allocation combination presented to the client during the asset allocation study.

Regardless of the asset allocation that is ultimately selected, there are two types of asset allocation that are used with clients: strategic and tactical.

Strategic asset allocation (SAA) is the asset allocation that, when integrated into the investment policy statement, is intended to satisfy the client's objectives and constraints. SAA is really the seminal element of the portfolio creation and management process. The typical method of selecting the strategic asset allocation is through the use of an asset allocation study. This process involves presenting the client, after a thorough fact-finding and profiling session (i.e., IPS inputs), with an array of possible asset allocations that may be appropriate for the client. The asset allocation study presents risk-and-return statistics for the array of asset mixes presented so that the clients can get a sense for the behavior he or she can expect from the selected allocation. Naturally, this process is not an exact science. Using historical or even forward-looking capital markets expectations cannot predict with precision how a portfolio will behave from year to year. Over the long run, however, behavior is more predictable using a strategic asset allocation.

Tactical asset allocation (TAA) is the process of making temporary adjustments to the asset class percentages selected in the SAA. These changes are based on projected short- to medium-term (defined as anywhere from a few months to five years depending upon the time horizon of the tactical decision) relative performance of asset classes in the client's portfolio. Some may interpret this as market timing. This is not the same thing. Market timing is defined as straying into asset classes outside the policy allocation in hopes of gaining short-term advantages. In practice, TAA can be thought of as tilting toward certain classes and away from others while still maintaining exposure to the classes that are in the client's policy allocation.

Some investment advisers don't explicitly break out asset allocation into strategic and tactical, but use a combination of both as they change asset allocation recommendations over time. Both strategic and tactical allocation selection are typically done using a modeling process that relies on assumptions of returns, risk, and correlations among asset classes. Many advisers don't take the time to dig in to the details of these assumptions. The next section does this, before we delve in to the key asset allocation considerations for UACs.

THE IMPORTANCE OF ASSUMPTIONS IN THE ASSET ALLOCATION SELECTION PROCESS

The most widely used implementation technique of modern portfolio theory's key tenet of diversification is *efficient frontier analysis*. Efficient frontier analysis, the process of minimizing risk per unit of return, is held in very high regard for many reasons, not the least of which is that is it based on the work of a Nobel laureate, Harry Markowitz. Mr. Markowitz's development of mean-variance optimization as a tool for investors and professionals is at the heart of asset allocation in practice. Many advisers use this tool with their clients because investors can attempt to obtain the highest Sharpe ratio in their portfolios by minimizing the volatility per unit of return by diversifying into multiple asset classes.

This process works because of a lack of perfect correlation between the asset classes in the portfolio construction; quantitatively, we call this the *covariance* among asset class pairs. Put simply, in one market environment, a given asset class may be falling while another one is rising, and another may be flat. In another market environment, the one that was flat may be rising, the one that was rising may be falling, and the one that was falling may be flat. The result is a smoothing of returns for the portfolio as a whole. We need to keep in mind, however, that the accuracy of the efficient frontier modeling process is based on assumptions of expected return, expected standard deviation (risk), and expected correlations among asset classes. The assumptions that are used for this analysis can cause the output to vary widely. Advisers need to understand the sensitivities of these assumptions so they can communicate effectively with their clients about the behavior of their clients' portfolios over time.

When advisers attempt to create efficient portfolios for their clients, they need to answer questions such as how many asset classes to include in the client's portfolio, which asset classes to use, and how much of the client's assets to allocate to each class selected. To answer these questions, advisers estimate inputs for each asset class of expected return, volatility of returns, and the correlations among all asset classes. They then optimize the mix of asset classes to create the efficient frontier, which represents the best possible combinations of risk and return for a given set of asset classes. So why all the fuss? The point is that the efficient frontier is a model in which assumptions drive the output. And assumptions of expected returns, volatility, and correlation very rarely come true to life. So advisers who want to add value to their client portfolios need to simultaneously examine history and look forward in making estimates—not an easy task. And, they need to realize that forecasts are nothing more than a best guess of the future.

The easiest place to estimate input assumptions is by using historical data. Using average return, standard deviation, and historical correlations you can back test and determine which portfolios have been optimal in the past. Obviously, using historical data only makes sense if you believe that history will repeat itself. A natural question here is, if you are going to use historical data, which historical period is best to use? Should one use a long period of time such as 100 years to capture the greatest amount of data possible, or use more mature capital market periods such as the last 30 years? And what about asset class maturity? Should one use one period for emerging markets bonds and another for Treasuries, reflecting the inception dates of these two asset classes? There is no right answer to these questions. They are a matter of judgment. There are some concepts to keep in mind, though. First, historical data should be assumed to have significant value, and changing estimates should have a clearly articulated logic. An example here is the correlation between U.S. large-capitalization equities and international large capitalization. Historically, these asset classes have been moderately correlated, but the case can be made that given the increasing integration of the global economies and capital markets, large multinational company equities will behave similarly regardless of where the companies are headquartered. Second, expected return estimates are going to have a large impact on the optimality choices of various asset mixes. Therefore, advisers need to carefully consider projected return estimates. Standard deviations and correlation assumptions have a lesser impact on optimality choices. Also, some return estimates include *alpha,* or outperformance, above an index, which typically distorts asset allocation models. Lastly, whatever methodology is used to determine assumptions should be applied consistently across asset classes.

THE IMPORTANCE OF ASSET ALLOCATION

Practitioners who rely on asset allocation to be the primary driver of returns recognize the pivotal role that strategic asset allocation plays in establishing the risk exposure a client can tolerate in his or her portfolio. One of the key benefits of the decision to diversify a portfolio into many asset classes is risk management. Although no asset allocation can prevent a portfolio from losing value in a severe market downturn, it can protect the portfolio in most market environments because when certain asset classes are falling, others are usually rising. Many advisers view asset allocation as highly important, based on a seminal article written in 1986 by Brinson, Hood, and Beebower (BHB), titled "Determinants of Portfolio Performance."[1]

BHB performed a study on the asset allocations of 91 large pension funds from 1973 to 1985. They replaced the pension funds' stock, bond, and cash selections with corresponding market indexes. The indexed quarterly returns were found to be higher than the pension plans' actual quarterly returns. The two quarterly return series' linear correlation was measured at 96.7 percent, with shared variance of 93.6 percent. On average, timing and security selection explained 6.4 percent of return variability. The contributions of timing and security selection to active returns were found on average to be negative, implying that spending time on these activities is not rewarded (on average).[2]

The authors interpreted the importance of asset allocation as the "fraction of the variation of returns over time" attributable to asset allocation on the basis of a regression analysis of the data.[3] What many financial advisers don't realize about this study is that it answered the question, "How much of the variability of returns across time for one portfolio is explained by asset allocation (or how much of a fund's volatility is explained by its policy allocation)?" rather than "What portion of a portfolio's return is explained by its asset allocation policy?" which is really what we as advisers want to know. This may seem like an insignificant distinction, but, in fact, it is very different.

In 2000, Roger G. Ibbotson and Paul D. Kaplan answered this second and more important question in a study titled "Does Asset Allocation Policy Explain 40, 90, or 100 Percent of Performance?" Ibbotson and Kaplan used five asset classes in this study: U.S. large-capitalization stocks, U.S. small-capitalization stocks, foreign stocks, U.S. fixed-income securities, and cash, examining the 10-year returns of 94 U.S.-balanced mutual funds versus the corresponding indexed returns. After adjusting for index fund fees, the active returns failed to beat index returns. The linear correlation of monthly index returns versus the actual monthly return series was measured at 90.2 percent, with a shared variance of 81.4 percent. Asset allocation explained 40 percent of the variation of returns across funds, and explained virtually 100 percent of the level of fund returns. Ibbotson and Kaplan confirm that on average, active management (that is, market timing and manager selection) adds literally nothing to returns.[4] This does not necessarily imply that an investor cannot be successful hiring active managers. Advisers should spend the majority of their investment policy creation time, however, on the asset allocation decision and less time on selecting active managers.

One final note is this: These studies do not include alternative investments such as hedge funds, private equity, or other private investments such as real estate or natural resources. In these asset classes, active management is almost assuredly what determines performance. In venture capital, hiring top decile (top 10 percent) managers is critical to investment success. It is not possible to invest in an index of venture capital, so manager selection is critical. In hedge funds, index returns are less than desirable. An approach that works well, therefore, especially for UACs who can allocate large sums to alternatives, is to get your active exposure in alternatives and index traditional investments, particularly highly efficient asset classes such as large-cap U.S. and large-cap international.

CONSIDERATIONS IN ASSET ALLOCATION FOR INDIVIDUAL INVESTORS

Individual investors in general, and UACs in particular, are characterized as unique, tax-paying, and diverse with their investment objectives; they have multiple time horizons, growth, and income needs, and varying risk toler-ances. What's a UAC adviser to do to keep it all straight? Have lots and lots of patience! To make matters more complex, many UACs have addi-tional constraints that must be worked around such as concentrated equity positions, operating business interests, philanthropic objectives, and many others. The task, therefore, of determining an optimal asset allocation is a customized process for each client and, as previously noted, is as much art as it is science. What is critical for UAC advisers to understand is that many UACs want to optimize an asset allocation for multiple objectives—and more often than not, this is simply not possible. One cannot simultaneously optimize for maximum income, maximum philanthropic donations, maxi-mum growth, and minimal taxes. It is certainly possible to have multiple objectives and create investment strategies for each of these objectives, but optimizing a single allocation for each one is not possible. UAC advisers need to help their clients determine what is most important to them, and, once that is established, tailor the asset allocation to the clients' key objectives.

Perhaps the best way to illustrate the process of customizing the asset allocation is to review the categories that comprise an investment policy statement. These are return objectives, risk tolerance, and constraints such as liquidity, time horizon, taxes, legal and regulation, and unique circum-stances. For clarity, there will be a segment in each of these sections called "impact on asset allocation" that will demonstrate what it is about each of these categories that affects the asset allocation process. The key is for advisers to learn how to have conversations with their clients about prior-itizing investment objectives so they can recommend the most appropriate asset allocation.

Return Objectives

Selecting a return objective is one of those subjects that often finds advisers and UACs ideologically distant. For example, advisers, who are grounded in asset allocation and capital markets principles understand that while a 9 percent return objective is difficult to achieve, it is well within the realm of possibility (assuming the client has the proper risk tolerance to withstand some volatility). To a UAC, especially one who created wealth or was part of the process that created wealth in a concentrated way such as holding a single stock, 9 percent sounds very unexciting. The good news is that most UACs don't *need* to earn more than 9 percent (although in some families the number of family members grows faster than the family's wealth and 9 percent is not enough!). Their basic needs are taken care of such that most could live very happy lives putting all of their money in municipal bonds. However, few, if any, UACs decide to put all of their money in municipal bonds. Why is that? Because most UACs *want* to earn more than 9 percent. Should they take on the risks necessary to earn a return higher than 9 percent? At the end of the day, it's up to the client to make that decision. But it is the job of the adviser to educate the client about the risks that must be taken to achieve a double-digit return.

It is therefore critical that a UAC's return objective be carefully defined, both quantitatively and qualitatively, with the emphasis being on the qualitative side. What UAC advisers need to do is help their clients define exactly what it is that they want their money to do for them. Return objective is a wonderful starting point because it gets UACs thinking about the broad subject of what long-term financial goals they have and how their existing wealth will help them achieve these goals. Return objectives are ironically one of the most important discussion points but are often backed into at the end of the process once the client has done significant thinking and planning about the question of what the family wants the money to accomplish. While quantitative measures are easy to judge ("Did I earn 9 percent or not?"), qualitative return objectives are not as easy, although they can certainly be evaluated. For example, a qualitative goal such as "to achieve returns that will provide an adequate spending income and maintain a fund's real purchasing power" can be concretely determined.

Impact on the Asset Allocation Decision   Return objective has a significant impact on the asset allocation decision. If the return objective is high, then an asset mix that emphasizes higher returns and higher-risk asset classes will be selected. If the return objective is low, then, naturally, the opposite is true. In the case of the client who is inclined toward a high return objective, UAC advisers need to carefully assess whether the client *wants* a high return objective or *needs* a high return objective. UA clients often take on more risk than is necessary simply because they think they ought to have a high return objective.

Risk Tolerance

When creating an asset allocation policy for a client, the natural complement to return objective is risk tolerance. As with return objectives, both qualitative and quantitative risk objectives are important considerations. Many practitioners begin the risk assessment process by administering a risk tolerance questionnaire that evaluates both quantitative and qualitative factors of an investor's risk tolerance. This usually results in the investor being categorized into one of four or five risk categories from low to high, based on the investor's willingness and ability to assume risk. But how can an adviser actually map the risk tolerance of the client to an allocation that is appropriate for the client? I believe that behavioral factors also need to be assessed because clients often overestimate their risk tolerance. In fact, I discuss this very subject later in the book. But from a purely risk assessment standpoint, there are several ways to do this. I discuss standard deviation, probability of a loss year, and shortfall risk as ways to match an allocation to risk tolerance.

Investors can quantify risk tolerance in terms of an acceptable level of volatility as measured by standard deviation of return. For example, an investor who is comfortable with the volatility associated with a standard deviation of return of 12 percent or less can eliminate allocations with greater than 12 percent volatility from consideration. The probability of a loss year is another way to quantify risk tolerance. In this method, an array of allocations can be presented to a client, some of which will have a high probability of a return that is less than zero and some of which will have a low probability of a return less than zero. A conservative investor might permit only a 10 percent chance of a negative return in any one year. A more aggressive investor might permit a 40 percent chance of a loss year in a given year. Finally, another way for an investor to quantify risk is in terms of shortfall risk, which is the risk that a portfolio's value will fall below some minimum acceptable level, such as the inflation rate or a spending rate, during a given time horizon. When shortfall risk is an important concern for an investor, an appropriate shortfall risk objective improves the description of the investor's attitude toward risk.

Impact on the Asset Allocation Decision   The willingness and ability to assume risk also has a significant impact on the asset allocation selection. Obviously, as risk tolerance increases, more risky asset classes will be included. UAC advisers need to differentiate between the ability to assume risk and the need to take risk. UACs often overestimate their need to assume risk while others overestimate their ability to tolerate risk.

Liquidity

Liquidity of a client's portfolio is a critical area and one that often gets overlooked. In general, significant liquidity requirements constrain the investor's ability to bear risk. The liquidity section of an investment policy statement for a UAC covers two primary areas. The first area pertains to how much liquid cash is needed to meet both *anticipated* expenses and cash needs such as capital calls for private investments, and any *unanticipated* demands for cash such as medical expenses or home maintenance. The second area pertains to the overall percentage of liquid, semi-liquid, and illiquid investments that are deemed to be permissible to hold in the portfolio.

Cash Liquidity   Cash requirements vary significantly for each client, as some clients depend upon portfolio returns (both income and capital gains) for their daily living expenses while others derive income from an occupation and don't need to make portfolio withdrawals for living expenses. In the former case, a predictable living expense amount (i.e., a spend rate) constitutes a high priority for the investment portfolio. Because of their predictability, anticipated expenses are typically paid for with cash that is reserved in some portion of the investment portfolio. In the latter case, cash reserves are less of an issue because cash is not needed for a spend rate and more of the principal of the portfolio can be invested. In either case, unanticipated cash needs can be met by a cash cushion, the amount of which is client-specific. In both cases, anticipated *negative liquidity events* such as home purchases, college expenses, major philanthropic gifts, or other major expenses also need to be planned for from a liquidity perspective. *Positive liquidity events* such as inheritance or other anticipated cash inflows can also be covered in the liquidity section of the investment policy statement, assuming the family is comfortable speaking openly about such topics.

Illiquidity in the Portfolio   UACs, especially those advancing in years, are sensitive to the overall level of illiquidity in their portfolios. Even though they have the ability, from an asset size perspective, to invest in private equity, private real estate and natural resources investments, hedge funds, and other illiquid or semi-illiquid investments, they often want to limit the amount of overall illiquidity in the portfolio to maximize flexibility of obtaining funds when and if they are needed. Although there is no hard and fast rule, I use 50 percent of the portfolio as a natural point at which to review liquidity needs of the client. In other words, if a client's portfolio is 50 percent or more in illiquid and semi-liquid investments, it's time for a conversation about it. Some clients may put a limit like 35 or 40 percent on their portfolios.

Impact on the Asset Allocation Decision   Some investors favor liquidity, and this decision can have a significant impact on the asset allocation decision. As previously noted, those clients who limit the amount of private equity and hedge fund investing in favor of more liquid equities can expose themselves to more day-to-day volatility (depending on which asset classes are ultimately chosen). High amounts of cash and bonds can also introduce a return drag into a long-term investment portfolio.

Time Horizon

The investment time horizon has a very large impact on the asset allocation selection. In particular, the time horizon essentially dictates the volatility that can be assumed in the portfolio. The shorter the time horizon, the less volatility the client can tolerate, and vice versa. Many advisers like to break up time horizons into short-term, medium-term, and long-term, but these phrases don't have universally accepted definitions. Whenever possible, I like to use ranges rather than absolute terms when describing a time horizon. For example, I label time horizons greater than 15 to 20 years as long-term, time horizons between 3 and 15 years as medium-term, and time horizons of less than three years as short-term. Medium-term can be the most open to interpretation; while I view 10 years as medium-term, some clients may perceive it as short-term and others may see it as long-term. In any event, portfolio allocations need to be constructed to account for the client's interpretation of time horizon.

A second and important aspect of time horizon is whether the investor faces a single- or multi-stage time horizon. Certain investors, particularly older clients, may be content with a single-stage time horizon such as 10 years. Most UACs, however, given their unique and complex nature, are better suited to a multistage time horizon that may dictate different asset allocations for different time horizons. UACs, once they establish objectives for themselves, often set risk-and-return objectives in a multigenerational context. A UAC may not be advanced yet in years but may still be planning for the grandchildren.

Impact on the Asset Allocation Decision Time horizon has a significant impact on the asset allocation decision because the time horizon selected can limit the amount of volatility that can be assumed by the client, and the type of investments the client will use. For example, a 5- to 10-year time horizon certainly has room for equities, but private equities are not going to work in this case.

Taxes

The issue of taxes is perhaps the most universal and complex investment constraint that exists when working with UACs. Taxation of income or property is a global reality and poses a significant challenge to wealth accumulation. Numerous taxes need to be dealt with: income tax, capital gains tax, wealth transfer tax, and property tax. For the purpose of this chapter, I am concerned mainly with the first two: income tax and capital gains tax. Wealth transfer is discussed in Chapter 15 and property tax is beyond the scope of the book.

With tax burdens of such magnitude, the individual investor must approach the investment process from an after-tax perspective. Just to give

TABLE 6.1 Tax Rates Around the World

Country	Income Tax	Gains Tax	Wealth Transfer Tax
Brazil	27.5%	15.0%	8.0%
Canada (Ontario)	46.4%	23.2%	0.0%
Chile	40.0%	17.0%	25.0%
China (PRC)	45.0%	20.0%	0.0%
Egypt	32.0%	0.0%	0.0%
France	48.1%	27.0%	60.0%
Germany	42.0%	50.0%	50.0%
India	30.0%	20.0%	0.0%
Israel	49.0%	25.0%	0.0%
Italy	43.0%	12.5%	0.0%
Japan	37.0%	26.0%	70.0%
Jordan	25.0%	0.0%	0.0%
Korea	35.0%	70.0%	50.0%
Mexico	30.0%	30.0%	0.0%
New Zealand	39.0%	0.0%	25.0%
Pakistan	35.0%	35.0%	0.0%
Philippines	32.0%	32.0%	20.0%
Russian Federation	35.0%	30.0%	30.0%
South Africa	40.0%	10.0%	20.0%
Taiwan	40.0%	0.0%	50.0%
United Kingdom	40.0%	40.0%	40.0%
United States	35.0%	35.0%	47.0%

Source: "The Global Executive," Ernst & Young, 2005.

readers an idea of the global reality of taxes, Table 6.1 illustrates the top marginal tax rates that existed around the world as of 2005.

Taxes negatively affect portfolio performance in two ways: periodically and cumulatively. The preferable method (if any taxation can be called preferable) is cumulative, which occurs when taxes are paid at the end of a given measurement period. Less preferred are periodic payments, which occur when a tax is assessed periodically throughout a measurement period; here, the beginning balance of the next period is reduced by the amount of the tax paid, and therefore funds that would otherwise compound at the portfolio growth rate do not do so. Table 6.2 highlights the effects of these two tax strategies on portfolio performance. At the top of the chart, a periodic tax of 20 percent, similar to an annual marginal income tax rate, is

TABLE 6.2 Comparison of Periodic and Cumulative Tax Effects

Year	Beginning Balance	10% Annual Return	Less 20% Tax	Ending Balance	Gain	Cumulative Gain
Periodic Tax 20%						
1	$1,000,000.00	$100,000.00	$20,000.00	$1,080,000.00	$80,000.00	
2	$1,080,000.00	$108,000.00	$21,600.00	$1,166,400.00	$86,400.00	$166,400.00
3	$1,166,400.00	$116,640.00	$23,328.00	$1,259,712.00	$93,312.00	$259,712.00
4	$1,259,712.00	$125,971.20	$25,194.24	$1,360,488.96	$100,776.96	$360,488.96
5	$1,360,488.96	$136,048.90	$27,209.78	$1,469,328.08	$108,839.12	$469,328.08
Cumulative Tax 20%						
1	$1,000,000.00	$100,000.00	-	$1,100,000.00	$100,000.00	
2	$1,100,000.00	$110,000.00	-	$1,210,000.00	$110,000.00	$210,000.00
3	$1,210,000.00	$121,000.00	-	$1,331,000.00	$121,000.00	$331,000.00
4	$1,331,000.00	$133,100.00	-	$1,464,100.00	$133,100.00	$464,100.00
5	$1,464,100.00	$146,410.00	-	$1,610,510.00	$146,410.00	$610,510.00
			Tax	$(122,102.00)		$(122,102.00)
				$1,488,408.00		$488,408.00

Source: Ernst & Young.

applied against investment returns (10 percent, in this case) over five years. In the lower part of the chart, a tax of 20 percent is subtracted from the beginning and ending balances (i.e., cumulative investment return) at the end of the five-year holding period, similar in concept to a capital gains rate tax. The difference in the ending balance of the portfolio values shows the benefit of deferring tax payments.

Given these two types of tax effects, the job of the UAC adviser is to minimize or eliminate, to the extent legally possible, the tax burden that occurs during the investment process. Tax strategies are naturally unique to each client, depending upon the content of current IRS regulations and the client's place of residence. Although tax minimization strategies often involve complex considerations, two basic strategies are fundamental and can be applied to almost every client. These are tax-deferral strategies and tax-reduction strategies.

Tax-Deferral Strategies   As we learned in the last section, periodic tax payments significantly inhibit the growth of a taxable portfolio. Taxable investors should always seek to defer taxes so that the time during which investment returns can be reinvested and compound can be maximized. Two strategies that facilitate this concept are *low turnover* and *tax loss harvesting*. Investment managers who focus on low turnover, which in effect means more buying and holding versus trading the portfolio, extend the average investment holding period of holdings, which postpones the triggering of taxable gains. Tax loss harvesting focuses on realizing capital losses to offset taxable gains while maintaining the investment performance of the portfolio. Both low turnover and tax loss harvesting strategies are intended to keep capital gains realization to a minimum, resulting in deferred tax payments.

Tax-Reduction Strategies   If taxes cannot be deferred, opportunities may remain to reduce their impact. When income tax rates exceed the capital gains tax rate, as they do in the current U.S. tax code (and in a number of countries as seen earlier in Table 6.1), advisers can recommend investment managers who employ a strategy of investments that are focused on capital gains versus ordinary income. Because the capital gains tax is assessed only at the time of sale, such strategies may also benefit from tax deferral as well as the lower tax rate. Investments that eliminate taxes altogether can also be employed in the portfolio. Tax-exempt bonds, for example, are the quintessential tax avoidance investment vehicle. Tax-exempt securities typically offer lower returns or involve higher expenses (including higher transaction costs) relative to taxable alternatives, and they are attractive only when the following relationship holds: Tax Free Return > [Taxable Return × (1 − Tax rate)].

Impact on the Asset Allocation Decision   Taxes have a huge impact on asset class and manager selection. The following are key considerations. For equity asset classes, indexing (versus active management) is an excellent choice because of its inherent tax efficiency. Long-term capital gains asset classes (at the time this chapter was written) are preferred over short-term capital gains (income tax) oriented asset classes. Here, hedge funds may take a lesser role in the taxable portfolio as do Treasury Inflation-Protected Securities, neither of which are particularly tax-sensitive investments. Real estate and energy, which are longer-term asset classes, are also excellent choices for the taxable portfolio. Optimizing a portfolio for *after-tax* returns is the best way to approach the asset allocation decision. I discuss asset location later in the book, which focuses on the best location for certain investments on the basis of obtaining the best tax treatment.

Legal and Regulatory Environment

In the context of the UAC asset allocation process, legal and regulatory constraints, with the exception of taxes, most frequently involve working with pools of investment capital that have some sort of legal restriction(s) on them, such as trusts or family foundations. I focus on trusts for the purpose of this chapter.

The use of trusts to implement investment and estate planning strategies is very common among UACs, and UAC advisers need to familiarize themselves with these strategies. In short, a trust is a legally established entity that holds and manages assets in accordance with specific guidelines. A trust is the legally recognized owner of whatever assets are held and is subject to taxes in the same ways that individuals are taxed. These assets vary and can include equities, bonds, real estate, real assets, and even art or coins. Trusts are not an investment strategy but are a way to implement an investment or estate planning strategy. The appeal of a trust is the flexibility and control afforded to the grantor; she can delineate how trust assets will be managed and distributed, both before and after her death.

The framework for investment decision-making within a trust often revolves around the conflicting needs and interests of current income beneficiaries versus those who will ultimately receive the corpus or principal of the trust, called the *remaindermen*. This conflict presents the trustee and portfolio manager of a trust with a challenge. Current income beneficiaries will typically desire that the trustee maximize current income through the selection of income-producing assets. The remaindermen beneficiaries will favor investments with long-term growth potential, even if this reduces current income. The trustee is responsible for considering the needs of both groups, under guidelines and criteria provided by the trust document. Most trustees have adopted the principles of modern portfolio theory and use a total return approach, which permits distributions from realized capital gains as well as income-oriented investments.

Impact on the Asset Allocation Decision   As is seen in this last section, legal and regulatory constraints can and do affect the asset allocation decision. In the case of trusts, there are often conflicting interests that must be managed, and the ultimate asset allocation selection can be greatly affected. UAC advisers need to work with these restrictions and simultaneously satisfy the needs of their clients, which is challenging but certainly possible.

Unique Circumstances

UACs often have unique circumstances that present challenges to their investment advisers. These circumstances constrain portfolio choices and add wrinkles to the asset allocation selection process. Such situations might include a concentrated equity position, certain business interests that need to be considered in the context of the overall portfolio, real estate holdings outside the liquid portfolio, socially responsible guidelines, or a host of others. UAC advisers need to consider carefully these unique circumstances because they can have a lasting impact on the asset allocation, which may lead to certain asset classes being either under or overrepresented in the portfolio.

Impact on the Asset Allocation Decision   UACs often have assets that they want accounted for when they create an asset allocation. These can be real estate holdings, concentrated equity positions, large bond portfolios, private business investments, and so on. If an ultimate asset allocation that excludes certain asset classes is selected, then the client needs to understand that the behavior of that allocation will be choppier or less even than that of a well-diversified portfolio. When taken as a whole, however, the portfolio may be just fine—or it may not, in the case of a concentrated equity position that is declining in value. When reporting on the portfolio, UAC advisers may be wise to include these assets in the reports to demonstrate the effect that unique circumstances had on the overall investment performance.

Now that we have covered the importance of asset allocation, we move next into investments used to execute an asset allocation strategy, starting with domestic and international equity.

CHAPTER **7**

Domestic and International Equity

The best way to own common stock is through an index fund.
—Warren Buffett

As was discussed in Chapter 4, nonfinancial issues are equally if not more important than financial issues to UACs. It is still incumbent upon UAC advisers, however, to deliver solid investment results. Because equities are core holdings in most UAC portfolios, UAC advisers need to have a firm understanding of how to best handle this part of the portfolio. Despite the long, grueling hours that went into my Chartered Financial Analyst (CFA) training, I do not focus any of this chapter on equity security analysis (do I hear a collective sigh of relief?)! The chapter focuses instead on developing an *equity investment strategy*, a way in which advisers to UACs should think about arriving at an equity investment allocation through a five-step process that is detailed here. Please note that any reference to *equities* means publicly traded equities.

In many ways, the equity strategy for UACs is the same as that for MA or IA clients—certainly the asset allocation and asset class selection processes are. What differs for UACs lies primarily in the implementation of the equity strategy: the managers selected (more institutional versus retail) and types of vehicles used (separate accounts and commingled vehicles versus mutual funds).

This chapter is organized as follows: I start with a brief introduction to equity securities and then proceed to outline a five-step process for arriving at an equity investment strategy that will encompass both domestic and international equities. Then I review each step in the process. First, the UAC adviser needs to examine the capital markets environment and answer the question, "How much do I want to allocate to equities?" You should notice that I said, *How much?* rather than *if*. Given that UACs have very long time horizons, it is unlikely that the general UAC will not want to have equities in her portfolio. Yes, it is true that some families decide to be only in alternatives or have a 100 percent bond allocation. But it is my experience, and my recommendation, that families with long time horizons have public equity exposure to take advantage of global growth. Next, assuming the equities are used in the portfolio, the question becomes which asset classes within equities are attractive, both domestically and internationally? I answer this question primarily through the use of valuation techniques. After that, I discern which substrategies or tactics within each equity asset class get employed, such as value or growth and using active or passive strategies. Once that is decided, the questions then to be answered include "How will the equity strategy be executed in regard to investment manager selection" and "Which vehicles will be used to manage the money?" Lastly, we will examine the performance analysis of equities.

INTRODUCTION TO U.S. AND INTERNATIONAL EQUITY SECURITIES

Individuals and institutions that invest in publicly traded U.S. and foreign equity securities own a share of the world's business fortunes. More U.S. residents have owned a piece of their country's corporations over the last decade than ever before, and with the awakening of wealth in emerging markets, more foreigners than ever own global stocks. Both U.S. and foreign equities have proven, over time, to be wise investments, 2008 notwithstanding. In the case of U.S. equities, no other asset class has performed better over the course of time. Professor Jeremy Siegel, author of the book *Stocks for the Long Run* (McGraw-Hill, 2002), shows that U.S. stocks have returned about 10.2 percent per year from 1926 through 2001 (Siegel arrives at that number by taking the product of 3.1 percent inflation, 4.1 percent dividends, and real capital appreciation of 2.7 percent; this return assumes the reinvestment of dividends and capital gains and no taxes).[1] Naturally, these healthy returns don't come without risk; domestic equities have also shown themselves to have one of the highest volatilities of any of the major asset classes. Depending on which source of information one uses, the standard deviation on American stocks has been approximately 17 percent per year.[2] This means that approximately 7 out of 10 years, the range of stock returns will be minus 7 percent to plus 27 percent. In the other three years, the range is even wider.

So why should UACs invest in equities rather than in other asset classes such as bonds? The answer lies in the *equity risk premium*, which is defined as the incremental return to equity investors for accepting risk above that of a lower risk investment in bonds. Roger Ibbotson of Ibbotson Associates and Yale University shows that U.S. equity holders have enjoyed returns 5 percent per year above those of bond holders.[3] For background, this analysis is rooted in the building-block methodology he developed based on the *premia* that asset classes have commanded over one another through the history of the capital markets. In short, stocks outperform bonds by a wide margin over the course of time. The amount one allocates to equities depends in large measure upon what one expects the risk premium on stocks to be in the future: the higher the risk premium, the higher the allocation.

With regard to foreign stocks of developed countries, investors can expect to earn a similar risk premium to that earned in U.S. equities. Naturally, there are differences between these two asset classes that will cause them to behave differently over time. Equities of various countries and markets outside the United States, for example, will react differently to economic trends and capital markets activity than domestic equities. Foreign currencies also play a large role in what equity returns are actually delivered to the U.S. investor. For instance, a country such as France may deliver only a 4 percent return on its equity, but if its currency, the euro, gains strength against the dollar or other currencies of, say, 5 percent, the return to the U.S. investor will be 9 percent.

It is my belief that UACs should hold both domestic and foreign large-capitalization equities as core portfolio holdings. A key concern, however, is the correlation between these two asset classes (and, for that matter, with nonequity asset classes), which I discuss shortly. Foreign equities have historically provided diversification benefits to investors due to a historical lack of perfect correlation with U.S. equities. Given the integration of the global economies, however, correlations have generally increased over the last two decades, and that trend may continue. Influences contributing to an increased general level of correlation among international markets are:

- An increase in the number of large multinational companies.
- Advances in communication and information technologies.
- Deregulation of the financial and banking systems of the G-7 countries, leading to major growth in international capital flows.
- Free-flowing foreign exchange between countries.

UAC advisers should strive to keep abreast of studies on cross-country correlations, of which there have been many over the past few decades. A recent study by Dr. Burhan Yavas and Fahimeh Rezayat is worth noting. Yavas and Rezayat examined the co-movements of American, Japanese, and German equity markets in a 2007 paper that sought to show the potential for increasing correlations among global markets. They examined the behavior of U.S., Japanese, and German markets during the period from January 4,

TABLE 7.1 Summary of Stock Market Co-Movements January 1999–February 2002

Rates of Market Change in Tandem	Positive Days	%	Negative Days	%	Total Days	%
All Three Markets in Tandem	129	15.7	117	14.3	246	30.0
U.S. and Japanese Markets in Tandem	227	27.7	217	26.5	444	54.2
U.S. and German Markets in Tandem	208	25.3	181	22.1	389	47.4
German and Japanese Markets in Tandem	181	22.1	166	20.2	347	43.3

Source: B. F. Yavas and F. Rezayat, "Integration among Global Equity Markets: Portfolio Diversification using Exchange Traded Funds," unpublished manuscript.

1999, to February 28, 2002, using the daily closing values of the Standard & Poor's 500 Index (S&P 500), the Nikkei 225 Index, and the DAX 30 to represent these respective stock markets. A simple data analysis indicated that during the study period, the three markets moved in tandem 30 percent of the days (15.7 percent positive and 14.3 percent negative). American and German markets moved concurrently 47.4 percent of the time, and Japanese and German markets moved in the same direction 43.3 percent of the time. Finally, the U.S. and Japanese markets moved together 54.2 percent of the time, as is shown in Table 7.1.[4]

These results show that there are indeed benefits to international diversification. In the same study, however, the authors examined the period six months before and three months after the terrorist attacks of September 11, 2001. The findings reported in Table 7.2 following the September 11,

TABLE 7.2 The Effect of September 11, 2001, on Stock Market Indexes

Indexes	Correlation Coefficients Before 9/11	Correlation Coefficients After 9/11	Jennrich Test
NIK & DAX	0.22	0.3	0.3185
NIK & SP	0.123	0.403	3.788***
DAX & SP	0.635	0.734	1.404*
SP & NIK	0.286	0.208	0.3071
SP & DAX	0.192	0.102	0.3748
DAX & NIK	0.275	0.23	0.1023

***significant at $\alpha=.05$; *significant at $\alpha=.20$
Source: B. F. Yavas and F. Rezayat. "Integration among Global Equity Markets: Portfolio Diversification using Exchange Traded Funds," unpublished manuscript.

2001, terrorist attacks indicate that the correlations between Germany and the United States increased significantly.

Similarly, the correlations between the Japanese and the U.S. markets increased significantly. Increased correlations among major equity markets demonstrated the spread of a crisis in confidence within the global investment community, which implies that a global shock affecting most of the equity markets in the same direction gave rise to increased correlations between the United States and the Japanese markets and between Germany and the United States—and, by extension, other markets around the world. UAC advisers need to be aware of this situation and understand that their clients may react negatively during severe market downturns.

THE FIVE-STEP EQUITY STRATEGY PROCESS

We can think graphically about developing an equity strategy as a five-step process that is illustrated in Figure 7.1.

First, we look at the overall capital markets environment. What is the current equity risk premium in equity markets globally? Where in the global economic growth are we? What is the trend in equity valuations? Answers to all of these questions (and more) will provide clues to the overall allocation to equities that is given in the portfolio. Next, we examine which equity asset classes look attractive and which look unattractive in the current macroeconomic framework. Which regions of the world look attractive? Do any currency issues need to be considered? After that, the question then becomes which subasset classes look attractive or unattractive, such as value or growth, or whether an active or passive management strategy should be employed. Once these questions are answered, the final implementation question is how should the investment managers be selected and which vehicles should be used to invest in each manager? Lastly, we need to understand how our managers are performing.

Capital Markets Analysis

Capital markets analysis focuses on both market and macroeconomic variables that influence valuations of asset classes. Valuations are the most

FIGURE 7.1　The Five-Step Equity Strategy

FIGURE 7.2   Capital Markets Analysis

important factor in selecting (and avoiding) asset classes, which in turn drive portfolio performance for clients. For equities, examining and forecasting market variables such as GDP growth, price/earnings ratios, inflation, dividend yield, real earnings growth, and interest rates is important in assessing asset class valuations in the current market environment. Table 7.3 shows a U.S. a forecast of GDP growth, inflation and short-term interest rates.

In addition to market fundamentals, macroeconomic variables need to be assessed and forecast. These variables include inflation, real GDP growth, unemployment, and many others.

World economic growth and valuation measures are shown in Figures 7.3 and 7.4.

Once market and macroeconomic variables are assessed and forecast, asset class returns, risk, and correlation expectations are made to identify the most attractive equity asset classes for inclusion in the portfolio. When selecting global equity allocations, using market capitalization weights of regions or countries is a simple and effective way to gain broad and balanced equity exposure globally. A simple way to do this is by using the weights of the MSCI Barra All Country World Index. As can be seen in Table 7.4, the United States represents about 42 percent of the world's equity capital markets. At the time this book was written, U.S. equity should represent, therefore, 42 percent of the equity allocation in a client's portfolio. Other asset classes can be viewed similarly.

Equity Asset Class Selection

After evaluating the overall capital markets environment, we need to investigate individual equity asset classes for their relative attractiveness or unattractiveness. (See Figure 7.5.) There are both quantitative and qualitative elements to this analysis. I use research from Hammond Associates and the environment as it existed in January 2008 as a test case to demonstrate the equity allocation process within the macroeconomic framework. I use five equity asset classes—U.S. large-cap, U.S. mid-cap, U.S. small-cap, international large-cap and international small-cap—for the major equity asset classes. All other types of equity asset classes, such as value or growth

TABLE 7.3 Interest Rate Forecast Summary

Global and Regional Aggregates	GDP growth, %				CPI inflation, %				Short term interest rates, %			
	2007	2008F	2009F	2010F	2007	2008F	2009F	2010F	Current	2008F	2009F	2010F
Global	4.8	3.4	1.2	3.1	3.5	5.5	2.6	3.0	4.32	4.25	3.81	4.05
Global ex U.S.	5.6	4.0	2.3	3.9	3.7	6.0	3.5	3.5	5.34	5.39	4.79	5.06
G7	2.3	0.9	-1.5	1.1	2.2	3.2	0.0	1.3	1.38	1.13	0.79	1.35
Developed Markets	2.5	1.0	-1.3	1.1	2.2	3.3	0.3	1.4	1.61	1.37	0.94	1.62
Emerging Markets	7.8	6.4	4.3	5.4	5.3	8.3	5.4	4.9	8.07	8.12	7.47	6.98
Emerging EMEA	6.4	5.3	2.4	3.5	7.3	11.7	9.2	7.2	11.28	10.79	10.55	9.29
Emerging Asia	9.4	7.7	6.2	7.1	4.3	6.8	2.7	3.4	5.24	5.36	4.91	5.08
Latin America	5.6	4.2	2.1	3.4	5.3	7.7	7.1	5.9	12.38	12.33	10.90	9.65
Americas	3.1	1.9	-1.2	1.4	3.5	4.7	1.5	2.6	3.92	3.62	3.28	3.07
EMEA	4.0	2.5	0.4	2.1	3.9	6.3	4.2	3.9	5.05	5.07	4.37	4.97
PacRim ex Japan	9.1	7.3	5.7	6.7	4.1	6.6	2.7	3.3	5.06	5.16	4.71	4.96
G-7												
Canada	2.7	0.6	-0.3	2.3	2.2	2.6	1.2	1.8	2.25	2.00	1.50	2.50
Euro area	2.6	1.0	-0.6	1.1	2.1	3.4	1.3	1.8	2.50	2.50	1.50	2.75
France	2.1	0.9	-0.7	1.1	1.6	3.2	1.1	1.7	2.50	2.50	1.50	2.75
Germany	2.6	1.4	-0.5	1.3	2.3	2.8	0.9	1.5	2.50	2.50	1.50	2.75
Italy	1.4	-0.4	-1.0	0.8	2.0	3.6	1.6	1.7	2.50	2.50	1.50	2.75
Japan	2.2	0.3	0.2	2.3	0.0	1.6	-0.5	0.1	0.30	0.30	0.30	0.75
U.K.	3.0	0.7	-1.6	1.5	2.3	3.6	0.9	2.3	2.00	2.00	1.00	3.00
U.S.	2.2	1.2	-2.5	0.5	2.9	3.8	-0.6	1.3	1.00	0.50	0.50	0.50

Source: Merrill Lynch.

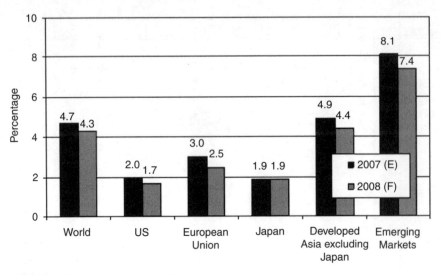

FIGURE 7.3 Macroeconomic Forecast
Source: IMF and Hammond Associates.

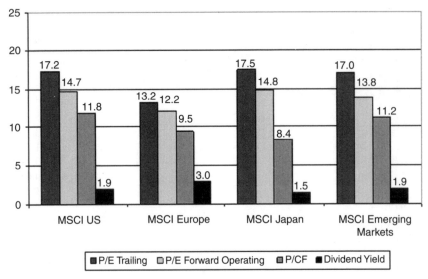

FIGURE 7.4 Global Valuation Measures
Source: Bloomberg, S&P/Citigroup and Hammond Associates.

TABLE 7.4 All Country World Index in USD (Month End May 30, 2008)

Market	Market Cap (BN)	ACWI
Australia	85.77	0.28%
Belgium	158.30	0.51%
Denmark	137.77	0.45%
Finland	223.40	0.72%
France	1,433.34	4.63%
Germany	1,195.28	3.86%
Greece	92.42	0.30%
Ireland	83.95	0.27%
Italy	502.62	1.62%
Netherlands	366.92	1.19%
Norway	158.36	0.51%
Portugal	43.33	0.14%
Spain	560.85	1.81%
Sweden	316.53	1.02%
Switzerland	913.06	2.95%
United Kingdom	2,841.34	9.18%
EUROPE	9,113.25	29.45%
Australia	887.17	2.87%
Hong Kong	291.96	0.94%
New Zealand	15.69	0.05%
Singapore	153.01	0.49%
PACIFIC ex JAPAN	1,347.83	4.36%
Japan	2,775.80	8.97%
EAFE	13,236.89	42.77%
Canada	1,268.13	4.10%
USA	12,858.69	41.55%
THE WORLD INDEX	27,363.70	88.42%
China	496.16	1.60%
Indonesia	54.27	0.18%
Korea	474.99	1.53%
Malaysia	80.64	0.26%
Philippines	13.95	0.05%
Taiwan	387.03	1.25%
Thailand	49.62	0.16%
EM FAR EAST	1,556.67	5.03%
India	228.31	0.74%
Pakistan	4.44	0.01%
EM ASIA	1,789.42	5.78%
Argentina	21.89	0.07%
Brazil	605.20	1.96%
Chile	44.98	0.15%

(*Continued*)

TABLE 7.4   (*Continued*)

Colombia	17.26	0.06
Mexico	175.06	0.57%
Peru	23.54	0.08%
EM LATIN AMERICA	887.95	2.87%
Czech Latin America	29.78	0.10%
Hungary	26.47	0.09%
Poland	58.53	0.19%
Russia	387.98	1.25%
EM EASTERN EUROPE	502.76	1.62%
Israel	85.22	0.28%
Jordan	3.29	0.01%
Turkey	42.57	0.14%
EM EUROPE & MIDDLE EAST	633.84	2.05%
Egypt	24.99	0.08%
Morocco	12.77	0.04%
South Africa	235.11	0.76%
Sri Lanka	0.98	
EM (EMERGING MARKETS)	3,584.08	11.58%

Source: MSCI Barra.

or other equity styles, are covered in the next section. There are many equity asset classes beyond those listed in Table 7.5 for both domestic and international equities, but this provides some of the primary examples.

Moving on to valuation, Figure 7.6 shows U.S. equity valuations as of September 2007. We see here that the largest U.S. stocks, as measured by the Russell Top 200, are undervalued relative to U.S. small-cap stocks, as measured by the Russell 2000, based on measures such as the price to earnings ratio (P/E) and price to cash flow ratio (P/CF). Therefore, when you decide which domestic equity classes to invest in, small-cap stocks are an asset class to underweight at the least or eliminate, based on your view of the prospects for small-caps moving forward. For U.S. equity exposure, large-cap stocks are now best.

On the international equity side, we can see that the same phenomenon exists in Figure 7.7: International small-caps are overvalued relative to

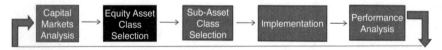

FIGURE 7.5   Equity Asset Class Selection

TABLE 7.5 Selected U.S. and International Equity Asset Classes

Broad Market U.S. Index	Russell 3000, Wilshire 5000, MSCI BMI
Largest U.S. Companies Index	Russell 200, S&P 100
Large-Cap U.S. Index	Russell 1000, S&P 500, MSCI 300
Mid-Cap U.S. Index	Russell Mid-Cap, S&P 400, MSCI 450
Small-Mid U.S. Index	Russell 2500
Small-Cap U.S. Index	Russell 2000, S&P 600, MSCI 1750
Micro-Cap U.S. Index	Russell Micro-Cap Index
Entire World Index	MSCI ACWI Index
Entire World Index without EM	MSCI World Index
Entire World Index without EM and North America	MSCI EAFE Index
Emerging Markets Index	MSCI Emerging Markets (EM) Index
Regional Index	MSCI EM Latin America Index
Regional Index	MSCI EM Europe, Middle East, and Africa Index
Regional Index	MSCI Europe Index
Regional Index	MSCI AC Far East ex Japan Index
Regional Index	MSCI BRIC Index

Source: Russell, S&P, MSCI Barra.

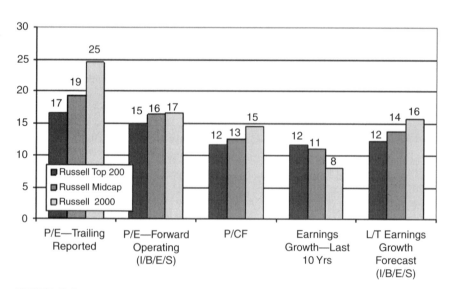

FIGURE 7.6 U.S. Equity Valuations
Source: Russell and Hammond Associates.

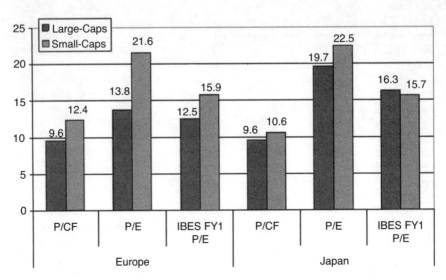

FIGURE 7.7   International Equity Valuations

international large-caps. The conclusion, therefore, is to underweight international small-caps relative to international large-caps. You may be wondering at this point: "What do you mean by underweight? What should the allocation to these two asset classes be, based on their relative valuation?" Generally, the answer to these questions should be answered in the context of overweighting or underweighting each asset class relative to the percentage that the asset class takes in the overall market capitalization of, in this case, international stocks. For example, in the case of international small-caps, this asset class represents approximately 20 percent of overall international equities. So if one underweights international small-caps, he might place a 10 percent weight of the international equity allocation there and overweight international large-caps by 10 percent.

After the decision is made as to which major equity asset classes should be included in the portfolio, specific sub-asset classes need to be decided upon such as value versus growth (style), any active equity strategies, and whether to use active or passive managers. This can be a complex decision, but one that is critical to the success of the client's portfolio.

Sub-Asset Class Selection and Active versus Passive Management

In the same way that the valuation analysis was performed in the last section, the identical methodology can be applied to sub-asset class decisions. (See Figure 7.8.) This is a more complex decision, however, because there are

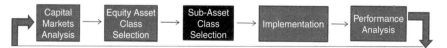

FIGURE 7.8 Sub-Asset Class Selection

many people who study various styles and equity strategies and valuation may not be the only factor at play. Academic research suggests that over the long run, for example, that value equities outperform growth equities. This concept is known as the relative price or value effect. Does this mean that a portfolio should *always* be tilted in this direction? This dogmatic of an approach may lead investors astray, as valuations can swing, making growth stocks a better bet when value is overvalued. Figure 7.9 demonstrates that in certain environments, like early 2008, growth equities were preferred to value as measured by the valuation premium of growth versus value.

In addition to growth and value, there are other equity strategies such as *cyclical,* which focuses on selecting equities depending on the stage of the economic cycle; *market timing,* which comes and goes in popularity and attempts to identify peaks and troughs of the market cycle (the Dow Theory is an example); *sector,* which attempts to identify the sectors of the market such as consumer discretionary, industrials, materials, and so on, that are both undervalued or expected to outperform other sectors of the market;

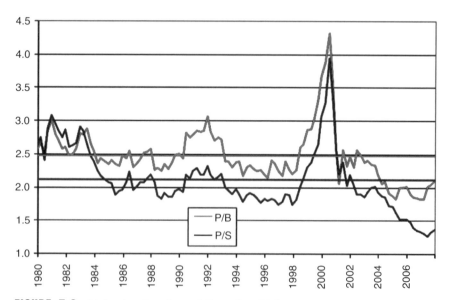

FIGURE 7.9 Valuation Premium of Growth to Value
Source: Hammond Associates.

quality, which attempts to identify those companies that enjoy a strong market position and are very financially sound (typically, large multinational companies); *contrarian,* which attempts to identify overlooked or out-of-favor equities that have good prospects for a rebound; and *momentum* that attempts to predict stock returns based on past price history. Many of these strategies can be found in both domestic and international equity investing.

Active versus Passive Management   Another major decision to be made in equity investing is active versus passive management. It goes without saying that the debate between active and passive management rages on. As many of you know, active fund management is based on two primary ideas:

- That securities markets are priced inefficiently.
- That managers have the ability to correctly time their investment decisions. Unfortunately for believers in active management, numerous studies have shown that doing either or both is difficult at best and impossible at worst.[5]

Those who believe in a passive or index-based approach acknowledge market efficiency and the inherent difficulty in predicting market movements. Some readers may know that I am a strong believer in behavioral finance and I am not sold on theories of market efficiency, but I am also a believer in passive investing over the long run. What gives? It is my belief that markets are efficient *enough* to make passive investing a better choice. Also, the behavior of active managers contributes to underperformance over time, the main culprit in my opinion being growth in assets (that is, a focus on asset gathering versus investing).

When it comes to trying to select securities that beat the market, the reason that money managers find it difficult to consistently beat the index is simply explained by the idea that the smartest people cannot outdo one another. Competent active managers all do the same thing: analyze the same data and the same economic statistics. The sheer number of people doing this work makes beating the market that much more difficult. Moreover, there is no academic research to demonstrate that active management outperforms indexing over the long term. In fact, Nobel laureate Bill Sharpe lays out a basic mathematical proof showing that the average passively managed investment will outperform the average actively managed investment over time.

If active and passive management styles are defined in sensible ways, it must be the case that: (1) before costs, the return on the average actively managed dollar will equal the return on the average passively managed dollar; and (2) after costs, the return on the average actively managed dollar will be less than the return on the average passively managed dollar. These assertions will hold for any time period. Moreover, they depend only on the laws of addition, subtraction, multiplication and division. Nothing else is required.

In short, there is little evidence that fund managers possess the ability to identify in advance those securities that will outperform the market. Research from Hammond Associates also confirms the difficulty of trying to beat the market, as noted in Table 7.6. Readers should also note that passive management is almost always more tax efficient than active management.

The reality of the situation, however, is that many UACs want active management because, although difficult to identify in advance, some managers do beat the market. What I recommend to clients is that they get their

TABLE 7.6 Active versus Passive Manager Analysis

Percentage of
Surviving Funds that
Have Outperformed
Their Index

Asset Class	Index	1 Year (%)	3 Years (%)	5 Years (%)	10 Years (%)
U.S. Large-Cap Growth	Russell 1000 Growth	61	55	60	78
U.S. Large-Cap Blend	S&P 500	48	45	39	39
U.S. Large-Cap Value	Russell 1000 Value	65	35	26	28
U.S. Mid-Cap Blend	Russell Mid-Cap Index	43	22	17	49
U.S. Small-Cap Growth	Russell 2000 Growth	54	48	39	83
U.S. Small-Cap Blend	Russell 2000	48	48	35	74
U.S. Small-Cap Value	Russell 2000 Value	79	56	28	46
International Large-Cap	MSCI EAFE-Net	55	53	41	53
International Small-Cap	S&P/Citigroup EMI-EPAC	59	38	41	67
Emerging Market Equities	MSCI EMF-Net	31	31	44	46

Source: Morningstar, PerTrac Financial Solutions, and Hammond Associates.

active management in alternative investments such as hedge funds, private equity, and private real assets, and index traditional investments such as stocks and bonds. But I still get pushback on this. A compromise that often works is a 50/50 blend of active and passive equity management. Over time, it is usually proven that passive wins.

Implementation

As noted earlier in the chapter, UACs have certain advantages over MA and IA individuals in making equity investments. I should quickly add that these advantages are not as pronounced as they are in the alternative investments such as hedge funds, private equity, and private real assets (energy, real estate, and so forth). In the case of equities, particularly foreign equities, there are certainly opportunities available to UACs to invest with managers that are simply not available to other investor classes. These managers cater to more institutional clients and family office clients with minimum investments of sometimes $1 million but in other cases $5 million or more. An example of this type of manager is Grantham, Mayo, Van Otterloo & Co. (GMO) in Boston. GMO has numerous investment products that are either closed to new investors or have high minimum investments such as $5 million per strategy.[6] I discuss two aspects of implementation in this section: key considerations for selection of equity managers and the types of vehicles that can be used. (See Figure 7.10.)

Manager Selection   Investment manager selection is a challenging endeavor for the UAC adviser, but the task is made somewhat more efficient by the higher amounts of capital being deployed. In short, when larger aggregate dollars are being invested, a universe of higher quality managers opens up. There are many factors to consider when choosing an equity manager. Many of these factors are qualitative rather than quantitative. We will first review some of the quantitative factors, and then move to the all-important qualitative factors.

Regarding quantitative factors, there are numerous things that an analyst can look at to evaluate the viability of an equity manager. I should state, for the record, that I am a strong believer in index investing. As we

FIGURE 7.10   Implementation of an Equity Strategy

reviewed in the last section, there are few, if any, managers who can consistently beat the market year in and year out. Bill Miller of Legg Mason did so for an impressive 15 years in a row from 1981 to 1995 with his fund, the Legg Mason Value Trust. In his sixteenth and seventeenth years, he was under his benchmark by approximately 1000 basis points in each year.[7] There are times that active managers are useful—particularly in down markets—but identifying which managers to hire is difficult. Some new research is emerging that shows that indexes are best held in up markets and active managers may be best in down markets because they will hold some amount of cash.[8] The trick, of course, is to know when markets are going up and when markets are going down!

In regard to quantitative and investment factors, it is naturally important to understand historical performance. Questions to be answered include: Has the firm exhibited an ability to add value to the benchmark over market cycles (three- to five-year periods)? How much value is added relative to the risk taken (i.e., what is the risk-adjusted performance)? Has the firm exhibited an ability to outperform peers over market cycles? Is the level of consistency of outperformance appropriate for the strategy? In regard to risk measurement, is the level of absolute and relative volatility appropriate given the strategy? Are the risk characteristics of the portfolio over time consistent with expectations? What are the sources of out- or underperformance (e.g., industry bets, stock selection, style biases) and do they match the manager's purported strengths? (I discuss this in more detail in the next section.) Is the manager tax efficient? If yes, how is that measured? And last, but certainly not least: Are the manager's fees competitive?

Equally important to historical performance is the manager's investment process. Is it well-defined and consistently applied? Are there any aspects to the investment process that provide a competitive advantage, such as extensive information and data sources, unique modeling capabilities, unusual perspectives, depth and quality of analytical resources, or experience of investment professionals? Is there something about the investment process that convinces you that historical performance can be repeated? Are the portfolio managers and research analysts experienced in managing this type of mandate? Is there significant experience among the professionals as a team? Do the investment and research professionals bring complementary skills to the portfolio management process?

In regard to qualitative factors, a key element is the strength of the organization and the firm's personnel. Questions to be answered include: How well has the organization been able to retain investment professionals and senior management? Has the firm increased staff as assets under management have increased? Are the investment professionals distracted by other responsibilities such as management, sales, and client service? Does the ownership structure align the employees' interests with those of clients and encourage long-term retention of key professionals? What succession plan, if needed, is in place? Is the firm's growth rate in assets appropriate for the given strategy? Are the firm's growth prospects, assets under management, and capital base sufficient to maintain a healthy business? Are compliance and back office systems adequate?

Equity Investment Vehicles   The next topic I address in this section is the types of vehicles through which a UAC can make equity investments. There are many, so I limit the discussion to the following: mutual funds, separate accounts, index funds, exchange traded funds, commingled funds, and limited partnerships/LLCs.

Mutual Funds   As most of you know, an equity mutual fund is a professionally managed fund that pools money from many investors and invests it in equities, both domestic and international. In a mutual fund, the fund manager, who is also known as the portfolio manager, trades the fund's underlying securities, realizing capital gains or losses, and collects the dividend or interest income. The investment proceeds are then passed along to the individual investors. The UAC may invest in mutual funds should the need arise, but most likely will invest in other types of accounts such as separate accounts or commingled funds.

Separate Accounts   A separate account allows an investor to choose an investment category that is customized to her individual risk tolerance and desire for performance. Unlike a mutual fund, the securities are held individually by the owner of the account (the investor). The best feature of a separate account is that it can be tax managed. Individual securities can be designated for tax losses or gains, unlike a mutual fund. Most UACs prefer separate accounts.

Index Funds   An index fund is a collective investment scheme (mutual fund or exchange-traded fund) that intends to replicate the movement of an index of a specific financial market, or a set of rules of ownership that are held constant regardless of market conditions. Examples are the S&P 500 or Russell 2000. Index tracking is achieved by holding all of the securities in the index in the same proportions as the index. Other methods of indexing include statistical sampling and holding representative securities. Many index funds rely on computer models to regulate which securities are purchased. The difference between the index performance and the fund performance is known as the *tracking error*. Many UACs invest in index funds. There is no real advantage, however, to putting higher dollar amounts to work in index funds.

Exchange Traded Funds   *Exchange Traded Funds* (ETFs) have been available in the United States since 1993 and in Europe since 1999.[9] ETFs combine index (and now active) funds and stock exchange trading together in one product. Funds and stock exchange investments are traditionally segregated. An ETF is a pool fund invested with a stated investment objective, for example, a tracker fund for the consumer discretionary sector or for a geographic region such as Japan. Shares owned in this fund by investors are in turn traded on an exchange. The benefits of an ETF are mainly liquidity and taxes. Unlike mutual funds, they can be traded any time during the trading day and have continuous pricing that mirrors the price performance of the underlying investments. Also, they don't have the built-in gains that can occur in mutual funds. They also have low annual management costs compared to other pooled investments. As with index funds, UACs can and do use ETFs, but there is no advantage of investment size with this vehicle.

Commingled Funds/Limited Partnerships/LLCs   Some equity investment firms offer commingled funds that are in effect private mutual funds. These funds are used by institutional managers that want the convenience of pooled funds but want to avoid the hassles of traditional mutual funds. Commingled funds have higher minimum investment sizes than traditional mutual funds. Equity managers can also offer limited partnerships or limited liability company investments, but these are not as common. Commingled vehicles use the IRS schedule K-1 versus a 1099 for tax reporting purposes. UACs often invest in commingled vehicles but do require more due diligence than mutual funds.

Performance Analysis

Understanding how your managers are performing is crucial to investment success. (See Figure 7.11.) There are literally hundreds of factors that one can examine to assess the performance of an equity manager. I examine four things in this section that UAC advisers need to be keenly aware of:

FIGURE 7.11   Performance Analysis

benchmark relative performance and peer rankings, style drift, attribution analysis, and considerations for manager termination.

Benchmark Relative Performance   An equity manager's returns should be measured against an appropriate benchmark and a well-defined peer universe. A typical expectation is that a manager will outperform his or her benchmark over a market cycle, as well as placing in the top 50 percent of the peer group over that period. It is important to keep in mind that every manager (including Bill Miller) will underperform at times. Performance should be monitored monthly or at least quarterly and significant deviations from expectations should be closely analyzed for any indication that investment process has changed.

While benchmark-relative performance changes over time, the types and level of risk taken by a manager in the quest to beat the benchmark should generally be stable. Equity managers who perform more aggressively than the benchmark (i.e., have a high tracking error and high volatility of returns) tend to maintain that level of aggressiveness over time. Risk can also be defined in terms of the characteristics of the manager's portfolio, commonly known as the *style bias* of a given manager. For example, some managers attempt to beat their benchmark by maintaining a deeper value bias than the benchmark. The risk of each portfolio should be evaluated on a quarterly basis and any significant change in a manager's risk profile or the level of risk assumed by the manager should be evaluated for its implications as to whether the manager's investment process has fundamentally changed.

We see in Figure 7.12 the Pzena large-cap value versus its benchmark, the Russell 1000 Value Index (DRI), and against its peer universe, U.S. large-cap value. The date range is October 2000 through December 2007.

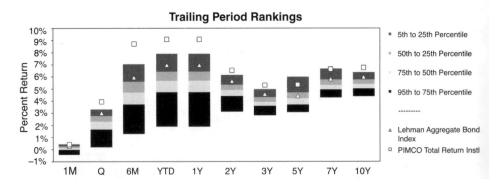

FIGURE 7.12   Benchmark and Peer Relative Performance
Source: © 2006 PerTrac Financial Solutions. All Rights Reserved.

Style Drift   Style drift occurs when a fund manager drifts away from the stated investment objective, and is a very common occurrence. Many funds bounce between two categories. Style drift could manifest as a shift within an asset class, such as from small-cap growth to small-cap value, or it could be a more serious shift from small core to mid-cap growth fund. Because we are hiring managers to play a position, similar to a baseball team, style drift is very important. If one invests in a fund expecting it to represent a certain style or category in the portfolio, one expects it to stay true to its category over time. If it doesn't, the portfolio can quickly become unbalanced.

We can see in Figure 7.13 that the Pzena Large-Cap Value Fund has stayed for the most part in large-cap value, but has strayed into growth at times. Note that some funds have the objective to find the most attractive style given the current market conditions.

Attribution   To what do we attribute a manager's performance? Is it stock picking, investing in the right style, or market timing? Were certain sectors over or underweighted? These are the questions that attribution analysis

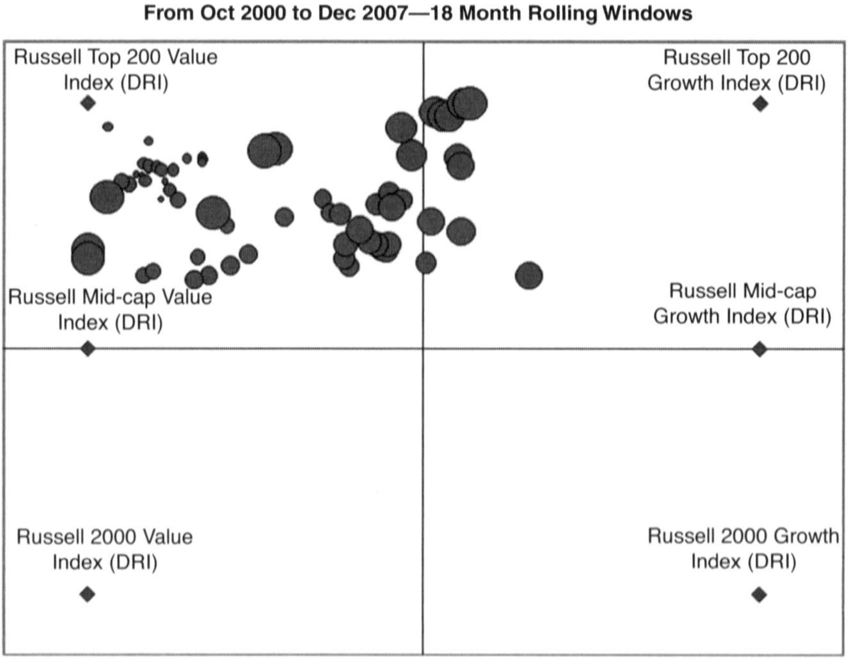

FIGURE 7.13   Style Analysis of Pzena Large-Cap Value
Source: © 2006 PerTrac Financial Solutions. All Rights Reserved.

attempts to address. Answering these questions for short periods, from a day to a quarter, requires a sophisticated process that must identify and price each security in the portfolio at least daily (some even argue that this should be done during the day at the time of any transaction). This kind of attribution analysis is costly and time consuming and is only practical for separately managed institutional portfolios. It is possible to do a more general attribution analysis using returns-based style analysis on any portfolio for which monthly or quarterly returns are available.

Most of a manager's returns are attributed to asset class returns. A U.S. equity manager's returns depend mostly on how well the U.S. stock market does. The second most important factor for an equity manager is investment style. Most growth stock managers perform well when growth stocks are in favor. Conversely they perform badly when growth stocks are out of favor. Our first goal is to find out how much of the manager's return comes from the general market and investment style. We accomplish this using a technique called style analysis. The next level of attribution analysis is sector analysis, which attempts to isolate how much exposure a manager had to a certain sector of, say, the S&P 500, and how much the fund had to that sector. Attribution analysis is lengthy and is best left for professional consultants to perform.

Terminating a Manager   So what good is all this analysis? It helps to decide whether to retain or terminate the equity manager. Changing managers is an important decision that must balance the opportunity cost of not changing to a new manager or strategy with the transactions cost and opportunity cost of changing managers. Every manager has periods of underperformance and every investment management organization has personnel changes. The fundamental question in any managerial change is whether a manager's recent underperformance or personnel change is a signal of future instability or underperformance. The following section identifies some specific factors that should trigger a review of a manager's continued role within an investment program. Advisers should resist, however, the urge to fire good managers for short-term underperformance. Even great managers go through periods of underperformance. Following the description of these factors is a description of the process used to review investment managers.

Personnel Changes   Virtually every organization has some level of personnel change over time. In fact, personnel change can be a positive influence on a firm, bringing new ideas and perspectives. The departure of professionals or the addition of new professionals who are key to either the firm's management or the investment process, however, should signal a need for review as to whether the original premise for retaining the firm is still in effect. In other words, are the reasons for originally anticipating competitive performance from this firm weakened, strengthened, or unaffected by this change?

Ownership Changes   Ownership changes may be a positive event, for example, when ownership of founding partners is more broadly distributed to the next generation of investment professionals at the firm. Ownership change, however, may also be a negative event, creating dissension and departures among the firm's professionals. In general, the firms which appear to have had the greatest success at generating organizational stability are those whose employees have a significant equity stake. Any significant change in ownership should be reviewed and evaluated for its likely impact on the stability and performance of the organization going forward.

Change in Strategic Direction   A firm's change in strategic direction may be signaled by new product introductions, a change in responsibilities among key personnel, or a change in ownership structure. Such events may indicate a lessening of focus on some of the firm's existing investment strategies. For example, a number of firms have reallocated existing research and portfolio management resources to new hedge fund products. This may be beneficial as a tool to retain talented employees who might be tempted to leave the organization, but may also dilute the resources devoted to more traditional strategies.

Now that we have covered equity securities, we move to fixed-income securities in the next chapter.

CHAPTER 8

Domestic and International Bonds

Imagine that a bond is a slice of cake. Now you didn't bake that cake, but every time you hand somebody a slice of that cake, a little bit comes off, little crumbs fall off. And you're allowed to keep those crumbs.

—Tom Wolfe, *Bonfire of the Vanities*
(Farrar, Straus and Giroux, 1987)

Most UACs have love-hate relationships with bonds. In 2008, anyone who held high quality bonds in general and government bonds in particular were very glad they did after witnessing the returns of nearly all other asset classes during that year. Growth-oriented clients traditionally shun bonds because they have historically delivered paltry returns in comparison to equities (or other higher-returning asset classes) over rolling 20-year periods. In fact, there has never been a 20-year period in which stocks trailed T-bills, and in only 2 percent of historical rolling 20-year periods have stocks trailed bonds. Table 8.1 shows the percentage of periods since 1926 when stocks underperformed bonds and T-bills.

Large and sophisticated institutional investors such as endowments and foundations have had tiny allocations to bonds of late—perhaps regretting allocating so little to bonds in the current market environment. For instance, Yale University showed an allocation to bonds of just 4 percent in their 2007 endowment report. In justifying such a low allocation, David Swenson, Yale's chief investment officer, notes: "Yale is not particularly attracted to fixed income assets, as they have the lowest historical and expected returns of the six asset classes that make up the Endowment. In addition, the government bond market is arguably the most efficiently priced asset class, offering few opportunities to add significant value through active management."[1] On the other hand, some investors are absolutely

TABLE 8.1 Percentage of Periods since 1926 in which
Stocks Underperformed Bonds and T-bills

	T-Bills (%)	Bonds (%)
1 Year	32	34
5 Years	23	24
10 Years	14	14
20 Years	0	2

Source: Hammond Associates.

smitten with bonds for their safety, income, potential deflation protection, diversification, and portfolio risk reduction benefits. Many UACs welcome the benefit of tax-exempt income from certain municipal government bonds. Other enlightened UAC advisers have broadened their investment horizons to include global and emerging markets bonds in their recommendations, because these bonds offer a wide investment opportunity set and good prospects for active management. For UAC advisers, familiarity with bonds and with creating a bond investment strategy is essential. Inevitably, the UAC adviser will encounter a bond-focused client and he or she can really score points by being ready to speak the language of bonds when that time comes. I start with the basics in this chapter; it is my experience that because bonds are underused, UAC advisers tend not to focus on fundamental concepts. Next, as in the last chapter, I discuss the major asset classes and types of bonds. I conclude the chapter with some investment strategy, manager selection, and performance evaluation considerations.

Although I do not go over a five-step process for developing a bond strategy as was done in the last chapter, you should know that the process for developing a bond allocation is essentially done in the same way. One starts with the macroeconomic environment, examining the capital markets environment to answer the question: "How much do I want to allocate to bonds?" Again, notice that I said, *How much?* rather than *if*. Given that UACs normally like to have risk reduction assets in their portfolios, and a ready source of liquidity if needed, it is unlikely that the general UAC will not want to have some bonds, however small the allocation might be. Bonds also provide valuable diversification to a portfolio. Figure 8.1 demonstrates the low correlation between stocks and bonds by comparing the correlation of the S&P 500 Index and the Lehman Brothers (now Barclays) U.S. Aggregate Index, the latter of which includes both government and corporate bonds. Correlation figures are based on total return.

Next, assuming bonds are used in the portfolio, the question becomes, "Which asset classes within bonds are attractive, both domestically and

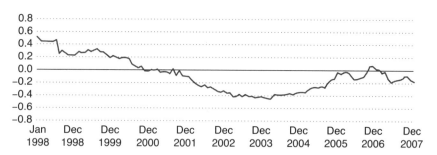

FIGURE 8.1 Correlations of the Lehman Brothers (Barclays) U.S. Aggregate
Index and the S&P 500
Source: Lehman Live, Standard & Poor's, 1/31/1998–12/31/2007.

internationally?" Again, the answer to this question is primarily found
through the use of valuation techniques. After that, the questions become
more specific: Which substrategies or tactics within each bond asset class get
employed, how will the bond strategy be executed, and which vehicles will
be used to manage the money? Lastly, the performance of bond managers
will need to be evaluated. All of these steps are taken much as they were in
the last chapter, but for the purpose of this chapter, I stick to fundamentals:
asset class descriptions, bond investment strategies, manager selection, and
performance considerations.

Before we begin, a note on mental accounting. For those advisers who
are graduating from MA or IA clients to UACs, it is important to know that
for the vast majority of UACs who take a diversified approach to an investment portfolio, bonds are not used for income per se. Municipal bonds, as
many of you know, have a legacy of providing income, but in my view this is
dated thinking. UACs should be counseled to think of bonds not as providing
income, but rather as a component of the overall portfolio that contributes to
its total return. Risk reduction, liquidity, and diversification precede income
in regard to a bond's importance. But there is still a tendency for those UACs
who may have viewed bonds as income producers in the past to see them
in this way, even when agreeing to a diversified portfolio approach. Sometimes mental accounting can be helpful, but in this case UA advisers should
encourage their clients to look at bonds in the context of the total portfolio.

INTRODUCTION TO BONDS

For those unfamiliar with the basics of bonds, there are a few key characteristics that both investors and advisers should be aware of. Note that for our

purpose here, I sometimes use the description of a single bond for simplicity. Keep in mind that what is explained in about a single bond can be extrapolated to describe groups of bonds that a bond manager could invest in. The bond characteristics you will learn about are maturity, redemption features, credit quality, interest, price (implying yield), and tax status. Together, these factors help determine the value of a bond and how well the bond (or bond manager) meets the investment objectives of a client.

Maturity

A bond's maturity refers to the specific date on which the investor's principal will be repaid. Bonds typically mature in a period of time from one day to 30 years. The maturity ranges of bonds generally fall into three categories: short term, intermediate term, and long term. Short-term bonds have maturities of up to five years; intermediate-term bonds have maturities of 5 to 12 years; and long-term bonds have maturities of 12 years or more. The maturity of a bond is important because the maturity date substantially affects the price and yield of a bond, and investors take a keen interest in when their principal will be repaid.

Bond Quality and Credit Ratings

Bond quality can range from the highest creditworthiness of U.S. Treasury securities, which are backed by the full faith and credit of the U.S. government, to below investment-grade (junk bonds), which are considered highly speculative. The way that investors and advisers can judge the quality of a bond—that is, the ability of an issuer to make its regularly scheduled interest payments and repay principal—is by relying on rating agencies that assign risk ratings to bonds when they are issued and monitor the development of these bonds during their lifetimes. These agencies rate bonds on several factors, which include the issuer's financial condition and management, quantitative and qualitative characteristics of the debt, and the general sources of repayment for interest and principal. Table 8.2 shows the ratings of the major rating agencies: Moody's Investor Service, Standard and Poor's Ratings Services, and Fitch IBCA agencies (the problems of these firms in view of the most recent subprime debacle notwithstanding).

As Table 8.2 indicates, the highest possible ratings are AAA from S&P and Fitch and Aaa from Moody's. Bonds rated BBB or above are considered investment-grade; bonds with ratings BB or below are considered junk bonds, or, more politely, high-yield bonds. Although the term *junk* may imply that these bonds should be avoided, there are certainly times when these securities can and should be part of a portfolio. The best time to invest

TABLE 8.2   Credit Ratings by Moody's, S&P, and Fitch

Credit Risk	Moody's	S&P	Fitch
Prime	Aaa	AAA	AAA
Excellent	Aa	AA	AA
Upper Medium	A	A	A
Lower Medium	Baa	BBB	BBB
Speculative	Ba	BB	BB
Very Speculative	B, Caa	B, CCC, CC, C	B, CCC, CC, C
Default	Ca, C	D	DDD, DD, D

Source: Moody's, S&P, and Fitch.

in high-yield bonds is when spreads have widened considerably; when the rate of interest paid on a junk bond is well over its long-term average spread over U.S. Treasury bonds, investors should consider them.

Interest Rates

Bonds normally pay interest to investors twice a year (semiannually) but can also pay monthly or quarterly. Interest can be paid on a fixed basis (i.e., the rate paid doesn't change over the life of the bond), it can float (the interest rate will float with prevailing rates over the life of the bond) or it can be paid at maturity along with principal. Some bonds, called payment-in-kind bonds, can actually pay interest with the issuance of more bonds, but this is a creative form of high-yield financing that I won't delve into. Zero-coupon bonds or *zeros* pay no periodic interest, but rather pay all interest and principal at maturity, usually compounded semiannually. To compensate for the lack of current interest payments with zeros, they are sold at a deep discount from their face value. Taxable investors need to be careful if the zero they invest in is taxable, because taxes accrue annually even though interest is paid at maturity.

Price and Yield

The price an investor pays for a bond is based on current interest rates, supply and demand, credit quality, maturity, and taxation. The yield of a bond is the return that is actually earned on the bond, based on the actual price paid and the interest payments to be received in the future. There are three main types of bond yields: current yield, yield-to-maturity, and yield-to-call. Current yield takes the price paid for the bond and divides it by the bond's interest payment. Yield-to-maturity sums the total amount of interest received on the bond from purchase until the bond's maturity, plus any gain earned if the bond is purchased below its face value (or minus any loss if it is purchased above its face value). Yield-to-call is calculated in the same way as yield-to-maturity, except that it assumes that the bond is called at the earliest point possible, and the investor receives the face value on the call date. Yield-to-maturity and yield-to-call, which are more informative than current yield, provide information on the total return received by holding the bond until it matures or it is called.

The way that bond prices move in relation to interest rate movements is often misunderstood by even professional investors and some financial journalists. When current interest rates *rise*, prices of outstanding bonds *fall* to bring the yield of existing bonds in line with higher-interest-paying new issues. The longer the maturity, the greater the risk that bond prices will fluctuate with changes in interest rates—a risk that investors will want to be compensated for. This concept can be shown by the *yield curve*. A normally shaped yield curve slopes upward and shows a fairly steep rise in yields between short- and intermediate-term issues; it shows a less pronounced rise between intermediate- and long-term issues.

If the yield curve is steep, it means the yields on short-term securities are relatively low when compared to long-term issues. If the yield curve is flat, it means the difference between short- and long-term rates is relatively small. When yields on short-term issues are higher than those on longer-term issues, the yield curve is said to be *inverted*, which suggests that bond market participants expect interest rates to decline; sometimes an inverted yield curve is a good indicator that a recession is at hand.

Bond Redemption

Many investors focus only on the maturity of the bond and can overlook features that can have material impacts on the expected life of a bond investment, such as call provisions and put provisions. Some bonds, particularly municipal bonds, have *call provisions* that allow (or under certain circumstances, require) the issuer to repay principal on a date before the bond's maturity date. The most common reason for a bond to be called is that the issuer has an opportunity to lower its interest cost because interest rates have gone down. Rather than focusing on yield-to-maturity, good bond managers focus on yield-to-call, which hypothetically assumes that the bond is called on the earliest date the issuer could call the bond. Bonds with call provisions usually must offer a higher annual return than bonds without call provisions to compensate for the option that a bond might be called before maturity. In the opposite case, some bonds have *put provisions,* which may require the issuer to repurchase the bonds at specified times before maturity at the option of the investor. Investors will normally exercise this option when interest rates have risen since the bonds were issued (or they simply want their money returned to them).

Tax Treatment

Different bonds naturally have different tax treatments. For example, interest on U.S. Treasury bonds is free of state and local income taxes but taxable at the federal level. Interest earned on municipal bonds is free of federal income tax, and in most cases, state and local income taxes. One might infer from this that taxable investors should always invest in tax-exempt securities. This is not always the case. The appropriateness of bond income that is taxable or tax-exempt depends on the taxable client's income tax bracket and other factors such as tax loss carryforwards and alternative minimum tax status. Another key factor is the type of account the securities are held in. Tax-deferred accounts such as company retirement accounts, 401(k)'s, or IRAs should hold taxable bonds in most, if not all, cases.

DESCRIPTIONS OF BOND ASSET CLASSES

We will now move to describing individual bond asset classes. The decision to invest in certain bond asset classes should factor in valuation as well as how the characteristics of the asset class meet the objectives of the client. For example, some UA investors may be subject to alternative minimum tax and taxable bonds may be more appropriate than municipal bonds. In other cases, a UAC may not wish to accept currency risk and global bonds may not be appropriate. It is up to the UAC adviser to not only understand valuations, interest rates, and currency characteristics of bond asset classes, but also to understand the client's needs and objectives to determine what is appropriate and what is not appropriate for the bond allocation. To help make these decisions easier, this section provides an overview of various bond asset classes. These are municipal bonds, United States government bonds (including government agency bonds and government-sponsored enterprise bonds), corporate bonds, foreign developed bonds, and emerging markets bonds.

Municipal Bonds

Municipal bonds are debt obligations issued by states, cities, counties, and other governmental entities to raise money to build schools, highways, hospitals, and sewer systems, as well as many other projects for the public good. When an investor purchases a municipal bond, she is lending money to a municipal issuer who promises to pay interest (usually semiannually) and principal on a specific maturity date. Municipal securities consist of both short- and long-term issues. Short-term securities, often called notes, typically mature in a year or less, while long-term securities, commonly known as bonds, typically mature in more than a year. Short-term notes are used by an issuer to raise money in anticipation of future revenues such as taxes, pending bond proceeds, or state or federal aid, or to cover uneven cash flows such as meeting unanticipated deficits or raising short-term capital for projects until long-term bond financing can be secured.

The two basic types of municipal bonds are general obligation bonds and revenue bonds. The principal and interest of a general obligation bond is secured by the full faith and credit of the issuer and is not backed by a specific project. These bonds are voter approved and supported by the issuer's taxing power. On the other hand, a revenue bond's principal and interest are secured by revenues derived from a specific project such as toll roads, hospitals, bridges, airports, sewage treatment facilities, and so on. While all municipal bonds can be separated into general obligation and revenue bonds, there are multiple types of municipal bonds in each category; describing them all here is beyond the scope of this chapter.

Tax Treatment of Municipal Bonds   Interest income received from investing in (most) municipal bonds is free from federal income taxes and, in most states, is also exempt from state and local taxes. Also, interest received from securities issued by U.S. territories and possessions is exempt from federal, state, and local income taxes in all states as well. Most states do not tax interest income arising from tax-exempt bonds issued by municipalities within the state; virtually all states, however, tax the interest received on out-of-state bonds. Sometimes, however, out-of-state bonds actually offer a higher after-tax yield than the tax-exempt bonds issued in one's own state. Take the example of a client who pays a 5 percent state income tax and the state taxes out-of-state bonds (but not in-state bonds) at 5 percent. What if an out-of-state bond was offering a 6.5 percent yield and an in-state bond was offering a 6 percent yield? Anything over a 6.32 percent out-of-state bond would be preferred to a 6 percent in-state bond. How is this calculated? The way to measure the tax-exempt advantage of a municipal security is to compare it to a comparable taxable investment. This is known as *taxable equivalent yield*. The formula for this is: tax-free yield divided by (1 – the appropriate tax rate). This formula can use federal, state, and local income taxes to calculate returns on the taxable bond investment.

There are several other tax issues of which you should be aware. Normal capital gains are taxed when you buy and sell municipal bonds in the secondary market before they mature. When a bond is sold, an investor may also recognize a capital loss if the sale proceeds (adjusted for selling costs) are less than the holder's tax basis. In such a case, capital losses are first applied against capital gains of the same type to reduce such gains. UAC advisers should also know that clients who borrow money to purchase bonds that are *not* exempt from federal income may, in some instances, claim an interest deduction on the debt that is incurred. However, the client may not deduct interest on indebtedness incurred to purchase bonds that *are* exempt from federal income. Without this interest disallowance rule, clients would realize a double tax benefit from using borrowed funds to purchase or carry tax-exempt bonds, since the interest expense would be deductible while the interest income is not taxable.

U.S. Government Bonds

There are certainly cases in which taxable clients should own taxable bonds, so reviewing these bonds is a worthwhile endeavor. This normally occurs when a UAC is subject to the alternative minimum tax or has a family foundation that is a tax-exempt entity. Some UACs like U.S. Treasury securities very much because of their safety; they are debt obligations of the United States government and are backed by the "full faith and credit" of the government through its ability to raise tax revenues and print money. U.S. Treasury securities are considered to have zero credit risk (although it is possible to purchase a credit default swap on U.S. Treasury securities), ensuring that interest and principal will be paid on time. I will take a brief pause here to reflect upon the sage words of Robert Rubin, the former U.S. treasury secretary and current vice chairman of Citigroup. In his book, *In An Uncertain World* (Random House, 2003), he notes "There are no provable absolutes."[2] But if there were, other than death and taxes, I think the next best thing we have to an absolute is that the U.S. government will pay interest and principal on time. Naturally, in exchange for this safety, interest rates are generally lower on Treasury securities than on other types of bonds that hold more risk. I cover four primary types of marketable Treasury securities here: Treasury bills, Treasury notes, Treasury bonds, and Treasury Inflation-Protected Securities (TIPS).

Treasury Bills   Treasury bills (or *T-bills*) mature in one year or less and do not pay interest prior to maturity; they are sold instead at a discount from their par value. T-bills are commonly issued with maturity dates of 28 days, 91 days, or 182 days through weekly auctions. T-bills are quoted on an annualized percentage yield to maturity. They are the closest thing that exists as a substitute for (taxable) cash. For those interested, T-bills can be purchased over the web from treasurydirect.com.

Treasury Notes   Treasury notes (or *T-notes*) have 2- to 10-year maturities and pay interest semiannually. They are commonly issued with maturity dates of 2, 5, or 10 years in denominations from $1,000 to $1,000,000. T-notes (and T-bonds) are quoted on the secondary market at percentage of par in thirty-seconds of a point. Thus, for example, a quote of 96:08 on a note indicates that it is trading at a discount: $962.50 (that is, 96 and 8/32 percent) for a $1,000 bond. Perhaps the most widely recognized bond of all U.S. Treasury securities is the 10-year T-note, which is often used as a proxy for the performance of the U.S. government bond market and to convey the bond market's forward-looking macroeconomic beliefs.

Treasury Bonds   Treasury bonds (or *T-bonds*) have the longest maturity, from 10 years to 30 years, and also pay interest semiannually. They are commonly issued with a maturity of 30 years. The U.S. federal government stopped issuing 30-year Treasury bonds (sometimes called *long bonds*) in October of 2001 because the government paid down a substantial portion of the federal debt in the last half of the 1990s, and the 10-year note replaced the long bond as a proxy for the U.S. bond market. Demand from large institutional investors, however, reignited interest in the long bond and it was reintroduced in February of 2006. The yield on the long bond is now commonly used as a proxy for long-term interest rates in general.

Treasury Inflation-Protected Securities   First issued in 1997, TIPS are inflation-adjusted bonds issued by the U.S. Treasury. Bond principal is indexed to the Consumer Price Index, a controversial, yet commonly used measure of inflation. The interest rate on TIPS is constant, but will pay different amounts of interest when multiplied by the inflation-adjusted principal, thus protecting the holder against inflation. TIPS are currently offered in 5-year, 7-year, 10-year, and 20-year maturities (30-year TIPS were once available but are no longer offered).

Interest payments from TIPS securities are federally taxed *in the year semiannual payments are received*. The inflation adjustment is also taxable each year. The implication of this tax treatment is that even though TIPS are intended to protect against inflation, the cash generated by TIPS is inversely related to inflation until the bond matures. For example, during a period of no inflation, the cash received will be identical to a noninflation indexed bond: The holder receives the coupon payment minus the taxes. During a period of inflation, the holder receives the equivalent cash flow (adjusted for inflation), but has to pay additional taxes on the inflation-adjusted principal. Because of this tax treatment, we often recommend that UACs get inflation protection from other real assets such as real estate or energy.

The Government-sponsored Enterprises Debt Market Government-sponsored enterprises (GSEs) are financing entities created by the United States Congress to facilitate loans to restricted groups of borrowers such as farmers and students. (GSEs are also sometimes referred to as federal agencies or federally sponsored agencies.) The Student Loan Marketing Association (commonly known as Sallie Mae), the Federal National Mortgage Association (Fannie Mae) and the Federal Home Loan Mortgage Corporation (Freddie Mac) are all privately owned corporations in that they have shareholders. While GSE debt was not explicitly guaranteed by the U.S. government, it now carries a guarantee that principal and interest will be paid on time. In assisting GSEs, the government provides access to large credit lines from the Treasury and important exemptions from tax and securities laws. The government has the power to regulate GSEs in various ways, including appointing directors to a GSE board. The most active issuers of GSE debt securities are Federal Home Loan Banks, Freddie Mac, Fannie Mae, Federal Farm Credit Banks, Sallie Mae, and the Tennessee Valley Authority. GSE debt can be attractive at certain times, especially during times of distress in the credit markets.

Corporate Bonds

Corporate bonds (or *corporates* as they are commonly known) are debt obligations of both public and nonpublic corporations. They are typically issued in $1,000 or $5,000 denominations and are divided into three groups: short-term notes (maturities of up to 5 years); medium-term notes and bonds (maturities of 5 to 12 years); long-term bonds (maturities longer than 12 years). There are five primary issuers of corporate bonds: utilities, financial services corporations, transportation companies, industrial corporations, and industrial conglomerates. These issuers can be domestic or foreign entities (foreign governments frequently issue bonds in the United States as well).

One of the most important factors in making an investment decision on a corporate bond is whether the bond is secured or unsecured. If a bond is secured, the issuer has pledged specific assets (collateral) that can be sold to pay off the bondholders in the event of a default. Most corporate bonds, however, are *debentures,* meaning that debt obligations are backed only by the issuer's "general creditworthiness" to repay interest and principal on time. Debentures usually have the extra protection, however, of a *negative pledge* provision. This requires the issuer to provide security for the unsecured bonds in the event that it subsequently pledges its assets to secure other debt obligations. The credit ratings agencies discussed earlier are used to determine how strong a company's unsecured bonds are.

High-Yield Corporate Bonds   High-yield bonds are issued by organizations that do not qualify for investment-grade ratings by one of the leading credit rating agencies discussed earlier. Issuers with a greater risk of default—that is, not paying interest or principal on time—are rated below investment grade (below BBB). These issuers must pay a higher interest rate to attract investors to buy their bonds and to compensate them for the risks associated with investing in organizations of lower credit quality. Entities that issue high-yield debt include many U.S. corporations, certain U.S. banks, various foreign governments, and some foreign corporations.

Mortgage-Backed and Asset-Backed Bonds   Mortgage-backed securities (MBS) and asset-backed securities (ABS) offer investors interest in pools of loans. In the case of MBS, these securities consist primarily of loans from government agencies such as the Government National Mortgage Association (Ginnie Mae) or the GSEs discussed earlier like Fannie Mae and Freddie Mac. The MBS market also includes private-label mortgage securities issued by subsidiaries of investment banks, financial institutions, and homebuilders, but these represent a small portion of the total mortgage-backed securities outstanding.

With ABS, the underlying loans can be anything from auto loans to credit card receivables to home equity loans, and usually carry some form of credit enhancement such as bond insurance, to make them attractive to investors.

Foreign Bonds   Large institutional investors and sophisticated private wealth clients are broadening their horizons to include foreign bonds. There are forces at work that are reducing clients' preference for domestic bonds, or their *home bias,* and the clients are diversifying internationally with their bond allocations. There are several key factors involved in this diversification trend. First, global bonds offer a wide opportunity set of bonds to invest in, which can provide opportunities to add alpha. Second, global bonds, particularly emerging markets bonds, have become a better investment because of a reduction in inflation volatility and country-specific inflation risks previously existent in international bond investing. Third, there has been a general decrease in the volatility of global growth rates and thus in country-specific business cycle risks, all of which are adding up to more capital flowing to foreign bonds. So what do we mean by foreign bonds?

Foreign bonds are issued by a foreign body, such as a government or corporation, and are denominated in a foreign currency that is traded in a foreign financial market. There are two main classes of foreign bonds, developed market bonds and emerging markets bonds, and each of these classes in turn contains two types of bonds: government and corporate bonds. Government bonds are backed by the country issuing the bonds and their agencies. Foreign corporate bonds are issued by major foreign companies, similar to Microsoft or IBM in the United States. Investing in foreign bonds carries the extra risk of currency fluctuations, which can result in a loss of value in an investment because the currency in which the investment is denominated depreciates against the home currency. Currency risk results from fluctuating global exchange rates, inflation, and interest rates. There are two types of currencies: currencies pegged to the U.S. dollar and currencies that are free-floating. Pegged currency values are those that move in line with the U.S. dollar and protect it from currency risk. The value of free-floating currencies, however, fluctuates completely independently from the U.S. dollar, posing a greater risk.

Developed Markets Bonds   Developed markets bonds are issued in developed countries such as France, Canada, Germany, and Japan, where financial markets and political systems are stable. Foreign developed bonds, like U.S. bonds, come in a wide array of maturities of varying credit quality. Some are dollar-denominated (these are known as *Yankee bonds*) but most are denominated in the currency of their home countries. Over the long term, yield spreads on foreign developed bonds will be virtually identical with domestic bonds of similar credit quality and duration. In the short run, however, bond prices (and implied yields) can vary widely among world bond markets. More importantly, exchange rates can fluctuate irrationally, which can have a major impact on returns. Foreign bonds, especially nondollar-denominated bonds, tend to have a low correlation to U.S. bonds, which makes foreign fixed income a good diversification tool.

Emerging Markets Bonds   Developing economies around the world are rapidly expanding the opportunity set for bond investors seeking the benefits of emerging market exposure, which include potentially attractive yields, rising credit quality, and diversification. The emerging markets comprise those nations whose economies are considered to be developing and include Africa, Eastern Europe, Latin America, Russia, the Middle East, and Asia (excepting Japan). Table 8.3 shows the three major emerging markets indexes.

Emerging markets have undergone fundamental changes in regard to disciplined fiscal and monetary policies, control of inflation, less-frequent currency devaluation, and a lower level of bond defaults. These policies have

TABLE 8.3 Three Major Emerging Market Indexes

As of 6/30/07	EMBI Global JPMorgan Emerging Markets Bond Index Global	ELMI + JPMorgan Emerging Local Markets Index Plus	GBI-EM Global Diversified JPMorgan Government Bond Index—Emerging Markets Global Diversified
Summary	EM External Debt Bonds denominated in U.S. dollars	EM Currency Money market securities denominated in local currencies	EM Local Debt Longer-term securities denominated in local currencies
Countries	Argentina	Argentina	Brazil
	Belize	Brazil	Chile
	Brazil	Chile	Colombia
	Bulgaria	China	Czech Republic
	Chile	Colombia	Hungary
	China	Czech Republic	Indonesia
	Colombia	Hong Kong	Malaysia
	Cote d'Ivoire	Hungary	Mexico
	Dominican Republic	India	Peru
	Ecuador	Indonesia	Poland
	Egypt	Israel	Russia
	El Salvador	Malaysia	Slovakia
	Hungary	Mexico	South Africa
	Indonesia	Peru	Turkey
	Iraq	The Philippines	
	Kazakhstan	Poland	
	Lebanon	Romania	
	Malaysia	Russia	
	Mexico	Singapore	
	Pakistan	Slovak Republic	
	Peru	South Africa	
	The Philippines	Taiwan	
	Poland	Turkey	
	Russia		
	Serbia		
	South Africa		
	Trinidad & Tobago		
	Tunisia		
	Turkey		
	Ukraine		
	Uruguay		
	Venezuela		
	Vietnam		

Source: JPMorgan.

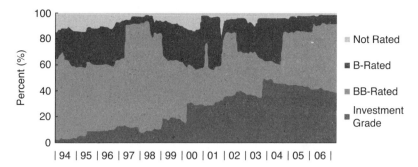

FIGURE 8.2   Market Capitalization Score Across Credit Ratings (JPMorgan EMBI Global Index)
Source: JPMorgan.

produced a steady increase in the credit quality of emerging markets bond issuers, with more than 40 percent of external debt now rated investment grade, as shown in Figure 8.2.

In another important structural change, most countries with emerging markets have shifted from policies in which the value of their local currency was fixed relative to the U.S. dollar to policies that allow the value of the local currency to float relative to the U.S. dollar. In 1996, more than 70 percent of developing countries pegged their currency to the U.S. dollar or ran fully dollarized economies.[3] Today, 85 percent of emerging markets countries allow their currency to float with little or no management.[4] A floating currency provides a mechanism to allow emerging markets countries to better cope with periods of volatility in the global financial system. For example, a downturn in growth in a country will typically lead to a decline in the value of the domestic currency. This action, in turn, makes that country's exports cheaper for foreign buyers and stimulates growth. Fixed currency regimes provide no way to adjust to financial shocks to the system and restore economic growth.

As the emerging markets asset class has evolved, the opportunity set for fixed-income investors seeking emerging markets exposure has steadily expanded, as illustrated in Figure 8.3. The combination of rising credit quality and fundamental improvements in emerging markets countries has attracted new investors, creating new borrowing options for emerging markets governments and corporations. The recent expansion of local currency bond markets, and the interest therein by institutional investors, will continue to help emerging markets fixed income become a well-recognized asset class.

Rather than spending time examining various bond investment strategies that our managers will be employing, such as laddering, bullet and barbell

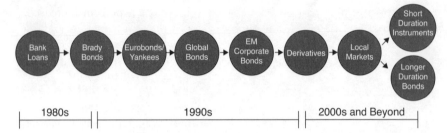

FIGURE 8.3 Emerging Markets Fixed Income: An Expanding Opportunity Set
Source: PIMCO Manager Selection and Performance Analysis of Bond Managers.

strategies, or bond swaps (we will leave those tasks to our bond managers), we should focus on developing an appreciation of key risks to be aware of when investing in bonds. These risks include interest rate risks, credit quality risks, volatility, and foreign exchange risks. Other factors such as cost should be considered when it comes to manager selection and performance evaluation. Because bond yields are relatively low now, there is a big debate between those who believe that active management is a useless endeavor in bonds versus those who prefer indexing.

We use throughout this section a comparative analysis of two large bond managers: the Pacific Investment Management Company (PIMCO Total Return Fund Institutional) and Vanguard (Total Bond Market Index Fund Institutional). PIMCO is an active manager while Vanguard is a passive manager. The funds are comparable because they have the same benchmark (Lehman Brothers Aggregate Bond Index), nearly identical average maturity (generally between 6.8 and 7.0 years) and very similar average credit quality (AA+ and AA1). As you will see, there are material differences in fees, performance, and volatility, and these factors give good indications of which manager is appropriate for which client. I first review some of the basic risks of bond managers: interest rate risk, credit risk, and foreign exchange risk (when investing in global bonds).

Interest Rate Risk

One risk that is nearly impossible to guard against is interest rate risk. Forecasting interest rates is an unrewarding task; many have tried and many have failed. Bond manager returns are highly correlated with changes in interest rates. As was reviewed before, when interest rates rise, bond values decline and vice versa. The easiest way to understand interest rate risk is to understand a bond concept called *duration*. Duration is a measure of a bond fund's sensitivity to changes in interest rates. The higher the duration, the more sensitive the bond manager's fund is to interest rate changes. As a very simple example, a duration of 5.0 implies that a 1 percent increase in interest rates will cause a 5 percent drop in the value of the manager's bond fund and vice versa. Weighted average maturity measures interest rate risk in a similar way: It is the weighted average time to maturity of the bonds in the portfolio, expressed in years. The higher the number, the more sensitive the portfolio will be to interest rates. Duration is a more precise measure of interest rate sensitivity. As with any financial instrument, there is no free lunch here. If you go with a short-duration fund, you can expect lower risk than a long-duration fund, but also lower returns over the long term. If you buy a long-duration fund, you will likely gain the potential to earn stronger long-term returns, at the expense of perhaps enduring large losses in the near term. For most investors seeking core bond exposure for their portfolios, we think intermediate duration funds—those with durations of three and a half to six years—are sound choices.

Credit Risks

Although most bond funds diversify credit risk very well, the weighted average credit quality of a bond fund will influence its volatility: the higher the volatility, the lower the credit quality and vice versa. When we look later at the comparison of PIMCO to Vanguard, we will see that although the Lehman Aggregate benchmark does not contain any junk bonds, PIMCO's guidelines allow investments in high yield securities (rated B or better) up to 10 percent of total assets, and will therefore be more volatile than the Vanguard fund.[5] You should know that investment-grade bonds can also cause volatility because sometimes the ratings agencies discussed earlier can be slow to issue downgrades. Figure 8.4 demonstrates the credit quality of the PIMCO fund as of March 2008.

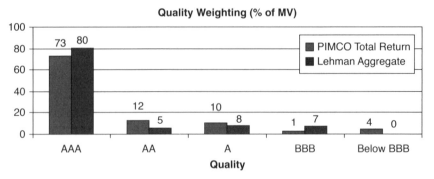

FIGURE 8.4 Credit quality of the PIMCO fund as of March 2008
Source: PIMCO.

Foreign Exchange Risk

Another cause of volatility in a foreign (or even domestic) bond manager's fund is foreign currency exposure. Changes in the value of currencies are more volatile than changes in the prices of bonds, and currency returns can often have a larger influence on a fund's total return than the bonds themselves! The PIMCO Total Return Institutional fund employs nondollar denominated foreign bonds and serves as a good example of a fund that contains foreign exchange risk (PIMCO normally hedges at least 75 percent of its exposure to foreign currency to reduce the risk of loss due to fluctuations in currency exchange rates).[6] Just as with noninvestment-grade exposure, foreign currency exposure is normally an immaterial part of funds benchmarked to the Lehman Aggregate Bond Index.

Fees and Expenses

Given that bond funds generally produce low yields relative to other asset classes, fees and expenses can have a substantial impact on net performance. Sometimes, expenses can eat up as much as 20 or 30 percent of a fund's yield at the retail level. Adding net value can be a difficult hurdle for even the best active bond managers. Passively managed funds can add value simply by charging lower fees. Looking at the two funds we have been discussing, the PIMCO Institutional fund's expenses are 40 to 43 basis points while the Vanguard fund institutional shares have a cost of just 7 basis points.[7] PIMCO needs to add value to help it overcome its fee differential. Another factor to consider vis-à-vis cost is trading costs (spreads) and taxes. Because bonds are constantly maturing and being called, even passive bond funds tend to have high turnover, which can lead to high trading costs and, potentially, tax bills. Passively managed funds tend to have lower turnover than actively managed funds and are therefore better on the cost side.

Analyzing Bond Managers

There are two predominant styles within fixed income management: *Core* and *Core Plus*. Core uses bonds mainly from the Lehman Aggregate Bond index. Core Plus is defined as a bond approach that makes extensive use (typically more than 10 percent) of securities outside the Lehman Aggregate Bond index. Evaluating bond funds does not have to be complex. You need only to focus on a few factors that provide insight into risk and return, which will then give you a feel for the fund's future volatility and return. The factors that we will look at here are style attribution, historical risk and return, volatility (standard deviation), and then the all-important Sharpe Ratio. Note that the 10-year standard deviation of the PIMCO fund is 3.9 percent, while the Vanguard Fund's is 3.5 percent, which is identical to the index.[8]

From Apr 1998 to Mar 2008—18 Month Rolling Windows

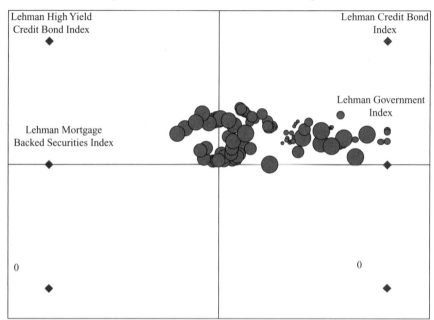

FIGURE 8.5 PIMCO Total Return Style Attribution
Source: © 2006 PerTrac Financial Solutions. All Rights Reserved.

Style Attribution   Style attribution is a measure that demonstrates where
the fund plays within the four major bond sectors: the Lehman Credit Bond
Index, the Lehman Government Bond Index, the Lehman Mortgage-Backed
Securities Index and the Lehman High Yield Index. Figures 8.5 and 8.6
compare the two funds we have been discussing.

The Vanguard fund tracks the Lehman Aggregate Benchmark very
closely. The PIMCO fund strays from the general style of the benchmark to
include high-yield and mortgage-backed securities, accruing higher risk but
with the potential for higher return.

Risk and Return   Understanding the risk-and-return characteristics of a
bond manager is essential. Figures 8.7 and 8.8 show two return/risk scat-
terplots of the PIMCO fund and the Vanguard fund. As you can see, the
PIMCO fund has a better return, but at higher risk.

The Sharpe Ratio   The Sharpe ratio is a measure of return per unit of risk.
Technically, the formula is return of the portfolio minus the risk-free rate

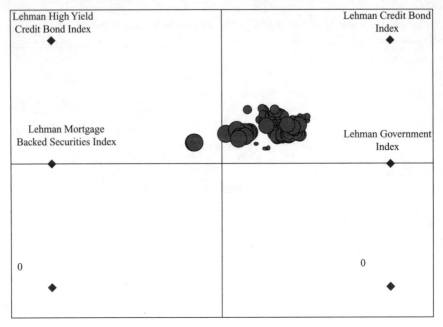

FIGURE 8.6 Vanguard Total Bond Style Attribution
Source: Vanguard.

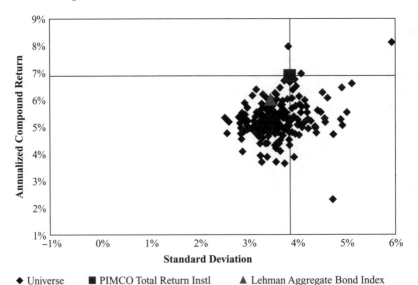

FIGURE 8.7 PIMCO Return/Risk Scatterplot (Since Inception)
Source: © 2006 PerTrac Financial Solutions. All Rights Reserved.

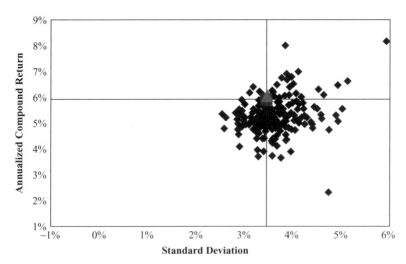

◆ Universe   ■ Vanguard Total Bond Market Index Inst   ▲ Lehman Aggregate Bond Index

FIGURE 8.8   Vanguard Return/Risk Scatterplot (Since Inception)
Source: © 2006 PerTrac Financial Solutions. All Rights Reserved.

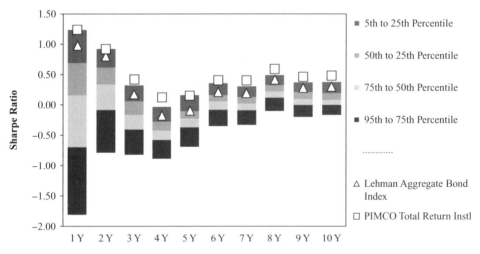

FIGURE 8.9   Sharpe Ratio Ranking of PIMCO Total Return Institutional Fund
Source: © 2006 PerTrac Financial Solutions. All Rights Reserved.

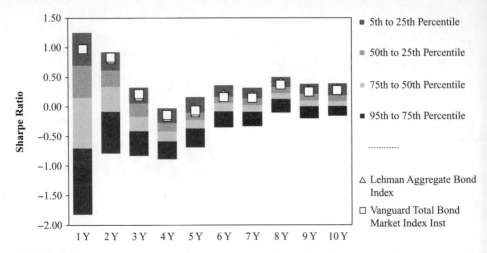

FIGURE 8.10 Sharpe Ratio Ranking of Vanguard Total Bond Market Index Institutional Fund

Source: © 2006 PerTrac Financial Solutions. All Rights Reserved.

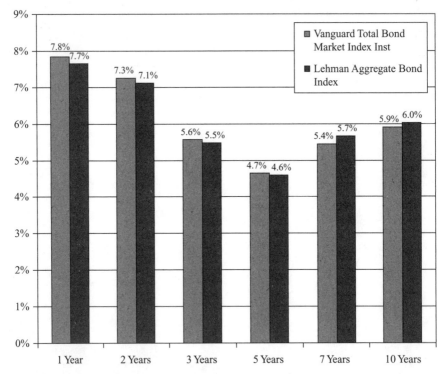

FIGURE 8.11 Returns versus Benchmark of the Vanguard Total Bond Market Fund for the Period Ending March 2008

Source: © 2006 PerTrac Financial Solutions. All Rights Reserved.

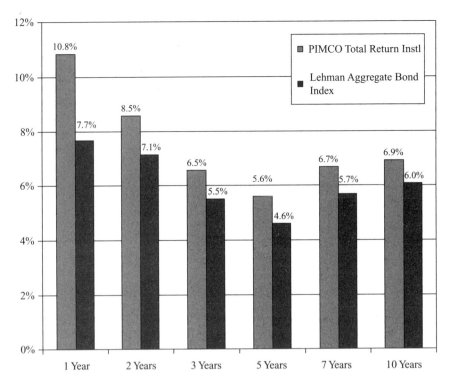

FIGURE 8.12 Returns versus Benchmark of the PIMCO Total Return
Institutional Fund for the Period Ending March 2008
Source: Vanguard and PIMCO.

divided by the standard deviation. Therefore, the higher the Sharpe ratio, the better. As you can see in Figures 8.9 and 8.10, the PIMCO fund has a very high Sharpe ratio compared to the benchmark and compared to the Vanguard fund. The Vanguard fund, which highly resembles the index, has a middling Sharpe ratio, which is to be expected. If one is going to hire an active manager, the Sharpe ratio chart should look like that of the PIMCO fund.

In conclusion, as Figures 8.11 and 8.12 confirm, the PIMCO fund has outperformed the Vanguard fund with less risk per unit of return. If one is comfortable with a slightly higher volatility, then the PIMCO fund might well be the right choice. If one prefers less volatility and wishes not to take active risk, the Vanguard fund is the better choice. It is up the UAC adviser to recommend to the client the fund that best meets the client's investment objective.

Now that we have covered both domestic and international bonds, we move to private equity in the next chapter.

CHAPTER 9

Private Equity

*Competition I don't worry about. Nothing can really solve the
problem of high prices.*
                    —Stephen Schwarzman, CEO, Blackstone Group

Although private equity goes through periods of lackluster performance
and funds may call capital without throwing off any cash returns (both
of which are happening in the current scarce credit environment that began in
2008), private equity has proven itself to be a rewarding undertaking over the
course of time. Allocations to private equity by UACs are substantial, despite
the fact that private equity partnerships are illiquid, usually have a life of 10
years or more, and return investor capital only at the discretion of the private
equity fund manager. You might ask, What is driving this trend? While the
key factor in real estate is location, location, location, the driver of private
equity's popularity is returns, returns, returns, as can be seen in Table 9.1.
Historically, early-stage venture capital has offered the highest returns of the
three primary categories of private equity, followed by buyouts, and then
mezzanine. But returns of various sectors of the private equity classes are
cyclical. In the late 1990s, venture capital topped the charts. In the early
2000s, as is typical during recession years, leveraged buyouts were a great
place to invest.

To get solid returns from this most illiquid of asset classes, careful planning and execution are required. UAC advisers must have detailed knowledge of what drives solid returns in private equity investing, the various
segments within it, and how to create a best-of-breed program. I discuss in
this chapter private equity as an asset class and best practices on creating
an institutional-quality private equity program by reviewing the following:
first, what private equity is and how it functions mechanically; second,
characteristics of individual private equity asset classes: buyouts, venture

TABLE 9.1 20-year Private Equity Returns for the Period
Ending December 2007

Fund Type	3 Year	5 Year	10 Year	20 Year
Early Stage VC	5.2	4.7	38.6	21.8
Later Stage VC	9.6	10	8.6	14.1
All Venture	8.7	8.2	18	16.6
Small Buyouts	5.5	7.1	3.9	21.4
Large Buyouts	9.2	13.9	7.3	12.4
Mega Buyouts	13.4	15.7	8.2	11.5
All Buyouts	12.2	14.5	7.8	12.4
Mezzanine	5.1	5.2	5.8	8.2
S&P 500	8.62	12.83	5.91	11.81
All Private Equity	11.3	12.4	10.1	13.6

Calculation Type: Pooled IRR; Primary Market: United States.
Source: Standard & Poor's, BMO Capital Markets, and International Monetary Fund.

capital, and special situations (mezzanine and distressed); and third, a process for creating a customized private equity program, including manager selection.

When this chapter was written, a golden age of private equity had come and, at least for now, gone. The stock market, partly responsible for such good times in private equity, has undergone a major correction. Credit markets, which were the fuel for the private equity fire, have all but seized up. Risk is being revalued. Things appear bleak for private equity, but this isn't the first time we've seen this type of cyclicality—and cyclicality leads to lower prices, which in turn lead to better returns. And as every great investor knows, understanding valuation is essential to investment success. Mr. Schwartzman must have seen the writing on the wall and known that the time to sell his firm was right around the corner. His quote at the beginning of this chapter foreshadowed times to come. As shown in Figure 9.1, prices for private equity were never higher historically than they were in 2006, the year before Blackstone Group went public.[1]

It is quite instructive to look at the factors that drove this most recent period in private equity and learn why it was such a good one. Several factors determine the quality of a client's experience investing in private equity: the private equity asset class one chose to invest in, the year the investment was made (a somewhat random factor), and the manager with whom one chose to invest. In regard to the first two factors, examining the years 2003

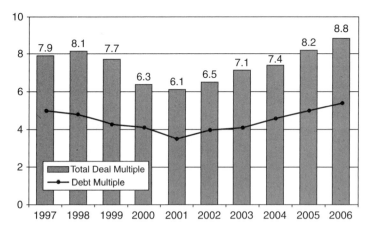

FIGURE 9.1 BUYOUT EBITDA Multiples 1997–2006
Source: Venture Economics/Thompson.

through 2006 (and into 2007) is instructive. During this period, free-flowing credit created a perfect environment for private equity firms like Blackstone, Thomas Lee, and Bain Capital to create astounding wealth for investors and general partners. Contributing factors included a relatively strong economy, low interest rates, strong corporate balance sheets, a robust stock market, lenders that were willing to provide capital aggressively, and low inflation. Moreover, access to capital markets in the form of M&A activity, company recaps, and IPOs were ideal ways for private equity firms to exit their private investments.

It is clear now that public equity markets were priced in 2000 to provide below-average returns after the popping of the technology stock bubble, and investors turned to private equity as a way to generate higher returns. With regard to the third factor, manager selection, UAC advisers need to understand that being in the right asset class (in the case of large buyouts) brought moderate to good returns, but being with the top managers brought great returns, as can be seen in Figure 9.2. Manager selection in particular is crucial to the success of a private equity program, but during this golden age, many private equity firms thrived simply because the environment was so beneficial.

Creating a solid private equity program is not for the novice. We will review some of the essentials here, but hiring professionals to oversee a program is highly recommended.

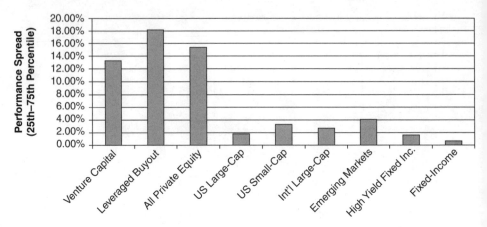

FIGURE 9.2   Performance Spread (Top minus Bottom Quartile Manager Return)
Source: Venture Economics and Morningstar.

WHAT IS PRIVATE EQUITY AND HOW DOES IT WORK?

Private equity used to be a fairly easy term to define. Simply put, if you couldn't sell your investment on an organized exchange or ask an investment manager for redemption in a reasonable amount of time, it was probably a private equity investment. But private equity has different meanings for different people. For instance, some people lump private investing in real estate and other real assets into private equity (I do not, and have a separate chapter for private real assets). Furthermore, a new term, *secondaries,* has arrived on the private equity scene, further clouding the definition. Secondaries are private equity interests that are bought and sold privately, providing liquidity to seller investors who want it and seasoned private equity investments for buyer investors who want those. Now that sounds a lot like a liquid market, doesn't it? Moreover, there are publicly traded private equity investing vehicles such as the aforementioned Blackstone Group, Apollo, and others. That doesn't sound like private equity, does it? Lastly, hedge funds have been entering the private equity scene through the use of side pocket investment pools and other tactics, further blurring the lines between private equity and hedge fund investing. So, for the purpose of this chapter, we need a definition. I define here private equity as illiquid, private partnership investing in three areas—buyouts, venture capital, and special situations (distressed and mezzanine)—by investment managers who are dedicated to raising multiple funds in these strategies (e.g., not a hedge fund with side pockets). Figure 9.3

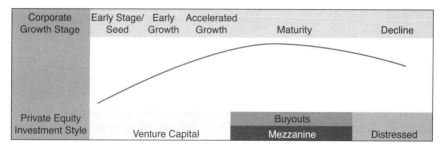

FIGURE 9.3 Spectrum of Private Equity Investing

below shows each of these areas of private equity along with the corporate stage of growth for each strategy.

Although investing in secondaries can be a sound private equity strategy, we will not include them in our working definition of private equity. Buying a fund interest in a secondary transaction is an alternative route to acquiring the investment, but at that point, you are still invested in the same assets as other limited partners. Lastly, publicly traded vehicles that engage in private equity investing are outside our definition, but the funds they raise to make investments are included. We will further define buyouts, venture capital, and special situations in the next section. With regard to special situations, there are many types, but we will limit our discussion to mezzanine investing and distressed investing.

So how does private equity work? Functionally, the way in which investors make investments in private partnerships could require a quite lengthy description, so our discussion of the relationship between the general partner (the manager) and the limited partner (the investor) and the process by which capital is invested is limited. I also assume that the discussion involves U.S. private equity managers (sorry, but I am going to display some home country bias) in regard to the relationship between the manager and the investor. You should know, however, that different countries treat the structure between investors and managers in different ways.

The General Partner–Limited Partner Relationship

Institutional-quality private equity partnerships are almost always structured as limited partnerships. A limited partnership has a fixed life, usually 10 years (though it can be longer). In a limited partnership arrangement, there is a general partner (GP) and a limited partner (LP). The GP is the managing partner and is responsible for the operations of the partnership and any debts taken on by the partnership—please note that portfolio company debt has no recourse to the LPs and documents rarely allow leverage at the fund level except to facilitate transactions. The general partner also picks the companies that the partnership will invest in, oversees its investments in them, and manages the process of exiting investments to create a return for its LPs. The GP typically invests the partnership's capital over the first three to five years, but the limited partnership will occasionally have investments that run beyond the fund's life. When this happens, the partnership term can be extended beyond the original term. In return for performing these services, the GP collects management fees and retains a percentage of ownership in the partnership. LPs invest money in the partnership and have limited liability, but are not involved in day-to-day management, and (usually) cannot lose more than their capital contribution. They receive income, capital gains, and tax benefits. In short, the LP is the investor and the GP is the manager, bound by a somewhat complex partnership agreement.

The specific document outlining the investment terms between the LPs and the GP is known as a Private Placement Memorandum (PPM). It is part marketing tool and part disclosure document. The PPM is designed to provide information to buyers (LPs) to protect sellers (GPs) from liabilities related to selling unregistered securities. A typical PPM contains a business description and terms of the security offered for sale, fees, historical returns, summary biographies of key personnel, and risk factors associated with the investment.

The PPM refers to another document called a Limited Partner Agreement (LPA), which is the actual binding agreement. The LPA establishes the rules of the operation of the fund, how the fund will be governed, and the limited partnership terms between participating parties. When there is a difference between the PPM and LPA, the LPA governs, so you should read it. A limited partnership investment is essentially a passive (flow-through) vehicle for the LP and the LP has virtually no sway over what investments are made or the terms of the investment partnership. The higher the quality of the manager, the less power the LP has in dictating anything related to the investment process. Despite this imbalance, some LPs still try to influence the investment process, with varying degrees of success. Assuming the investor has done the requisite due diligence and decided to invest, the LP completes the subscription documents and makes a capital commitment.

The Way Capital Flows in a Private Equity Investment

All investors in a private equity fund commit a specific cash amount to be invested in the fund partnership over a specified period of time, usually

10 years. This amount is known as the limited partner's *capital commitment.* The sum of all LP capital commitments plus the GP commitment equals the total size of the fund (the general partner must also make a capital commitment to participate in the fund). In practice, the way in which LP investors make their investments is through a capital call structure, meaning that money gets *called,* usually in a three- to five-year period as the GP needs money to make investments. Such calls are due on as short as five days notice, so sufficient funds must be available for when the capital call notices arrive. The requirement to fund a capital call is legally binding, so this kind of investing is serious business. The general partner then uses called capital to complete portfolio investments.

The good part comes when investments are realized and capital is distributed. The returns that an investor receives from a private equity fund can be both income and capital gains realized from investments (less expenses and any liabilities). Once an LP receives his initial capital investment returns, subsequent distributions are considered profits. The partnership agreement outlines both the timing of distributions to the LPs and how profits are divided among the LPs and GPs. Once a fund is substantially committed, and assuming the manager is successfully investing its funds and sees continuing opportunities in the marketplace, the GP will then go about raising its next fund and will ask its existing investors if they want to invest again, or *re-up*.

Private Equity Management Fees

Acting as the investment manager, the GP charges a management fee to cover the costs of managing the partner's capital. The management fee (paid quarterly over the life of the fund) often tails off in the later stages of a fund's existence. The way in which fees are charged is negotiated with investors upon formation of the fund. The Blackstone Group, which has been involved in some of the biggest corporate buyouts during the latest private equity boom, has about $50 billion of assets under management and charges its investors a 1.5 percent management fee (and charges the companies it invests in other fees that it splits with investors)—not a bad business model.[2] The firm also takes a 20 percent *carried interest* fee on profits made by its funds when it realizes profits. Carried interest is the term used to describe the profit split of proceeds to the general partner. This is the general partner's fee for carrying the management responsibility of the fund (plus the liability, if any) and for providing the necessary expertise to successfully manage the fund's portfolio of investments. There are many variations on the fees charged and the profits split between the LPs and the GP, both in the amounts and how they are calculated, but a 2 percent management fee plus a 20 percent carried interest is typical.

THREE PRIMARY TYPES OF PRIVATE EQUITY INVESTMENTS

We now move to examine the three types of private equity investments made: buyouts, venture capital, and special situations. These three were chosen because they are the most commonly used strategies used by institutional investors and sophisticated family offices.

Buyouts

A *buyout* is a strategy in which a private investor group acquires control of a corporation, division of a corporation, or even a product line of a corporation with a capital structure that is 50 percent to 80 percent debt (the days of 90% leverage are over). Once the investor gains control of the company, the buying group has the leeway it needs to do what it wants. A typical buyout strategy involves trying to grow the target company by acquiring similar companies and combining them in a roll-up strategy to try to gain efficiency through eliminating redundant business lines (e.g., accounting departments) and increasing the multiple at which it can sell the company by increasing its size. The bigger the company, the safer its revenue stream and, theoretically, the more valuable it is.

No one knows for sure when the first leveraged buyout deal occurred, but most market observers agree that it was carried out after World War II ended. The U.S. business climate after World War II was permeated with a Depression-era mentality, and American CEOs considered carrying debt to be an imprudent way to conduct financial affairs from about the late 1940s through the early 1960s. Creating conglomerates during the 1960s became a fashionable business strategy and, as a result, American companies began to become unprofitable because of too many layers of management and lack of proper strategic direction. Seeing an opportunity to unlock value, early private equity investors began to buy companies or divisions with leverage but did so in relative obscurity.

The buyout business continued to evolve through the 1970s, and by the 1980s, Buyout transactions were becoming more visible. Of note during that decade was a deal done by a group called Wesray Capital. They purchased a company called Gibson Greeting Cards for $80 million and put in only $1 million of their own equity capital to effect the transaction, borrowing the rest. A year and a half later, Gibson went public at a valuation of $220 million.[3] Quite a coup! Congress soon began examining the practice of the leveraged buyout closely for legislation and the media devoted a substantial amount of coverage to high-profile leveraged buyouts. Junk-bond king Michael Milken created a buyout world unto himself during the 1980s in which the use of high-yield bonds proliferated to affect many buyouts. His activities, it turned out, involved some illegal procedures and by the 1990s the buyout went somewhat out of fashion. But like most fashions, it came back, and the decade of the 2000s has seen a major resurgence in buyout activity until the credit crunch of 2008. If history is any guide, another wave of buyouts will occur once the economy improves and credit begins flowing again.

How a Buyout Transaction Works Mechanically, a buyout can be extremely complex on large transactions or relatively simple on small ones. A small buyout—a relatively simple transaction—works very much like buying an investment real estate property. The prospective investor puts down a percentage of the purchase price (which often depends upon market conditions), and borrows the rest of the money to effect the transaction in hopes of collecting income on his assets and seeing his property increase in value through appreciation over time. With a home purchase, there is typically one lender (e.g., a local bank); in a small buyout structure, there is typically a single lender providing senior debt capital. In more complex transactions, there may be numerous providers of outside capital, debt, and sometimes equity (beyond the down payment equity). Senior bank debt (which in the home-buying analogy is the mortgage) is normally provided by one or more large commercial banks and usually consists of two parts: a revolving credit facility and term debt. A revolving credit facility (a *revolver*) acts much like a credit card that the company can use for working capital. Term debt, secured by the assets of the company, has a maturity of 5 or 10 years, depending on how the deal is negotiated, and has numerous repayment options which are too varied to review here.

When needed to effect a transaction, there is sometimes another layer of (usually unsecured) debt capital in a buyout transaction that is below the senior debt called *mezzanine* (so called because it fits between bank debt and the equity). Mezzanine debt's returns are higher than senior debt because of higher risk, but not as high as common equity's. Some mezzanine lenders will require equity participation in the deal in the form of warrants that are essentially a call option on common equity. In addition to the debt component of a buyout, another source of financing for leveraged buyouts is preferred equity. Preferred equity is between mezzanine debt and common equity in the capital structure of the company and is often attractive to investors because its dividend payment represents a return on investment while its equity ownership component allows holders to participate in equity appreciation.

Preferred interest is often structured as payment-in-kind (PIK) dividends, which means that any interest is paid in the form of additional shares of preferred stock. Buyout firms will often structure their equity investment in the form of preferred stock, with management, employees, and warrant holders receiving common shares. Figure 9.4 shows a typical buyout structure. I discuss how to create a buyout investment strategy later in the chapter.

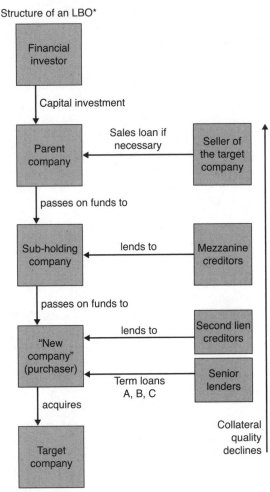

Structure of an LBO*

*Corporated acquisitions by a financial investor using a large proportion of debt.

FIGURE 9.4   Typical Buyout Structure
Source: Deutsche Bundesbank.

Venture Capital

Unlike buyout capital, which is provided to mature companies, venture capital is provided to young, rapidly growing companies in the interest of taking the company to an IPO or similar exit. As with buyout funds, venture funds are limited partnerships that have as investors pension funds, endowments and foundations, companies, and UACs. Not all venture capitalists invest in start-ups; some invest in companies at various growth stages of the business life cycle. Start-up investing is typically done before there is a real product or company organized (also known as *seed-stage investing*). Early-stage investing provides capital to young, growing companies. Late-stage investment funds a company that is nearly profitable or that is already profitable but requires capital to accelerate growth (also known as *expansion-stage investing*—or as some venture capitalists describe it: "*Roll out investing* versus *find out investing*!").

The venture capital industry has grown from a small investment pool in the 1960s and early 1970s of mainly angel investors (wealthy people with management expertise or retired businessmen and -women who are looking for first-hand business development) to a mainstream asset class today, a significant part of the institutional and corporate investment realm. General Georges Doriot is considered to be the father of the modern venture capital industry. In 1921, Doriot, a young veteran of World War I, became the first French-born student to enroll at Harvard Business School. He later joined the faculty, teaching manufacturing strategy. After becoming an American citizen and helping with the war effort of World War II, he co-founded American Research and Development Corporation (AR&DC) with Ralph Flanders and Karl Compton in 1946. AR&DC developed a company that was to become Digital Equipment Corporation.[4] When Digital Equipment went public in 1968 it provided AR&DC with 101 percent annualized return on investment (ROI), a stellar return.[5] It is commonly accepted that the first venture-backed start-up is Fairchild Semiconductor, funded in 1959 by Venrock Associates, the venture capital arm of the Rockefeller Family.[6] Since then, venture capitalists have nurtured the growth of some of the United States's best technology companies, including Google, Microsoft, Apple, DEC, Compaq, Sun Microsystems, and Intel.

Venture capital firms come in many shapes and sizes. They can be generalists, investing in various industry sectors, geographic locations, or stages of a company's life cycle. Others specialize in one or two industry sectors, such as semiconductors or software, or may invest in only one geographic area. Some firms are relatively small, seed-stage focused with a few million dollars under management, while others have billions of dollars of assets under management invested globally. Regardless of size or specialty, venture capitalists add value by getting actively involved in the companies they invest in, taking board seats and guiding growth. Many venture capitalists consider themselves to be entrepreneurs first and financiers second.

Of all the private equity strategies, venture capital is the riskiest. Venture capitalists look at hundreds of investment opportunities annually before investing in only a few selected companies with favorable investment opportunities. The venture capital business has become much more competitive over the years. Without an IPO or similar exit strategy returning many times the invested capital, moderate returns will likely result because some investments in the fund will be total losses. Venture capitalists mitigate the risk of venture investing by developing a portfolio of young companies in a single venture fund and often co-invest with other venture capital firms.

Venture capitalists usually seek to exit their investments in three to seven years, but sometimes that time stretches much further. An early-stage investment may take 7 to 10 years to mature, while a later-stage investment may only take two years. It is incumbent upon UAC advisers to assess potential duration of a strategy and ensure that it is congruent with the client's appetite for liquidity. Venture capital is neither a short-term nor a liquid investment, and permanent loss of capital is a real possibility. But with careful diligence and expertise, one can be a successful venture capital investor.

Special Situations

Mezzanine Financing   To continue the description from the previous section, mezzanine financing is a hybrid form of capital that is so named because it exists in the middle of the capital structure and generally fills the gap between bank debt and the equity in a transaction. Structurally, mezzanine financing is junior to the bank debt that is taken on to finance a leveraged buyout and senior to common stock. The need for it depends a lot on how aggressive senior bank lenders are. If banks are lending aggressively, mezzanine financing may not be needed. If banks are less aggressive, mezzanine financing may be needed. Mezzanine financing is compensated for its lower priority and higher level of risk with higher interest rates than senior debt. Rates of return on mezzanine depend on current market conditions but can be greater than 12 percent. Mezzanine financing is a hybrid because it is a blend of traditional debt and equity financing. Compared with equity financing, mezzanine financing usually converts to equity ownership in the event of a default on the loan (i.e., the investor gets the keys if the loan isn't paid back) and typically comes with equity participation in the form of warrants in the case of a profitable exit. All in, mezzanine investors are typically looking for a total return of 15 to 20 percent.

While mezzanine debt is more costly than straight bank debt, it permits equity investors to use less of their capital to finance a deal. The primary risk with mezzanine, aside from debt not being repaid, is the ability of the mezzanine capital provider to realize the value of its equity. Sales, recapitalizations (refinancing), or IPOs are all ways in which the equity piece can be monetized. When credit conditions are tight, as they were when this chapter was written, mezzanine lenders have a strong leg to stand on in regard to dictating better returns for themselves. Although typically not the case, some mezzanine lenders provide strategic assistance to a deal.

Distressed Investing *Distressed* investing involves the acquisition of stocks, bonds, or other assets (e.g., trade or financial claims) of companies in or near bankruptcy or those that are experiencing strategic, operational, or serious financial challenges. Prices of distressed companies' securities fall in anticipation of financial distress when their holders choose to sell rather than remain invested in a financially troubled company. Distressed investing is in many ways taking advantage of emotional stress: in times of crisis, asset managers, investors, and other market participants may behave in an economically irrational way whether the probability of bankruptcy is real or just perceived. On the other hand, there are professional investors who specialize in researching distressed securities and understand the risks and rewards of buying distressed securities at bargain prices, seeing value where others see potential disaster.

There are two basic types of distressed investing: distressed for control and non-control. With control, an investor is basically trying to buy the equity of a company through buying the debt of same and having the company go through a Chapter 11 reorganization process. Chapter 11 gives the company legal protection to continue operating while working out a repayment plan, known as a plan for reorganization, with a committee of its major creditors. While distressed situations of this kind frequently involve mature companies that are in decline, opportunities can also arise as a result of good companies with poor balanced sheets. Non-control investing or Chapter 7 (liquidation) bankruptcy involves a complete liquidation of the company. Distressed securities can also include bank loans and other privately placed debt of the same or similar entities with acute operating or financial problems or both. Generally, a distressed investor focuses mostly on the bank debt, trade claims, and bonds when looking for bargain-priced securities. Although there are various definitions of the word *distressed,* a common rule of thumb is that a distressed security is one that trades at a 10 percent discounted price-to-yield over comparable duration U.S. Treasury (risk-free) bonds.

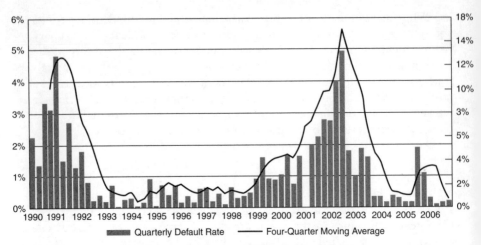

FIGURE 9.5 Quarterly Default Rate and Four-Quarter Moving Average 1991–2006
Source: Altman, E. and Ramayanam, S., "Special Report on Defaults and Returns in the High-Yield Bond Market: 2006 in Review and Outlook," New York University Salomon Center Leonard N. Stern School of Business, February 2007.

Private equity distressed managers focus on the following things to make money for their clients: seeking assets that are trading at a substantial discount to intrinsic value, attempting to control or at least influence the resolution of creditor issues, resolving the source of distress, and, if they are successful, exiting the investment at a profit. Distressed fund managers differentiate themselves by the types of securities or assets they acquire, the level of control they seek, and the liquidity (hence the time horizon) of the securities they invest in. Most distressed investments come about as a result of recession or general economic slowness. Additional factors that may contribute to a distressed cycle include a breakdown in the credit cycle, corporate malfeasance, scandals, or other crises of confidence that expose financial weakness in companies or cause a general withdrawal of liquidity from the capital markets. Figure 9.5 illustrates the historical cyclical pattern of credit default rates.

CREATING A CUSTOMIZED PRIVATE EQUITY PROGRAM

Now that we have reviewed the major strategies of private equity, we are ready to create the private equity program for the client. The first step in implementing a private equity portfolio for the UAC is to decide whether she will establish an allocation to private equity and, if so, what percentage of the portfolio will be allocated there. The inclusion of private equity strategies in an individual or family office private equity portfolio is driven largely by the same factors that influence the overall asset allocation decision: return objective, risk tolerance, liquidity requirements, and time horizon, among others. The overriding consideration for most investors, however, is liquidity. Private equity capital can be tied up for many years, for which investors need to be compensated. Clients should not bother investing in private equity unless they believe they can earn a marginal return over public equity securities which varies according to market conditions (but 500 basis points above the S&P 500 is about right).

Once an allocation to private equity is made, the next step is to determine how much money will be allocated each year. This is typically done with a cash flow private equity commitment model. In rough terms, for every percent allocation to private equity (in dollars), clients should make regular annual commitments of one third of a percent to meet the target. Clients should not shoot for the entire allocation in one or two years. They should strive instead for *vintage year diversification*, which, as in wine collecting, helps prevent an investor from investing too much in a single bad year. Private equity returns have good years and bad years. If substantially less than a third of the commitment is invested annually, there will be a reduced likelihood of reaching a target private equity allocation within a reasonable time horizon; any more, and one risks too much allocated to a single vintage year. In addition to providing vintage year diversification, this approach allows clients to adjust commitments for the inherent unpredictability in performance and cash flows, as well as allow the client to address changing opportunities within the broad landscape of private equity.

In Table 9.2, which illustrates a sample client with a total portfolio of $100,000,000 and a 12 percent allocation to private equity, the client reaches his target allocation in the sixth year of the program.

Once the client decides how much to allocate to private equity, the next question is how to access private equity: either investing in *direct* limited partnerships having interest in underlying companies, or investing in a fund of multiple private equity partnerships *(fund of funds)*. Which way is best depends on the amount of capital being invested, administrative capability, due diligence resources, and access to top managers. With regard to capital, there is some debate about what account size is appropriate to invest in LPs, but certainly at annual commitments of $30 million to $40 million, funds of funds are less attractive. Even at this level though, if the investor has little or no administrative help, a fund of funds might be the best option. If a direct approach is used, portfolio size may still limit the number of managers that can be used in a given year and tilt the portfolio toward managers with

TABLE 9.2 Illustration of Private Equity Commitment Schedule

Target Allocation: 12 percent
Total Portfolio Market Value: $100,000,000
Target Private Equity Assets: $12,000,000
Projected Portfolio Growth Rate: 2.50 percent

Year	Commitment	Cumulative Commitments	Estimated NAV	Target NAV	Est. % of Target Allocation Invested	Est. % of Total Portfolio
2007	$4,200,000	$4,200,000	$585,900	$12,000,000	4.9%	0.6%
2008	$4,200,000	$8,400,000	$2,260,860	$12,000,000	18.8%	2.3%
2009	$4,200,000	$12,600,000	$4,774,560	$12,000,000	39.8%	4.8%
2010	$4,200,000	$16,800,000	$7,781,760	$12,300,000	63.3%	7.6%
2011	$3,000,000	$19,800,000	$10,556,460	$12,607,500	83.7%	10.0%
2012	$3,000,000	$22,800,000	$12,461,400	$12,922,688	96.4%	11.6%
2013	$3,000,000	$25,800,000	$13,570,200	$13,245,755	102.4%	12.3%
2014	$3,000,000	$28,800,000	$13,695,900	$13,576,899	100.9%	12.1%
2015	$3,000,000	$31,800,000	$13,418,100	$13,916,321	96.4%	11.6%
2016	$4,200,000	$36,000,000	$13,185,900	$14,264,229	92.4%	11.1%
2017	$4,200,000	$40,200,000	$13,283,160	$14,620,835	90.9%	10.9%
2018	$4,200,000	$44,400,000	$13,719,960	$14,986,356	91.5%	11.0%
2019	$4,200,000	$48,600,000	$14,418,360	$15,361,015	93.9%	11.3%
2020	$4,200,000	$52,800,000	$15,178,560	$15,745,040	96.4%	11.6%

Source: Hammond Associates.

TABLE 9.3   Risk, Return, and Liquidity Characteristics of Private Equity Strategies

Private Equity Strategy	Return Profile	Risk Profile	Liquidity Profile
Buyout	10–25%	Moderate	4–6 Years
Special Situations—Mezzanine	8–15%	Low	3–4 Years
Special Situations—Distressed	8–20%	Moderate	3–5 Years
Venture Capital	0–40%	High	3–9 Years

broader opportunity sets rather than narrowly defined specialists. If size is not an issue and direct investing is preferred, top notch due diligence is required to evaluate individual funds. Having access to top fund managers is also essential.

After deciding whether a direct or fund of funds approach will be used, the next consideration is establishing risk and return parameters for the private equity portfolio, similar to how one addresses the task for the entire portfolio. An investor's risk-and-return profile will play a role in selecting a manager because some private equity managers are significantly more conservative in approach than others. This is why composition of the private equity portfolio is critical to the success of the private equity investor. Clients can choose from a variety of risk-and-return profiles within various private equity strategies, all with varying degrees of return expectations, volatility, and duration. Table 9.3 shows the risk, return, and liquidity characteristics of private equity strategies that can be used when creating a private equity portfolio for a client.

The allocation of private equity assets among the three primary strategies (buyouts, venture capital, and special situations) is important because, as we just noted, each strategy has its own risk-and-return expectations. In general, venture capital investments, which have the highest expected return, also have the most risk, as measured by volatility of returns. In fact, some loss-averse investors avoid venture capital altogether because of the *J-curve* associated with venture capital in which returns in the early years are negative before (one hopes) turning positive in later years. Venture investors must have a long time horizon and must not expect any distributions for the first five years of the investment. Buyout funds tend to have a lower risk profile because the underlying companies usually have cash flow and are more mature businesses than venture companies. Buyouts, therefore have a lower expected return than venture capital. Certain market conditions, however, can change the risk-and-return profiles of these two categories, such as those of the early-to-mid 2000s when buyouts clearly led the way after venture capital suffered from the late 1990s tech boom and bust. Buyouts return capital more quickly than venture capital investments, but not as quickly as special situations funds. These funds have a more senior claim on target companies' assets and will thus have a lower expected return and risk than both venture capital and buyout investments. Special situation funds also have a shorter time horizon with capital both called and distributed more quickly than in venture and buyout investments.

Finding the right mix for the individual client varies because each client is different. Some clients have greater liquidity needs than others. Some may simply want to focus only on buyout strategies, while others would rather take a barbell approach, combining lower-duration strategies such as mezzanine with longer-duration strategies such as venture capital. In any case, investors should have a baseline strategy mix between the three primary private equity classes with tilts that can be put on as both market conditions and investor preferences change. For example, a baseline mix between the three classes might be 33 percent buyout, 33 percent venture, and 33 percent special situations. But say, for example, that a given client does not have the required liquidity tolerance for venture capital. An appropriate baseline mix for that client might be 50 percent buyouts and 50 percent special situations—with a tilt away from large buyouts and toward special situations of 60 percent special situations and 40 percent buyouts. Each of the categories of private equity tends to be cyclical and imperfectly correlated to the other categories. Therefore, diversification across both category and fund vintage year is important.

Final Selection of Private Equity Managers

Once the investor has determined the amount of the commitment, the vehicle (fund of funds or direct), and which sectors to allocate to, she must make a final decision about which private equity managers she will perform the requisite due diligence on and commit capital to. I review in this section best practices for selecting investment managers, and address the due diligence considerations to implement the private equity allocation.

The selection of and access to the best managers is the key driver of performance for a private equity program, whether that be a direct program or a fund of funds. As we saw earlier in the chapter, the difference between the performance of a 25th percentile manager and a 75th percentile manager is substantial: The lowest spread among private equity segments (13.3 percent for venture capital) is more than three times that of the widest public equity class (4.1 percent for emerging markets equities).

Six key characteristics of managers are critically important for private equity (and for that manner, all alternative investment managers) so they can offer the investor a chance at success in the private equity area. These are: seasoned professionals, competitive advantage, disciplined approach, strong track record, GP–LP alignment of interests, and industry standard structure and fees.

- *Seasoned Professionals:* Chances for success in private equity investing increase dramatically when investors hire GPs with professional investment teams that are staffed with experienced professionals who have successfully worked together over a meaningful period of time.
- *Competitive Advantage:* Investors should look for GPs who possess a differentiated and sustainable competitive advantage and an ability to create economic value through strategic guidance and operating improvements at the portfolio company level.
- *Disciplined Approach to Deal Sourcing:* GPs that foster a disciplined and proactive approach to sourcing activities will have a robust deal flow, which should lead to superior investment opportunities.
- *Strong Track Record:* GPs that have a propensity to outperform their peers by historically generating a top-quartile track record are preferred.
- *Aligned GP–LP Interests:* GPs with a substantial investment of personal capital in their funds who have a high hurdle rate before they get a preferred return are preferred. In addition, GPS who offer LPs the opportunity to replace the GP in certain circumstances are preferred.
- *Industry Standard Terms and Fees:* Investors should seek out GPs who structure their partnership in line with industry norms and help provide downside protection in the event of adverse developments.

Due Diligence

The process of screening and selecting appropriate private equity managers requires a significant investment of time. If an investor conducts his own due diligence, he must begin with a review of the fund materials, including the PPM. If the fund appears worth pursuing, potential investors should meet with the management team and conduct a quantitative and qualitative analysis of the team, strategy, track record, and terms. Investors at this stage of the process should also conduct reference checks with both portfolio executives and other investors. As the last step, an investor should conduct an on-site visit with the manager and make the final decision whether or not to invest. Table 9.4 shows a sample due diligence review based on AICPA guidelines.

The last step is to put it all together into a strategic private equity plan, detailing the allocation, the amount of commitments, the strategies that will be pursued, and the managers who will be committed to. Finally, actual commitments can be made and the private equity investment process begins in earnest.

TABLE 9.4 Due Diligence Summary Review

Procedures Completed?
Hold face-to-face meeting
Conduct on-site visit
Evaluate investment strategy, process, and portfolio
Review key documents
Evaluate how the specific allocation fits with the clients investment objectives
Solicit information regarding the team or firm from knowledgeable third parties
Check references
Conduct a third-party background check
Review and negotiate legal documents
Complete a formal investment memorandum

Source: Hammond Associates.

Private equity can be an excellent source of additional return for UACs and family offices. But UAC advisers need to know that unless one invests with the absolute top managers, it simply an asset class to avoid. Capital is tied up for many, many years and the return premium needs to be high enough to account for this illiquidity. Why earn public equity-like returns with illiquidity? Unless one is highly skilled at picking private equity managers, and has the time and resources to perform world-class due diligence, it is best to bring in a group of professionals to perform this task.

CHAPTER 10

Hedge Funds

You need to be in the top 10% of hedge funds to succeed.
—David Swensen, Yale University's Chief Investment Officer

Hedge funds are a challenge for even the most experienced UAC advisers. They often bring more questions than any of the other asset classes, and the answers are rarely black and white. This is especially true given the discouraging results hedge funds had in 2008. Also, with their inherent tax inefficiency and limited information available to investors, UACs are often asking what the right amount is to allocate to hedge funds in the taxable portfolio. Other questions abound: Are hedge funds an asset class? Are long-only hedge funds a good idea? Are hedge funds going to be regulated in the future? What are the different hedge fund strategies? What is a side pocket? How much leverage is appropriate for a hedge fund? I will answer some of these questions in this chapter. The short answer to all of these questions, however, is that unless you have a very well qualified staff of people selecting the funds and creating a portfolio of funds that work well together, you should not be investing in hedge funds (and even then success is not assured). In my experience, the top 10 percent may not be good enough.

I provide in this chapter a very broad overview of some key aspects of hedge funds that UAC advisers should be aware of when advising their clients. I review the history of hedge funds, the legal environment of hedge funds, hedge fund strategies, and finally, some ideas on selecting managers. I undertake first the task of trying to define a hedge fund. As you read this chapter, you may notice there are no references to any academic studies on hedge funds; this is intentional. Because there isn't a widely accepted database on hedge funds like there is for other manager types (e.g., bonds, private equity, or real estate), academic studies on hedge funds should be taken with a grain of salt. The most important determinant of success with hedge fund investing is, without question, manager selection. And only those with deep experience with hedge fund investing should be entrusted with that task.

WHAT IS A HEDGE FUND?

The Merriam-Webster online dictionary does a simple, articulate job of defining a hedge fund: "an investing group usually in the form of a limited partnership that employs speculative techniques in the hope of obtaining large capital gains."[1] Despite the hoopla surrounding hedge funds, the term *hedge fund* has no exact legal definition. Perhaps the best way to describe a hedge fund is to identify what it is *not*. One way to do that is to understand the differences between investing in a hedge fund and investing in a mutual fund or other regulated investment vehicle. One of the better summaries of these differences has been compiled by the Investment Company Institute as seen in Table 10.1. The key differences between a hedge fund and a mutual fund are the degree of regulatory oversight, the fees charged, leveraging practices, pricing and liquidity practices, and the characteristics of the typical investors who use each investment vehicle.

Most hedge funds today share some common characteristics. UAC advisers may find that knowing these can go a long way toward explaining to a client what a hedge fund is. The key characteristics that we will review are active risk, broad mandates, limited liquidity, high fees, limited transparency, unique trading tactics, and lack of benchmark. There are certainly others, but this covers most of the important common characteristics.

Active Risk

Hedge funds managers, by definition, are not going to be the investment managers whom investors turn to for systematic or market risk (i.e., *beta*). Hedge funds take on specific or active risk and expect to be rewarded for doing so by producing *alpha*, which is defined as risk-adjusted excess return. Indeed, what would be the point of investing in a manager that charges a 2 percent management fee and 20 percent incentive fee for beta exposure? Hedge funds are supposed to be able to do things that will earn themselves unique sources of alpha, such as having better and faster access to information, superior analysis of same, the best talent money can buy, and more. When you hire a hedge fund manager, you are hiring what is supposed to be skill beyond that available in traditional asset classes or simple systematic market exposure.

TABLE 10.1 Comparison of Mutual Funds to Hedge Funds

	Hedge Funds	Mutual Funds
Regulatory Oversight	Unlike mutual funds, hedge funds are not required to register with the SEC. They issue securities in private offerings not registered with the SEC under the Securities Act of 1933. Furthermore, hedge funds are not required to make periodic reports under the Securities Exchange Act of 1934. Like mutual funds and other securities market participants, hedge funds are subject to prohibitions against fraud, and their managers have the same fiduciary duties as other investment advisers.	Mutual funds are investment companies that must register with the SEC and, as such, are subject to rigorous regulatory oversight. Virtually every aspect of a mutual fund's structure and operation is subject to strict regulation under four federal laws: the Securities Act of 1933, the Securities Exchange Act of 1934, the Investment Company Act of 1940, and the Investment Advisers Act of 1940. The Investment Company Act is the cornerstone of mutual fund regulation. It regulates the structure and operation of mutual funds and requires funds to safeguard their securities, forward price their securities, and keep detailed books and records. In addition, the 1933 Act requires that all prospective fund investors receive a prospectus containing specific information about the fund's management, holdings, fees and expenses, and performance.
Fees	There are no limits on the fees a hedge fund can charge its investors. A hedge fund manager typically charges an asset-based fee and a performance fee. Some have front-end sales charges, as well.	Federal law imposes a fiduciary duty on a mutual fund's investment adviser regarding the compensation it receives from the fund. In addition, mutual fund sales charges and other distribution fees are subject to specific regulatory limits under NASD rules. Mutual fund fees and expenses are disclosed in detail, as required by law, in a fee table at the front of every prospectus. They are presented in a standardized format so that an investor can easily understand them and can compare expense ratios among different funds.

(Continued)

TABLE 10.1 *(Continued)*

	Hedge Funds	Mutual Funds
Leverage Practices	Leveraging and other higher-risk investment strategies are a hallmark of hedge fund management. Hedge funds were originally designed to invest in equity securities and use leverage and short selling to hedge the portfolio's exposure to movements of the equity markets. Today, however, advisers to hedge funds use a wide variety of investment strategies and techniques. Many are very active traders of securities.	The Investment Company Act severely restricts a mutual fund's ability to leverage or borrow against the value of securities in its portfolio. The SEC requires that funds engaging in certain investment techniques, including the use of options, futures, forward contracts, and short selling, cover their positions. The effect of these constraints has been to strictly limit leveraging by mutual fund portfolio managers.
Pricing and Liquidity	There are no specific rules governing hedge fund pricing. Hedge fund investors may be unable to determine the value of their investment at any given time.	Mutual funds are required to value their portfolios and price their securities daily, based on market quotations that are readily available at market value as determined in good faith by the board of directors. In addition to providing investors with timely information regarding the value of their investments, daily pricing is designed to ensure that both new investments and redemptions are made at accurate prices. Moreover, mutual funds are required by law to allow shareholders to redeem their shares at any time.
Investor Qualifications	A significantly higher minimum investment is required from hedge fund investors. Under the Investment Company Act of 1940, certain hedge funds may accept investments from individuals who hold at least $5 million in investments. This measure is intended to help limit participation in hedge funds and other types of unregulated pools to highly sophisticated individuals. Hedge funds can also accept other types of investors if they rely on other exemptions under the Investment Company Act or are operated outside the United States.	The only qualification for investing in a mutual fund is having the minimum investment to open an account with a fund company, which is typically around $1,000, but can be lower. After the account has been opened, there is generally no minimum additional investment required, and many fund investors contribute relatively small amounts to their mutual funds on a regular basis as part of a long-term investment strategy.

Source: http://www.ici.org/funds/abt/faqs_hedge.html.

Broad Discretion

Hedge fund managers have a great deal of flexibility to pursue various investment styles, asset classes, security types, and trading techniques. For example, one of the main differences between a hedge fund manager and a traditional equity manager is that the hedge fund manager can concentrate his or her portfolio in only a few securities or have thousands of them. Those securities can be of varying sizes and styles. This flexibility affords the manager the leeway she needs to adapt to various market conditions as they change. By contrast, a traditional equity manager who follows a certain size and style such as large-cap growth cannot change his investment strategy outside of large-cap growth, even if large-cap may be falling out of favor. In addition, a traditional equity manager has limits on the amount of cash she can hold, whereas hedge fund managers can hold as much cash as they deem necessary.

Limited Liquidity

Perhaps the thorniest issue with investing in hedge funds is the liquidity (redemption) terms that hedge funds offer. Most hedge funds have an initial period during which the investor cannot pull money out of the fund. This is known as a *lock-up period,* the length of which varies by fund. Although lock-up terms have varied widely historically, a typical lock-up period is two years, but some are one year while others are three years; beyond three years is unusual. Even after the lock-up period has passed, investors typically can only redeem on certain dates. Some funds only offer annual liquidity, which can be redeemed on a specific day each year. Others have semiannual, quarterly, or sometimes monthly liquidity. Investors are often required to give notice of their desire to redeem their investments, typically ranging from 30 to 90 days in advance. While these terms can appear burdensome, hedge funds often have good reasons for these types of liquidity terms. They do not want to begin engaging in a trading strategy that might take time to implement and realize value and then have investors pull money out. Also, some funds invest in illiquid securities, and selling at distressed prices because investors want liquidity reduces returns to remaining investors. Some funds also offer side pocket investments that are essentially private equity investments that are illiquid. Even when an investor redeems from a fund, he or she will not receive liquidity from side pockets until the investment is sold or goes public.

High Fees

Hedge fund managers charge fees that are well beyond those of traditional investment managers. Fees are divided into two areas: management fees and incentive fees. Management fees usually range from about 1 to 3 percent of assets under management. Incentive fees permit the hedge fund manager to participate in the positive performance of the fund. Incentive fees typically range from 15 to 25 percent of the annual realized or *unrealized* gains. There are certain hedge funds that charge well above these ranges. One of the issues with this type of fee structure, of course, is that managers have an incentive to assume excessive risk to maximize income. This is not always in the best interest of the investor. Many hedge fund managers use a tool called a *high-water mark*. A high-water mark is a measure of prior losses occurring in a fund that must be recouped by new profits before an incentive fee is paid. A few funds include a *hurdle rate,* a minimum rate of return performance level that the fund manager must achieve if he is to receive an incentive fee.

Limited Transparency

Many investors would like to know what a hedge fund is doing so they can assess the risks embedded in the manager's strategy and holdings before investing their capital. Hedge fund managers prefer not to show investors or anyone else what they are doing, mainly to protect their intellectual property: the holdings and strategies in their funds. Thus, a tension exists between investors and managers that is not easily resolved. This lack of transparency is part of what gives hedge funds their aura of mystery. Those responsible for doing due diligence on managers must penetrate this aura and uncover details. Managers are gradually getting more comfortable about revealing information. At the end of the day, trust is paramount. With such limited regulation, a hedge fund that is intent on defrauding investors will likely be able to succeed.

Unique Trading Tactics

Hedge fund managers use three basic trading tools that go beyond traditional management so they can achieve alpha: short selling, leverage, and derivatives. Short selling allows managers to profit from declines in securities prices by borrowing someone else's shares and buying them back at a later time. Leverage, or borrowed money, is used to magnify returns on various investment strategies such as small security pricing discrepancies. Derivatives permit hedge fund managers to take meaningful positions in a certain segment of the market synthetically, or without actually owning the underlying security. These three tactics are used throughout the hedge fund world, although to varying degrees, with certain strategies using some more often than others, depending on the need.

Lack of Benchmark

Hedge fund managers are in the business of making money. Some in the industry refer to this as absolute returns. In the pursuit of absolute returns, hedge fund managers are unconstrained in their investment strategies. They, as such, have no formalized benchmark to beat (although some hedge fund managers do compare themselves to certain benchmarks, such as cash plus 4 percent or an individual strategy benchmark such as a convertible arbitrage benchmark). Traditional managers must concern themselves with tracking error to their benchmarks, while hedge fund managers don't need to do so. Additionally, traditional investors are used to classifying their managers into style boxes (large-cap growth, small-cap value, etc.), while hedge fund managers have no such style box to be placed into.

HEDGE FUND INVESTING BY UACs AND FAMILY OFFICES

UACs and Family Offices are fairly heavy users of hedge funds. Evidence of this fact is noted in a recent survey done by accounting firm Rothstein Kass. They contacted 147 substantial single family offices in the Americas, Europe, and the Far East and found that 107 or 73.3 percent of them were using hedge funds. They then interviewed these 107 family offices and found that the median allocation to hedge funds was 22.8 percent. (Families interviewed for this survey had an average of $774.8 million in assets and were distributed as follows geographically: Americas, 58.9 percent; Europe, 21.5 percent; and Far East, 19.6 percent.)[2] Another source of information on this subject is the Family Office Exchange in Chicago. In a September 2008 survey of their membership, the weighted average percentage of assets overseen by the family office allocated to hedge funds was 16 percent. In this same survey, the top quartile of hedge fund allocations was 28 percent.[3] In short, family offices and other UACs are investing in hedge funds in a substantial way. Why? Well, the answer lies in the promise that hedge funds attempt to deliver on equity-like returns with bond-like volatility. But, as we've seen in 2008, there's no such thing as a free lunch. We will now review some key concerns that family offices have with hedge funds.

In the same Rothstein Kass survey, participants were asked to express concerns they had with hedge funds. "Lack of transparency" overwhelmingly ranked the highest with nearly 73 percent of participants citing this concern. Next on the list was the length of the lock-up periods. Style drift,

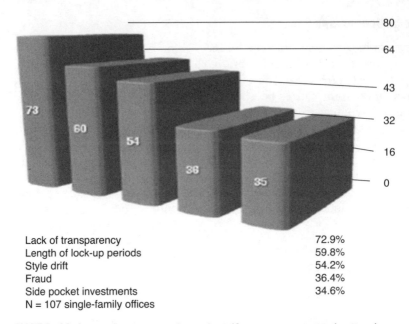

Lack of transparency	72.9%
Length of lock-up periods	59.8%
Style drift	54.2%
Fraud	36.4%
Side pocket investments	34.6%
N = 107 single-family offices	

FIGURE 10.1   Key Concerns of Family Office Investors in Hedge Funds
Source: Rothstein Kass.
http://www.rkco.com/pdflib/on_the_rise_9-30-08.pdf.

fraud, and side-pocket investing rounded out the top five. These results can be seen in Figure 10.1.

We reviewed many of the concerns noted in Figure 10.1 in the last section. One area that we have not discussed, and one that generates many questions, is side-pocket investments. For those readers who may be unfamiliar with them, let's take a few moments to review the basic structure of side-pockets realizing that there are many deviations from the following description. As many readers know, hedge funds can invest in both liquid and illiquid investments. With liquid investments, valuation is easy: read the newspaper and see a price quote. With illiquid investments, valuation can be a thorny issue. Many hedge fund managers address the valuation issue by carving out hard-to-value assets from the rest of the portfolio and placing them in special purpose vehicles, better known as side-pockets. Side-pocket investments are not included in fund NAV calculations and each side-pocket investment is owned in a separate vehicle. Once an investment is placed into a side-pocket, only existing investors participate in the gains or losses generated from the sale of the investment. When an investment is realized, side-pocket proceeds are transferred into the fund; those investors who were invested in the side-pocket are entitled to more (less) of the fund when there is a gain (loss) on the investment.

A key benefit of side-pockets is that generally speaking, investments that are chosen to be in a side-pocket are expected to have good returns due to some special characteristics of the investment. In addition, management fees are typically charged on side-pocket investments at cost, while incentive fees are typically charged on the basis of actual realized proceeds. On the other hand, side-pockets present due diligence challenges. For example, pricing illiquid investments is difficult and rigorous analysis is often required to understand a manager's pricing and valuation policies. In addition, the added flexibility afforded to managers in the use of side-pockets can potentially hide poor performance as managers can place unprofitable portfolio investments in side-pockets.

A HISTORY OF HEDGE FUNDS

Some might say that an obscure scientific researcher named Karl Karsten, who forecast economic and business conditions and created a fund to exploit his research, was the first hedge fund manager.[4] In actuality, the first recognizable hedge fund was started in 1949 by Alfred Winslow Jones. Jones was a U.S. magazine reporter and former sociologist born in Australia. He graduated from Harvard in 1923, and after some colorful overseas activities, landed back in the United States as a staff writer at *Fortune* magazine. During his time there, he wrote an article titled "Fashions in Forecasting," which inspired him to try the stock market himself. So, with $40,000 of his own money and $60,000 from others, he founded an investment company called A.W. Jones & Co. His investment strategy relied on two key aspects of the hedge fund (detailed earlier), short selling and leverage. His fund borrowed funds so that it could invest in far more securities than it had capital for and he identified not only stocks he expected to increase in value, but also stocks he expected to fall. By betting that some stocks would fall, Jones hedged his position—hence the term *hedge fund*—and reduced the effect that a change in the general stock market would have on his investments.[5] So, how did he do?

A 1966 *Fortune* article, "The Jones Nobody Keeps Up With," reported Jones's returns—325 percent over the previous five years, 670 percent over the previous decade.[6] His success brought hedge funds to the attention of American investors and an industry was born during the bull market of the 1960s. But by the 1970s, the bear market had taken hold and the hedge funds that grew out of the Jones era took heavy losses. The recession of 1973–1974 put many hedge funds out of business, with the stock market falling nearly 50 percent by 1975. From 1975 to about 1982, the market was effectively flat, and some saw an opportunity to create new funds, eyeing an eventual upturn in the markets. In 1984, Sandra Manske started a company called Tremont Partners to track hedge fund performance. At that time, she identified 68 hedge funds, although there may have been more.[7]

Some hedge fund managers did well in the period from 1980 to 1985. In 1986, for example, an article came out in *Institutional Investor* magazine describing the performance of Julian Robertson's Tiger Fund as having a compound return of 43 percent in its first six years of existence. Robertson expanded his strategies from Jones's long-short strategy (which Robertson also used) to directional strategies based on macroeconomic research, now referred to as global macro. Robertson also used derivatives such as options and futures.[8] Just when things were looking up for hedge funds, they hit a brick wall: the stock market crash of 1987.

On October 19, 1987 (now referred to as Black Monday), the Dow Jones Industrial Average fell 22 percent and many hedge funds lost substantial sums.[9] Robertson's Tiger Fund lost over half of its value. But by 1989, the stock market gained back what it had lost and several global macro funds had extremely good returns. For example, George Soros's Quantum fund made $1 billion when it forced the British pound to exit from the European Monetary System. That event, however, coupled with another event in 1994 in which several global macro funds had leveraged bond bets that lost large amounts of money when the Fed unexpectedly raised interest rates, raised concerns that hedge funds were contributing to financial instability.[10]

It wasn't until 1997, when a financial crisis led to sharp declines in Asian currencies, that hedge funds were blamed for some destabilizing actions. According to Eichengreen et al. (1998) and Brouwer (2001), hedge funds sold between $7 billion and $15 billion of the Thai currency (baht) in 1997.[11] But another debacle in 1998 would top even the Thai baht events. A fund called Long Term Capital Management (ironically named considering its fate) had borrowed 96 percent of its capital (totaling $100 billion) and lost nearly all of it on a bet that low-quality and high-quality bond spreads would narrow. Shortly thereafter, the Fed stepped in and orchestrated a consortium of 14 banks to pony up $3.5 billion to save the fund. On August 17th, 1998, when the Russian government devalued its currency, there was a flight to quality and LTCM was out of business. The Fed's intervention in this matter raised serious questions about bailing out greedy investors and creating a moral hazard at the same time. Ten years later, we would see other controversial acts by the Fed—the bailout of Bear Stearns (among others like Fannie Mae and Freddie Mac) with the orchestration of its sale to JPMorgan Chase. Ironically enough, Bear Stearns was one of the only major New York banks that didn't participate in the 1998 bailout of LTCM![12]

When this chapter was written, hedge funds were managing over $1.5 trillion dollars, according to Hedge Fund Research, a research firm in Chicago.[13] Contrast that number to the asset level in 2000, when hedge funds managed about $500 billion.[14] Assets have effectively tripled in that time! The hedge fund industry is a global business and the focus is not just on the traditional money centers of New York and London. Asia is becoming a large focus of attention. Brazil has a robust hedge fund industry. The best and brightest are opting out of traditional Wall Street jobs and joining hedge funds. Wealthy individuals, who were the first customers of hedge funds, are no longer the only ones who want to invest. Today, the largest customers are often nonprofit organizations, pension funds, and other institutions. As noted earlier, David Swensen has put a sizable share of Yale University's endowment in various hedge funds and has earned outsized returns.[15] The bottom line is that hedge funds are here and here in a big way. But investing in them has some tricky legal aspects that we now review.

THE LEGAL ENVIRONMENT OF HEDGE FUNDS

In the United States, three sets of regulators oversee the financial services industry. The Securities and Exchange Commission (SEC) oversees publicly traded securities, including the corporations that issue them and the broker-dealers that make markets for them. The Commodity Futures Trading Commission (CFTC) oversees the futures industry. The Federal Reserve, the Office of the Comptroller of the Currency, and the Office of Thrift Supervision oversee the commercial banking and thrift industry. These agencies were created on the basis of the idea that the U.S. government should regulate financial companies that deal with the general public. Hedge funds, however, do not deal with the public and are therefore treated differently from the general investing public, falling outside the direct jurisdiction of these regulators. Hedge funds use some well-established loopholes that are conveniently built into the securities law code and can legally operate beyond the reach of these regulatory bodies.

The first area we will cover will be how hedge funds are affected by the Securities Act of 1933 (also known as the truth-in-securities law). This Act requires that firms issuing publicly traded securities register with the SEC and file disclosure reports to ensure that these firms provide the general public with all relevant information to make their investment decisions. Technically, for the purpose of this Act, an offering in a hedge fund is considered a public offering of securities. But since most hedge funds don't want to register with the SEC, they structure their offerings as private placements, which are exempt from registration. Under the safe harbor provision of Rule

506 in Regulation D, a hedge fund may qualify if the fund has no more than 35 *nonaccredited* investors and does not engage in solicitation. The SEC's definition of an *accredited* investor is an individual who has more than $1 million in financial wealth or earned more than $200,000 ($300,000 for married couples) in the previous two years. The SEC's definition of non-solicitation is essentially word-of-mouth communication among clients or prospects with a preexisting relationship with the hedge fund.[16]

The next item under discussion is the Securities Exchange Act of 1934. This Act gives the SEC power to regulate securities brokerage firms that deal in the secondary market.[17] It affects hedge funds in two ways. First, hedge funds consider themselves traders rather than dealers. If considered dealers, they would be required to register with the SEC. Second, hedge funds have fewer than 500 investors. If they had more, they again would be required to register with the SEC. Hedge funds are usually exempted from registration as broker-dealers and the associated costly reporting requirements as long as they trade only for their own investment accounts.

The Investment Advisers Act of 1940 regulates investment advisers. This Act requires that persons or firms compensated for advising others about securities investments must register with the SEC and conform to statutory standards designed to protect investors. By having fewer than 15 clients, as defined under rule 203(b)(3)-1 of the Act, and by not soliciting business from the general public, a hedge fund manager may be exempted from registration as an investment adviser. However, the definition of *client* came under fire because hedge funds were typically counting an entire fund as one client, and in July 2004, the SEC approved a new rule, 203 (b)(3)-2, which changed the definition of a client. Hedge funds still have to register with the SEC if they serve more than 15 clients. The new rule stipulated, however, that advisers to "private funds" can gain eligibility for registration exemption if they have lock-ups longer than two years.[18]

The Investment Company Act of 1940 gave the SEC the authority to regulate investment companies. An investment company is defined as any issuer that is engaged primarily in the investing or trading in securities. This is, in effect, the mutual fund industry. Hedge funds, which look a lot like mutual funds, attempt to qualify for registration exemption under Sections 3(c)1 and 3(c)7 of the Act. Those exemptions are for funds with 100 or fewer investors (a *3(c)1 fund*) and funds in which the investors are *qualified purchasers* (a *3(c)7 fund*). A qualified purchaser is an individual with more than $5 million in investment assets or an institutional investor with more than $25 million. Hedge funds must be sold through a private placement to comply with 3(c)(1) or 3(c)(7), and thus cannot be offered or advertised to the general public under Regulation D. Although it is technically possible to have nonaccredited investors in a hedge fund, the exemptions under the Investment Company Act, combined with the restrictions contained in Regulation D, effectively require hedge funds to be offered solely to accredited investors or qualified purchasers.[19]

The Commodity Exchange Act of 1974 created the Commodities Futures Trading Commission (CFTC), which regulates futures markets in the United States and "protects market participants against manipulation, abusive trade practices and fraud."[20] The CFTC has the exclusive right to oversee futures trading, floor traders, futures exchanges, and a host of other commodities market participants. Financial companies that offer trading advice in futures contracts must register with the National Futures Association (NFA), which is the futures industry's self-regulatory body. If a hedge fund trades futures and options on futures on behalf of its investors, it may be required to file as a commodity pool operator with the CFTC. Certain hedge funds may qualify for exemption from their requirements in registration, disclosure, and record maintenance, but the rules are complex.[21]

The bank regulators noted earlier (e.g., the Fed, the Comptroller of the Currency, and the Office of Thrift Supervision) do not have any direct authority over hedge funds, since hedge funds are not banks. We now turn to the strategies that hedge funds pursue.

HEDGE FUND STRATEGIES

There are many different investment strategies used by hedge funds, each offering various degrees of risk and return. Knowing and understanding the characteristics of the many different hedge fund strategies is essential because all hedge funds are not the same—investment returns, volatility, and risk vary enormously among the different hedge fund strategies. Some strategies that have low correlations to equity markets are able to deliver consistent returns with extremely low risk of loss, while others may be as volatile, or more so, than mutual funds. While some hedge funds attempt to deliver 50 percent plus returns, the primary aim of many hedge funds is to reduce volatility and risk while attempting to preserve capital and deliver positive (absolute) returns under all market conditions.

There are as many different descriptions of hedge fund strategies as there are hedge funds. Therefore, we have to settle on one way if we are to communicate clearly in the section.[22] Although this is not an endorsement of HFR, I use their four-category methodology for describing hedge funds. A chart of these strategies is contained in Figure 10.2. After the descriptions of the hedge fund strategies are given, I discuss how a hedge fund strategy can be put together for an individual client.

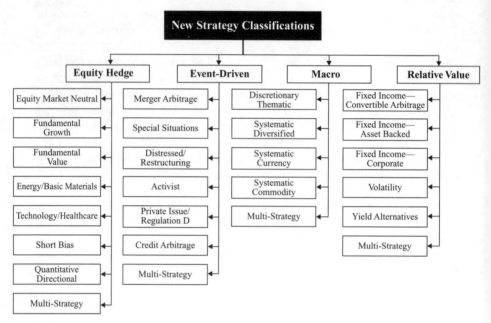

FIGURE 10.2 HFR Hedge Funds Strategy Classification System
Source: Hedge Fund Research, Inc. "Hedge Fund Strategy Classification" January 2008.
https://www.hedgefundresearch.com/pdf/new_strategy_classifications.pdf

Equity Hedge

These investment managers maintain positions both long and short in primarily equity and equity derivative securities. A wide variety of investment processes can be employed to arrive at an investment decision, including both quantitative and fundamental techniques. Strategies can be broadly diversified or narrowly focused on specific sectors and can range broadly in their levels of net exposure, leverage employed, holding period, concentrations of market capitalizations, and valuation ranges of typical portfolios. EH managers would typically maintain at least 50 percent, and may in some cases be substantially entirely invested in equities, both long and short. Substrategies of Equity Hedge are as follows:

> *Equity Market Neutral*—These strategies employ sophisticated quantitative techniques of analyzing price data to ascertain information about future price movement and relationships between securities and select securities for purchase and sale. These can include both factor-based and statistical arbitrage trading strategies. Factor-based investment strategies include strategies in which

the investment thesis is predicated on the systematic analysis of common relationships between securities. In many, but not all cases, portfolios are constructed to be neutral to one or multiple variables, such as broader equity markets in dollar or beta terms, and leverage is frequently employed to enhance the return profile of the positions identified. Statistical arbitrage trading strategies consist of strategies in which the investment thesis is predicated on exploiting pricing anomalies that may occur as a function of expected mean reversion inherent in security prices. High frequency techniques may be employed and trading strategies may also be employed on the basis of technical analysis, or opportunistically, to exploit new information the investment manager believes has not been fully, completely, or accurately discounted into current security prices. Equity market neutral strategies typically maintain characteristic net equity market exposure no greater than 10 percent long or short.

Fundamental Growth—These strategies employ analytical techniques in which the investment thesis is predicated on assessment of the valuation characteristics on the underlying companies, which are expected to have prospects for earnings growth and capital appreciation exceeding those of the broader equity market. Investment theses are focused on characteristics of the firm's financial statements in both an absolute sense and relative to other similar securities, and more broadly, market indicators. Strategies employ investment processes designed to identify attractive opportunities in securities of companies that are experiencing or expected to experience abnormally high levels of growth compared with relevant benchmarks growth in earnings, profitability, sales, or market share.

Fundamental Value—These strategies employ investment processes designed to identify attractive opportunities in securities of companies that trade a valuation metrics by which the manager determines them to be inexpensive and undervalued when compared with relevant benchmarks.

Energy and Basic Materials—These strategies employ investment processes designed to identify opportunities in securities in specific niche areas of the market in which the manager maintains a level of expertise that exceeds that of a market generalist in identifying companies engaged in the production and procurement of inputs to industrial processes, and are implicitly sensitive to the direction of price trends as determined by shifts in supply and demand factors, and the direction of broader economic trends. Energy and basic materials strategies typically maintain a primary focus in this area or expect to maintain in excess of 50 percent of portfolio exposure to these sectors over various market cycles.

Technology and Health Care—These strategies employ investment processes designed to identify opportunities in securities in specific niche areas of the market in which the manager maintains a level of expertise that exceeds that of a market generalist in identifying opportunities in companies engaged in all development, production, and applications of technology and biotechnology as related to the production of pharmaceuticals and the health care industry. Though some diversity exists as a substrategy, these strategies implicitly exhibit some characteristic sensitivity to broader growth trends, or in the case of the later, developments specific to the health care industry. Technology and health care strategies typically maintain a primary focus in this area or expect to maintain in excess of 50 percent of portfolio exposure to these sectors over various market cycles.

Short-Biased—These strategies employ analytical techniques in which the investment thesis is predicated on assessment of the valuation characteristics on the underlying companies with the goal of identifying overvalued companies. Short-biased strategies may vary the investment level or the level of short exposure over market cycles, but the primary distinguishing characteristic is that the manager maintains consistent short exposure and expects to outperform traditional equity managers in declining equity markets. Investment theses may be fundamental or technical in nature and the manager has a particular focus, above that of a market generalist, on the identification of overvalued companies and would expect to maintain a net short equity position over various market cycles.

Quantitative Directional—These strategies employ sophisticated quantitative techniques of analyzing price data to ascertain information about future price movements and relationships between securities and select securities for purchase and sale. These can include both factor-based and statistical arbitrage trading strategies. Factor-based investment strategies include strategies in which the investment thesis is predicated on the systematic analysis of common relationships between securities. Statistical arbitrage trading strategies consist of strategies in which the investment thesis is predicated on exploiting pricing anomalies that may occur as a function of expected mean reversion inherent in security prices. High frequency techniques may be employed and trading strategies may also be employed on the basis on technical analysis or opportunistically to exploit new information the investment manager believes has not been fully, completely, or accurately discounted into current security prices. Quantitative directional strategies typically maintain varying levels of net long or short equity market exposure over various market cycles.

Multi-Strategy managers would typically have no more than 50 percent exposure to any one, distinct equity hedge substrategy.

Event-Driven

Investment managers who maintain positions in securities of companies currently or prospectively involved in corporate transactions of a wide variety, including but not limited to: mergers, restructurings, financial distress, tender offers, shareholder buybacks, debt exchanges, security issuance, or other capital structure adjustments. Security types can range from most senior in the capital structure to most junior or subordinated, and frequently involve additional derivative securities. ED exposure contains a combination of sensitivities to equity markets, credit markets, and idiosyncratic, company-specific developments. Investment theses are typically predicated on fundamental characteristics (as opposed to quantitative), with the realization of the thesis predicated on a specific development exogenous to the existing capital structure.

> *Merger Arbitrage*—These strategies employ an investment process primarily focused on opportunities in equity and equity-related instruments of companies that are currently engaged in a corporate transaction. Merger arbitrage involves primarily announced transactions, typically with limited or no exposure to situations that come before or after the announced date or situations in which no formal announcement is expected to occur. Opportunities are frequently presented in cross-border, collared, and international transactions that incorporate multiple geographic regulatory institutions. They typically involve minimal exposure to corporate credits. Merger arbitrage strategies typically have over 75 percent of positions in announced transactions over a given market cycle.
>
> *Special Situations*—These strategies employ an investment process primarily focused on opportunities in equity and equity-related instruments of companies that are currently engaged in a corporate transaction, security issuance or repurchase, asset sales, division spin-off, or other catalyst-oriented situation. These involve both announced transactions as well as situations that come before or after the announced date or situations in which no formal announcement is expected to occur. Strategies employ an investment process focusing broadly on a wide spectrum of corporate life

cycle investing, including but not limited to distressed, bankruptcy, and post-bankruptcy security issuance, announced acquisitions and corporate division spin-offs, asset sales, and other security issuances affecting an individual capital structure focusing primarily on situations identified through fundamental research, which is likely to result in a corporate transaction or other realization of shareholder value through the occurrence of some identifiable catalyst. Strategies effectively employ primarily equity (greater than 60 percent) but also corporate debt exposure, and in general focus more broadly on post-bankruptcy equity exposure and exit of restructuring proceedings.

Distressed/Restructuring—These strategies employ an investment process focused on corporate fixed-income instruments, primarily on corporate credit instruments of companies trading at significant discounts to their value at issuance or obliged (par value) at maturity as a result of either formal bankruptcy proceeding or financial market perception of near-term proceedings. Managers are typically actively involved with the management of these companies. They are frequently involved on creditors' committees in negotiating the exchange of securities for alternative obligations, either swaps of debt, equity, or hybrid securities. Managers employ fundamental credit processes focused on valuation and asset coverage of securities of distressed firms. Portfolio exposures are concentrated in instruments which, in most cases, are publicly traded; in some cases, actively; and in other cases, under reduced liquidity but in general for which a reasonable public market exists. In contrast to Special Situations, Distressed Strategies employ primarily debt (greater than 60 percent) but also may maintain related equity exposure.

Activist—These strategies may obtain or attempt to obtain representation of the company's board of directors in an effort to affect the firm's policies or strategic direction and in some cases may advocate activities such as division or asset sales, partial or complete corporate divestiture, dividend or share buybacks, and changes in management. Strategies employ an investment process primarily focused on opportunities in equity and equity related instruments of companies that are currently or prospectively engaged in a corporate transaction, security issuance or repurchase, asset sales, division spin-off, or other catalyst-oriented situation. These involve both announced transactions as well as situations that come before or after the announced date or situations in which no formal announcement is expected to occur. Activist strategies are distinguished from other event-driven strategies in that, over a given market cycle, activist strategies would expect to have greater than 50 percent of the portfolio in activist positions, as described.

Private Issue–Regulation D—These strategies employ an investment process primarily focused on opportunities in equity and equity-related instruments of companies that are primarily private and illiquid in nature. These most frequently involve realizing an investment premium for holding private obligations or securities for which a reasonably liquid market does not readily exist until such time as a catalyst such as a new security issuance or emergence from bankruptcy proceedings occurs. Managers employ fundamental valuation processes focused on asset coverage of securities of issuer firms, and would expect over a given market cycle to maintain greater than 50 percent of the portfolio in private securities, including Reg D or PIPE transactions.

Credit Arbitrage—These strategies employ an investment process designed to isolate attractive opportunities in corporate fixed income securities; these include both senior and subordinated claims as well as bank debt and other outstanding obligations, structuring positions with little or no broad credit market exposure.

Macro

Investment managers who execute a broad range of strategies in which the investment process is predicated on movements in underlying economic variables and the impact these have on equity, fixed income, currency, and commodity markets. Managers employ a variety of techniques, both discretionary and systematic analysis, combinations of top -down and bottom-up theses, quantitative and fundamental approaches and long- and short-term holding periods. Although some strategies employ RV techniques, macro strategies are distinct from RV strategies in that the primary investment thesis is predicated on future movements in the underlying instruments, rather than realization of a valuation discrepancy between securities. In a similar way, while both macro and equity hedge managers may hold equity securities, the overriding investment thesis is predicated on the impact movements in underlying macroeconomic variables may have on security prices, as opposed to EH, in which the fundamental characteristics of the company are the most significant to investment thesis.

Discretionary Thematic—These strategies are primarily reliant on the evaluation of market data, relationships, and influences, as interpreted by an individual or group of individuals who make decisions on portfolio positions. Strategies employ an investment process most heavily influenced by top-down analysis of macroeconomic variables. Investment managers may actively trade in developed and emerging markets, focusing on both absolute and relative levels of equity markets, interest rates or fixed-income markets, currency, and commodity markets; frequently employing spread trades to isolate a differential between instruments identified by the investment manager to be inconsistent with expected value. Portfolio positions are typically predicated on the evolution of investment themes the manager expects to materialize over a relevant time frame, which in many cases contain contrarian or volatility-focused components.

Systematic Diversified—These strategies have investment processes typically as a function of mathematical, algorithmic, and technical models, with little or no influence of individuals over the portfolio positioning. Strategies that employ an investment process designed to identify opportunities in markets exhibiting trending or momentum characteristics across individual instruments or asset classes. Strategies typically employ quantitative processes that focus on statistically robust or technical patterns in the return series of the asset, and typically focus on highly liquid instruments and maintain shorter holding periods than either discretionary or mean-reverting strategies. Although some strategies seek to employ counter-trend models, strategies benefit most from an environment characterized by persistent, discernible trending behavior. Systematic diversified strategies would typically expect to have no greater than 35 percent of a portfolio in either dedicated currency or commodity exposures over a given market cycle.

Systematic Currency—These strategies typically have investment processes as a function of mathematical, algorithmic, and technical models, with little or no influence of individuals over the portfolio positioning. Strategies that employ an investment process designed to identify opportunities in markets exhibiting trending or momentum characteristics across currency assets classes, frequently with related ancillary exposure in sovereign fixed income. Strategies typically employ quantitative processes that focus on statistically robust or technical patterns in the return series of the asset, and typically focus on highly liquid instruments and maintain shorter holding periods than either discretionary or mean-reverting strategies. Although some strategies seek to employ counter-trend models, strategies benefit most from an environment characterized by persistent, discernible trending behavior. Systematic currency strategies typically would expect to have more than 35 percent of a portfolio in dedicated currency exposure over a given market cycle.

Systematic commodity—Systematic commodity strategies typically have investment processes as a function of mathematical, algorithmic, and technical models, with little or no influence of individuals over the portfolio positioning. Strategies that employ an investment process are designed to identify opportunities in markets exhibiting trending or momentum characteristics across commodity assets classes, frequently with related ancillary exposure in commodity-sensitive equities or other derivative instruments. Strategies typically employ quantitative processes that focus on statistically robust or technical patterns in the return series of the asset, and typically focus on highly liquid instruments and maintain shorter holding periods than either discretionary or mean-reverting strategies. Although some strategies seek to employ counter-trend models, strategies benefit most from an environment characterized by persistent, discernible trending behavior. Systematic commodity strategies typically would expect to have more than 35 percent of a portfolio in dedicated commodity exposure over a given market cycle.

Multi-Strategy Strategies employ components of both discretionary and systematic macro strategies, but neither exclusively both. Strategies frequently contain proprietary trading influences, and in some cases contain distinct, identifiable substrategies such as equity hedge or equity market neutral. In some cases, a number of substrategies are blended together without the capacity for portfolio level disaggregation. Strategies that employ an investment process is predicated on a systematic, quantitative evaluation of macroeconomic variables in which the portfolio positioning is predicated on a convergence of differentials between markets, not necessarily highly correlated with each other, but currently diverging from their historical levels of correlation. Strategies focus on fundamental relationships across geographic areas of focus both inter- and intra-asset classes, and typical holding periods are longer than trend-following or discretionary strategies.

Relative Value

Investment managers who maintain positions in which the investment thesis is predicated on realization of a valuation discrepancy in the relationship between multiple securities employ a variety of fundamental and quantitative techniques to establish investment theses. Security types range broadly across equity, fixed income, derivative, or other security types. RVA positions may also be involved in corporate transactions, but as opposed to ED exposures, the investment thesis is predicated on the realization of a pricing discrepancy between related securities as opposed to the outcome of the corporate transaction.

> *Fixed-Income–Convertible Arbitrage*—These include strategies in which the investment thesis is predicated on realization of a spread between related instruments in which one or multiple components of the spread is a convertible fixed-income instrument. Strategies employ an investment process designed to isolate attractive opportunities between the price of a convertible security and the price of a nonconvertible security, typically of the same issuer. Convertible arbitrage positions maintain characteristic sensitivities to credit quality of the issuer, implied and realized volatility of the underlying instruments, levels of interest rates and the valuation of the issuer's equity, among other more general market and idiosyncratic sensitivities.
>
> *Fixed-Income–Asset-Backed*—These include strategies in which the investment thesis is predicated on the realization of a spread between related instruments in which one or multiple components of the spread is a fixed-income instrument backed by physical collateral or other financial obligations (loans, credit cards) other than those of a specific corporation. Strategies employ an investment process designed to isolate attractive opportunities between a variety of fixed-income instruments specifically securitized by collateral commitments that frequently include loans, pools and portfolios of loans, receivables, real estate, machinery, or other tangible financial commitments. The investment thesis may be predicated on an attractive spread given the nature and quality of the collateral, the liquidity characteristics of the underlying instruments, and on issuance and trends in collateralized fixed-income instruments, broadly speaking. In many cases, investment managers hedge, limit, or offset interest rate exposure in the interest of isolating the risk of the position to just the yield disparity of the instrument relative to the lower-risk instruments.
>
> *Fixed-Income–Corporate*—These include strategies in which the investment thesis is predicated on the realization of a spread between related instruments in which one or multiple components of the spread is a corporate fixed-income instrument. Strategies employ an investment process designed to isolate attractive opportunities between a variety of fixed-income instruments, typically realizing an attractive spread between multiple corporate bonds or between a

corporate and risk-free government bond. Fixed-income–corporate strategies differ from event-driven–credit arbitrage in that the former more typically involve more general market hedges that may vary in the degree to which they limit fixed-income market exposure, while the latter typically involve arbitrage positions with little or no net credit market exposure, but are predicated on specific, anticipated idiosyncratic developments. Volatility strategies trade volatility as an asset class, employing arbitrage, directional, market neutral or a mix of types of strategies, and include exposures which can be long, short, neutral or variable to the direction of implied volatility, and can include both listed and unlisted instruments. Directional volatility strategies maintain exposure to the direction of implied volatility of a particular asset or, more generally, to the trend of implied volatility in broader asset classes. Arbitrage strategies employ an investment process designed to isolate opportunities between the price of multiple options or instruments containing implicit optionality. Volatility arbitrage positions typically maintain characteristic sensitivities to levels of implied and realized volatility, levels of interest rates, and the valuation of the issuer's equity, among other more general market and idiosyncratic sensitivities.

Yield Alternative—These strategies employ an investment thesis that is predicated on the realization of a spread between related instruments in which one or multiple components of the spread contains a derivative, equity, real estate, MLP, or combination of these or other instruments. Strategies are typically quantitatively driven to measure the existing relationship between instruments and, in some cases, identify attractive positions in which the risk-adjusted spread between these instruments represents an attractive opportunity for the investment manager. Strategies employ an investment process designed to isolate opportunities in yield-oriented securities, which can include equity, preferred, listed partnerships (MLPs), REITs, and some other corporate obligations. In contrast to fixed-income arbitrage, yield alternative contain primarily non-fixed-income securities, and in contrast to equity hedge strategies, the investment thesis is more predicated on the yield realized from the securities than on price appreciation of the underlying securities. Multi-strategies employ an investment thesis that is predicated on the realization of a spread between related yield instruments in which one or multiple components of the spread contains a fixed income, derivative, equity, real estate, MLP, or combination of these or other instruments.

MANAGER SELECTION

Whether a client is using a fund-of-funds manager approach or investing directly with individual hedge fund managers, getting the best managers available and crafting a strategy that contains diversified risk exposures are essential. To accomplish these tasks effectively, a family needs to do one of two things: hire a staff of hedge fund research analysts or hire a consultant. Hiring a staff of research analysts is viable for a very large family office that has the ability to manage and retain sophisticated investment professionals that are experienced in hedge fund due diligence and monitoring. Engaging a consultant to assist the family office investment personnel is a cost-efficient way to get specialized hedge fund expertise and supplement a family office's core resources. The good news for family offices that are in the process of creating a hedge fund program is that they can choose top-quality service providers who can custom-create high quality hedge fund portfolios.

By way of review, hedge funds can add valuable return and diversification benefits to an overall portfolio if implemented professionally. Hiring managers that have no unique characteristics is a potential disaster waiting to happen. Also, when creating a hedge fund portfolio, it is important to select managers who are differentiated from one another. When markets turn down, or liquidity becomes an issue, similar to what happened in the latter half of 2008, investors with hedge funds that have similar holdings found themselves with large, unexpected losses. Be sure to consult experienced professionals when creating a hedge fund portfolio.

Now that we have covered hedge funds, we move next to another asset class normally uncorrelated to equities, real assets.

Real Assets

When future historians look back on our way of curing inflation they'll probably compare it to bloodletting in the Middle Ages.
—Lee Iacocca

Inflation protection is of paramount importance in any portfolio, especially that of the UAC, given the additional hurdles of taxes and fees. Real (or *hard*) assets, which are tangible—as opposed to financial assets, which are intangible—maintain their value over long periods of time because of their positive correlation to inflation. They usually also provide valuable diversification benefits to a portfolio. The rationale for holding real assets in an investment portfolio is to generate attractive nominal rates of return and provide a hedge against unexpected inflation. While stocks do tend to pass on the long-run effects of inflation, there have been periods (during the 1970s, for example) when inflation was high and stocks did poorly. Unlike financial assets such as stocks and bonds, which are valued primarily on the basis of discounted cash flows, real assets generally have intrinsic value, and can be valued on the basis of future cash flows they generate as well as replacement costs. By contrast, stocks and bonds tend to perform better when the rate of inflation is stable or slowing. Faster inflation lowers the value of future cash flows paid by stocks and bonds because those future dollars will be able to buy fewer goods and services than they would today. During the 1980s and 1990s, for example, inflation fell and stocks and bonds experienced bull markets.

Real assets also tend to be inherently tax efficient because of their long holding periods, with some offering special tax advantages, such as depreciation and long-term capital gains tax rates when held for 12 months or more, and generally provide some level of cash flow during the holding period. Real estate, for example, pays out net income from operations, and timber generates a yield from harvesting trees and other fees. Oil and gas will generate income from the sale of oil and gas reserves.

The inflation-hedging properties of real assets can vary in responsiveness to near-term inflation. Producing oil and gas investments will tend to generate higher near-term returns during periods of inflation, since the source of inflation is often a spike in energy prices from an external source like OPEC or general economic growth that would eventually show up in higher energy prices. Real estate keeps up with inflation by increasing rents over time and through higher replacement costs as general price levels rise. Timber tends to fight inflation due to both the ties between economic growth and end demand for paper and lumber and the general increase in land value over time—and the best part is that trees grow, which produces value. Scarcity of supply affects all of the traditional real assets and is an important driver of returns. Supply and demand for raw materials like timber, oil, and gas are reflected in commodity prices. When it comes to real estate, the key value drive is the location (scarcity) of property which is reflected in the prices paid for specific buildings relative to their replacement cost.

So, stocking the portfolio with inflation protection assets is essential. As much as 20 percent of the portfolio should be dedicated to real assets. Although there are numerous assets that might qualify as real (including artwork and wine), we will stick to institutionally investable asset classes in this chapter. These are real estate (both public and private), natural resources (both public and private), and commodities. Inflation-protected bonds will not be covered here. Treasury Inflation-Protected Securities were covered in Chapter 8 and are not particularly well suited for taxable investors given their tax-inefficient structure. Tax-exempt inflation protection bonds are not readily available to most investors and can trade down significantly during turbulent times, so these are also not covered. I first discuss the general benefits of real assets in the portfolio.

THE PORTFOLIO BENEFITS OF REAL ASSETS

In addition to the robust nominal returns generated by real assets, they usually provide valuable diversification benefits. With regard to returns, from 1996 to 2006, real assets dominated global stock and bond returns, as can be seen in Figure 11.1. Real asset returns ranged from 7 percent for TIPS to 19 percent for Master Limited Partnerships (MLPs). Stock and bond benchmarks returned 6 to 10 percent over the same period. Annualized volatility, as measured by standard deviation, ranged from 2 to 15 percent for real assets, as compared to 6 to 17 percent for financial assets.

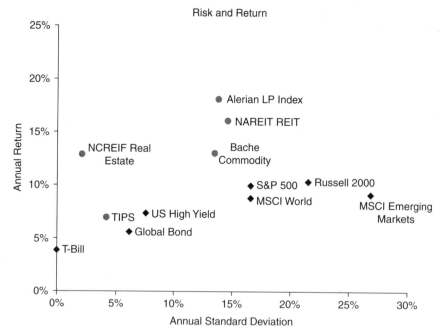

FIGURE 11.1 Returns of Traditional and Real Assets 1996–2006
Source: Alternative Investment Analytics LLC.

Real assets offer diversification benefits and their returns tend to be weakly correlated with equities and bonds (except Inflation-Protected Bonds). Real assets have a relatively high positive correlation to U.S. stocks, but a low correlation with bonds, which provides diversification benefits to the portfolio as can be seen in Table 11.1. If a deflationary period were to occur, real assets would likely underperform other asset classes.

REAL ESTATE: A LONG-TERM INFLATION HEDGE

Although real estate did not appear to be an inflation-fighting asset from 1996 to 2006, there is a substantial amount of literature that came out in the 1980s evidencing the ability of real estate to hedge inflation over long periods of time. In 1985, a group of researchers named Fogler, Granito, and Smith examined the positive relationship between real estate returns and inflation. They offered two possible explanations for the observed relationship: first, that there is simply a positive relationship between the two variables, or

TABLE 11.1 Real Asset Indexes March 1996–December 2006 (Quarterly Data)

	TIPS	NAREIT All	NCREIF National	Bacho Commodity	Alerian Master	MSCI World	Lehman Global	U.S. Inflation
Annualized Mean	7%	16%	12%	13%	19%	10%	6%	3%
Annualized Std. Deviation	4%	15%	2%	14%	12%	17%	6%	1%
Sharpe Ratio	0.62	0.81	3.76	0.66	1.22	0.34	0.26	n/a
Maximum Drawdown	−3%	−24%	0%	−21%	−11%	−46%	−6%	−1%
Maximum Return	8%	19%	5%	18%	18%	21%	9%	2%
Minimum Return	−3%	−11%	1%	−11%	−11%	−18%	−3%	−1%
Correlation with MSCI World	(0.52)	0.33	0.19	(0.11)	(0.07)	1.00	(0.17)	(0.28)
Correlation with Lehman	0.47	0.05	(0.04)	(0.17)	0.07	(0.17)	1.00	(0.26)
Correlation with U.S. Inflation	0.05	(0.13)	(0.09)	0.50	(0.03)	(0.28)	(0.26)	1.00

Source: Alternative Investment Analytics LLC.

second, that the relationship is explained by changing investor expectations concerning the inflation-hedging ability of real estate. The authors concluded that the second explanation was valid, but rejected the first.[1]

In 1987, another group of researchers named Hartzell, Hekman, and Miles examined the inflation protection of a commingled real estate fund (CREF) using two tests that used Treasury bill rates as a proxy for expected inflation. They concluded that commercial real estate was a complete hedge against both expected and unexpected inflation.[2] In 1989, Rubens, Bond, and Webb examined the inflation-fighting ability of residential, commercial, and farmland real estate and four types of financial instruments, both as individual assets and as parts of portfolios. They found that all three types of real estate are at least partial inflationary hedges and that portfolios that include real estate realize an increase in inflation protection.[3]

So if we agree that over time, investing in real estate will protect against the effects of inflation, how does the UAC invest? Ideally, clients with the typical low liquidity needs and long time horizon will invest in real estate the way they do in private equity: in private partnerships. As we saw back in Chapter 9, a private investment program is best achieved with vintage year diversification, and we will need to do the same with private real estate. As for portfolio construction in the UAC's private real estate portfolio, that is a matter of risk appetite. Generally, the UAC will want a core, diversified fund as an anchor. If additional return is desired, satellite strategies such as those in the value-added and opportunistic strategies (defined later) can be implemented. During the five or so years it takes to get a private strategy fully invested, liquid real estate investment trusts (while on the volatile side) can act as a proxy for private real estate while the vintage year diversification takes effect. I now review the various vehicles through which UACs can make real estate investments and then discuss various strategies that investment managers in private real estate undertake on behalf of their investors.

How to Invest

As noted earlier, during the time that UACs are investing in private real estate partnerships, they can use (a collection of) publicly traded real estate investment trusts, or REITs, which operate in much the same way that mutual funds do for stocks. A REIT is a company that owns, and in most cases operates, income-producing real estate (although some REITs are only in the business of financing real estate). To be a REIT, a company must distribute at least 90 percent of its taxable income to shareholders annually in the form of dividends. According to NAREIT, the National Association of Real Estate Investment Trusts, there are 146 REITs in the Financial Times Stock Exchange (FTSE) NAREIT All REIT Index that are publicly traded REITs and real estate operating companies in the United States.[4] One can either invest in an index of REITs (sponsored by companies such as Vanguard or Dow Jones/Wilshire) or invest in an active manager of REITs through a mutual fund structure. The advantages of investing this way are that publicly traded REITs have daily liquidity, usually a substantial dividend that can be reinvested if desired, no capital calls (so one can get invested immediately) and relatively low cost. The disadvantages are that REITs tend to be correlated with equities generally and small-cap stocks in particular, and their volatility (we saw a steep drop in REIT valuation in the 2007–2008 market correction after a substantial seven-year run of REITs). Although REITs are liquid daily, they are long-term investments and should not be viewed as trading vehicles.

On the private side, there are two basic types of funds, closed-end and open-end (again borrowing from the mutual fund side of the business). Open-end funds are typically structured as private REITs, private partnerships, or limited liability companies. They usually offer quarterly investment and redemption options and allow for the reinvestment of income and capital gains. Although these are private partnerships that invest in privately traded properties, open-end funds permit investors to invest all of their money up front and typically offer the investor liquidity after an initial lock-up period (similar to a hedge fund's) of two or three years.

Open-end funds offer investors the ability to establish a core investment in a broad range of real estate properties. The life of an open-end fund is not fixed; it stays open for as long as an investor wants to remain in the fund. The one risk of investing in open-end funds (and REITs, for that matter) is buying in at peak prices. In contrast, closed-end funds, which I review next, can be selective about when to invest and their investor can benefit from this selectivity.

Closed-end funds are either limited partnerships or LLCs with finite lives of 7 to 10 years. Unlike open-end funds, closed-end funds call capital over time to fund portfolio investments. Capital is returned rather than reinvested after a property is sold, and the fund terminates once the last property is sold. The advantage of closed-end funds is that the interests of these managers are aligned with those of their investors; managers have an incentive to sell properties at a profit and return cash since they are focused on individual portfolios. On the downside, these funds have no liquidity and can take years to fully fund. Lastly, the fees on these are higher than those of open-end funds or REITs at about 1.5 percent for core strategies.

Strategies

The types of strategies employed by real estate investment groups generally fall into four groups: core, core-plus, value-added, and opportunistic. These

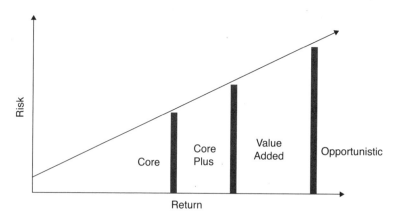

FIGURE 11.2 Risk-and-Return Spectrum for Various Real
Estate Strategies

strategies follow the risk-and-return spectrum from left to right, as can be
seen in Figure 11.2. Core strategies rely primarily on income for their returns.
Opportunistic strategies have nearly no income and rely on capital gains for
their returns. Risk is low for core strategies and high for opportunistic
strategies. Core-plus and value-added have both income and capital gains
characteristics and fall between these two extremes. Additional drivers of
return in a real estate fund are capital improvements, reducing vacancy
rates, leverage, and active management, including selling at the right time
and buying at below-market prices. We will review each strategy now and
demonstrate how each of these return drivers is used. Incidentally, when we
get to energy investing later in the chapter, there are four strategies that will
fall along a similar risk-and-return spectrum.

Core   Core real estate funds are multibillion-dollar investment portfolios
of mostly stable, income-producing properties. These funds are generally
open-ended with low or no leverage. The holding period of a property in a
core fund is 7 to 10 years and net return targets are in the range of NCREIF
index returns of 7 to 10 percent (NCREIF, the National Council of Real
Estate Investment Fiduciaries, publishes an index of the gross returns of
large core real estate funds). Core returns are primarily composed of income
(6 to 7 percent) rather than capital gains (1 to 3 percent). The cost for
investing in core funds generally runs 1 percent.

Core-Plus   After core, the next strategy on the risk-return spectrum is
core-plus. These are also large funds and generally seek returns of 10 to
13 percent. Buyers of core-plus properties often use slightly more leverage

than core investors (typically 40 to 60 percent of a property's value). Core-plus investments are relatively safe, but provide the owner with the opportunity to increase return in exchange for taking some risk. For example, a buyer may acquire an office building that is well occupied, but needs minor renovations, such as upgraded lobbies or common areas, with some leases expiring over several years. After completing upgrades, a property owner can sign new leases with higher rates, increasing the investment's yield. The cost of a core-plus fund is about 1 to 1.5 percent.

Value-Added   The value-added investor takes on more risk and for higher reward, seeking returns of 12 to 17 percent, normally with a 50-50 split between income and capital gains. Value-added investors seek properties that have been poorly managed or neglected by inexperienced or inattentive owners. Fund managers typically improve the properties, bring occupancy to market levels, and then sell to core real estate investors. Value-added investments rely on a fund's understanding of a given market's trends, demographics, and tenant needs to be successful. The value-added space is broadly populated with a large number of smaller funds that manage anywhere from $200 million to $2 billion in equity capital and can be either open- or closed-end. The cost for a value-added fund will run between 2 and 4 percent, depending on the fee structure, profit interest received by the manager, and gross returns.

Opportunistic   The riskiest real estate investors reside in the opportunistic category. The strategies employed in opportunistic are fairly similar to value-added except that opportunistic investors take more development and vacancy risk, and employ leverage of up to 80 percent to generate net returns of 18 percent or more. These are closed-end funds that resemble private equity partnerships in structure and pricing. These funds seek properties with value-added characteristics, but take more development, leasing, and vacancy risks. They are structured as closed-end limited partnerships with holding periods of about three years. Above-average returns are typically driven by shorter holding periods rather than additional value production. Buyers of opportunistic real estate may buy properties that have been foreclosed or those sourced from distressed sellers. Fees on opportunistic funds can be up to 5 or 6 percent all in.

NATURAL RESOURCES

Beside real estate, the other primary real asset is the broadly defined area of natural resources. Common natural resources are oil, gas, grains, metals,

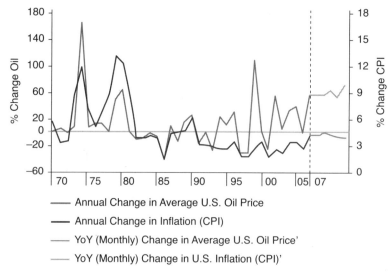

— Annual Change in Average U.S. Oil Price

— Annual Change in Inflation (CPI)

— YoY (Monthly) Change in Average U.S. Oil Price'

— YoY (Monthly) Change in U.S. Inflation (CPI)'

I Data reflect year-over-year changes for the first four months of 2008.

FIGURE 11.3 Inflation versus Oil Prices for the Period 1970 through 2006
Source: Oil and Gas Journal database, US Bureau of Labor Statistics,
and Bloomberg.

and other commodities of many different kinds. Energy (i.e., crude oil and
natural gas), basic commodities, and timber are the most widely recognized
natural resources investments, and I now switch our focus to these three
areas, discussing how to make investments in natural resources. Natural resources are one of the most underused but best inflation-fighting investments
a UAC can make. In Figure 11.3, we see how well crude oil, for example,
tracks inflation. Since 1970, oil prices have tended to correlate positively
with general price increases, particularly during periods of relatively high
inflation. The correlation between oil prices and inflation has been less pronounced in recent years, as domestic inflation has been relatively low and
commodity prices have enjoyed a period of relative strength.

Energy

There are three segments of the energy industry: the upstream, the midstream, and the downstream. Companies involved in upstream activities are
exploring and extracting energy products from under the ground and under the ocean. Midstream companies provide the tankers and pipelines that
carry crude oil to refineries. The downstream includes market participants

involved in refining, marketing, and distributing energy products, including local gas stations that serve the end user. An integrated oil company is involved in two or more of these activities. Most private energy investment funds are focused on upstream and midstream activities. These funds invest in domestic oil and gas wells, with an emphasis on owning what are called *proved reserves*. As the name implies, there is evidence that oil or gas is present and is being pumped from the ground at these sites. Some funds also pursue exploration activities. Others invest in midstream assets such as pipelines and energy-related technologies. The overriding risk when investing in energy is a change in the underlying commodity price compared to the price assumed when the investment is made. Another risk factor is production costs. In 2005, the cost to purchase reserves and pump oil from the ground was approximately $25 per barrel. In 2008, the cost was between $35 and $40. Most energy investments hedge price exposure for some period of time, which offers a level of protection, but can limit the upside and the inflation sensitivity.

As was mentioned earlier, the spectrum of risk and return available in the energy markets is similar to real estate strategies. In real estate, core funds derive most of their return from income. In the energy world, comparable funds are known as *royalty funds*. These funds' target returns are typically 8 to 10 percent in a stable price environment, but can increase in rising price environments. The core-plus real estate fund's energy equivalent is a *resource fund* whose primary strategy is to buy reserves and create value, mainly by cutting costs and improving operations. Returns expectations are 12 to 15 percent, net of fees. The value-added energy strategy is a resource fund or a private equity fund that invests in proved reserves and will pursue lower-risk drilling and reengineering activities to increase production. The target return on these funds is 15 percent net of fees. The last category is opportunistic. Here, the primary activity is drilling wells. This is a higher risk, higher reward scenario. Many of these investments are made by private equity funds. Expected returns in these funds are above 15 percent, but have a higher degree of risk than other types of energy funds.

Tax Benefits   For the benefit of potential energy investors, the U.S. Congress provides tax incentives to stimulate domestic natural gas and oil production financed by private sources. All revenues from oil exploration and development projects are subject to a depletion allowance from the U.S. government. The primary investment activity in an oil or gas property is known as a *working interest*. A working interest is held directly or through an entity that does not limit the liability of the taxpayer, but is not considered a passive activity by the IRS, regardless of whether the taxpayer materially participates in the activity. Thus, the owner of a working interest in an oil or gas property is permitted to deduct losses attributable to the working interest against other income without limitation under passive loss rules. Working interest holders will pay taxes on only 75 to 85 percent of total oil and gas income. With royalty- or income-oriented funds, income is taxable but unit holders receive a pass-through of proportionate shares of depreciation or tax credits to which the underlying property owner is entitled. Some resource funds actively drill and will write off the associated expenses. Private equity funds are oriented more toward drilling, and when underlying companies are sold, gains are long-term. Thus, private equity is the energy investment vehicle offering the most tax benefits.

Commodities

Commodities are raw materials used to create consumer products and include energy, industrial and precious metals, agriculture and livestock, and soft commodities, perishables like coffee and sugar. Commodities have evolved as an asset class with the development of commodity futures exchanges and investment vehicles that track commodity indexes. Futures and options contracts can be traded on hard and soft commodities globally. This has created a tremendous demand for commodity-based investments. According to Barclays Capital, there is currently approximately $175 billion invested in allocations tracking commodity indexes.[5] The S&P GSCI (Standard and Poor's–Goldman Sachs Commodity Index) Total Return Index and the Dow Jones–AIG (American International Group) Commodity Index are two commonly used benchmarks that define the composition of the commodities market. Both indexes are based on a basket of collateralized commodity futures returns, rather than simply futures price returns over a period of time. Each index calculates returns from three distinct sources (hence the classification, *total return*):

- Interest earned from the cash collateral committed to trading in the futures (generally Treasury bills)
- Change in futures contract price which, when added to the above, should approximate the return on the reference index
- Return from rolling the futures into further dated contracts as they approach expiry which has been a positive contributor over the long-term, but recently has had a negative impact

The S&P version is a world-production weighted index (similar in concept to a market capitalization weighting for equities). The Dow Jones–AIG

TABLE 11.2 Two Commonly Used Benchmarks in the Commodities
Market

Commodity Group	% Weight in DJ–AIG Commodity Research Total Return	% Weight in S&P GSCI Total Return Index
Energy	36	74
Agriculture	34	13
Precious Metals	9	2
Industrial Metals	13	7
Livestock	7	4

Source: AIG, S&P, as of 12/31/2007.

Commodity Index is both liquidity (two-thirds) and production (one-third)
weighted, with constraints on individual commodities (15 percent) and
commodity groups (33 percent) as of the January 2008 rebalancing period.
While each index intends to represent the commodity market, construction
and methodology differences result in varying portfolio compositions (see
Table 11.2).

Ways to Invest (Speculate) in Commodities   There are four primary ways
to add commodities to a portfolio:

1. Buying the physical commodity: This approach offers pure exposure to
   the underlying commodity, but delivery, storage, and spoilage may be
   problematic.
2. Investing through the futures or derivatives market: This method has
   predominantly been limited to large institutional investors with the
   resources and experience to administer complicated futures portfolios
   themselves, or to use a total return swap and manage the related coun-
   terparty risk.
3. Investing in pooled vehicles such as mutual funds: Until recently, mutual
   funds presented the most viable option for individual investors or small
   institutions because they provide convenient access to commodity-linked
   investment at reasonable costs and low investment minimums.
4. Exchange Traded Notes (ETNs): ETNs provide a new way to access
   difficult-to-reach markets such as commodities. ETNs are unsecured
   debt securities that deliver exposure to the returns of an asset class
   or market with the trading flexibility of an equity. ETNs linked to
   commodity indexes are designed to allow investors cost-effective access
   to the returns of popular commodity benchmarks, minus an investor fee.

TABLE 11.3 Returns and Standard Deviation of Commodities versus Other Asset Classes

	1-Year Return %	3-Year Return % Annualized	5-Year Return % Annualized	Standard Deviation % Annualized*
Dow Jones–AIG Commodity Index Total Return	21.80	12.10	15.71	14.40
S&P GSCI Total Return Index	38.62	8.42	16.05	20.86
S&P GSCI Crude Oil Total Return Index	54.76	8.78	22.22	28.26
S&P 500 Index	−5.08	5.85	11.32	9.18
Lehman U.S. Aggregate Index	7.67	5.48	4.58	3.60
MSCI EAFE Index	−2.70	13.32	21.40	11.30

*Based on monthly returns, calculated for the period 3/31/03–3/31/08.
Sources: Dow Jones, AIG Financial Products Corp., S&P, Lehman Brothers, MSCI Inc., Bloomberg.

Commodities as an asset class outperformed traditional assets such as stocks and bonds through early 2008. The Dow Jones–AIG Commodity Index returned nearly 16 percent annually over the five years that ended March 31, 2008, as can be seen in Table 11.3. By 2009, prices of commodities collapsed due to the global recession.

Commodity prices were driven higher by a number of factors, including increased demand from emerging markets countries that need basic commodities to support manufacturing and infrastructure growth. The commodity supply chain had also suffered from a lack of investment, creating bottlenecks and adding an insurance premium to the returns of many commodity futures. Although there were many fundamental factors at play, some industry observers promulgated the idea that speculators drove up commodities during this period. When this chapter was written, oil fell from a peak of $147 to below $40; we can draw a conclusion as to whether speculators contributed to this volatility. In addition to the potential returns, commodities offer investors diversification benefits. The Dow Jones–AIG Commodity Index's returns have been largely independent of stock and bond returns, as Table 11.4 illustrates.

Commodity investing in the fashion mentioned above is both passive and speculative. There is no expected return outside of the changes in price levels for commodities. Therefore, if commodity prices are flat, there is no return. Commodities can also be volatile as we saw in the second half of 2008.

TABLE 11.4 Correlations between Commodities and Other Asset Classes

Dow Jones–AIG Commodity Index Total Return	1.00
S&P GSCI Total Return Index	0.88
S&P GSCI Crude Oil Total Return Index	0.70
S&P 500 Index	0.08
Lehman U.S. Aggregate Index	0.01
MSCI EAFE Index	0.22

Source: Dow Jones, AIG Financial Products Corp., S&P, Lehman Brothers, MSCI Inc., Bloomberg (3/93–3/08), based on monthly returns.

Operating investments that are linked to commodities are preferred over passive investments because they make money even in flat commodity price environments. Such investments are expected to generate positive returns during periods of commodity price inflation, but operating companies can be hedged against the types of reversals we saw in late 2008.

Timber

UACs and Family Offices have been investing in timber for decades. Timber investing, however, has gained significant interest from large numbers of UACs in the past decade because of its growing institutional quality, steady returns, and inflation protection. Because trees grow, unlike other assets, timber returns have also been proven to be weakly correlated with returns on traditional investments, like stocks or bonds, and have a relatively low systematic or market risk (i.e., beta).[6] Timberland has also been shown to be directly related to inflation, making timberland investments good for preserving capital during periods of inflation. Timberland returns have also been high relative to their level of volatility (although estimating the volatility of an illiquid asset class is difficult at best).[7] Investors need to keep in mind, however, that timber is one of if not the most illiquid and long-term of all asset classes if people make investments through a limited partnership structure. In addition, timber is highly tax efficient because most harvesting activity and land sales are treated as long-term taxable gains.

The number of global timberlands owners, funds managers, fund of funds managers, listed vehicles, and institutional funds in North America, Europe, Australia, Latin America, Africa, and Asia have grown so much recently that DANA Limited has been able to identify and profile or list more than 600 global players in the timberlands business.[8] Markets for timber are both global and local, depending on the product. For pulpwood (which is considered to be of lower value), it is usually inefficient to transport it more

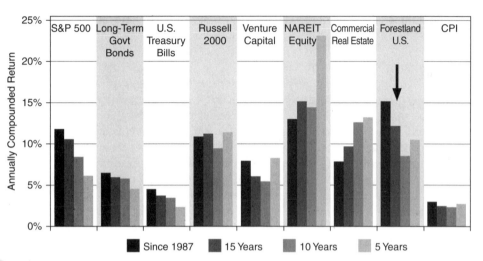

FIGURE 11.4 U.S. Forestland Returns versus Other Asset Classes since 1987
Source: Forest Systems and Forest Research Group.

than 100 or so miles. For higher value timber, global shipments are economically feasible. Institutional and private equity timberland investments have moved from being an obscure asset class pursued only by pioneering investors to a mainstream investment for an increasing number of foundations, pension funds, endowments, private equity or hedge fund firms, and family offices. Investors should note, however, that many commingled timber funds have some mix of international timber exposure and that this activity contains some risks not present in U.S. investing. These risks include currency risks, transportation (export) risks, political risk, and capital repatriation risks. Figure 11.4 shows the returns for U.S. forestland compared with other asset classes.

Institutional investor participation in the asset class has been facilitated by the creation of timberland investment management organizations (TIMOs). TIMOs are organizations that invest in timberland on behalf of the investors mentioned earlier. Investments are completed either on a separate account basis or through a commingled limited partnership structure. In just three years, from 2004 to 2007, the area of timberland owned by forest products companies halved, while areas managed by TIMOs increased by 120 percent, by private investors almost 110 percent, and by timber REITS by 35 percent. Of the top 10 company timberland owners in 1981, only one (Weyerhaeuser) had any significant core holdings left by early 2008.[9]

TIMO-only investments have increased more than 300 percent from $9.0 billion in 1997 to more than $29 billion in early 2008.

Investment Dynamics of Timber   Timber returns are affected by three main factors: the stumpage price or the price for a given type and category of tree (price per pound), the growth rate of the trees which determines the amount of wood fiber, plus the underlying land value. Supply and demand, and, by extension, prices for wood products are subject to cyclical fluctuation. Factors such as residential construction activity, home remodeling, and other manufacturing uses of wood all affect pricing. Of the lumber consumed in the United States, almost 40 percent is used for new residential home construction and another 30 percent is used for home repair and remodeling.[10] Macroeconomic conditions such as interest rates, weather events and seasonal trends, population growth trends, and consumer preferences all affect timber prices. The good news for timber investors is that demand for timber is expected to continue to increase over the next 20-plus years, particularly as emerging markets continue their growth despite the economic downturn of 2008.

There are seven components, as shown in Figure 11.5, of timber returns that influence the three factors to arrive at the total return to the timber investor. These factors are biological growth, active and opportunistic harvesting, acquisition and disposition strategies, value increases, other active management activities, land enhancements, and price appreciation. *Biological growth* is simply the gross increase in total timber based on biological tree growth. *Active/opportunistic harvesting* involves, for example, focusing on harvesting certain trees that are currently garnering high prices over other types of trees that are not currently priced as favorably. *Acquisition and disposition strategies* involve making smart land purchases and selling land opportunistically. *Value increases* involve trees getting bigger which produce higher value wood products to sell. *Other active management strategies* are, for example, buying an adjoining parcel of land to increase access points for better harvesting. *Land enhancements* are things like building roads and harvesting in such a way that the tract is visually more appealing. *Price appreciation* is the real return (inflation) component of timber.

In addition, environmental and regulatory issues can affect timber returns. For example, the placement of the northern spotted owl on the endangered species list resulted in changes to harvest practices on both public and private timberland. These changes in harvest practices resulted in an increase in the value of private timberland by restricting the ability to harvest federal timberlands. This development was a primary reason for the unusually high returns for timberland in the late 1980s, particularly in the

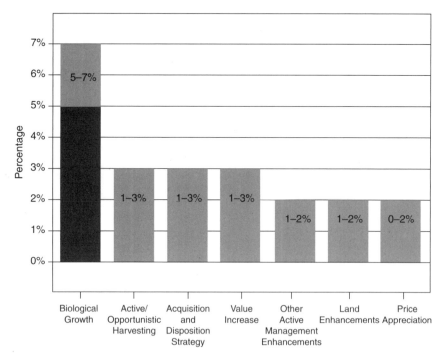

FIGURE 11.5 Timberland Investment Return Components
Source: Timbervest.

Pacific Northwest region. In the future, other wildlife species could be put on the endangered species list, further affecting the value of timberland. Legislation was introduced in Congress in 1994 banning the exporting of logs from privately owned timberlands. This ban was already in place for federal lands. While the legislation didn't pass, it is indicative of the regulatory risks associated with timber investing. If such legislation had passed, it likely would have resulted in lower domestic log prices.

Timber Returns NCREIF's Timberland Property Index is the leading source of institutionally verifiable timber return information. Total returns for timber are broken down into an income component and a capital return component. The income return is calculated as EBITDDA (earnings before interest expenses, income taxes, depreciation, depletion, and amortization). Income is generated mainly by timber harvesting, but may also include other activities such as the sale of development rights and even hunting or fishing leases. Capital returns are mainly a reflection of changes in market value due

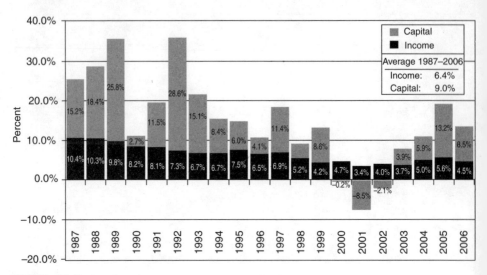

FIGURE 11.6 Timber Return Components 1987–2006
Source: National Council of Real Estate Investment Fiduciaries.

mainly to biological growth of trees, but it also includes land sale proceeds. Income and capital returns tend to move together. When timber prices are higher than average, both income and capital returns rise because timber managers harvest more wood and higher prices for timber mean higher appraised values for timberland. Figure 11.6 contains historical performance, volatility, and correlations for the NCREIF Timber Index compared to other indexes for 10 years, ending December 31, 2006.

The NCREIF Timberland Property Index has exhibited some decline in its rate of return since inception. Overall, forestland total return has averaged a healthy 15.7 percent since the inception of the index.[11] The index, however, has some flaws. It has a small number of participants and manager returns are largely based on appraisals, which in turn may be based on the sales of very small parcels of timber. The historical data supporting much of the timber investment thesis are also skewed by events such as the spotted owl legislation. Moreover, very few timber funds have ever been liquidated to prove that the returns are genuine. The main ways that timber managers can add value relative to each other is by buying cheap or selling dear (they generally manage the trees the same way), but most sizable properties are sold at auction, and timber funds haven't sold enough property to make return calculations meaningful.

How to Invest in Timber   For most family offices, a limited partnership is the most appropriate vehicle for investment. These limited partnerships typically have an initial term of 9 to 10 years with subsequent annual or multiyear renewal periods that generally last no longer than three or four years. Capital is typically drawn down over one to three years. Management fees vary by partnership but usually range from 100 to 150 basis points of capital committed. Limited partnerships generally have a profit-sharing component after the limited partners receive a preferred return of about 8 percent. This profit split is in the 15 to 20 percent range after a preferred return. Timber investment managers generally do not employ leverage. After the initial investment period, cash distributions can range from 1 to 5 percent a year. In the later years of the partnership, cash distributions are higher as timber tracts are sold. Lower cash flow investments can often lead to higher returns because younger forests can often be bought at a lower price, since the timber is not ready to be harvested. The targeted real return net of all fees for timber limited partnerships is approximately 6 to 8 percent. (Real expected return is gross of investment management fees but net of all timber management operating costs and inflation.) Another way to get timber exposure is through publicly traded timber real estate investment trusts (T-REITs). The advantage of a T-REIT is immediate liquidity. The disadvantage is that T-REITs have quarterly debt service and dividend requirements. This means they must constantly harvest timber, eliminating the flexibility afforded to private timberland investments, which can refrain from harvesting in poor pricing environments. In addition, because T-REITs are publicly traded, they can trade at prices that do not reflect the underlying net asset values and have higher volatility than private investments.

In addition to taxes and fees, inflation is a significant wealth dissipater. Left unprotected, a portfolio can be ravaged by the effect of rising prices. UACs and their advisors often leave inflation out of the equation when it comes to calculating how much money one will have available in the future. As we saw earlier in the chapter, the inflation rate since 1998 has been approximately 2.5 percent; in the 1980s, the country experienced double-digit inflation at times. Since that time, the price of goods and services has increased about 80 percent. An item costing $1,000 in 1980 costs about $1,800 today. Real assets can play a significant role in combating the impact of inflation. UAC advisers need to familiarize themselves with real assets and use them whenever possible. I now move to Part III of the book: Multigenerational Considerations for Ultra-Affluent Clients.

Three

Multigenerational Considerations for Ultra-Affluent Clients and Family Offices

Selecting an Adviser

No road is long with good company.
—Turkish Proverb

Near the end of a selection process in which my firm was a finalist for investment adviser to a substantial family office, I was asked about the best way for the family to select their new adviser. On the surface, this seems like a great opportunity to boast. There is a natural and substantial temptation to point to a stellar investment performance record, a vast array of top quality services, and one's own superb qualifications to be the family's new trusted adviser. But this temptation should be resisted. You need to put yourself at risk, but the risk can pay off handsomely. The risk-taker's response to that question is: "Choose the one you feel the most comfortable working with." If a prospective adviser hasn't done the work to get the client comfortable with the process and described what it's like to work with the adviser, asking this question will likely fall flat. But if you have done the work, you may just get a new client. The trick, of course, is to get the client to feeling comfortable with you. To get to that point, advisers should understand who they are and what types of clients are likely to be a good fit for them.

This chapter will help readers understand how advisers are categorized and how clients fit their needs with the various methods of delivering financial advice. There is no one right way of delivering advice. If there were, all financial services companies would go out of business except the ones that followed the only model that worked. Underlying all successful financial service firms' relationships with their clients is one fundamental aspect: Trust. Without it, a client-adviser relationship has little chance of flourishing. We witnessed in 2008, one of if not the most egregious violations of trust in financial advisory history with the Bernard Madoff scandal. UACs will be more skeptical than ever when selecting an adviser. I first review the importance of trust by examining a study performed by the Wharton School at the University of Pennsylvania and State Street Global Advisors, and then review the various methods of delivering financial services, both new and old, and the client types that are appropriate for each one. I discuss at the end some questions commonly asked by UACs that advisers should family arize themselves with.

TRUST: THE KEY INGREDIENT

In my experience, trust is the bedrock of the client-adviser relationship. Many advisers know this intuitively, but do not pay the requisite attention to the issue. There are critical times when trust is evaluated by the client, and knowing when these times arise is crucial for success, particularly with UACs. But you don't have to take my word for it. Figure 12.1 shows the results of 866 individuals who completed an online survey given by State Street Global Advisors and the Wharton School held between June 14 and June 29, 2006. Two identical survey tracks (i.e., lines of questioning) were presented to two groups, the first consisting of 500 consumers and the second of 366 financial advisers. Financial advisers comprised a wide range

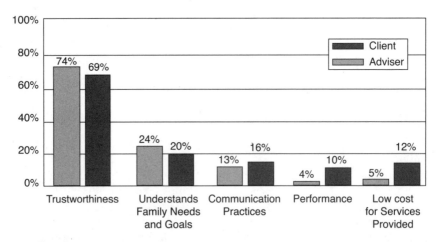

FIGURE 12.1   The Importance of Trust: Most Important Characteristics of a Financial Adviser
Source: State Street Global Advisors and The Wharton School.

of investment and financial service professionals, and clients represented an equally wide range of portfolio sizes.[1]

Needless to say, both clients and advisers put trust at the top of the list as one of the most important characteristics of a financial adviser. But trust has not always been there in the financial advisory business. In this article, Charlotte Beyer, CEO of the Institute for Private Investors (IPI) in New York, was quoted as saying that at one time wealth management was a business "shrouded in mystery—and very, very high profit margins." The article goes on to say, however, that: "Since the model has changed, via a transition from product to service, many financial advisors have had to master the art of a new sales tactic. Call it the 'sales-free sale,' this approach is now an essential part of every successful advisor's repertoire. The distinction is noteworthy because there is much less of an emphasis on pitching stocks and mutual funds, and more on personal counseling and education."[2] This quote encapsulates the approach demanded by UACs.

The article also notes that there are three basic levels of trust: trust in technical competence & know-how, trust in ethical conduct and character, and trust in empathic skills and maturity.[3] It should go without saying that most clients are seeking an adviser whose level of competence and know-how inspires trust. When a UAC meets an adviser for the first time, she will be constantly evaluating the person, silently asking, "Can I envision this person becoming a part of my inner circle?," "Does this person know what he is doing?," and "Could I work with this person for a long time—is this person trustworthy?" Many advisers make the mistake of believing that technical investment knowledge is enough to engender trust. Not true. Being able to help families with soft issues, like coping with family matters and generational concerns, engenders deep trust. Without the personal dimension, the client's trust in the adviser to handle personal issues and sensitive information with empathy and tact, the client will not feel connected to the adviser. Wharton Professor of Finance Richard Marston notes that "increasingly the value of financial advice is not really managing the money, but in the 'softer' advisory elements—personal counseling and instruction. The advisor has to understand the logic behind the advice and work the argument through with the client so the client really understands it."[4]

Trust must continually be earned but can easily be lost. And, as I have said before, temporary subpar investment performance is not a relationship- or trust-killer. Advisers to UACs must remember that things like professionalism, fee transparency, underpromising and overdelivering, and making time for clients are what affects the level of trust that a client has in an adviser. In regard to professionalism, advisers often forget that real money is at stake in the investment process, and taking losses lightly or paying little attention to small accounts affects trust. Advisers also need to keep in mind that all staff members who touch the client need to be properly trained. Clients form impressions of the adviser based on interactions with staff as well as the adviser.

Regarding fee transparency, Mitch Anthony, a Minneapolis-based consultant to the financial advisory industry, sums it up: "No matter how much you think you realize the level of distrust over fees, we underestimate it. It's easy for the industry to say we're changing the way we do business because we want to build trust with our clients, and then come out with a bunch of touchy-feely ads, but all it does is increase the level of cynicism to the consumer."[5] Advisers need to be transparent about fees with UACs. Period. Another mistake that advisers often make is over-committing themselves to clients before they become clients. Things like this are said: "You should expect consistent double-digit returns from this portfolio over time" or "I make myself available to all my clients day or night and on weekends." Now these may be genuine statements, but if they do not materialize, trust can be damaged. Lastly, with respect to making time for clients, some advisers push off too much of the advisory work onto subordinates. The client is hiring, first and foremost, the adviser—not the assistants!

In short, advisers who can build and deliver on these three levels of trust—competence, ethics, and empathic skills—create the right environment for satisfying and long-lasting relationships with clients. We now move to understanding how advisory firms can be classified and what clients are appropriate for each type of firm.

HOW UACs SELECT AN ADVISER

UACs have had many business models to deal with over the years. These models have thankfully evolved to the point where for some firms, their service offerings are working effectively because they deliver outstanding, comprehensive service offerings. For those advisers who have not evolved, it is important for you to know what is working and what isn't. It is useful to see where the industry was years ago to put into perspective where it is now. To that end, I begin this section with a brief history of how UACs have historically been served. I then discuss new, more updated business models that are proving effectual. I end this section with a discussion of how asset size dictates which business model is appropriate for a given client.

History of How UACs Have Traditionally Been Served

For better or worse, bank trust departments were the default choice of ultra-affluent clients for many, many years. America's great fortunes were in the .hands of the J. P. Morgans and the Bessemer Trusts of the world from about the turn of the twentieth century to about the 1980s. Then new entrants came on the scene about 30 years ago and UACs had more choices. Wirehouse brokers got in on the action. Independent investment advisers had developed the wherewithal to service larger clients. Consultants like Cambridge Associates began to emerge. With all of the new entrants came a plethora of business models to choose from. Even the most sophisticated of families had trouble deciphering the buzzwords, financial products, fee arrangements, and the rest of it so they could make a good decision for their family's future. It's even more complex today. Fund managers are targeting UACs directly. Private banks offer their own products. Brokers offer other firms' products. Coming full circle, some fund-of-fund managers now offer asset allocation advice! What's a client to do?

Historically, wealth advisory firms have been judged on two dimensions: *type of platform* and *level of transparency*. There is a tremendous amount of important information contained in these seemingly innocuous dimensions. I delve into these subjects in detail and provide examples of financial services firms that fit into cross-sections of these dimensions. Generally speaking, UACs want to hire independent, objective advisers who get paid by their clients and not by fund managers, brokers, custodians, or anyone else. But this is not always the case. I discuss questions further on that clients may ask prospective advisers wishing to be retained.

Type of Platform

Financial services firms have generally fallen someplace along a spectrum of *open platform* or *closed platform*. When we say open platform, we refer to firms that offer clients the ability to gain access to so-called best-of-breed services, offered (usually) by third-party vendors. The adviser diagnoses a client's key issues without a specific solution in mind, and then decides which service provider fills the client need the best. The advantage of open platforms is that they offer the client the opportunity to get an objective solution to a problem. The disadvantage of this type of solution is that it is usually more complicated and is labor intensive in that staff is needed to manage the process of interfacing with a number of different vendors that need to be coordinated to be effective. A closed platform is one in which a broad array of services are offered by a single provider, with the client usually adapting his needs to the services being offered. The advantage to this model is its simplicity: The client can take care of a multitude of issues with one firm. The disadvantage is that the advice given may not be objective and the services that are offered may not be of the best quality.

Level of Transparency

Transparency is the ability for the client to truly understand the service offering being provided to him. This is crucial to those advisers who wish to serve UACs. Some firms that aspire to serve clients of this class lack transparency and wonder why they are not gaining traction in this space. Transparency is not necessarily just about fees. It's also about education and getting the client to understand the details of managing wealth. Regarding fees, UACs want to know in detail what fees they are being charged at every level of their financial management. For example, they want to know not only what their consultant or other adviser is charging them, but they want to know what the custodial fees are, what the mutual fund fees are, what the index funds are charging, and, especially, what the alternative managers are charging for management and incentive fees. Some firms take pride in laying out the fees for the entire wealth management supply chain. Others choose not to disclose the full array of costs associated with their offerings or the underlying providers that help deliver services to the end client.

Regarding education, some firms educate their clients about any wealth management subject that the client wishes to know. These topics can range from how custodians charge fees, to how structured products function, to various models of how private equity firms charge fees, and many others. Other firms don't consider it a useful endeavor to educate clients about wealth management topics. Either they don't have the time or patience to do so, or they simply want to keep their clients in the dark about how their advisory business operates. It should be noted here, though, that some business models of delivering financial services are based on convenience, such as an outsourced chief investment adviser model. These models may have a somewhat closed platform and not be of the highest transparency, but not because the provider is attempting to keep clients in the dark. The client may simply not wish to be concerned with transparency or the fact that the platform is closed because she fully trusts the service provider.

Figure 12.2 charts these two dimensions and the associated types of firms that tend to have business models falling along them. You should take note that many of the types of firms in Figure 12.2 have evolved and strengthened their business model. I next discuss the evolution of the business models of firms serving UACs.

Evolution of Business Models Serving UACs

UACs have enjoyed a much improved service offering over time, as can be seen in Figure 12.3. Investment advisory services were the lead service offering by advisers years ago. Services offered under this model were the

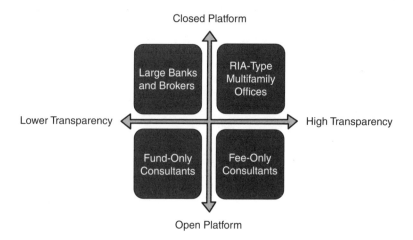

Closed Platform

Large Banks and Brokers

RIA-Type Multifamily Offices

Lower Transparency

High Transparency

Fund-Only Consultants

Fee-Only Consultants

Open Platform

FIGURE 12.2 Common Business Models of Financial Services Firms

basics of asset allocation, manager search, and performance measurement. As the industry evolved, a wealth advisory model emerged. Under this model, the basic investment services were offered and functional services were added such as tax and estate planning, budgeting, and bill paying. Finally, the family office and multifamily office offering built upon the two categories of services in the wealth advisory model and added soft services such as family governance and philanthropic services. It is critical for an adviser that the client is served by the most appropriate model. The next section discusses how this is done.

Client Segmentation

As can be seen in Figure 12.4, wealth level can be used as a determinant of where a client best fits along the continuum described in the last section. According to Family Office Exchange, for those UACs with between $50 million and $250 million, the multifamily office offering is likely to be the most appropriate service model. For those UACs with more than $250 million, the single family office is likely to be the most appropriate service offering. This is naturally a rough guideline but does a good job in initially segmenting clients by their needs.

I should point out that there are certainly going to be exceptions to what is presented in Figure 12.4. For example, a family with $300 million and a significant number of trusts and an operating business that requires significant banking or investment banking services may feel that the best

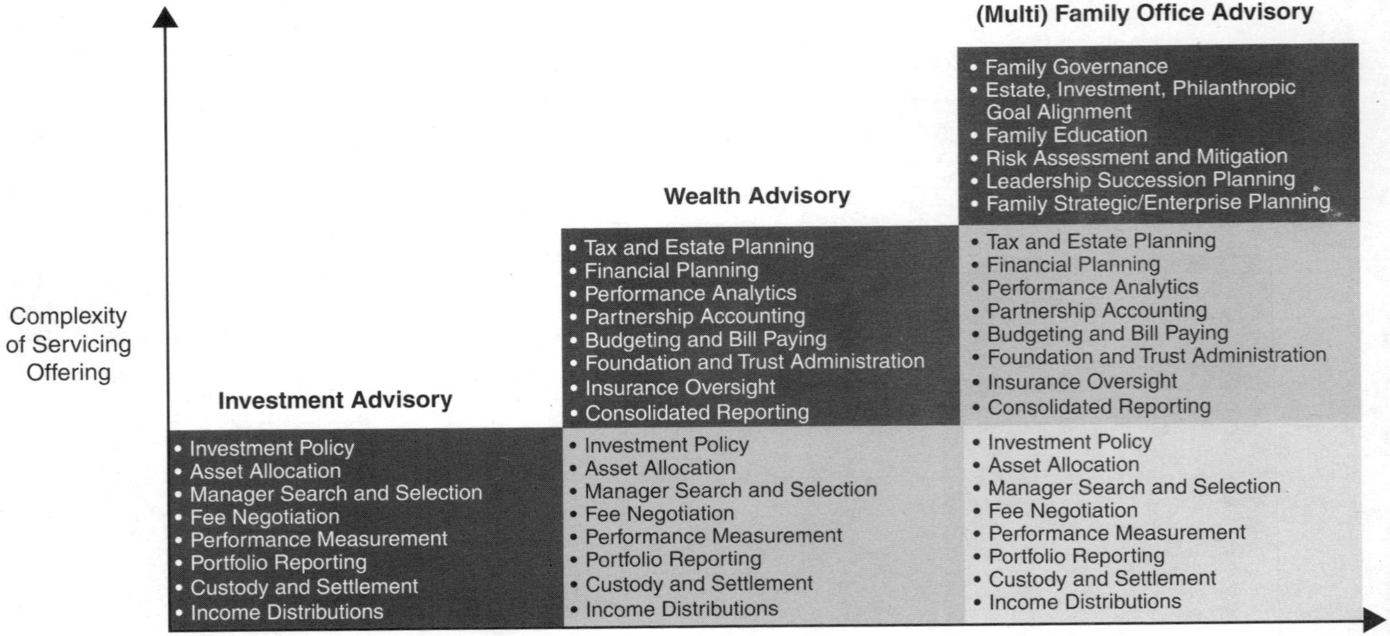

FIGURE 12.3 Evolution of Family Wealth Offering
Source: Family Office Exchange. All rights reserved.

Average Client Assets	Type of Firm	Value Proposition
$1–10 Million (Investable Assets)	Investment Advisory Firms	• Coordination of investment diversification process • Access to all asset classes through single adviser • Semi-open architecture to access multiple providers • Standard offering for most providers today
$10–50 Million (Investable Assets)	Wealth Advisory Firms	• "Nearly wealthy" can access services available to centimillionaires • Planning, execution, and oversight from single provider • Integration of ownership structures, investment strategies, and risk management services • Typically no lifestyle management services
$50–250 Million (Investable Assets)	Multifamily Offices	• Implementation of financial planning process • Depth and breadth of professionals for continuity • Better risk management process • Better information platform for better decision-making • Greater expertise and continuity in client relations
Over $250 Million (Investable Assets)	Dedicated (Single) Family Offices	• Fully dedicated resources • Most comprehensive range of services • Full-scale integrated across disciplines • Implementation of custom strategies • Oversight of "special projects" • Broadest definition of "assets" • Formalized governance for intergenerational issues

FIGURE 12.4 Client Segmentation by Wealth Level
Source: Family Office Exchange. All rights reserved.

place for personal financial services is with a large commercial family office firm. They can get one-stop shopping, and convenience is at a premium for this family. Another family with $400 million may have just sold a business and may no longer need the services of a large bank or broker. This family, now in the wealth management business, doesn't wish to open a single family office but wants convenience, education, and transparency, and may wish to employ a multifamily office. Yet another family, a single-family office with a staff of two or three professionals and relationships with lawyers, CPAs, and family counselors, may wish to augment their investment capabilities with an independent fee-only consultant. Finally, a different family may wish to outsource the entire investment process to an outside investment consultant who takes discretion on their funds, leaving the family free of the investment decision-making process. Regardless of what option a family chooses, UACs seek certain fundamental qualifications. These are reviewed in the form of questions that may be asked of advisers in the next section.

QUESTIONS FOR PROSPECTIVE ADVISERS

Advisers are often ill-prepared for tough questions about how their service offering stacks up against the competition. UACs communicate with one another freely and share resources so they can ensure that they are getting the best advice. One way of sharing information is to share lists of questions with one another. Advisers need to be aware of questions they might be asked so that they can be prepared. Broad categories of questions are as follows:

- Firm knowledge (broken down into three subcategories—history, ownership, and growth trends).
- Knowledge of service offerings and fees.
- Client relations knowledge.

These questions are not intended to be those answered in a request for proposal as was shown in Chapter 3. These questions are to be answered verbally during a client interview. The objective of the adviser is to get the client comfortable with the approach her firm takes to serving UACs.

Firm Overview: History, Ownership, and Growth Trends

UACs want to know about your firm and as a representative of that firm, you need to be able to communicate some essential information. Questions that might arise are:

- When was the decision made to serve ultra-affluent clients and how did your firm decide that it was particularly well suited to serve this client type?
- When did your firm begin serving ultra-affluent clients?
- How does your firm define ultra-affluent?
- What is your firm's ownership structure?
- How has the ownership changed over time?
- If there are members of a founding family involved in running the firm's business, what percentage of the family's assets are managed by the firm?
- How many employees are at your firm?
- How many employees are in the following categories:
  - Consultants, relationship managers, or portfolio managers
  - Research professionals
  - Tax and accounting professionals
  - Other family specialists (philanthropy, family counseling, and so forth)
  - Marketing and IT professionals
  - Operations and administrative staff
- How are relationship managers compensated? If they are paid incentive compensation, how is that calculated?

Growth Trends

- What is the process by which your firm acquires new clients?
- How many new clients have you gained in each of the past three years?
- How many new clients have you lost in each of the past three years?
- How many relationship managers or consultants have been added in the past three years?
- What are the current assets under advisement and how has that changed over the past three years, including a breakdown of both assets gained and assets lost?
- How many employee hires and resignations or terminations have been made over the past three years?
- How many accounts does the average relationship manager handle?
- What, if any, new services offerings is your firm introducing in the next 12 to 18 months?

Services Offerings and Fees

- When delivering services to clients, do you receive any fees from anyone except your clients? If so, under what circumstances? How is this information disclosed?

- Does your firm have any proprietary investment products?
- If so, are these products required to be used by clients?
- Does your firm offer noninvestment services such as tax and estate planning or wealth transfer, family philanthropy, counseling, bill paying, and so on? If so, do you integrate these services with investment advice?
- Do you help family members develop their goals and strategies, if needed?
- Do you provide clients with performance measurement and analytics?
- Do you provide client education?
- How do you charge for your services? Is there a published fee schedule?
- What is the minimum account size or minimum fee?
- Do you offer any performance-based fees?
- What is your ideal or target client profile?
- How do you ensure the confidentiality of client information?

Client Relations

- How many relationships does your firm serve?
- Does your firm serve only taxable clients?
- How are relationship management teams structured?
- How many points of communication does the client have with your firm?
- How frequently do you meet with clients?
- What are the different ways you communicate with clients (i.e., telephone, meetings, research mailings, online)?
- Do you have regularly scheduled reviews? If so, how often do they occur?
- Do you publish research? Please list any regular research papers clients receive and when they are sent out.
- Do clients have online access to their reports?
- How many clients have terminated your services in the past three years? Can you explain the reasons for their departure?
- Please provide the following documents:
  - Description or chart of the relationship management team with descriptions of the role of each team member
  - The firm's organization chart
  - Sample performance reports and quarterly reports
  - Sample investment policy statements
- Please provide references of three clients that have worked with your firm for at least three years.

CONCLUSION

Selecting an adviser is an incredibly important task. As you can see through the questionnaire, many detailed questions requiring thoughtful answers can and will be asked of any candidate wishing to serve a UAC or family office. Advisers are often ill-prepared for tough questions about how their service offering stacks up against the competition. The best way to get prepared is to review the questions in this section and prepare both written and verbal responses to them. Advisers will be in a much better position to win a new client when thoughtful responses are provided.

CHAPTER 13

Selecting a Custodian and Investment Vehicle Structure

One of the unique aspects of working with UACs over other client types is that advisers need to gain knowledge of two important back office issues: custody and investment vehicle structures. The right custodial relationship and investment vehicle structure can have a positive economic impact on the families being served; conversely, having an inefficient back office structure can be costly. Moreover, having the wrong custodial and vehicle structure can inhibit the family's (and adviser's) ability to get a clear picture of assets and performance. If the monthly or quarterly process of putting reports together is chronically plagued by lateness, errors, or incomplete information, decisions based on this information will be less than optimal. Thus, even the most dedicated wealth management professionals, who may not wish not to immerse themselves in the details of any back office functions, will be at a disadvantage if they do not understand custody and the considerations that go into creating an appropriate investment vehicle structure. As with the last chapter, there is not one right solution for everyone. The custodial decision and investment vehicle structure decision is unique for each family.

I address these two topics in this chapter. I begin with a review of custodial services, move to an overview of the major custodians (in the global family office space, there are numerous custodians with excellent capabilities), and then highlight some key areas of evaluation when it comes to selecting a custodian. In the second half of the chapter, I present various investment vehicle structures and discuss the pros and cons of each. Administrative considerations for selecting an investment vehicle structure are discussed at the end.

CUSTODIAL SERVICES

Custody has long been thought of as the proverbial back office of the securities industry. Firms offering custody have traditionally served two main functions: safekeeping assets and processing transactions. At one time, custody was an important business for many banks. Over the past several decades, however, the business has been commoditized and some players have dropped out. The players who remain in the business attempt to provide value-added services to augment basic custody services. These value-added services can be important to family offices. One area that confuses both client and adviser alike on the subject of custody is the differences between brokerage custody and bank custody. As a general rule, families of substantial wealth use bank custodians—but not always. What is sometimes overlooked with this issue is that with brokerage custody, ownership of the assets can be in "street name" versus direct ownership by the client. With street name ownership, a client's asset becomes part of the firm's balance sheet. With bank custody, direct ownership of the assets is the norm. Another difference between brokerage custody and bank custody has to do with transparency of fees (there is a section on fees later in this chapter). If you are unsure of how your assets are held, or how you are being charged for custody, call your custodian. The remainder of this chapter is focused on bank custodial services. Today, the bank custody business can be broken down into two main areas: basic custodial services and master custodial services. Basic custodial services are traditional services like the safekeeping of assets, transaction processing, corporate actions, proxy voting, tax reclamation, securities lending, income collection, and some others. These services can be provided on a domestic or global basis. Master custody builds upon the basic custody services whereby the custodian becomes the book of record for a client. The custodian consolidates assets, does partnership accounting where needed, and provides year-end tax information, thereby concentrating all asset information in one contact. If desired, consolidated reports can be created by the master custodian, significantly reducing the burden on the family to create this information. The relationship between the custodian and the family office is illustrated in Figure 13.1. I next review some of the major players in the global custody business.

Major Custody Players

Global Investor magazine publishes an annual global custody survey, the 2007 results of which are presented in Tables 13.1 and 13.2. The survey measures customer satisfaction by means of questionnaires completed by fund managers with respect to the services of custodians. In 2007, 1,254 questionnaire responses were received, of which 1,025 qualified. For a response to qualify, the primary business of the respondent must be either asset management, insurance, or the management of a pension fund. The respondent must also deal with two or more global custodians. Each response is carefully screened to ensure that it meets the set criteria. Banks must receive a minimum of 25 qualified responses to qualify for the overall ranking, of

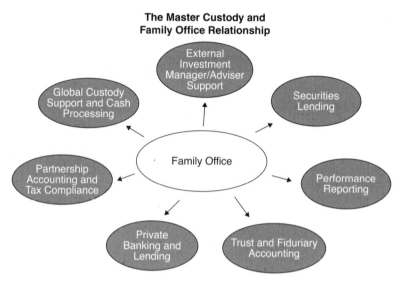

The Master Custody and Family Office Relationship

FIGURE 13.1 Custodial Relationship
Source: BNY Mellon.

which at least five must be from outside the bank's domestic market. For the purpose of the survey, Europe is treated as a single market.[1]

The ranking methodology of this survey entails respondents rating their counterparties on a scale of 1 to 10 (1 being very poor and 10 being excellent) across 25 separate service categories encompassing securities services and treasury services. Respondents were also asked to give each service

TABLE 13.1 Overall Survey Rankings: Unweighted

		Score
1	RBC Dexia Investor Services	73.31
2	Pictet & Cie	71.66
3	Mellon Group	70.41
4	Northern Trust	69.29
5	Brown Brother Harriman	64.63
6	State Street	62.25
7	Citi	61.45
8	JPMorgan	59.41
9	HSBC Securities Services	58.39
10	Investors Bank & Trust	57.83
11	The Bank of New York	57.25

Source: Global Investor Magazine.

TABLE 13.2 Overall Survey Rankings: Weighted

		Score
1	State Street	81.27
2	Mellon Group	80.88
3	RBC Dexia Investor Services	75.51
4	Northern Trust	74.8
5	JPMorgan	70.73
6	Citi	69.43
7	HSBC Securities Services	69.2
8	The Bank of New York	67.56
9	Brown Brother Harriman	67.21
10	Investors Bank & Trust	60.59
11	Pictet & Cie	47.42

Source: Global Investor *magazine*.

category an importance rating from 1 to 10 (1 being unimportant and 10 being very important). In the survey, responses were scored in three ways: unweighted, weighted, and footprint. In the unweighted scoring, the rating and importance scores are multiplied together to produce a category score for each of the services. Each of the service category scores is then averaged, and the average scores are added together and divided by 25 (the number of categories). To avoid bias from those respondents who are more diligent, if a respondent neglected the importance component a default average (based on the first 100 qualified responses) is used. In the weighted scoring, fund managers with more assets under management have a greater influence on the rankings. The respondents are split into three categories (as to their assets under management) and the following weightings applied:

0.5 = the smallest 25 percent (representing the fewest assets under management).
1.0 = the middle 50 percent.
1.5 = the largest 25 percent.

Although it is not shown, in the footprint calculation, the score is calculated for each custodian as its total unweighted score multiplied by its number of qualified responses.[2]

Custodial Selection Questions

As mentioned previously, there is no one right custodial relationship for a family and careful consideration needs to go into the selection of a custodian. To aid families in the selection process, a request for proposal (RFP) is usually submitted to a small number of highly qualified custodians. The RFP asks questions that normally fall into the following categories: organization and background of the custodial institution, family office business characteristics, regulatory and compliance, client service and administration, investment manager relations, securities processing, asset pricing, income collection and cash management, custody and safekeeping, accounting and reporting, systems, data processing and online capabilities, risk and performance services, securities lending, transition, and fees. Some RFPs will also ask questions on banking services and fiduciary services but I will not cover these areas in this chapter.

Organization and Background Questions   It is important for UACs to understand the commitment of their potential custodian to the custody business and also the stability of the organization. The following questions are designed to help gain insight into these issues:

- How is the custody division of your firm structured?
- What is your firm's credit quality and financial strength?
- Please describe your firm's current custody business:

	Under $50 million	$50–150 million	$150–500 million	$500 million– 1 billion	$1 billion plus	Total
Number of Clients						
Total Assets ($, MM)						

- Briefly summarize your firm's perceived competitive advantages within the custody, private wealth management, and family office industry.
- Please provide the size (total portfolio assets) of your five smallest and five largest custody relationships and family office relationships.
- How many clients have you added in each of the past three years? How many clients have you lost in each of the past three years?
- Has your firm been the subject of any litigation or investigation by a regulatory authority within the last three years relative to this service area? If so, please describe.

Private Wealth Custodial Services   UACs and family offices are taxable investors who are not always well served by institutionally focused firms. These questions are designed to understand the custodian's commitment to private wealth clients:

- Briefly describe the organization of the custody division that services private wealth. Is your family office custody effort part of your overall custody operation, or separate?

- What services do you offer as part of your private wealth platform that is beyond what you offer institutional custody clients?
- What are your organization's particular strengths in the private wealth area?
- How many private wealth families does your firm work with?
- Please describe any services related to tax compliance that you offer to families.

Regulatory and Compliance   It is important for UACs to understand the internal and external risk controls of the custodial firms being evaluated. This is best understood by requesting an SAS 70 report. In addition, these questions can be asked:

- How do you monitor legislative and regulatory changes affecting master trust administration? How are these changes communicated to clients and throughout your organization?
- Provide a detailed summary of your organization's internal control structure.
- Provide copies of the organization's most recent audited financial statements and auditor's management letter.
- Describe your fiduciary role and responsibility as custodian.

Client Service and Administration   At the end of the day, client satisfaction is all about the people servicing the account. UACs need to feel comfortable with whom they will be working. These questions are designed to gain insight into the professional background and capabilities of those people servicing the custodial relationship:

- How many professional staff members at your firm are devoted exclusively to the delivery of custody services for the private wealth clients?
- What approach to account administration is used (e.g., individual relationship manager, account teams, account administrator with support group)?
- How many accounts does your typical relationship manager or account administrator manage?
- Comment on any personnel turnover your organization has experienced in the past three years.
- What training is provided to customers?
- How do you monitor client satisfaction?

Investment Manager Relations   Most UACs and family offices have an open architecture approach to investing their assets. Therefore, their custodian needs to be able to interface with multiple managers effectively and efficiently. Asking these questions will help gain insight into this important issue:

- Describe how your organization interacts with investment managers. Explain your procedures for notifying the investment managers of trades and cash balances.
- How many investment managers do you work with?
- How do you monitor investment manager satisfaction?
- Do you provide investment managers with access to a remote inquiry service? If so, what online information or reports are available to them?

Core Custodial Services The following four areas are the core services of any custodian: securities processing, asset pricing, income collection and cash management, and custody and safekeeping. Without the ability to do these core functions well, a custodian candidate would likely be removed from the list. The following questions will help evaluate a custodian's ability to deliver these core services.

Securities Processing

- What is the organization structure of your trade settlement group?
- What worldwide depositories does your institution use to settle securities?
- What options are available for trade communication?
- What are your procedures to monitor and resolve failed trades? How do you compensate for income lost for failed trades?
- How do you process trades?
- How do you handle information on corporate activities such as tender offers, exchange offers, and so on?
- Please describe how you handle and report proxy information.

Asset Pricing

- What sources do you use for pricing each category of securities and when are prices available?
- How do you value difficult-to-price assets such as private placements?
- What procedures and control points do you have in place to ensure that securities are priced accurately?
- How do you identify and communicate pricing discrepancies?

Income Collection and Cash Management

- Describe your policies concerning the following:
  - Collection and crediting of interest and dividend income.
  - Automatic investment of cash balances.

- When does income become available for investment?
- Describe your cash management services used for short-term cash reserves.

Custody and Safekeeping

- Describe your physical securities safekeeping facilities.
- What are your firm's depository memberships and what are the services you use at these depositories?
- Describe your system for the registration and custody of assets, including depositories used.
- Describe where and how the receipt and delivery of physical securities occurs and how are they secured.
- Describe your securities settlement process.
- Describe your procedures and capabilities for settling and accounting for same day cash trades.
- How and when do you record and report corporate actions?
- What is the source of your pricing data for stocks, bonds, options, convertibles, and futures contracts, including how frequently prices are updated?
- Do asset valuations include accrued income and pending transactions?
- How are valuation differences resolved between the investment manager and the master custodian?
- How do you price securities not available from a pricing service, such as private placements?
- Can the client specify alternative pricing sources?
- What procedures do you have in effect, if any, to investigate unusual or significant pricing changes from the previous pricing period?
- How do you handle corrections and reversals (i.e., as adjustments or as offsetting purchases and sales)?

Accounting and Reporting   UACs and family offices need to account for their data in three basic ways: trust accounting, portfolio accounting, and tax accounting. These questions are designed to evaluate a custodian's ability to account for and report data:

- Describe your accounting system (trade date or settlement date, accrual, or cash basis). Can you provide reports on any of these accounting bases?
- What is the lag time between trade execution, availability of online transaction data to the client, and the posting of the transaction to your accounting system?

- Do you support automated interfaces to general ledger and family office accounting systems?
- Do asset valuations include accrued income and pending transactions?
- How do you report interest and dividend income? Do you break out between taxable and nontaxable, and by state, if applicable?
- Do you have the capacity to capture and report brokerage commissions generated by an account? By transaction?
- How do you report gains and losses? Do you track short-term versus long-term, cumulative, and year-to-date?
- Do asset valuations reflect pending transactions?
- Do asset statements have the capability to show accrued income?
- What reports are provided as part of your standard package? How frequently are they produced?
- Do you have a 24-hour help desk available?

Data Processing and Online Capabilities   Many UACs have unique needs when it comes to seeing their data. They may want others to have access as well, such as their CPA or investment consultant for example. In addition, data must be secure. These questions cover these issues:

- Discuss the hardware and software systems in the place that support your Custody Department. How long has the current software been in place?
- Do you provide online services to your clients? How long has it been offered? How many clients are currently using it?
- What provisions are made for training of client personnel on the online system?
- What equipment and software is necessary for clients to obtain online services?
- What security features are provided?
- Describe your online system for clients and investment managers. Describe the information available; for example, pending trades, accounting information, asset lists by account including market value, transaction history, summary of account market values for the portfolio, securities on loan, or performance management tools.
- How current is the information that is accessed? How many hours a day is the system available?
- How many prior months of holdings and transactions data can be reviewed?
- Does your online system provide the client and investment manager with investable cash balances each morning?
- What backup and recovery capabilities are in place in case of malfunctions or emergencies? Where is the backup system located?

Risk and Performance Services   Understanding how investments are performing and how they are reported is critical. These questions assess a custodian's capabilities in these areas:

- Describe your firm's performance measurement and analysis capabilities.
- Can you provide for accounts not in your custody?
- Can different accounts be combined online for performance reporting? Can reports be customized?
- Describe how your performance is calculated.
- List the indexes available and dates of availability.
- Can you backload data?
- How many and what types of reports are available, and when?
- Do you offer an investment manager compliance product?

Securities Lending   Some clients decided to earn extra income from securities lending (although some wish they had never got involved in this area after some problems surfaced in 2008 with securities lending). Still, some clients are doing it. These questions will help in deciding whether to engage in securities lending:

- Do you provide securities lending services? If so, please describe your program.
- With how many borrowers do you have business relationships? How are these brokers selected? How often is creditworthiness reviewed?
- What types of collateral do you require?
- How is cash collateral invested?
- What are the risks in securities lending and how do you manage these risks?
- How do you coordinate your securities lending activities with the client's investment manager(s)?
- What percentage of collateral do you require? Do you mark to market daily?
- To what degree are your securities lending clients insured against losses from participation in your program?
- Explain your security loan allocation system and the basis on which you make such applications to all clients. How do you provide equal opportunity to all participating clients to lend their securities?
- How is the income generated from securities lending split between the client and you?
- Have any of your clients experienced any negative loans? What is the bank's policy for minimizing the risk of negative loans?
- Please describe the securities lending reports you provide.

Transition   Transitioning from one custodian to another is never easy. It is important to have a team of professionals who are experienced in making transitions and will put together a plan and stick to that plan during the transition. These questions should help you assess a custodian's abilities in this area:

- Please describe the conversion process (who is responsible for coordinating activities, who participates, what activities must occur, etc.). Please specify if you have a dedicated conversion team.
- Please provide a sample timetable including the type and amount of resources to be provided by the client.
- How do you handle transactions and claims that are in process during the transition or conversion period?
- Do you require a blackout period?

Fees   There are two key areas to be aware of when it comes to fees: transparency of fees and understanding how fees are actually charged (which are not necessarily the same thing). Asking these questions is a good start toward understanding fees:

- Please provide a breakdown of your fees:
  - Initial setup fees
  - Asset charges
  - Active manager or separate account fees
  - Line item fees
  - Performance measurement fees
  - Partnership accounting fees
  - Other fees (use of online system, etc.)
  - Total estimated fee—first year
  - Total estimated fee—subsequent years
- Please disclose any other fees that haven't been addressed that could be incurred.

What a Family Office Should Look for in a Custodian

After asking these questions, one should have a very good idea of how a custodian fits the needs of a given family. The best advice to UACs and family offices who are in search of a custodial relationship is to think not only about today, but also try to think about what the family structure might look like in five or ten years or longer. Regardless of complexity, the chosen custodian should have a key set of attributes:

- Financial strength.
- A broad and deep service offering to fit a unique set of needs.

- A commitment to the custody business.
- A reasonable price for services provided.
- Top quality technology.
- A dedicated client relationship team.
- Accuracy and timeliness.
- Global capability.

INVESTMENT VEHICLE STRUCTURE

Another one of the challenges of working with UACs, especially those with multigenerational wealth, is that they usually (but not always) have a spider web of accounts, trusts, partnerships, and companies that is difficult to visualize without drawing on paper. This complexity often leads to challenges in making good tax planning and investment choices. In my experience, there are many families that would like to restructure their investment vehicle structure or would start over if they could by using more modern techniques of pass-through vehicles like partnerships, limited liability corporations, and limited liability limited partnerships. These structures allow families to aggregate family assets for the purpose of lowering management fees and gaining access to top-tier investment managers with high minimum investments. Eligible accounts can be trusts, individual accounts, or other limited partnerships. Another major benefit of partnerships is the ability to track each partner's cost and tax basis as they enter the pool and to allocate gains and losses based on an individual's participation in the pool rather than on a pro rata basis at year's end.

The process for executing one of the pass-through entities described earlier is relatively straightforward, and thus the use of partnership structures has accelerated. An attorney drafts a limited partnership or limited liability agreement, which defines the rights of the general partners and limited partners. The agreement typically places restrictions on the ownership of partnership interests, and usually contains language saying that the partnership cannot be terminated until a specified future date unless all participants agree. The last step is subscribing to the partnership by transferring cash or assets into the name of the partnership and receiving in return units of a limited interest in the partnership. Because these pools are restricted to family members, they are exempt from most governmental oversight.

As the use of partnerships has grown, families are now crafting many unique and interesting structures that help them accomplish their specific goals. When setting up multiple partnerships, the primary consideration is the trade-off between flexibility of investing and the cost and work effort of managing the investment vehicle structure. The greater the number of partnerships, the greater the ability to invest in specific investment styles and managers—but the cost and effort required for partnership accounting and tax preparation also increases with each partnership. I now review four partnership structures and discuss their pros and cons.

A Pool for Every Investment Manager

Option I, shown in Figure 13.2, is the ultimate in flexibility. This approach is generally used by families with multigenerational wealth who have numerous trusts and individual accounts, with each account owner wanting to select his own individual investment managers. In this scenario, the family is not put in the position of having to seek consensus on which managers to invest in; they establish the partnership structure to facilitate co-investing. This approach usually comes as a result of a family member selecting a particular investment manager and then asking the family office to establish a pool for that manager. The family office hires the manager and then offers other family members access to that manager. Each family individually decides then whether they want to invest with that manager (they can usually gain access at a later time if they wish). This flexibility gives rise to a multitude of pools, and it is not uncommon in these circumstances to have as many as 40 to 50 unique pools!

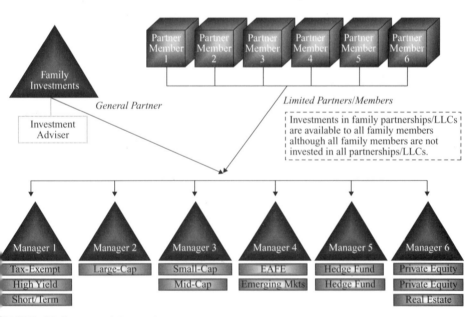

FIGURE 13.2 A Pool for Each Manager
Source: BNY Mellon.

The major advantage for the family is the ability to hand-pick managers they want to invest with. The major cons are obvious, more pools to account for and more costs related to preparing tax returns and the requisite K-1s.

A Pool for Multiple Managers within a Specific Style

Like Option I, Option II, shown in Figure 13.3, provides a great deal of flexibility, but it begins to narrow the number of pools that need to be maintained. With this strategy, the family creates a suite of pools based on style mandates. For example, a set of pooled investments might be large-cap equity, small- and mid-cap equity, international developed equity, international emerging markets equity, tax-exempt fixed income, hedge funds, and so on. In this structure, the account holders focus their attention on the style classes, and the general partners of the partnership determine which managers should be in a partnership. If a family member is enamored with a particular investment manager, the manager would have to fit into one of the style pools. If there are already managers in that style pool and a new manager becomes part of the pool, it would be left up to the general partner,

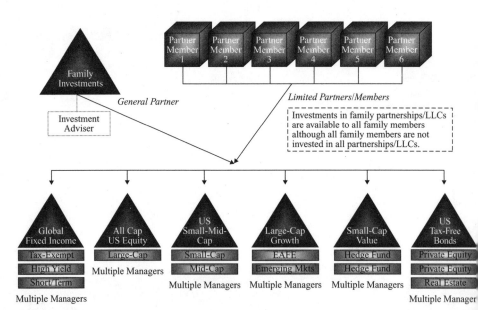

FIGURE 13.3   A Pool for Multiple Managers within a Specific Style
Source: BNY Mellon.

family office, or family investment committee to decide how that manager would be allocated money vis-à-vis the other managers.

The advantage of this option is similar to that of Option I in that there is flexibility in investing choices. The disadvantage is the need for an interim step in the accounting as you consolidate multiple managers within a style together before you can complete the process. Also, there are still more than just a few partnerships that need to be maintained (usually at least 10).

A Pool at the Asset Allocation Level

Option III, shown in Figure 13.4, may be the most popular of all the options because it establishes pools along the standard lines of asset allocation strategy. An example of this would be to have pools for fixed income, all cap U.S. equity, U.S. mid or small equity, international equity, hedge funds, and alternative assets. Thus, it is similar to Option II but limits the number of pools to about six or seven because managers are more narrowly grouped, by asset allocation strategy rather than by style. Account owners determine the asset allocation strategy but the family office or investment committee decides how many dollars go to each manager and style. The advantages of this option are similar to the previous two. The disadvantages are that

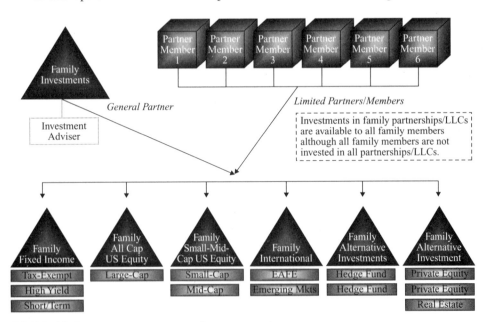

FIGURE 13.4 A Pool at the Asset Allocation Level
Source: BNY Mellon.

the family is still responsible for half a dozen or more pools and needs to consolidate all managers and styles within one asset allocation strategy before completing the process.

A Single Family Pool

Option IV, shown in Figure 13.5, is the least flexible for the family members, because they invest in only one total pool. The pool establishes a single asset allocation for all participants and the determination as to how to invest the dollars within the pool rests with the family office or investment committee. These structures retain some popularity, primarily with first- and second-generation families in which the family agrees to go along with the office's investment decisions. The benefit of this system is clearly having only one partnership to report on. The drawbacks are the lack of individual flexibility on setting investment strategy and the need to wait until all information is received before tax forms can be produced. An additional drawback is that the single pool has both liquid and illiquid investments in the same pool (to solve this problem, some families will establish two family pools: one for illiquids and one for liquid investments). This option works best when

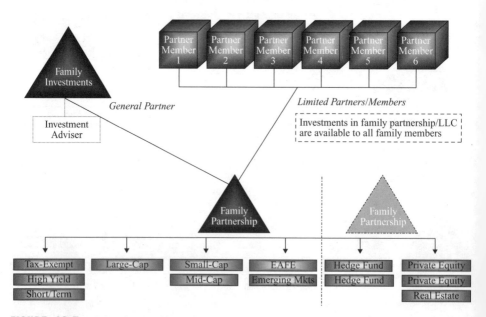

FIGURE 13.5   A Single Family Pool
Source: BNY Mellon.

the pool operates on a *fixed sharing ratio* strategy. A fixed sharing ratio is a situation in which all members agree to accept the same allocations across the different investment strategies. Some families have set up this type of strategy, but allow family members to invest differently across the asset classes or managers. This is referred to as allowing *variable sharing ratios* within the pool. Even though this does allow for only one pool to report on for tax purposes, one still needs to account for which members are invested in what strategies. Thus, a family can save on tax preparation costs, but may still be saddled with a more complex accounting requirement where accountings need to be done when variable sharing is allowed.

Formation Decisions

There are several important issues that need to be considered when creating a partnership to facilitate co-investment among family members. Establishing these vehicles requires a considerable amount of thought and consideration, and can affect family relationships. The administrative issues I cover next have long-lasting effects, so careful consideration is required.

Selection of Partners and Share Classes   When creating a pool, the family must establish who is eligible to participate in the pools, who serves as general partner, how manager selections decisions should be made, and so on. When creating partnerships, there are also options to establish multiple classes of units similar in concept to common stock and preferred stock. The family must decide whether participants get special rights and whether all classes have the same say in the partnership.

Expense Considerations   Families always look to keep costs down. Paying for the accounting and tax filings for these structures is a serious considera-tion, as is the ability to provide investment flexibility.

Timing of Entry and Exit from Partnerships   A key consideration when forming partnerships is when to allow new members in or existing members out. The greater the flexibility in allowing members in and out, the more frequently an account can be rebalanced. This decision also impacts other important benefits of a pool like liquidity discounts, creditor protection, or the ability to borrow against partnership interests.

Transition   Transition involves the ability to impose restrictions on the transfer of interests in the pool. An example would be the ability to transfer an interest to younger generations and still maintain control.

Contributions   A new partnership needs to include language speaking to the frequency and timing at which a member can make contributions into the pool. Also, whether contributions can be in cash or contributed property is an important consideration to note since the complexity of the accounting increases if a member contributes securities in lieu of cash.

Distributions   On a periodic basis, the partnership will most likely distribute income (at a minimum to cover the tax liability passed through on the K-1) and occasionally may decide to distribute cash or property. An agreement needs to specify how this is done.

Withdrawals and Transfers   This issue concerns when to allow a member of the pool to leave and whether that departure can be a complete or partial withdrawal. There are benefits to having multiple participants in a partnership for co-investing, but when a meaningful participant in a pool divests, those benefits may be lost (i.e., per capita management fees may increase as the size of a pool decreases). To help manage the impact of divestment, most agreements have a notification time frame (a 90-day notice) clause with the proviso that the member in control has the right to waive the notification. This allows the general partner a little time to make the appropriate adjustments, if needed.

Cash or Accrual Accounting   Accounting for the partnerships can be done on a cash basis or accrual basis. There is no right or wrong way, but tax rules prevent families from switching methodologies in the same year.

Allocations   Allocation of income and expenses is essential to partnership accounting, and to ensure fairness there needs to be language governing these allocations. In addition, the allocation of gains and losses can be handled in several different manners: aggregation, layering, or the traditional pro rata method. If the agreement is silent on this point, it is usually left to the tax matters partner or managing partner-member to make these decisions; most new partnership agreements, however, spell this out.

Valuations   All pools need to provide updates to the values each member has in the pool. How values are determined should be clearly prescribed. For example, prices for securities might be calculated using the closing price as listed by major independent pricing services. When prices and quotes are not available from independent pricing services, quotes from the investment managers or other authorized parties can be used. Valuations can be calculated daily (like mutual funds), weekly, monthly, quarterly, or annually. The more frequent the valuation, the greater the cost of accounting. At a minimum, valuations must be calculated on the basis of the limited partner's right to subscribe and redeem. If a pool holds illiquid investments, this can cause delays in the calculation of unit values, which in turn may hold up asset allocation decisions and other important matters.

Performance Measurement Considerations   Each member of the pool is entitled to know how her investments are performing. Performance by manager, style, asset allocation strategy, and total partnership is important regardless of the option chosen. If illiquid investments are included in a pool, then further performance considerations are involved.

Administration and Recordkeeping   Most agreements spell out the frequency of reporting on each partner's participation in the pool. Most pools make reports available on a quarterly basis to allow the participants to make any adjustment to their tax estimates.

Special Elections   The agreement must specify whether it allows for special elections under Section 754 of the IRS code. An example seen in a number of these agreements regards a step-up in the basis upon the death of a partner. In this election, the cost basis is reset to the value at the date of death. You should confer with your tax adviser when considering the 754 election.

Passive Activity Losses   Passive activities are trade or business activities in which one does not materially participate. Losses from passive activities and how they should be treated should also be covered in the agreement.

Authority to Act   Making decisions on behalf of a pool usually rests with the general partner, who maintains control of the management and conducts the business of the pool; the tax matters partner, who is responsible for all matters relating to the tax treatment of the pool; and the managing member, who is empowered to manage the activities.

Succession Planning   There should be language in the agreement that outlines how the pool will be operated if one of the individuals with control resigns or is incapacitated.

CONCLUSION

Gaining knowledge of back office issues such as selecting a custodian and creating an investment vehicle structures is one of the less glamorous activities of the UAC advisers but is needed nonetheless. The right custodial relationship and investment vehicle structure can have a very positive economic impact on the families being served; conversely, having an inefficient back office structure can be costly. As with other areas that we have discussed, bringing in professionals to assist in these areas is not only the right thing to do, it is fairly easy to do because there are numerous experts in the field. We move next to the all-important task of the considerations that go into creating a family office.

CHAPTER 14

Considerations for Creating a Family Office

Riches are for spending.
—Sir Francis Bacon

Creating a family office is a heady subject. There are practices of major advisory firms devoted to family offices: tax, estate planning, banking, and investments. There are also networking organizations, executive recruiters, conferences, and outsource service providers (bill pay, dog walking, etc.)—and then there are the family offices themselves. The subject matter of this chapter could fill an entire book. I just stick to some key topics so that you can become familiar with what families consider when deciding whether to create a family office. The main issues are defining the family office, reasons to create a family office and some of the challenges involved, administrative considerations, and finally, forming a private trust company. I focus in this chapter only on single family offices (SFOs), as opposed to multifamily or any other type of family office. Before we get into these key considerations, a brief introduction to the subject is in order.

Going back to a concept I discussed in Chapter 4, families of substantial wealth want to avoid the dreaded "shirtsleeves to shirtsleeves in three generations" disease that has plagued many once-great fortunes. Recall that the number of wealthy families that have maintained prosperity for three or four generations is modest. A prime benefit of a family office is that it can protect families from the dissipation of wealth decades after the original creator of the wealth has passed on. There are good examples of both successful and not-so-successful wealth-preserving families, even between branches of the same family. One such example is that of the offspring of Cornelius Vanderbilt, founder of the old New York Central Railroad.

Since 1949, William A.M. Burden & Co., a New York–based family office group, has been successfully guiding one branch of the Vanderbilt fortune, the Burdens.[1] Six generations after Vanderbilt made his fortune, the Burdens continue to grow and prosper.

By pooling their money and following a sound investment strategy, 43 of the descendants of the Commodore's great-great-grandson William A. M. Burden—Kellys, Rosengartens, MacDonalds, and Burdens—remain individually and collectively wealthy. Other non-Burden Vanderbilt descendants' wealth has greatly diminished. What was missing for the non-Burden descendants? They lacked the three things that most SFOs exist for:

1. A mechanism to take control of the family's financial and administrative affairs.
2. Garnering superior investment results and taking advantage of asset size to achieve economies of scale.
3. A venue to provide family members with customized services such as tax management, philanthropy facilitation, and education.

This chapter will help you understand what a family office is and how families go about deciding if a single family office is for them. A common question at this stage is "How much money does it take for an SFO to make economic sense?" Stephen Martiros and Todd Millay of CCC Alliance in Boston have the following answer to this question: "We define 'family office–scale wealth' as the amount of financial assets required to retain well qualified, full-time, in-house professionals (e.g., accountants, lawyers, investment advisors) regardless of the actual structure used. This is generally estimated to be from $50 million to $100 million in assets. Regardless of whether they have established a formal family office, any family with over $50 million in assets should understand the framework of a family office."[2]

Another perspective on the subject comes from a 2008 study performed by Campden Research and Merrill Lynch on European family offices:[3]

> It all depends on the family office strategy and the services that the family wants, but it must be around the €250 million to €300 million mark to support the minimum €3 million cost base needed to support a professional asset management operation. Estimates of €100 million to €150 million and sometimes more are typically snobbish and just plain wrong. You can run a family office with assets of between €30 million and €50 million; it all depends on how many people the family office is providing services to, what kinds of services, and the balance of in-house and outsourced services.

It appears that CCC and the Campden/Merrill study have fairly consistent answers on this subject: It depends! So, let's try to get some clarity now by defining what we mean by a family office.

WHAT IS A FAMILY OFFICE?

We will focus on SFOs in this chapter, but this is not the only type of family office, and it's good to have a working knowledge of all types. Prince and Grove researched over 650 family offices and identified three different types of family office structures: the classic single family office, in which one wealthy family handles all of their affairs internally; the multi-family office (MFO), which caters to more than one family, from five or six to upwards of 50; and a commercial family office (CFO), which is primarily a wealth management firm that has created a platform to provide family office services with considerably fewer overall assets.[4] Within the SFO world, we can refine our definition even further by again turning to Stephen and Todd from CCC. They note that each SFO is designed for the level of wealth, type of assets, complexity, and objectives of the family it serves. While the specific design and activities of family offices vary widely, they can be categorized on the basis of activities performed in-house. In "A Framework for Understanding Family Office Trends," Stephen Martiros and Todd Millay have this to say:

> Family offices follow three templates: administrative, hybrid, or comprehensive. In an administrative family office, advisory and investment management services are managed through contracts with external service providers. The administrative family office typically directly employs staff to provide some level of bookkeeping, tax, or administrative services—often on a part-time basis. Families that utilize an administrative family office template typically have an asset base of $50 million to several hundred million dollars. Overhead costs for this model range from $100,000 to $500,000.

> The hybrid family office keeps functions strategic to the family's objectives in-house, and outsources nonstrategic functions. Some families hire family members for certain strategic activities, when the family member has a demonstrated expertise or when privacy and continuity of management are top concerns. In addition to administrative functions, hybrid family offices employ experts in tax, legal, and/or asset allocation. Certain investment management functions may be kept in-house particularly where it leverages a

family's industry expertise—e.g., real estate investing. Families that utilize a hybrid family office template typically have an asset base of $100 million to $1 billion. Overhead costs for this model range from $500,000 to $2,000,000 or more.

The comprehensive family office is designed to provide services for families who desire the maximum degree of control, security, and privacy. All functions, including administrative, tax, legal, risk management, and core investment management, are provided by in-house employees. Specialized investment management activities such as hedge fund, venture capital, private equity, or emerging market investments may be sourced externally depending on each family's objectives, budget, and their ability to recruit and retain such talent. Families that utilize a comprehensive template typically have assets greater than $1 billion. Overhead costs for this model range from $1,000,000 to $10,000,000 or more when performance bonuses are included.[5]

CHALLENGES OF WEALTH

Which type of SFO is appropriate often depends on what objectives a family is trying to achieve. These objectives, in turn, are often related to the challenges that the family faces. Family offices are often designed to overcome some of the invisible forces that can work to dissipate wealth; money alone cannot sustain a family's legacy. Families need to create an environment where members understand what values they want to preserve. Next-generation family members need a venue in which they can take on the responsibilities of stewardship of the family's wealth. Without an appreciation for the responsibility of ownership, wealth can dissipate. Beyond just taking responsibility, the family needs leadership. The family office can help develop competent leaders across family branches and new generations of a family. Families can sometimes grow faster than the wealth can sustain the lifestyle of the entire family. If wealth is to keep up with the growth of the family, risks will need to be taken. A family office can help family members understand and balance risk and opportunity across the family's assets. One of the most potentially debilitating of forces of wealth is that it can zap beneficiaries' motivation. Family office services and staff can help empower beneficiaries to achieve individual personal goals.

One of the most important elements of family sustenance over generations is a proper family governance structure. Family offices can be instrumental in executing a family governance structure that can develop a strategic direction for the family, along with a decision-making process that the family will support. As part of the long-term planning process, I encourage families to establish an effective family governance process or a strategic plan to help grow the human capital that exists in every family. Family members with the aptitude and interest should be offered the opportunity to become part of the family business, which in this case is managing wealth. It is inevitable that family members will have varying levels of interest and skills, so the process needs to be flexible enough to accept involvement or delegation to other family members. In all cases, the emotional and intellectual development of family members is critical to the prosperity of future generations. A governance system needs to be in place that will stand the test of time—that is, as family members enter and leave the family, a structure needs to be in place to ensure that the family understands its history, legacy, and values. Figure 14.1 shows the importance of various factors to families considering establishing a family office.

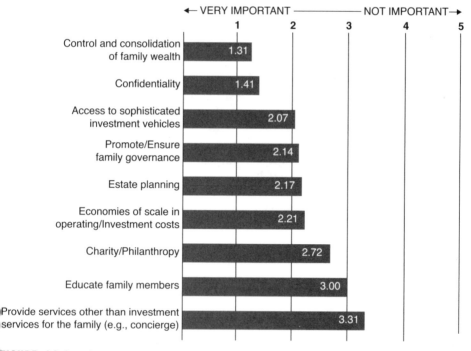

FIGURE 14.1 The Importance of Various Factors when a Family is Establishing a Family Office

Source: The Merrill Lynch/Campden Research European Single Family Office Survey, 2008.

PRACTICAL REASONS TO CREATE A FAMILY OFFICE

Just as there are different types of family offices, there are different reasons why families might want to create family offices. I have seen over the years many family office structures designed to meet numerous objectives. For those families that have been managing wealth for a generation or longer, the family office process typically consists of an arrangement wherein staff perform tasks dictated by past and present needs. Occasionally, these structures fail to evolve along with the family's present and future needs, as families and assets have grown. Clearly, as families' needs change, so too should the family office structure. Given the ever-changing composition of families with significant means (births, divorces, graduations, etc.), many family offices are continually searching for effective long-term processes for serving their family clients, in regard to both administration and investment decision making. The processes that work for one family may not necessarily work for another. To act against the hidden forces that can dissipate wealth, there are some practical, proactive steps that families can take to help themselves by creating a family office. These are asset management proficiency, economies of scale, education, and philanthropy management.

Asset Management Proficiency

To endure over multiple generations, wealth requires diligent oversight. Whether they like it or not, family members need to engage in the financial management process, and those who are not interested in doing so will likely be at a disadvantage. Blocking and tackling issues such as portfolio diversification, personal financial planning, and tax compliance can often be efficiently and effectively delivered by centralizing these activities in a family office. Proper accounting of assets, performance measurement, and consolidation of asset management are critical but often lacking. Family offices can help create the structure needed to gain proper asset management proficiency.

Economies of Scale

One of the best ways to leverage the family office setting is to gain cost savings through aggregation of a family's financial services, such as consulting fees, tax compliance, master custody, insurance, and so on. Also, associated buying power can assist in gaining access to the best strategic advisers, such as investment consultants, estate planners, tax planners, and philanthropic advisers. With the right oversight, the family office can provide individual family members with customized services by aggregating services that are common to all family members. Doing this effectively, however, requires experienced family office professionals that can properly diagnose financial issues and recommend good alternatives to family members.

Education

Educating and training younger generation family members on financial matters is very helpful and allows them to become functioning members of the financial family. Sometimes, these family members can end up working in the family office. The SFO can plan and coordinate family educational meetings and other events to foster continued family group interaction. By virtue of its office space, the family office offers family members the opportunity to conduct educational activities.

Philanthropy Management

Family offices can be critical in overseeing mission development, grant-making, foundation management, and reporting. By centralizing philan-thropic activities and finding issues of common concern, families can have a greater impact. At the same time, successful philanthropic efforts in family offices design their mission to be flexible enough to respond to individual family members' needs. When family foundations are formally managed through the family office, younger family members can be moved to get in-volved in philanthropy. Figure 14.2 shows some additional practical reasons that families set up family offices.

CHALLENGES OF RUNNING A FAMILY OFFICE

Running a family office is difficult. There are a host of challenges that families face when establishing an SFO, and I discuss four major ones: attracting and retaining talented staff, regulation and compliance, family dynamics, and back office functions.

Attracting and Retaining Talented Staff

A full-service family office can offer an array of services in-house, includ-ing financial planning, investment management, estate and trust advice, in-surance and risk management, philanthropic oversight, and other personal services. The proper delivery of these services requires talented individuals. Because SFOs are usually small organizations, attracting and retaining talent can be challenging. In fact, according to the 2008 Merrill Lynch/Campden Research European Single Family Office Survey, this was the most

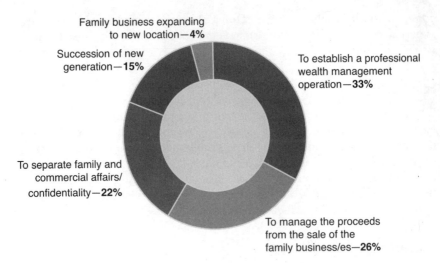

FIGURE 14.2   Practical Reasons for Establishing a Family Office
Source: The Merrill Lynch/Campden Research European Single Family Office
Survey, 2008.

challenging issue faced by respondents.[6] This topic is discussed in more
detail later in the chapter.

Regulation and Compliance

If an SFO serves multiple family members, it may need to be registered or
regulated. Family offices organized as registered investment advisory firms
are regulated by the Securities and Exchange Commission. Family offices
organized as private trust companies are regulated by banking laws. While
there are benefits to regulation, there are also risks. Improper family office
oversight could result in negative publicity or adverse legal action. Assuming
the family office hires a staff, it takes on the legal responsibilities of being an
employer—meaning that it must now deal with laws regarding employment,
antidiscrimination, compensation, and much more.

Family Dynamics

When a family creates its own office, it takes on the responsibility of managing complex intrafamily personal relationships. This can sometimes be
tricky. For example, if a family member is invited run the family office and
is not properly trained to do so, family members may squabble and personality conflicts may arise. In addition, these complex family dynamics can

make it difficult for outside professionals to perform well because the family office can become a venue for family members to act out their conflicts.

Back Office Processes

An often overlooked aspect of the successful SFO is the right back office to support the complex financial structures of wealthy families. Many families use spreadsheet-based programs to keep track of family wealth, to their disadvantage. Families need to upgrade to software that can manage complex, intergenerational investment programs for members. Affluent families often have numerous investment relationships, and asset allocation and rebalancing are difficult to determine without the right back office or technology solution. Family members are demanding that they get information at their fingertips on brokerage, trust accounts, and pooled entities. Without the proper back office solution, information flow is poor, and prudent decisions are often not possible.

SERVICES PROVIDED BY A FAMILY OFFICE

As we learned earlier, there are three types of family offices: administrative, hybrid, or comprehensive. The services offered by family offices vary, depending on the goals of the family group, the size of the family, and the amount of the assets. For the administrative family office, the focus is compliance. This involves recordkeeping and reporting required of the family. Investment services are completely outsourced. In-house services associated with an administrative office are the following:

- Bookkeeping.
- Oversight of master custody services.
- Delivery of consolidated financial reporting.
- Coordination of pooled fund accounting.

At the hybrid family office, services can include those offered at an administrative office but can also include personal financial services such as tax compliance, budgeting and cash planning, and even personal security. In this situation, most of the investment management functions are outsourced to third-party providers, but some investment functions, such as asset allocation, may be done in-house. Hybrid family office services delivered in-house include:

- Tax compliance.
- Budgeting and cash planning.

- Coordinating personal banking.
- Personal security.
- Paying bills.
- Asset allocation.

The last type of single family office is the comprehensive office. Here, all functions of the administrative and hybrid offices are performed in-house, as are core investment functions such as investment policy, asset allocation review and rebalancing, manager selection, and even security selection. An investment consultant may be hired who will in turn recommend other specialized investment managers such as venture capital funds and hedge funds. The comprehensive office typically employs a Chief Investment Officer, and that person leads a staff charged with oversight of the investment process. In addition, the comprehensive family office will deliver services for wealth transfer, generational planning, and philanthropy, and can coordinate the delivery of these services to each family member. The following is a list of services that a comprehensive office will perform beyond those listed earlier.

- Investment policy oversight.
- Selection of investment managers.
- After-tax performance measurement and analysis.
- Rebalancing the strategic asset allocation.
- Wealth transfer.
- Executing economies of scale purchasing.
- Trustee responsibilities.
- Administration and compliance of philanthropy.
- Philanthropic grant-making coordination.
- Philanthropic program analysis and assessment.
- Integration of the various disciplines for each individual family member.

It is important to note that although there are three categories of family offices, there are many overlapping versions of these types.

ADMINISTRATIVE CONSIDERATIONS FOR ESTABLISHING A FAMILY OFFICE

As we saw in the last section, the decision to deliver services in-house or externally is a critical one that requires careful planning and oversight. In any case, family offices should endeavor to control the quality of any service that is delivered to their clients, as best they can. Naturally, this is easier when those services are delivered in-house. But if the family office is to provide

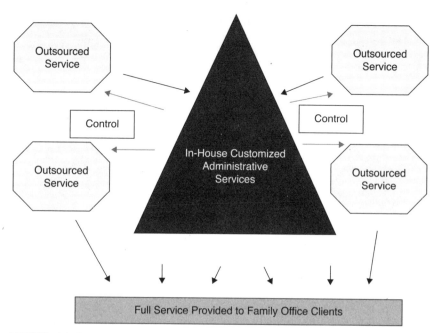

FIGURE 14.3 Coordination of In-House and Outsourced Services for Family Office Clients

customized, high quality services to its clients, coordination and control are essential. Figure 14.3 depicts the process of coordinating in-house and outsourced services.

To get an idea of what families do in practice, we can turn again to the 2008 Merrill Lynch/Campden survey. Thirty families of varying size across Europe (see Figure 14.4) were questioned about their practices of delivering services in-house versus outsourcing. Figure 14.5 shows the results, which demonstrate that family offices rely significantly on third-party providers. Offices that wish to have the maximum degree of control, security, and privacy will deliver more of these services in-house.

Costs and Pricing of Family Office Services

Believe it or not, families often forget that someone actually has to pay for the services of a family office! The type of family office structure will naturally dictate the cost of operation. As we learned earlier, overhead costs for an administrative office are about $100,000 to $500,000. Hybrid family offices cost anywhere from $500,000 to $2 million to run, while a comprehensive

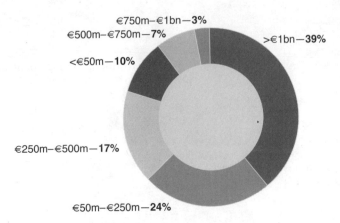

FIGURE 14.4 Size of Family Offices in the ML/Campden 2008 SFO Survey
Source: The Merrill Lynch/Campden Research European Single Family Office Survey, 2008.

office can be upward of $10 million. The Merrill Lynch/Campden survey provides some good data on the costs of running a family office. Surveyors determined that the average cost of running a single family office is 62 basis points. The details behind these numbers were:

- For single family offices of less than €250 million, the cost is 89 basis points, and over €1 billion it is 48 basis points.

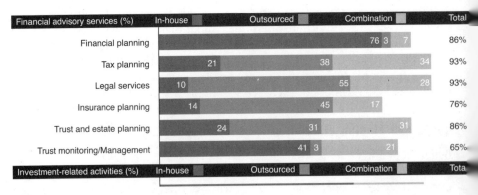

FIGURE 14.5 Outsourced versus In-House Delivery of Family Office Services
Source: The Merrill Lynch/Campden Research European Single Family Office Survey, 200

- Outsourced services account for less than 25 percent of costs for 58 percent of single family offices, although they account for more than 75 percent of costs for 21 percent of participants.
- Single family offices with an internal investment management function need to have at least €250 million to justify the €2.5 million to €3 million spend required.
- Single family offices that outsource the bulk of their services can be supported by a lower base of assets under management (roughly €50 million to €100 million).[7]

Family Office Fee Structures

The family office is usually paid for in whatever way makes the most financial sense for all clients involved. Some key factors that are usually considered when developing a fee structure are simplicity, fairness, tax efficiency, asset size, and services provided. For simplicity's sake, fees need to be straightforward and transparent, and they need to be accounted for in an efficient way. If a fee structure can't be explained or calculated easily, problems will arise. Fairness is obvious. If some family members are resource hogs while others are subsidizers, tensions may result. Some form of tracking mechanism may be required to ensure fairness. Younger members of the family may be discouraged from joining the family office if they are being charged unfairly; this prevents younger generations from getting involved with the office, which can be a serious long-term negative. Regarding tax efficiency, those entities that can deduct fees on their income tax forms should be allocated the maximum fees. Additionally, fees can be allocated to older family members so as to minimize estate taxes. Asset-based fees are typical in the family office. There is an inherent fairness to this method, and it is easy to calculate and administer. Asset-based fees do not, however, measure other services being used. Some offices will therefore charge a flat fee based on an estimate of the complexity of the client's needs and the time required to meet those needs. Other families will charge an asset-based fee and then have an a la carte menu of services from which clients can choose, charged on an hourly basis. The allocation of family office costs to clients is complex and often ambiguous. In practice, the best way for a family to determine whether their cost structure reflects reality is to compare the cost of the services they receive to the cost of purchasing those services externally.

Attracting and Retaining Talented Staff

As we saw earlier in the chapter, attracting and retaining talented staff members is challenging. In fact, this issue is of paramount importance to

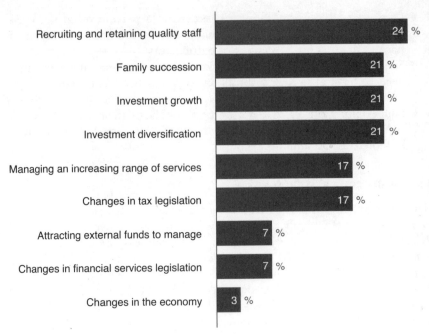

FIGURE 14.6   Key Challenges Facing Family Offices
Source: The Merrill Lynch/Campden Research European Single Family Office
Survey, 2008.

family offices, as can be seen in Figure 14.6, a summary of key challenges
faced by family offices today.

One of the ways in which family offices can solve this problem is by
permitting the family office staff to participate in the success of investment
partnership strategies. There has been a growing trend of establishing a link
between the family office and family pools. The concept of rewarding the
office for handling investments can help keep the office staff engaged while
allowing for the expensing of certain payments. The following scenario is
an example of how a family office could structure this relationship through
a profit-sharing arrangement: The family office enters into a management
service agreement with the family investment partnership. As a result, the
office becomes a management company for the investment partnership and
is responsible for paying for the costs of managing the partnership's assets.
In return for accepting this responsibility, the management company accepts
an allocation of profit (*profits interest*) from the investment partnership.

The economic considerations of this arrangement revolve around the
formula(s) and the percentage(s) used to calculate the profits interest. It can

be a simple single-tier calculation of a percentage of the annual profits each year, or a complex multi-tier calculation that uses multiple formulas and percentages. For example, a management company may receive a first-tier priority allocation consisting of a percentage of the assets under management. A second-tier allocation may also be employed, taking a percentage of the residual profits (if any) after the first-tier allocation. Other economic considerations in this structure would include whether to use a high watermark and whether to make the formula cumulative if profits are insufficient to cover a first-tier asset base formula.

Some income tax considerations include whether the management company will be respected by the IRS as a trade or business as well as being respected as a separate and distinct partner in the investment partnership. Some other considerations include the following:

- Ownership of the management company (usually the younger generation).
- Choice of entity for the management company (S-corps are the entity of choice).
- Whether the management company will make an initial capital contribution (usually at least 1 percent of the investment partnership's asset value).
- Whether to include or remove hard-to-value assets (typically remove real estate and private equity investments).
- Funding working capital cash flow needs of the management company (usually by way of a line of credit).
- Whether or not the management company needs to register as an investment advisory company (usually not an issue for the federal government, but it could be problematic for some states).

The major benefits of using incentives such as this include offering key employees of the management company economic rewards as well as an incentive system that aligns the family's goals and objectives with those of the key employees. It also provides the family with the ability to transfer entrepreneurial risk of funding the investment advisory and management cost necessary to manage the assets of the investment partnership to the management company. Another tax benefit to the structure might be wealth transfer if the younger generation owns the management company and the management company is successful at building up equity over the years. The management company may also be able to take an ordinary deduction (above-the-line) for the costs it incurs under the management agreement, while the investment partnership will most likely treat these costs as a

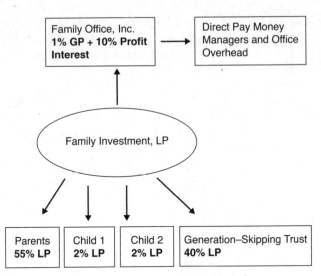

FIGURE 14.7 Profit Interests Structure Example
Source: BNY Mellon Bank.

portfolio deduction, not deductible for the alternative minimum tax, and subject to a 2 percent of AGI limitation for regular income tax purposes. Figure 14.7 depicts an example of the aforementioned arrangement.

CONSIDERATIONS FOR ESTABLISHING A PRIVATE TRUST COMPANY

As you learned in Chapter 1, there is a substantial amount of money held in trust in the United States, and some families have the majority of their assets in trust. Oversight of these assets is usually done by either individual trustees or *corporate* (commercial trust company) trustees. Despite the oversight benefits of a corporate trustee, most wealthy U.S. families choose individuals rather than trust companies to serve as trustees, even for complex trusts holding very substantial assets. Why? For one, there is a general feeling among wealthy families that corporate trustees have suffered from a lack of continuity, and therefore quality, of late. Convenience is also a culprit here. An individual can serve as trustee without meeting any regulatory qualifications, and without being licensed or demonstrating any special skills or experience. There is a middle-ground solution that wealthy families are turning to called a private trust company (PTC). A private trust company is, essentially, a company formed for the specific purpose of acting as trustee of a single trust, or a group of related trusts. I now review the factors that are relevant in making the choice to form a PTC rather than having individual trustees.

Continuity

Relying on individual trustees (ITs) to properly oversee trust assets over the course of time makes a large assumption: a continuous flow of qualified trustees. At any given time, ITs can be prevented from doing their jobs by personal issues such as careers, physical location, health, age, motivation, and competing commitments. Moreover, being an IT involves some level of personal liability, which can discourage some from becoming trustees in the first place (although most families and trusts provide indemnities to the individual trustees because insurance coverage is often limited or unavailable). A PTC can obviate reliance on individual trustees for continuity.

Regulation

ITs require little in the way of formal government regulation, but do have a fiduciary duty to future generations. Trust companies are subject to government rules and regulations (capital requirements, accounting, etc.), which increase cost but improve oversight. What is the right balance? No one wants to deal with excessive regulation and additional costs, but sometimes these are warranted. Although a trustee's job is routine, more formality brings more organization, and an organized process in trust management can bring better decisions and prevent mistakes. A corporate trustee does not guarantee results, but following a prudent process is highly recommended—and that process should be documented. The incremental cost and burden of a private trust company is real, but it can be worth the price to get better, more organized oversight.

Control

Often, the family's overarching desire is for more control over its assets and family office processes. But the lack of oversight over ITs can sometimes inhibit this control. A PTC often encourages broad family participation and communication on trust matters, which improves oversight and control. So long as the PTC structure grows and adapts with the changing needs of new generations of the family, it should be effective. However, a PTC also needs to maintain control over personal information to prevent unnecessary disclosure to family members. Before establishing trustees, families need to

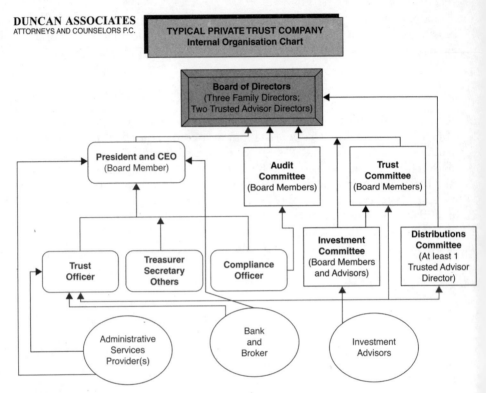

FIGURE 14.8 Example of a Private Trust Company Structure
Source: 2006-7 Duncan and Associates A&C P.C., All Rights Reserved.

evaluate which method will be better for maintaining privacy. Figure 14.8 shows the level of control that a PTC brings.

Taxes

The type of trustees the family chooses also has tax implications at both the federal and state level. Some states tax income earned by trusts according to where the individual trustees reside, and many states apply multiple tests to determine whether they will tax a trust's income. These issues are easier to manage if the trustee is a PTC. At the federal level, the expense of operating a trust company is much more likely to be fully deductible than the expense of ITs. Of particular relevance here is the deductibility of investment advisory fees. These issues can be suitably addressed whether the family uses a PTC or an IT, but a PTC can perhaps bring a more organized framework for maximizing tax benefits.

CONCLUSION

Establishing a family office is a serious decision requiring the consideration of many complex factors. By knowing these key considerations, UAC advisers can be better equipped to help their clients weigh the pros and cons of setting up a family office. As is always the case, make sure to bring in professional help if the conversation on this subject goes beyond the scope of your capabilities. Your clients will appreciate your candor and recognize that you are doing the right thing for them by bringing in additional help.

CH

Wealth Transfer Planning

Riches ... very seldom remain long in the same family.
—Adam Smith

I have discussed throughout this book how nonfinancial issues can torpedo a family's wealth accumulation. A potentially even more dangerous wealth dissipater, transfer taxes, can have a seriously negative effect as well. Without proper planning, wealth can evaporate quickly. Consider that as families move from one generation to the next, a typical family's membership doubles. The family's wealth needs to be spread over more per capita if the wealth doesn't double as well, net of spending, taxes, and inflation. Let's take the following simple example: suppose a family starts with 15 family members, and that number doubles every 25 years. Further suppose that the net growth of the family's asset is 2 percent after spending, inflation, and taxes—not an unreasonable amount. Lastly, suppose that the family does no wealth transfer planning and the parents die after 35 years. A chart illustrating this family's wealth might look like Figure 15.1.

Advisers who want to work with UACs need to have at least a basic understanding of estate planning strategies, which are at their core legal strategies designed to mitigate taxes, enhance wealth, and protect the dissipation of assets. Complex planning is naturally the domain of trust and estate lawyers; hundreds of different permutations of well-established wealth transfer tools can be implemented in various combinations to efficiently transfer wealth from one generation to another, and these are little understood by the average financial adviser. There are, however, some very basic ones that can transfer substantial amounts of wealth, and UAC advisers need to be conversant in these basic planning tools and have an understanding of popular advance planning techniques as well. As we have discussed earlier, bringing in a specialist is the best way to add value to areas that are beyond the skill

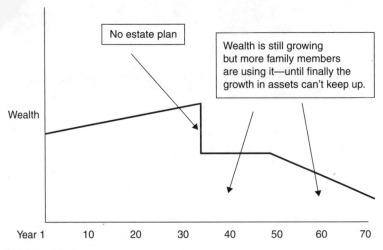

FIGURE 15.1 Example of Wealth Dissipation

set of the UAC adviser. Because every wealth transfer plan is customized, UAC advisers need to leverage their experience with the client to help analyze a situation along with one or more trained wealth transfer professionals to create a solution. It is important to remember that wealth transfer plans must have a clear business objective and benefit. These advanced planning strategies are not supposed to be tax shelters, but business transactions with a subsidiary tax benefit. It is essential, therefore, that wealth transfer plans are categorized as bright-line transactions—meaning that there is no question about their legitimacy—and this standard must be upheld by all professionals that the UAC adviser brings into a client relationship.

Many advisers don't know that a significant amount of wealth can be transferred using the very simplest of estate planning strategies, such as taking advantage of the annual gift tax exclusion amount (currently $12,000) and the lifetime gift tax exemption (currently $1 million).[1] Thus, this chapter is a review of some of the basics. It also delves into some advanced topics such as planning with life insurance, estate freezing techniques, and family limited partnerships.

Given the vast array of wealth transfer options available and the number of decisions to make, UACs are often bewildered by the integration of estate planning with investment strategies and tax advice. This bewilderment can be mitigated if the adviser can make complex concepts easy to comprehend. This chapter should be able to help you do that. To start with, let's analyze what UACs can do with their wealth once they have all the material things they desire (homes, cars, airplanes, jewelry, etc.) and enough money has been carved out for basic living expenses (with an emergency reserve). With what's left over, there are really only three basic things that can be done: pursue charitable endeavors, pay taxes, or pass it on to living and potential future generations. Many families struggle when deciding among these three areas, especially about how much they want to pass on to their children while making sure that family members develop values, morals, and a desire to be productive members of society. Some families are charitably inclined while others are less interested in philanthropy. Most clients want to minimize tax payments, but you might be surprised by the occasional family that wants to pay more than their fair share of taxes. Many clients are stuck in limbo because they are fearful of committing to a wealth transfer plan when they haven't yet decided on a personal spending plan or amounts of charitable giving. Lastly, some families are fearful of causing disputes among heirs.

Before I jump in with the basic techniques, I first discuss the reality of wealth transfer and the opportunity to be of service. The bottom line is that UACs are not planning as much as they should. Evidence of this is provided in a 2008 study done by Bank of America Private Wealth Management, which finds that the majority of owners of ultra-high-net-worth family businesses are leaving their professional and personal interests vulnerable through inadequate business succession, asset protection, and estate planning. While these families are highly successful in building and managing their businesses, they are often less successful when it comes to transitioning their companies from one generation to the next, with only 15 percent of family-owned companies lasting past the second generation. Conducted by Prince & Associates, Inc. and Campden Research, the study surveyed 242 second- and third-generation business owners with interests valued at a minimum of $300 million and mean value approaching $730 million.

The study reports that "Owners of ultra-high-net-worth family businesses often have a team of advisors focusing on an array of needs such as wealth management, tax strategies and succession planning, without addressing the bigger picture. Given the near-term and long-term complexities with managing a successful family business, it is crucial that these families think about the wealth tied to their business and their personal fortune in a holistic, strategic manner."[2] Many clients avoid wealth transfer planning because it involves the subject of death and funerals. What clients need to keep in mind is that wealth transfer planning focuses on life after death. An effective estate plan designates who gets what and when they get it. Without a proper plan, this may not happen, especially if the courts have to decide. Many families become divided after the death of a parent because of the lack of a proper estate plan. UAC advisers should recognize that they can be of significant value to their clients by asking questions and recognizing that planning needs to take place.

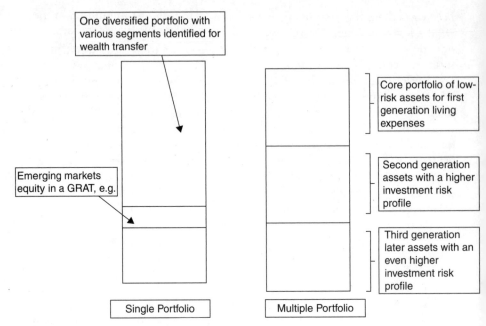

FIGURE 15.2   Different Investment Portfolios Accomplishing Similar Wealth Transfer Objectives

As a final introductory note, readers should know that there is no one right way to design an estate plan vis-à-vis the family's investment portfolio or the notion of setting aside a core amount of money with which to live out the rest of their lives. Some clients choose to have a single pool of capital that has a single asset allocation with embedded wealth transfer strategies. For example, a portfolio like this could have emerging markets stocks in a wealth transfer vehicle such as a grantor-retained annuity trust (defined later). Others may designate different investment portfolios with different asset allocation strategies to serve various wealth transfer purposes. Figure 15.2 illustrates this idea. It is important to know that both methods can be effective and it is typically the preference of the clients, often depending on the existing investment vehicle structure, that determines how a given family approaches this decision.

ESTATE PLANNING BASICS

A basic estate plan includes a will or living trust, an advance health care directive (also known as a durable power of attorney for health care), and a general durable power of attorney. Beyond these fundamentals, there are a variety of basic gifting techniques that can be used to minimize federal transfer taxes, of which there are three to be aware of: the estate tax, the gift tax, and the generation-skipping transfer tax. The *estate tax,* currently at a top rate of 45 percent, is a federal government tax that applies upon death to the transfer of assets to someone other than a spouse or charity (there may also be state estate taxes, but these go beyond the scope of this chapter). Currently, there is a $2 million estate tax exemption amount. The *gift tax* is a tax that is levied on lifetime gifts that are in excess of the gift tax exemption amount, which is currently $1 million. Nonexempt gifts are taxed at a top rate of 45 percent. The *generation-skipping transfer (GST) tax* is a 45 percent tax placed on transfers above the GST exemption amount of $2 million for those families intent on transferring money to multiple generations. Taken together, these taxes make effective wealth transfer planning difficult. A simple, yet effective method of minimizing these taxes is to give assets away to beneficiaries while the donor is still living. The following discussion will assume that we are discussing residual monies outside of those needed for living expenses.

Annual Exclusion Gifts

Under the current transfer tax scheme, a donor may give $12,000 each year to any beneficiary, without any gift tax consequences. There are also other payments, such as school tuition and medical expenses, that can be made without incurring a gift tax so long as payments are made *directly* to the education institution or medical provider by the donor. Let's look at a simple example of giving away the annual exemption of $12,000. Suppose an older couple has two children, each of whom is married, and each of whom has one young child. This couple could give away a total of $144,000 each year without using up any part of their lifetime exemption by giving $12,000 to each child, each child-in-law, and each grandchild, for a total of six individual recipients from each grandparent ($72,000 in gifts from the grandmother and $72,000 in gifts from the grandfather). If this set of grandparents did this each year for 20 years, assuming a 7 percent compounded rate of return before taxes, they could transfer over $6.3 million to their beneficiaries tax free. A gift to a 529 college savings plan is also an effective transfer mechanism. In the initial year, a gift of up to five times the annual gift tax exclusion amount (five times $12,000 at current rates) can be made without the imposition of a gift tax. This uses up an equal amount of the annual gift tax exemption for the year of the gift plus the next four years. It must be noted though, that if the donor dies within the five-year period after the transfer, a proportionate amount of the gift will be included in the donor's estate for estate tax purposes.

Lifetime Gift Tax Exemption

To some families, $6.3 million doesn't really make a dent in the estate. The next basic technique involves gifting beyond the annual exemption gifts just discussed and into something called the *lifetime gift tax exemption* (LGTE). While the current $2 million exemption for gift and estate tax in total increased to $3.5 million by 2009, the LGTE is scheduled to remain at $1 million throughout this period. This exemption amount arises by way of an estate or gift tax credit given during lifetime or at death without any estate or gift tax. Although it may seem counterintuitive, it is best to use the LGTE as soon as is practical. Many people assume that they should avoid making taxable gifts, and leave their assets to their heirs at death because they incorrectly think that it makes the most sense to delay paying taxes as long as possible. It is best to make gifts while paying current taxes because transferring assets early allows the income and growth on the transferred assets to accrue to beneficiaries without transfer taxes and without increasing the size of the donor's estate. To demonstrate the effectiveness of this strategy, assuming a 7 percent compounded rate of return before taxes, a $1 million LGTE gift removes over $3.8 million over 20 years from the taxable estate of the donor.

Advanced Gifting Concepts and Strategies

Which assets are best to give to beneficiaries? To answer this question, one needs to consider the cost basis of the asset under consideration for gifting. Upon death, the assets in an estate receive a step-up (or step-down) in basis to their value as of the date of death (implying that if the asset is sold shortly after death, there should be little or no capital gains tax due). When an appreciated asset is given away during one's lifetime, however, the donor's tax basis carries over to the recipient and that recipient will therefore not receive a step-up in basis upon the death of the donor. It is therefore generally more tax efficient to give away assets with a relatively high tax basis, or to give away assets that the recipient is unlikely to sell. Gifts can also be made to beneficiaries through irrevocable trusts established for their benefit. The funds in these trusts may be used as either a safety net for beneficiaries during their lives (with the idea that the funds are really intended to pass to the next generation) or they may be distributed to the beneficiaries at a particular age during their lifetimes.

Three such trust vehicles in this area are a Crummey trust, an intentionally defective trust, and a generation-skipping trust. By way of background, for a gift to qualify for an annual or lifetime exclusion, it must be a gift of a "present interest." This means that the gift must be made outright to the recipient and not be controlled by the donor. A *Crummey trust* (named for the person who won a court case for the establishment of this type of trust) is one whereby the beneficiary has the right to withdraw a certain amount out of contributions made to the trust that year (usually the amount of the gifts made by the donor that year). If the beneficiary doesn't withdraw the permitted amount within a certain period of time (typically, 15 or 30 days after the beneficiary is given notice of the right to withdraw funds), then the beneficiary loses the right to demand withdrawal at a later date, and the assets remain in the trust to be distributed as designated in the trust document. For example, it can be set up so that the assets are distributed in thirds, when the recipient reaches ages 27, 37, and 47. This way, gifts are made but spending of the funds is controlled.

To further provide value to beneficiaries, it is possible to create a grantor trust for income tax purposes called an *intentionally defective trust*. This simply means that the trust is designed to have the income taxes paid by the grantor, the person who created the trust. Structuring a trust this way has the effect of depleting the taxable estate and at the same time increasing the assets in the trust, which is thus not subject to estate taxes upon the donor's death. Alternatively, a trust can be set up so that the assets will continue in trust for the beneficiary's entire lifetime, and then pass on to the beneficiary's descendants. This is called a *generation-skipping trust* and can give the beneficiary the right to benefit from the assets, but, if drafted properly, provides two important benefits that an outright gift does not: (1) the assets in the trust are exempt from the claims of most of the beneficiary's creditors, and (2) the assets in the trust escape estate taxes when the beneficiary dies. It is possible to set up a generation-skipping trust to give the beneficiary a great deal of power and control, or to limit the rights and power of the beneficiary. This kind of trust may make sense if the donor is trying to protect a child from himself if the child has problems with creditors, has a drug or alcohol addiction, is developmentally disabled, or is a poor money manager.

Estate Freezing Techniques

If these gifting strategies will not remove enough taxable assets from the estate, *freezing* techniques can be used to further reduce the taxable estate. In very general terms, freezing is an estate planning technique designed to limit the growth of capital property held during lifetime by transferring future growth in the capital property to heirs. The most common freezing techniques involve the use of *grantor retained trusts* (GRTs). In a GRT, the donor gives assets to a trust irrevocably for a fixed number of years, after which the trust assets are either distributed to the beneficiaries, or remain held in trust for them. There are four main types of GRTs: a grantor retained annuity trust (GRAT), a grantor retained unitrust (GRUT), a grantor retained income trust (GRIT), and a qualified personal residence trust (QPRT). While there are many techniques involving GRTs, I examine GRATs, which are a very popular estate transfer technique, in detail later in this section. In addition to GRTs, there are a few other estate freezing techniques to be aware of. These are private annuities, sales to an intentionally defective irrevocable trust, and self-canceling installment notes (SCINs).

Private Annuities   A *private annuity* is a promise by someone (e.g., a child) to pay a fixed amount of money to a donor every year for the rest of the donor's life. A person buys an annuity by paying money, or selling an asset, to the person who has promised to make the payments to the buyer. The amount of the payment is based on a life expectancy table, and an IRS-determined interest rate, as well as the amount of the annuity. The promise must be unsecured, so the buyer is relying on the creditworthiness of the person making the promise. The payments the buyer receives are partially ordinary income, with the balance either a tax-free return of investment (basis) or capital gain. The person making the payments will invest the money so she will pay tax on the income, but doesn't get a deduction for the payments made to the buyer. Thus, effectively, the income earned on the money transferred is taxed twice (once to the person making the payments and again to the recipient.) However, when the donor or recipient dies, assuming the trust has not been depleted, the remaining money or assets transferred will pass to beneficiaries without estate or gift tax liability.

Sale to an Intentionally Defective Irrevocable Trust   Another technique is to sell an appreciated asset to an *intentionally defective irrevocable trust* (IDIT). An IDIT is treated as a grantor trust for income tax purposes, but treated as an irrevocable trust for gift and estate tax purposes. What this does is freeze the current value of the asset being sold to the trust. Unlike a regular installment sale, gains for income tax purposes on the sale to an IDIT aren't reported. Such a sale defers gains on the sale until the asset is sold by the IDIT to a third party, or until death, whichever occurs first. If the asset is sold during lifetime, then the grantor pays capital gains tax on the sale.

Self-Canceling Installment Notes   With a *self-canceling installment note* (SCIN), the donor lends money or sells an asset to another person, typically a child, in exchange for a promissory note that provides for the payment of interest and principal over a specified time period, but also provides that if the donor dies before the note is repaid, the balance will be canceled and the note will be forgiven. Because the child may benefit by not having to repay the balance if death occurs, the child must pay either a higher rate of interest than usual or a bonus added to the principal of the note; the amount of the interest or principal bonus must be calculated by an actuary. The term of the note must be arranged such that the note is repaid during actuarial life expectancy. The interest received is taxable as ordinary income. If money is lent to another person, the principal repayments are generally tax-free; but if an asset is sold to another person, the principal repayments are part return of capital and part capital gain.

Grantor Retained Annuity Trusts

A Grantor Retained Annuity Trust, or GRAT, is an irrevocable trust established by the creator of the trust (the grantor), who transfers assets to the GRAT while retaining the right to receive fixed annuity payments, payable at least annually, for a specified number of years. After the expiration of the term, the Grantor will no longer receive any further benefits from the GRAT. The remaining trust principal comprising the GRAT at the end of the term interest can be either distributed to specified beneficiaries (such as the children of the grantor), or held in further trust for the benefit of one or more individuals. If the grantor survives the initial term of the trust, that is, the term during which the grantor is to receive annuity payments from the GRAT, the remaining principal of the GRAT will be excluded from the grantor's gross estate for federal estate tax purposes.

The primary advantage of establishing a GRAT is that the assets transferred by the grantor to the GRAT are valued at a discount for federal gift tax purposes. This is because the value of the gift will equal the fair market value of the assets initially transferred to the GRAT, reduced by the present value of the future annuity payments that the grantor will receive during the initial term. How large the discount will be depends on the length of the initial term of the GRAT, the amount of the fixed annuity payments that will be made from the GRAT to the grantor during the initial term, and the applicable federal rate of interest in the month that the assets are transferred, as announced by the Internal Revenue Service. In other words, the transfer of property to a GRAT constitutes a gift equal to the total value of the property transferred to the GRAT, minus the present value of the retained annuity interest held by the grantor.

Using a simple example, assume that grantor X, age 70, transfers $2 million of assets to a GRAT that provides the grantor the right to receive an annuity of $140,000 per year (7 percent of the value of the assets initially transferred to the GRAT), payable annually, for a 15-year period. Assume also that the applicable federal rate announced by the IRS in the month that the property is initially transferred to the GRAT is 6.0 percent. Based on applicable IRS tables, the value of the retained interest is about $1.2 million, which means that the value of the gift being made by the grantor to the GRAT upon creating the GRAT is about $800,000. Assuming grantor X is still living at the end of the term, the trust beneficiaries will receive the balance of the assets composing the GRAT, which may exceed $2 million, depending on whether the GRAT is able to earn an amount in excess of the annuity payments that are made to the grantor over the 15-year term.

Another benefit of a GRAT is the taxpaying character of the trust. For federal income tax purposes, a GRAT is treated as a grantor trust, so during the term of the GRAT that the grantor receives annuity payments, he is taxed on all income earned by the GRAT, including capital gains. This taxation results in additional estate planning benefits because the taxes paid by the grantor reduce the grantor's estate, rather than reducing the value of the assets gifted to the grantor's beneficiaries. One disadvantage of a GRAT is that it is irrevocable. The trust agreement can provide for some flexibility, but any time a trust is created that cannot be amended by the grantor, there is always the risk that a change in the grantor's life circumstances may make the trust less desirable during the trust's term. This disadvantage, however, is no worse than the risks inherent with making outright gifts, because then the recipients of gifts can spend the money as they choose. As a final note on GRATs, if the grantor dies before the expiration of the GRAT, the GRAT's assets will be includible in the gross estate of the grantor for estate tax purposes. The grantor can protect against this occurrence, however, by establishing an irrevocable trust that purchases a life insurance policy for the initial term of the GRAT.

Rolling Grantor Retained Annuity Trusts   The goal of a GRAT is for the trust assets to earn returns that exceed the IRS section 7520 rate. This rate is often referred to as the trust's *hurdle rate,* because the GRAT's earnings must top that rate for the GRAT to work. Thus, longer-term GRATs tend to perform better because returns have a longer window to increase, similar to the example we used in the previous section. GRATs also typically do well in a low-interest-rate environment because the grantor can lock in a low IRS hurdle rate, increasing chances of success. As interest rates increase, however, GRATs become riskier. The length of a trust term and the hurdle rate are two key factors in the success of a GRAT.

So, one can improve the chances of outperforming the hurdle rate by choosing a long trust term, but a long term increases mortality risk and, as discussed earlier, if the grantor fails to outlive the term of the GRAT, the assets are included in the grantor's estate. A strategy has been developed to address this risk: rolling GRATs (RGs). RGs are an alternative to traditional GRATs that may allow for enhanced performance without mortality risk.

The technique involves creating a series of short-term GRATs (typically two or three years) with each successive GRAT funded by annuity payments from the previous ones. By using short trust terms, mortality risk decreases. Over the longer term, rolling GRATs stand a good chance of successfully transferring wealth, and in many cases outperforming a single, longer-term GRAT.

With a GRAT, poor market performance in the early years can make it difficult for the trust to ultimately succeed. RGs eliminate this problem. Moreover, the success of a single long-term GRAT usually depends upon low interest rates at the inception of the GRAT, while the success of a series of RGs does not depend on a lower initial interest rate. RGs also allow the transfer of wealth to beneficiaries sooner and offer the option to stop creating GRATs if asset growth rates drop too low or the Grantor believes that enough wealth has been transferred. Finally, even if a single GRAT does not perform, either because the grantor dies during the term or the trust doesn't outperform the hurdle rate, the money simply goes back into the grantor's estate and there is no harm done, except for the fees paid to create the structure.

Life Insurance Planning

Life insurance can play a significant role in wealth transfer planning, but UACs do not usually use it for income replacement. More commonly, they use it to provide liquidity to a decedent's heirs to cover the estate tax bill that will be payable on the person's death. Another use is for the funding of a buy-sell agreement so that the decedent's interest in a business can be repurchased by another party. Also, when someone wants to leave a major asset like a business to one child, life insurance can provide the resources to allow other children to receive assets of equal value. There are other complex planning techniques involving life insurance and many different types of life insurance policies. Again, consult wealth transfer professionals before embarking upon any wealth transfer plans involving life insurance.

Irrevocable Insurance Trusts   An *irrevocable life insurance trust* (ILIT) is used to remove the proceeds of an insurance policy from the estate of the insured. If the insured person holds certain direct or indirect powers over an insurance policy on her own life, the proceeds of the policy will be subject to estate taxes upon death. The powers that cause this to occur include the rights to name beneficiaries, to directly borrow against the cash value of the policy, and to cash in the policy. Families often set up ILITs to own the insurance policy, with a friend or relative serving as the trustee to keep life insurance proceeds from being taxed as part of the insured person's estate. An irrevocable insurance trust is commonly structured as a Crummey trust to allow the annual gifts to qualify for the $12,000 annual exclusion from taxable gifts. Annual gifts are made to the trust to provide the trustee with funds to pay the insurance premiums. Generally, the trustee should apply for new insurance policies, but an existing policy can be used under certain conditions. If the insured applies for or owns the policy and dies within three years of transferring the policy to the ILIT, then the policy proceeds are taxed in the insured's estate. This three-year rule can be avoided if the policy is sold to the insured's ILIT so long as the ILIT is structured as an intentionally defective grantor trust. There can also be income tax consequences if an existing policy is transferred to an irrevocable trust or if the insured has borrowed against the cash value of the policy.

Split-dollar (and Family Split-dollar) Insurance Plans   A basic split-dollar insurance strategy involves dividing the ownership or benefits of a cash value insurance policy between two people. One person pays all or part of the premium each year, and upon the insured person's death, that person is entitled to regain all of the premiums paid (or possibly all of the cash value of the policy). The rest of the policy proceeds are paid to the insured person's beneficiaries. A split-dollar arrangement allows a cash value insurance policy to be purchased with very little or no outlay by the insured person. A family split-dollar arrangement uses the same concept to fund an irrevocable insurance trust without gift taxes by having the insured pay the portion of premium which represents the addition to the policy's cash value. This type of arrangement is still being used, but some of the economic benefits have been eliminated since 2003 rulings on split-dollar regulations changed certain rules with this strategy. Regulations under IRC §61 now govern split-dollar insurance arrangements. Taxation of these arrangements is defined under IRC §61 or §7872. UAC advisers should know the rules governing this strategy.

A split-dollar life insurance arrangement is any arrangement between an owner and a nonowner of a life insurance contract that satisfies the following criteria:

- Either party to the arrangement pays directly or indirectly all or a portion of the premiums on the life insurance contract including a payment by means of a loan to the other party that is secured by the insurance contracts;
- At least one of the parties to the arrangement paying premium under the paragraph above is entitled to recover (either conditionally or unconditionally) all or any portion of those premiums, and such recovery

is to be made from, or is secured by, the proceeds of the life insurance contract; and

- The arrangement is not part of a group term insurance plan described in Section 79 unless the group-term life insurance plan provides permanent benefits to employees (as defined in §1.79-0). Reg. §1.61-22(b)(1).[3]

Check with counsel on the viability of split-dollar insurance for each UAC relationship.

Charitable Gift Planning

Many UACs use charitable gift planning to accomplish their charitable goals and reduce income, gift, and estate tax burdens. It is tempting to use these strategies just for the tax benefits, but there should be charitable intent for them to work properly. I review three popular vehicles: charitable remainder trusts, charitable lead trusts, and private foundations.

Charitable Remainder Trusts   A *charitable remainder trust* (CRT) is an entity in which property or money is earmarked for a charity, but the donor (the grantor) continues to use and receive income from it for a specified number of years or until his death. Trust beneficiaries receive the income during the term of the trust and the charity receives the principal at the end of the term. The grantor avoids capital gains taxes upon the sale of assets donated to the trust, and also receives a current income tax deduction for the fair market value of the remainder interest of the property in the trust. In addition, the assets are removed from the donor's estate, reducing subsequent estate taxes. While the contribution is irrevocable, the grantor may have some control over the way the assets are invested, and can switch from one charity to another as long as the charity is a qualified charitable organization.

CRTs come in three types: charitable remainder annuity trusts (which pay a fixed dollar amount annually), charitable remainder unitrusts (which pay a fixed percentage of the trust's value annually), and charitable pooled income funds (which are set up by the charity, enabling many donors to contribute). Charitable remainder trusts provide distributions to beneficiaries for a period of up to 20 years or for the life or lives of the beneficiaries. When the initial term ends, the assets remaining in the trust can pass to a family-controlled charity. A charitable remainder unitrust gives the current beneficiary a fixed percentage of the value of the assets in the trust, recalculated each year. Thus, if the value of the assets increases, the payout increases; but if the value of the assets declines, the payout will decline as well. A charitable remainder annuity trust gives the current beneficiary a fixed dollar amount each year, which never changes. A charitable remainder trust is often used when a person wants to sell appreciated assets, because the trust pays no current capital gain tax on a sale. Money that otherwise would go to the government in taxes on a sale will instead be held in the trust and can be invested. Distributions from the trust will be taxed to the beneficiary as ordinary income, capital gain income, or tax-free income, depending on the type of income earned by the trust.

The donor can be the trustee of the trust, and can retain the right to change the charitable beneficiaries. A unitrust can be designed so that distributions don't exceed the current income of the trust. It is also possible to design a unitrust so that distributions are limited to the current income of the trust pending a sale of an asset (such as raw land), but this limit is removed after the sale. If a CRT is set up during the donor's lifetime, the donor is entitled to an income tax deduction for some part of the value of the assets transferred to the trust. The amount of the deduction will depend on what kind of trust (unitrust or annuity) is used, current interest rates when the trust is funded, the payout rate, how long the noncharitable beneficiaries will receive benefits, the type of asset given to the trust, and the type of charity (public or private) that is chosen to receive funds at the end of the trust's life. Charitable trusts can also be set up upon death. This is done when the donor wants to provide a benefit to someone for a period of time or for a lifetime and get an estate tax charitable deduction.

Charitable Lead Trusts   A *charitable lead trust* (CLT) is a trust that the donor establishes either during life (called an *inter vivos* trust) or at death (called a testamentary trust). The income from the trust flows to a charitable organization, typically for a set number of years. After that period, the assets in the trust are distributed to a beneficiary of the grantor, typically one or more family members. The CLT can have an interesting distinction from other similar trusts, depending upon how it is set up. Because the assets will one day be transferred to another person, it can be considered a *nongrantor* trust. This means that the trust assets are not owned by the person who established the trust, and the assets are not going to be returned to her someday. (A grantor trust is one in which the assets will eventually be distributed back to the donor and the donor is subject to tax on the assets.)

If the trust is set up as a nongrantor trust for income tax purposes, then no income tax deduction is received when the trust is funded, but distributions to charity from the trust will be deductible against the trust's income. If the CLT is set up during the lifetime as a grantor trust for income tax purposes (i.e., the donor is taxed on the income earned by the trust each year), then the donor can claim an income tax deduction when the trust is funded, but will not get an income tax deduction on distributions made from the trust to charity. A CLT is often set up under a living trust or will. The estate gets an estate tax deduction for a portion of the assets going into the trust. The size of the deduction will depend on what kind of CLT is used, the payout rate, the prevailing interest rates when the trust is funded, and the length of the charitable term. A CLT works well if one has assets that are likely to increase in value far faster than the IRS-provided interest rate.

Private Operating (Family) Foundations Many UACs set up family foundations to accomplish their charitable goals and must give away at least 5 percent of the assets (adjusted to account for debt and cash reserves) each year. Many people do not know the difference between a private foundation and a public foundation. UAC advisers should know the difference.

> *The Foundation Center defines a private foundation as a nongovernmental, nonprofit organization having a principal fund managed by its own trustees or directors. Private foundations maintain or aid charitable, educational, religious, or other activities serving the public good, primarily through the making of grants to other nonprofit organizations.*

> *To understand what a private foundation is, it helps to understand what it is* not. *Every U.S. and foreign charity that qualifies under Section 501(c)(3) of the Internal Revenue Service Code as tax-exempt is a "private foundation"* **unless** *it demonstrates to the IRS that it falls into another category. Broadly speaking, organizations that are* **not** *private foundations are public charities as described in Section 509(a) of the Internal Revenue Service Code.*

> *Another difference between private foundations and public charities is that public charities generally derive their funding or support primarily from the general public, receiving grants from individuals, government, and private foundations. Although some public charities engage in grantmaking activities, most conduct direct service or other tax-exempt activities. A private foundation, on the other hand, usually derives its principal fund from a single source, such as an individual, family, or corporation, and more often than not is a grantmaker. A private foundation does not solicit funds from the public.*[4]

In addition, there are differences in tax treatment between private and public foundations. Significant limitations on income tax deductions exist on gifts that are made to private foundations. Generally, cash gifts to a private foundation are deductible up to 30 percent of the donor's adjusted gross income (AGI) and noncash gifts may be deductible up to 20 percent of the donor's AGI. In some cases, the donor's deduction is based on the smaller of the donor's income tax basis or the value of the asset given away. By comparison, cash gifts to public charities are generally deductible up to 50 percent of the donor's AGI, while noncash gifts are generally deductible up to 30 percent of the donor's AGI. In most cases, a donor's deduction on a gift to a public charity is based on the value of the asset and isn't limited to the donor's income tax basis.

Family Limited Partnerships

Oddly, while *family limited partnerships* (FLPs) are extremely popular among UACs, they are not referred to or defined in Internal Revenue Code. This is so because an FLP is simply a limited partnership whose partners are family members. Like other limited partnerships, it consists of two types of partners, general and limited, and is typically structured as a fixed-term partnership. General partners control all management and investment decisions and bear 100 percent of the liability. Limited partners do not participate in the management of the FLP and have no liability. An FLP is a flow-through entity, meaning that owners report partnership income and deductions on their personal tax returns. By combining investments together into an FLP, a family's investment fees are significantly reduced; instead of maintaining separate accounts or trusts for each child, the partnership can hold one account, and the children or trusts for children can own partnership interests.

In terms of structure, generally senior family members (e.g., parents) contribute assets to an FLP in exchange for a small general partner interest and a large limited partner interest. They then give some or all of the limited partner interest to their children and grandchildren, directly or in a trust. Even though the parents have given away the limited partnership interests, they, as the general partners, still retain full control over all the assets in the partnership. Another benefit of creating an FLP is that transfers of limited partnership interests have gift and estate tax benefits. First, transfers of LP interest are eligible for the annual gift tax exclusion. Gift tax is normally due on the value of the gifts above the annual exclusion, but parents can use their $1,000,000 lifetime gift tax exemption to counteract this tax. Since the gift has been completed, all appreciation on the assets is transferred out of the parents' estates. Also, by transferring assets to children, parents remove them from the parents' estate for federal estate tax purposes, while retaining control over the decisions and distributions of the investment.

The value of limited partnership shares can be discounted when transferred to family members, since the limited partners cannot control investments or distributions—although the IRS can take exception to discounts in the 50 percent range, the 20 percent range is usually more acceptable. When this chapter was written, the IRS was intensely scrutinizing the viability of FLPs. So please consult an expert in this area before discussing FLPs with your client. A properly structured FLP also protects assets from claims of future creditors. Creditors cannot force distributions from, vote for, or own the interest of a limited partner without the consent of the general partners. And in the event of a divorce, where a limited partner ceases to be a family member, the partnership documents usually require a transfer back to the family for fair market value, keeping the asset within the family structure. Also, because of an FLP's flexibility, family members who are owners can usually amend the partnership agreement as family circumstances change.

CONCLUSION

We have barely scratched the surface of wealth transfer. But UAC advisers should have at least a cursory understanding of the concepts presented in this chapter. As always, consult professionals who are skilled in these areas before recommending any strategy to your clients.

Special Topics for Ultra-Affluent Clients and Family Offices

Concentrated Equity Risk Management

My dream is big, OK?
—Masayoshi Son, Founder of Softbank

It has been reported that Mr. Masayoshi, the founder of dotcom darling company Softbank, lost a total of $75 billion with the rupture of the technology stock bubble in 2000. Softbank's stock price is down 98 percent from its bubble peak.[1] In fact, according to *Forbes* magazine, the total wealth of the Forbes 400 members dropped by about $350 billion to $872 billion between 2000 and 2002.[2] There is a clever term that has been created to account for this level of financial loss: Swils. This term stands for "Sudden Wealth Loss Syndrome." Numerous examples of Swils exist. When this chapter was written, the most recent example was James Cayne, the former chairman of the brokerage firm Bear Stearns. At one time, his stake in the firm was worth approximately $1 billion. In March of 2008, after his firm imploded, he sold his holdings for $61 million.[3]

Mr. Cayne actually did not do so badly compared to some. Take the case of Mr. Warren "Pete" Musser. Mr. Musser founded Safeguard Scientific, a Pennsylvania-based technology company that was another casualty of the dotcom era. He went from being a billionaire to having a negative net worth of $15 million in a matter of weeks. Mr. Musser refused to sell or protect any of his Safeguard stock and had also leveraged it using margin loans to buy shares in other risky companies. When the music stopped, his margin calls wiped him out and then some.[4] And let's not forget domestic diva Martha Stewart. At one point, (specifically, the day her company went public in 1999) her ownership in her company was worth $1.3 billion. Several years later, when she was mired in an insider trading scandal, her wealth had dropped about 70 percent.[5] There are numerous other examples we could use. But the point is this: When exposed to the risks of a single stock position, it is best to take steps to protect oneself. I review several common strategies for protecting concentrated equity positions in this chapter. As I have said before, it is best to bring in a specialist to help with these matters. They are complex, with many tax consequences. First, I first define what we mean by a concentrated equity position.

WHAT CONSTITUTES A CONCENTRATED EQUITY POSITION?

UACs with concentrated stock are rich on paper but lack two key qualities: liquidity and diversification. The definition of a concentrated equity position is, however, highly variable, depending on the client's individual situation. Considerations such as risk tolerance, the client's overall portfolio asset allocation, the desired and required returns, total wealth, and other factors influence how one defines a concentrated stock holding. A frequently overlooked scenario is one in which a client's current income, health and retirement benefits, and investment assets are tied to a single company's fortunes. In this case, even a small allocation to the company's stock may be considered concentrated, given the more substantial total exposure. Some clients I have worked with over the years have used the word *diworsification* to describe taking a concentrated position and moving it into a diversified portfolio. Clearly, they believe they can get rich by holding a concentrated stock portfolio. What does the academic literature say about what is considered concentrated versus diversified?

In the past, some researchers have suggested that adequate diversification could be achieved with 15 to 30 equally weighted stocks.[6] Campbell et al. (2001) reported that over the last few decades, however, there has been a noticeable increase in the volatility of individual stocks relative to the market. At the same time, they claim, there has been a general decline in the correlations among individual stock returns. Campbell and his colleagues concluded that "the R^2 of the market model for a typical stock has also declined, while the number of stocks needed to obtain any given amount of portfolio diversification has increased."[7] As a result, to assume that a small number of stocks will be representative of the future risk and return of the broad market is more problematic now than in the past, especially during periods like 2008.

TABLE 16.1 S&P 500's Largest 20 Companies, According to Floating Capitalization

No.	Company	Price	Floating Capitalization (in millions)	% of Total
1	ExxonMobil	81.64	415,274.03	5.12
2	Procter & Gamble	62.8	185,074.88	2.28
3	General Electric	17.07	179,291.01	2.21
4	AT&T	29.42	173,372.06	2.14
5	Johnson & Johnson	60.65	168,277.56	2.08
6	Microsoft	20.33	155,528.41	1.92
7	Chevron	76.52	154,386.04	1.9
8	Wal Mart	57.18	127,846.18	1.58
9	Wells Fargo	30	126,720.25	1.56
10	Pfizer	18.27	123,193.43	1.52
11	IBM	87.37	117,377.92	1.45
12	JPMorgan Chase	31.35	117,009.41	1.44
13	Cisco Systems	16.96	99,302.27	1.22
14	Verizon Communications	34.64	98,394.38	1.21
15	Bank of America	14.33	91,622.92	1.13
16	Coca-Cola	45.9	91,325.28	1.13
17	Philip Morris International	44.12	89,256.25	1.1
18	Hewlett Packard	36.81	88,940.37	1.1
19	PepsiCo	55.97	86,928.16	1.07
20	Intel	15.2	84,542.40	1.04

Source: http://www.indexarb.com/capitalizationAnalysis.html (January 2, 2009.).

Although the number of stock holdings needed to achieve reasonable diversification continues to be debated, it is fair to say that the trend is toward more, rather than fewer, stocks. One might measure concentration by looking at market weights in an index like the Standard & Poor's 500. As can be seen in Table 16.1, at year-end 2008, Exxon Mobil (representing 5.1 percent of the capitalization-weighted S&P 500) was the index's largest company, and Pfizer (representing 1.5 percent) and Intel (at 1 percent) were the index's tenth- and twentieth-largest companies, respectively.

Using a thoroughly diversified 20-stock portfolio (a more aggressive estimate) implies that no stock should represent more than 5 percent of an individual's equity holdings. In an asset allocation framework, this means that for a client with an allocation of 50 percent stocks, no one security should represent more than 2.5 percent of the aggregate portfolio. In practice, some clients hold single stocks that make up 40 percent or even more of their portfolios. Let's look at why this is.

Why Do Some Clients Hold Concentrated Equity Positions?

Many clients, intent upon diversifying a large single-stock position, choose to sell all or a portion of the security outright. For these clients, the reduction of stock-specific risk is paramount, and the diversification benefits outweigh the cost (the tax on the gain) incurred to sell the stock. After all, by selling the security, a client only surrenders a portion of the gain, while she could lose far more by continuing to hold the stock. However, some clients may decide to continue to hold concentrated equities for a variety of reasons. Some of the most common reasons include:

- Desire to defer capital gains or to potentially eliminate capital gains due to a cost basis step-up at death.
- Desire to participate in the stock's future returns.
- Dividend received on the stock is used to fund the investor's annual living expenses and lifestyle.
- Legal or contractual selling restrictions; company insiders, executives, and affiliates face regulatory and company-specific restrictions that may impose lockup periods, trading windows, and other insider restrictions that may limit their ability to sell or hedge a position. A second example of a contractual restriction is a clause in a trust agreement that forces a beneficiary to continue to hold the stock of the company that made the grantor wealthy.
- Psychological reasons such as endowment bias (reviewed in Chapter 3), which occurs when a person irrationally keeps something he already owns simply because he finds more value with previously owned objects.

Desire to Defer Capital Gains   Many clients hold concentrated equity positions because they would prefer not to realize capital gains on sales. In some cases, the capital gains may be significant if their cost basis is very low. Some clients, however, erroneously inflate the impact of the capital gains tax (currently 15 percent on long-term gains for those in the higher marginal tax brackets), by not recognizing that the tax is assessed only on the gain realized and not the entire position value. For example, if a client sells a stock position that is 50 percent profit, the client would surrender only 7.5 percent (15 percent of 50 percent) of the position's value to capital gains tax.

The 7.5 percent cost in this example can be considered the primary cost of diversifying the holding. The benefits attained by diversifying are a significant reduction of downside risk, an ability to participate in the returns of the broad stock market, and an ability to reallocate the proceeds to other asset classes. Another way to look at this is to consider that for a certain

7.5 percent loss of principal, the client is moderating the uncertainty of the stock's future performance, which may be significantly worse than that of the overall market.

For certain clients who are of advanced age or in poor health, liquidation of the holding may not be advisable, given the step-up in cost basis that occurs at death. Since step-up results in the elimination of the accumulated capital gain—either in part or in whole—the portfolio may be diversified in a more tax-efficient manner after the step-up. One consideration is that tax laws can change, and there is no guarantee what the applicable IRS Tax Code will be in the future.

Desire to Participate in the Stock's Future Returns   Some of the world's greatest fortunes have been accumulated by holding a single stock. Observers of stock market history know this, and the allure of getting rich this way is strong and has led many investors down the path of chasing the returns of a single company as opposed to building a sustainable risk-adjusted diversified portfolio. Relative to the market, the concentrated stock must provide much higher returns to compensate for its much higher risk. By adjusting the returns for risk, the cost of diversification in our previous example is reduced.

Illiquid or Restricted Stock Holdings   The challenge of selling an illiquid stock holding can be a daunting task for even sophisticated investors. Some stocks may be illiquid because they trade infrequently, making it difficult to dispose of a large number of shares in a timely and cost-effective manner. Buyers may not always be readily available, and those that are available will likely want to receive a discount for the shares, because they know that the large sell order could potentially depress the stock's price. A trader who specializes in the niche area of liquidating illiquid securities, based on the shareholder's fact pattern and goals, should have the expertise and ability to carefully balance the investor's desire for the *immediacy of execution* (time certainty) against the *execution price of the transaction* (price certainty).

Restricted stock, also known as letter stock or restricted securities, refers to stock of a company that is not fully transferable until certain conditions have been met. Upon satisfaction of those conditions, the stock becomes transferable by the person holding the award. There are numerous factors that influence the valuation of restricted securities, including:

- The nature and length of the restriction.
- Certain rights attached to the restricted securities, such as registration rights.
- The transferability of the restricted securities.
- The underlying financial strength of the company.

- The liquidity (daily volume, bid/ask spread, etc.) of the stock.
- The availability of publicly traded option contracts on the issuer's stock.
- The ability to pledge the restricted shares as collateral in a hedging transaction.

Because the shares are illiquid and the purchaser inherits the seller's restrictions, such assets typically sell at a discount from the market price of their unrestricted counterparts. Relevant real-world transactions of restricted stock give the best precedents for determining applicable discounts to apply to particular restricted securities.

CONCENTRATED STOCK RISK MINIMIZATION STRATEGIES

A UAC with a concentrated low cost basis position seeking to diversify their portfolio has a choice:

1. Sell the stock, pay the capital gains tax, and use after-tax proceeds to build a diversified portfolio.

   Or

2. Implement a strategy, using some combination of financial instruments, which will defer triggering the capital gains tax and should eliminate some of the risk of the position.

If a stock position has more than doubled, a UAC in most instances will wish to pay less tax than more tax. Once they determine they would like to avoid triggering a large capital gain, the UAC should determine their goals and decide if they are simply trying to protect concentrated positions with some appreciation in the underlying stock (hedging) or if the UAC also wishes to gain access to cash by borrowing against their hedged position (monetization).

When hedging a low basis position, it is important for a UAC to work with both an experienced capital markets expert who can help a UAC implement their objectives through a capital markets based transaction and also a trained tax professional who can tell a UAC the expected tax results of his plan. The tax considerations, for even the very basic hedging and

---

The author gratefully acknowledges Michael Lynch from Twenty-First Securities Corp. for his substantial contribution to this section on concentrated stock risk minimization strategies.

monetization strategies described in this chapter, are extremely complicated and this chapter is too short to review all of the nuances in detail.

This following section reviews a few of the many different strategies available to a UAC including:

- Generating portfolio income
- Hedging strategy:
  - Put purchase
  - Zero premium collar
- Monetization
- Exchange funds (diversification)

The decision to use a particular strategy depends on many factors. Generally, as clients move along the investor life cycle continuum, they become more concerned with wealth preservation than wealth creation. Therefore, a monetization strategy may be more relevant to younger investors who may want to take proceeds and invest them, whereas an older investor may simply be interested in protecting wealth. There are two important factors to consider that we will look at when deciding the best course of action for a particular client fact pattern. These are risk and diversification, as shown in Figure 16.1. It is very important in any case to consult key advisers such as legal, accounting, derivative and tax professionals when contemplating any of these structures for substantial wealth.

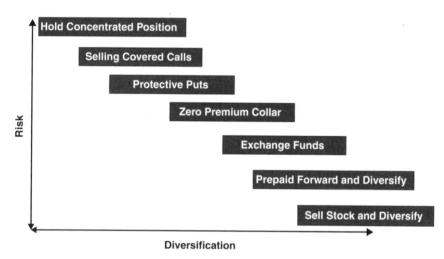

FIGURE 16.1   Diversification and Risk Levels of Concentrated Stock Sell Decision

We will now discuss each of these strategies. Conveniently, the most risky strategy and the least risky strategies don't require much explanation. The least risky strategy is to sell the concentrated position and invest the after-tax proceeds into a diversified mix of assets. The most risky strategy is to hold the concentrated position without any downside protection.

Portfolio Income: Covered Call Writing

Covered call writing is the sale of a call option on a stock owned by the investor. In exchange for an upfront premium *received*, the seller or writer of a call option has the obligation (if the call option is exercised) to deliver the underlying stock at a predetermined price (strike price) on or before a certain date (expiration date). The seller of the call option establishes a short position in the call option.

The sale of a call option generates portfolio income on a concentrated equity position beyond dividends. By selling a call option on the underlying equity and receiving a premium, the client retains any increase in the underlying stock price up to the call strike price and forgoes any appreciation of the stock price above the call strike price. In this strategy, a client offsets a portion of any potential stock price depreciation by the amount of premium received but covered call writing should not be used as a standalone hedging strategy as the downside protection is limited to the call premium generated.

If the call option has not been exercised prior to expiration of the option (assuming the use of American Style options) and the stock price is below the strike price of the call option, the call option will expire worthless and no further action is taken.

If the stock price is above the strike price at expiration, the writer of the call option could:

1. Deliver their low basis shares to settle the obligation of the contract.
2. The writer of the call option could purchase new shares in the market and deliver the higher basis shares to settle the obligation.
3. Repurchase the short call option prior to expiration.

Suppose a client owns shares in HIJ Corp. that are trading at $100 per share. The client would like to believe HIJ stock will trade within a narrow range over the next 12 months and wouldn't mind generating additional income in the meantime. In consultation with her adviser, the client decides to sell a one-year call option on 100,000 shares of stock with a strike price of $120 for an upfront premium of $20. Table 16.2 shows the outcomes at three prices: $40, $110, and $140.

TABLE 16.2 Covered Call Outcomes

Stock Price at Expiration	Call Strike Price	Call Exercised?	Call Value at Expiration	Call Premium	Ending value (Pre tax)
$40	$120	No	$0	$20	$60
$110	$120	No	0	$20	$130
$140	$120	Yes	($20)	$20	$140
$160	$120	Yes	($40)	$20	$140

The advantage of selling covered calls is that the client receives an up-front premium while holding a long position in the stock (income generation and tax deferral). Also, the client would retain the voting rights of the stock and continue to collect any dividends.

A covered call writing program can be used as an effective structured selling program for an investor. An investor may be desirous of pairing down their concentrated position at a target price that is above the current market price of the stock. Instead of placing a sell limit order (where no premium is received by the investor) for the stock above the current market price, an investor could sell a call option whose strike price plus the upfront premium is equal to the target sales price. If the call option is exercised, the investor's shares are called away at the call option's strike price and the investor has met their goal of pairing down their position at the target sales price without necessarily needing the stock to ever trade at or above the target price.

> *Example: An investor would like to sell shares at $40 when the stock is trading in the market at $28.*
>
> *The investor could sell a call option with a $35 strike price and receive a $5 premium upfront.*
>
> *If the call option is exercised at or before expiration, the investor effectively sells their shares at $40.*

The disadvantage to selling covered calls is that the client forgoes stock price appreciation above the call strike price of the option and the client is at risk if the underlying equity declines beyond the premium received. There are also tax implications of these strategies that must be considered including the capital gain tax triggered if the investor elects to deliver their low basis shares to settle the call obligation and the tax analysis required so that the call option sold meets the criteria for a qualified covered call and the investor does not inadvertently cause the dividend paid by the stock to be taxed at ordinary rates.

Hedging: Protective Put

A protective put involves the purchase of a put option on a stock owned by an investor. In exchange for an upfront premium *paid*, the investor has the right, but not the obligation, to sell the underlying stock at or before the expiration date of the option if the price of the stock is less than the put strike price. The investor establishes a long position in the put option.

Clients can protect a concentrated equity position from a decline in market value by purchasing a put option. The long put position effectively locks in a minimal sales price for the stock or establishes a floor on their position while deferring the capital gains tax.

If the stock price falls below the put strike, the investor can exercise the put option and sell the stock at the put strike price. Alternatively, the client may choose to sell the put option and collect the value of the put option.

Suppose a client owns shares in XYZ Corp. that are trading at $100 per share. The client is concerned about the potential for an overall decline in the stock market over the next 24 months and wants to protect the gains of her stock position. After consulting her adviser, the client purchases a two-year put option with a strike price of $80 for premium of $10 per share (or 10 percent of the stock value). Table 16.3 shows examples of a client's outcomes at a stock price expiration of $40, $110, and $120. Figure 16.2 is the payoff diagram of a protective put.

The advantage of a protective put is that the client is fully protected against a declining stock price below the put strike (minus premium paid) and maintains full upside in the appreciation of the underlying equity (minus premium paid). Also, the client would retain the voting rights of the stock and continue to collect any dividends.

The disadvantage of a put purchase is that the client pays an upfront premium (which is generally expensive) for the downside protection and the option may expire as worthless if the stock price is higher than the put strike price at expiration. The investor would have some downside exposure from the price of the stock when the put is purchased down to the put option

TABLE 16.3 Protective Put Outcomes

Stock Price at Expiration	Put Strike Price	Put Exercised?	Value of the Put	Premium Paid for the Put	Ending Value (Pre-Tax)
$40	$80	Yes	$40	$10	$70
$110	$80	No	0	$10	$100
$120	$80	No	0	$10	$110

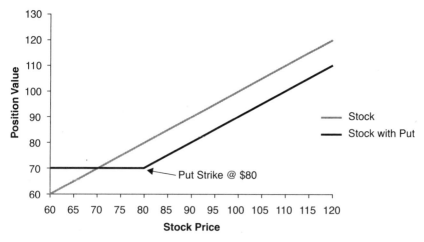

FIGURE 16.2   Payoff Diagram of the Protective Put

strike price. Also, any dividends received on the underlying stock would not be qualified dividend income and would be taxed at ordinary rates.

Zero Premium Collar

With a zero premium collar, the investor sells a call option on a stock owned by the investor that generates a premium (cash inflow) and simultaneously purchases a put option (cash outflow) with the same expiration date. The cost of the put option is equal to the premium generated by the sale of the call option (net of transaction costs).

The zero premium collar establishes a minimum sales price, or floor, for the underlying stock at the strike price of the put option. In order to finance the put purchase, the investor sells a call option with the same expiration date that will generate enough premium to fully cover the cost of the put. The investor forgoes any upside appreciation above the call strike price and effectively establishes a cap on the position.

If the stock price is between the put and the call strike price at expiration, both options expire worthless and the client retains the stock.

Alternatively, in physical settlement, if the put or call option is in the money at expiration, the client may choose to sell shares at the put strike price if the stock price is below the put strike price or deliver the shares to settle the short call obligation if the price of the stock is above the call strike price. The investor can also sell the put option or repurchase the short call option prior to expiration.

TABLE 16.4 Zero Collar Premium Outcomes

Stock at Expiration	Put Exercised?	Call Exercised?	Put Value	Call Value	Stock + Option End Value
$60	Yes	No	$20	$0	$80
$110	No	No	$0	$0	$110
$150	No	Yes	$0	($30)	$120

For simplicity, suppose a client owns shares in DEF Corp that are trading at $100 per share. The client is interested in protecting most of the current value of his stock position and is willing to limit the upside appreciation in the stock to pay for the protection. After consulting his adviser, the client enters into a one-year collar by purchasing a put option with a strike price of $80 (80 percent) and selling a call option with a strike price of $120 (120 percent) on 250,000 shares of stock. The client did not pay anything out of pocket at the outset of the transaction because the premium generated from the sale of the call option financed the purchase of the put option (including any transaction costs). Table 16.4 shows the potential outcomes at stock prices of $60, $110, or $140. Figure 16.3 shows the payoff diagram for this example.

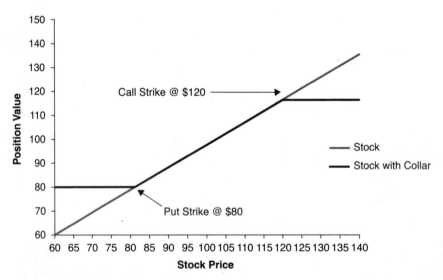

FIGURE 16.3 Payoff Diagram for Zero Premium Collar

On the expiration date, the following examples of the client's potential outcomes apply:

The advantage of this structure is that the client reduces downside risk in the underlying equity below the put strike price and participates in the stock appreciation up to the call strike price. Also, the client would retain the voting rights of the stock and continue to collect the dividend. The investor can customize the strike prices and maturity to best fit his unique circumstances if they utilize an OTC or E-Flex option.

The disadvantage of a zero premium collar is that the client's ability to participate in the underlying stock appreciation is limited to the strike price of the call option. Also, any dividends received on the underlying stock would not be qualified dividend income and would be taxed at the ordinary rates.

Monetization

Investors also have the ability to borrow against hedged positions. A monetization strategy is simply a collar (floor and cap) combined with a margin loan. The put call parity states that different financial instruments can be combined to produce the same economic results. There are a number of different strategies available in the market that produce the economics of a collar and margin loan but the tax treatment of each of the different structures can vary substantially. It is important, with a tax adviser, to carefully evaluate an investor's fact pattern, tax status, use of proceeds, and the characteristics of the underlying stock (e.g., dividend or nondividend paying stock) before selecting any monetization strategy to insure that the client achieves their desired pretax economics and after tax result.

The economics of a collar loan can be achieved by a number of different commonly used strategies including (but not limited to):

1. Prepaid variable forward
2. Nonrecourse loan in conjunction with the sale of qualified covered calls
3. Options-based collar with a margin loan
4. Swap (with collar-like economics in the contract)

An example of the different tax results of the strategies listed above (that all provide the same economics) would be the tax results of a nonrecourse loan combined with the sale of qualified covered call versus a prepaid variable forward. If a stock pays a dividend and an investor utilizes a prepaid variable forward to monetize their position, the dividend paid on the stock would not be qualified dividend income and would be taxed at the ordinary rates. If the investor used the nonrecourse loan to monetize the stock, the dividend should be taxed at the lower 15 percent rate (assuming the call options are qualified covered calls). Also, the interest expense paid on the nonrecourse loan should be currently deductible at the 35 percent rate versus deferred, and capitalized if the prepaid variable forward is utilized.

The prepaid variable forward, however, is the most utilized monetization strategy on Wall Street due to its prepackaged nature, lack of restrictions on the use of proceeds, and administrative ease, but in many cases does not provide the most efficient tax results.

A prepaid forward contract allows a client to receive an upfront payment (typically, 75 to 90 percent of the current market value of held shares) in exchange for delivery of a variable amount of shares or cash in the future. Since the contract establishes floor and cap prices that dictate how many shares (or cash equivalent) are returned at a given market price at the expiration of the contract, the investor is protected against downside risk of the stock limited to the amount of upfront credit they receive while enjoying appreciation potential up to the cap. The agreement allows the client to enter the forward sale without paying taxes on the sale until the maturity of the agreement. At maturity, if the stock price is below the floor, the client delivers to the sponsor of the contract 100 percent of the shares (or a cash equivalent payment) in the contract and retains the upfront credit. Above the cap, the client delivers a number of shares equal in value to the floor price plus the difference between the stock price and the cap price. If the stock price is between the floor price and the cap price, the client will deliver the number of shares equal in value to the floor price. Once the proceeds of the prepaid contract are received, the client will usually invest the proceeds in a diversified portfolio of assets.

Suppose a client owns shares in ABC Corp and she would like to monetize this position without realizing an immediate taxable gain. After discussions with her adviser, the client decides to enter into a prepaid forward contract with a floor price of $80 and a cap price of $100 on 200,000 shares of stock. The time frame for these contracts is usually not less than one year and not more than five years. Table 16.5 shows the percentage of shares or how much cash the client must deliver at the expiration of the contract. Figure 16.4 is a payoff diagram of the prepaid forward contract.

There are several key factors that investors should consider when entering into a prepaid forward transaction. On the one hand, the client will reduce risk by establishing a floor price and receiving proceeds up front. On the other hand, the client forgoes stock price appreciation above the cap price. The IRS is currently scrutinizing some of the prepaid variable forward

TABLE 16.5 Obligations at Maturity of the Prepaid Forward Contract

Stock Price at Expiration	Number of Shares Delivered	OR	Amount of Cash Delivered per share	Shares Remaining (if stock settled)
$50	100% of Shares		$50	0.0%
$80	100% of Shares		$80	0.0%
$100	80% of Shares		$80	20.0%
$110	81.8% of Shares		$90	18.2%
$120	83.3% of Shares		$100	16.7%
$130	84.6% of Shares		$110	15.4%

contracts that were structured aggressively, and essentially gave up the risks of ownership to the client (client lent their shares to the dealer at the initiation of the trade and gave up voting rights and all dividends, the contracts did not provide a cash settlement alternative, and the upfront credit was tied to the dealers' short sale price when hedging its exposure) and these transactions could possibly trigger a sale under common law. Thus, a client who has entered into any of these transactions or is considering doing so should consider seeking immediate tax advice from a qualified professional.

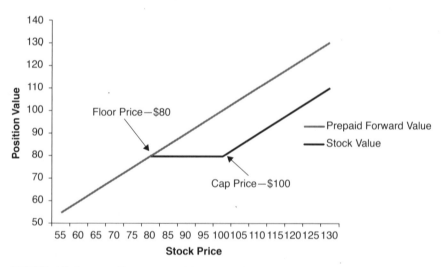

FIGURE 16.4 Payoff Diagram of the Prepaid Forward Contract

Exchange Funds

Exchange funds allow an investor to contribute low-basis securities into a partnership without triggering a taxable event and achieving immediate diversification. An investor contributes stock into a partnership comprised of a diversified pool of securities with other qualified investors, and in exchange, the investor receives a pro rata share of the partnership. After seven years, the investor typically has the option to redeem its interest in the fund and receive a diversified basket of securities equal in value to the investor's pro rata ownership of the partnership or continue the investment in the partnership. If the investor elects to redeem its ownership interest after seven years, the diversified basket of securities retains the low-cost basis from the original contribution.

There are exchange funds for publicly held stock and private stock (pre-IPO or private equity). For public exchange funds, at least seven years must pass between the times an investor deposits stock into the partnership before a basket of stocks can be returned to the investor. The partnership must hold at least 20 percent of the portfolio in qualifying assets in order for the exchange of contributed securities for partnership units to be nontaxable. The qualifying assets are typically illiquid securities made up primarily of real estate investments.

Exchange funds have been in existence for many years, but Congress tightened the rules substantially in 1997 by creating a new class of investors called *qualified purchasers* (QPs). The Securities and Exchange Commission defines QPs as investors with more than $5 million of investable assets. To meet the 1997 requirements, the operators of exchange funds were required to form partnerships that are not offered to the general public but only to QPs. SEC rules require that the partnerships be treated as private placements, rather than public offerings to investors. Eaton Vance in Boston is the largest of the public stock exchange fund providers and many of the large wire house brokerages such as Goldman Sachs sponsor exchange funds.

After seven years, an investor can elect to withdraw from the exchange fund without triggering a taxable event. When the investor redeems their partnership units of the exchange fund, the partnership returns a basket of securities from the partnership's pooled assets. The basket of securities returned to the investor have a cost basis equal to the cost basis of securities originally contributed to the exchange fund by the investor seven years earlier. As a result, the client with too much in one stock can diversify her holdings without triggering a taxable event.

Private equity exchange funds differ from public exchange funds in that the main objective of private equity exchange funds is to provide investors with downside risk protection should their stock become worthless before they achieve an IPO or acquisition event. The need for diversification is much greater with private stock than it is with public stock because public stock can be sold at any time. When a liquidity event occurs in a private equity fund, proceeds are immediately distributed to limited partners, rather than being held or reinvested. The objective of private exchange funds is liquidity as well as diversification. EB Exchange Funds is the best-known firm specializing in exchange funds for private equity.

CONCLUSION

Protecting equity positions is very important. Many wealthy families have obtained wealth by concentrating their investments in a single stock. From an investment standpoint, that is an incredibly risky strategy. At some point, the goal of the client moves from wealth creation to wealth preservation. The strategies contained in this chapter are designed to assist UAC advisers to help their clients protect their wealth. Be sure to consult experts in this area before embarking upon any of these strategies.

CHAPTER 17

Family Governance

Govern a family as you would cook a small fish—very gently.
—Chinese Proverb

James E. Hughes, Jr., author of two excellent books on family governance and leading authority on the subject, sums up what this chapter addresses with the title of chapter one of his book *Family Wealth—Keeping it in the Family* (Bloomberg, 2004): Long-term wealth preservation as a question of family governance. Hughes points out something that most UAC advisers know intuitively, but may not know how to communicate to their clients: Preserving wealth over multiple generations is a question of human behavior choices, not the best estate plan or investment managers. And that human behavior needs to be codified in a compact or agreement among its members if each generation is to successfully overcome the natural forces that can dissipate a family's energy, and therefore wealth.[1] A system of family governance is the codification of the family's values and a plan to engage members in that system through its stated mission. *Family Wealth* and Hughes's other book *Family: The Compact Among Generations* (Bloomberg, 2007), are essential reading for UAC advisers. This chapter provides some insights from my own experience as well as a primer on the subject of family governance.

When dealing with a family with multigenerational wealth, UAC advisers must navigate a complex system of attitudes, economic and social backgrounds, generational views, and varying values, and when these varied forces collide, they can test the strength of family bonds. Family relationships are most at risk when traumatic events such as illness, divorce, or an unfair inheritance occur. Even normal activities such as organizing a family get-together can bring differences among family members to the surface. Ultra-affluent families, with their long-term wealth at risk, need a common way of communicating and understanding one another. Money can lead family members to want to disengage from the family because they can afford to be independent. Perhaps the biggest divide occurs between older generations who have needed to work for themselves to create wealth and newer generations who simply take their affluence for granted.

GENERATIONAL DIVISION

In my experience, it is generational division that causes the most problems for families. First, as just noted, there is the work ethic issue: older generations, particularly those who were exposed one way or another (either personally or through relatives) to the Great Depression, understand the concept of hard work and know that being deprived of resources is a normal part of life. New generations, who have no such perspective, have little reason to work hard and have no concept of deprivation. Normal life for new generations of UACs consists of going to the best schools, taking vacations to high-end resorts, dining out on a regular basis, being seen by the best doctors, and on and on ad infinitum. At the extreme, some family members are led to believe that private jet travel, limo drivers, and black-tie affairs are necessities and not extravagances. So, for older generations, the question becomes how to instill the new generation with a strong work ethic, financial and behavioral discipline, and a tradition of family values, all of which are necessary for perpetuating future generations' high quality of living. The only way this issue will be tackled is if families have leadership, but a difficult challenge awaits these leaders.

The brave souls who take on the challenge and assume a position of family leadership must possess outstanding communication skills as well as a commitment to perpetuating their family through the upcoming generations. In their excellent paper titled *Spread the Wealth: Seven Realities for Affluent Family Leadership,* Gregory T. Rogers and Kelly Costigan note: [2]

> *In fact, a new paradigm for family leadership would seem to be in order: one that is collaborative; equipped with a sharp global outlook and business smarts; diplomatic; and, dare we say it, tough and shrewd enough to manage the often conflicting family dynamics, opposing interests, and personalities of several generations. To make a difference, leadership of a family will also depend on an input-process-feedback loop that supports the growth of each individual, exposes all members to life-skill experiences and strives to build a foundation of respect across generations known and yet to come. The "old school" approach of keeping family members insulated from the hard work and responsibilities that come with affluence is over.*

In short, the challenges of modern life will require a strong leadership structure. A properly structured family governance system can be of significant help to this leadership task.

FAMILY GOVERNANCE: AN ESSENTIAL PART OF SUCCESSFUL WEALTH TRANSFER

A family governance system goes beyond the traditional elements of wealth planning (financial and wealth transfer planning, tax strategies, investment management, etc.) and delves into qualitative elements such as family dynamics, shared family values, mission statements, philanthropy management, and family education. By bringing in the qualitative side and implementing a family governance system, families can not only perpetuate wealth, but also help members handle contentious family issues that can put long-term wealth objectives at risk. When the family is facing its toughest challenges, it is important to come back to a core set of guiding ideologies.

Properly implemented, family governance serves the UA family as a mediation device and a decision-making tool. As a mediation device, a codified family governance system can help manage the competing interests of various family groups by defining each group's roles and responsibilities (and boundaries) and supporting the family's collective mission. As a decision-making tool, family governance can serve as a process that enables family members to make decisions without conflict and communicate the family's values, vision, and mission to family members and to the public. But success is not guaranteed just because a family governance system is in place. Many families have successfully developed their values, vision, and mission, but fail to implement them. They don't realize that family governance is an ongoing process that continually needs to be refined.

Implementing Family Governance

Unless specially qualified, UAC advisers should bring in specialist professionals who are trained to deliver family governance advice. It is essential that UAC advisers get to know who these people are and bring them into a situation when the timing is right. That does not mean, however, that one should delegate the entire job of understanding family governance dynamics to outside specialists. Advisers must get involved and understand what is driving families to behave the way they do; and doing so means understanding the process. So, to make things easier, this section explores family governance through a mini-case-study of a hypothetical family, the Incredibles, who are establishing a family governance system. The process followed for this case study is from a resource we discussed in an earlier chapter, "Family

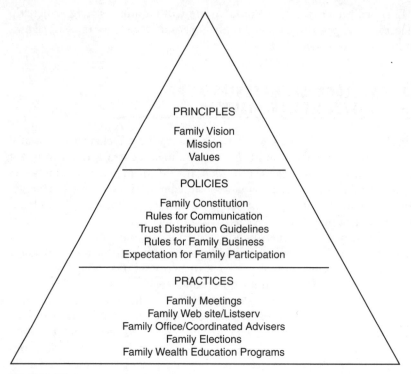

FIGURE 17.1   Triangle of the Components of a Family Governance System
Source: Family Governance: A Primer for Philanthropic Families.

Governance: A Primer for Philanthropic Families" put out by the National Center for Family Philanthropy. The author, Patricia Angus, focuses on three crucial elements of family governance: principles, practices, and policies. These three elements form a triangular structure: family principles at the top of the triangle, the principles lead to family policies, and the family practices are the implementation of the system, as is shown in Figure 17.1.[3] This triangular system can be informal and casual or have formal structures and processes, depending on the needs and culture of the family.

THE INCREDIBLE FAMILY

The Incredibles are a first-generation family of substantial wealth that has just sold their manufacturing company for $250 million. Mr. and Mrs. Incredible have four children, Dash, John, Prince, and Mary, and eight grandchildren. Both John and Mary are married, with four young children each, while Prince and Dash are single playboys. Mr. and Mrs. Incredible came from lower-middle-class families and worked tirelessly together to build their company, Stretchy Clothing, Inc. They are worried about the effect of wealth on their children and grandchildren, and they want to leave the legacy of a positive work ethic in their family. They recently completed a wealth transfer plan with a series of trusts and planning that will establish some guidelines about how the money left to future generations will be distributed. But they want to take things one step further and have recently embarked on a quest to establish a system of family governance for the benefit of present and future generations. They are working with their UAC adviser, Jack, and have brought in a specialist in family governance, Paul. Paul is a big believer in the principles, policies, and practices method of establishing and implementing a system of family governance, and Paul and Jack are helping the Incredibles develop one of their own.

Principles: Vision, Values, and Mission

Paul explains that for a family to establish a system of governance, the family must first discover its unique set of principles—its values, its vision, and its mission. These principles form the foundation of the family's ethos and must be shared and supported by the family, as they in turn will influence the family's policies and practices. And while it is tempting for family members to want to include personal aspirations in establishing the family's principles, Paul explains that the personal aspirations of family members must be set aside and that family members should respect each other's differences. To help develop the principles section of the family governance program for the Incredibles, Paul asks three key questions. To give you a frame of reference, each question includes a discussion section. At the end, the answers that the Incredibles gave will be revealed. The first step is to define the family's values.

Question 1: What Are the Incredible Family's Shared Values?   What is a value? As commonly accepted, *value* is defined as the quality or worth of something. What is a family? A family is defined as the basic unit in society traditionally consisting of two parents rearing their children. When we put values in the context of a family, we get *family values:* a set of valued social standards that provide a foundation for raising children and perpetuating a family. Social values are often reinforced by spiritual or religious beliefs and associated traditions. Family values are often simply behaviors that have been passed down from generation to generation. The values a family

develops are the basis of how young family members learn, grow, and function in the family and in society. To make the task of defining values easier, we can think of values in three categories: work, leisure, and intimacy (i.e., love). These values are critical to long-term family success, and it is very important to balance them. Many families get too focused on either work or leisure and neglect intimacy. Some focus on only work and cause serious stress on the family unit. In either case, without incorporating intimacy into our relationships, our lives can become unsatisfying. Traditional values concepts that fall under intimacy include things like how a family member views a marriage and commitment, physical gestures such as hugging and kissing, how members display emotions, how they share common interests, and last, but not least, what role spirituality plays in the family.

There is a useful exercise a family can do to identify both the values of the family and the values of its individuals. To start the exercise, each family member is given a blank sheet of lined paper, divided in into three columns. The first column is used to identify the activities that the family values, in any order. Then, in the second column, the individual prioritizes the list based on how important each activity is to the family. In the third column, the activities are ranked in terms of how much time is actually spent doing each. Naturally, the point of the exercise is to identify how the family needs to change its behavior to act out what it values most. The values in bold are those that the Incredibles indentified with. Charlotte Roberts, co-author of *The Fifth Discipline Fieldbook* (Doubleday, 1994) provides a sample list of values.[4]

Achievement	Democracy	Honesty
Advancement and promotion	Ecological awareness	Independence
	Economic security	Influencing others
Adventure	Effectiveness	**Inner harmony**
Affection (love and caring)	Efficiency	Integrity
Arts	Ethical practice	Intellectual status
Challenging problems	**Excellence**	**Involvement**
Change and variety	Excitement	Job tranquillity
Close relationships	Fame	Knowledge
Community	Fast living	Leadership
Competence	Financial gain	Location
Competition	Friendships	**Loyalty**
Cooperation	Growth	Market position
Country	Having a family	Meaningful work
Creativity	Helping other people	Merit
Decisiveness	Helping society	Money

Nature	Purity	Serenity
Being around people who value others	**Quality of what I take part in**	Sophistication
Order (tranquillity, stability, conformity)	Quality relationships	Stability
	Recognition (respect from others, status)	Status
Personal development		Supervising others
Freedom	Religion	Time freedom
Physical challenge	Reputation	**Truth**
Pleasure	Responsibility and accountability	Wealth
Power and authority		**Wisdom**
Privacy	Security	Work under pressure
Public service	Self-respect	Work with others
		Working alone

Question 2: What is the Incredibles' common vision for the family and its future generations? A family vision can be reduced to the following question: What is the family all about now and where is it going in the future? A family's vision is composed of its shared values, the legacy it wants to create, and what it will contribute to the community at large. The benefit of having a family vision is that it provides the family with a unique philosophy and a direction so that family members know what the family stands for and where it is going. Moreover, a vision can help mediate family conflicts if they arise because the shared vision can guide members toward a solution to the conflict, and helps family members to learn from the experience instead of having the conflict cause problems. Some families have difficulty creating a vision. There are some questions that, when answered, can help to create a vision for a family. These are:

- What is our family all about today, and what do we want to be in the future?
- What makes us proud as a family?
- How do we want to treat one another on a daily basis?
- What is it about our family that we like the most?
- What about our family can we improve?
- How are we perceived by the community?
- What types of charitable activities do we want to participate in?
- What families do we admire? What can we learn from these families?

Incredibles' Answer Our vision is to be a close, supportive, and loving family that works hard, while taking time for healthy leisure activities. In addition, we want to contribute to the community through our family foundation, the Incredible Generosity Foundation.

Question 3: What is the Incredibles' Mission?   One of my favorite quotes from Yogi Berra, the baseball philosopher, is "When you come to a fork in the road, take it."[5] Families come to many forks in the road, and if a family does not know what it stands for, wrong turns could result. On the other hand, there are successful families who have a clear sense of their values, vision, and mission and have encapsulated that information into a Family Mission Statement (FMS) to help them decide which path to take when the inevitable forks appear. Families in need of multi-generational values transfer will find that a FMS provides an ideological foundation that the family can continually look to for guidance.

An FMS is the backbone of a family governance system because it describes the family's commitment to its members and their community. However, FMSs are often met with suspicion and resistance when they are being created. In our example, Paul might hear a younger family member ask a senior family member, "Why do we need to do this? Don't we know who we are?" While it may be true that the family knows itself, families who execute a meaningful mission statement will reap a substantial return on the investment. Once it is completed, many family members refer to the FMS for guidance frequently. When creating an FMS, the family should attempt to get the widest possible participation. When many family members are involved, all can appreciate and understand their history and better understand the present so that planning for the future is easier and more gratifying for the entire family. One way to help family members accept a family mission statement is to refer to many successful businesses that use them. One company that comes to mind is Johnson and Johnson. This is their mission statement (what they call their credo):

We believe our first responsibility is to the doctors, nurses, and patients, to mothers and fathers and all others who use our products and services.

In meeting their needs everything we do must be of high quality.

We must constantly strive to reduce our costs in order to maintain reasonable prices.

Customers' orders must be serviced promptly and accurately.

Our suppliers and distributors must have an opportunity to make a fair profit.

We are responsible to our employees, the men and women who work with us throughout the world.

Everyone must be considered as an individual.

We must respect their dignity and recognize their merit.

They must have a sense of security in their jobs.

Compensation must be fair and adequate, and working conditions clean, orderly, and safe.

We must be mindful of ways to help our employees fulfill their family responsibilities.

Employees must feel free to make suggestions and complaints.

There must be equal opportunity for employment, development, and advancement for those qualified.

We must provide competent management, and their actions must be just and ethical.

We are responsible to the communities in which we live and work and to the world community as well.

We must be good citizens—support good works and charities and bear our fair share of taxes.

We must encourage civic improvements and better health and education.

We must maintain in good order the property we are privileged to use, protecting the environment and natural resources.

Our final responsibility is to our stockholders.

Business must make a sound profit.

We must experiment with new ideas.

Research must be carried on, innovative programs developed and mistakes paid for.

New equipment must be purchased, new facilities provided, and new products launched.

Reserves must be created to provide for adverse times.

When we operate according to these principles, the stockholders should realize a fair return.

This credo represents the core beliefs that lead Johnson and Johnson philosophically. The statement does not outline daily communications or weekly operating procedures, but rather communicates the long-term leadership goals and values of the organization. Notice how it encourages employees to make suggestions and fulfill their family obligations. Family mission statements are flexible and should be amended and updated as needed. As promised, the Incredibles' mission statement is contained below.

The Incredible Family Mission Statement Our first responsibility is to the growth and development of all Incredible family members. We must always be aware of the mental and physical state of each member of the family so that we can react to any adverse changes in any family member. We must always strive to develop our children in a way that respects them as individuals and supports their needs while helping them to become functioning members of society. The family's values and vision, as created by the family members, should always be kept in mind when senior family members are developing and mentoring younger family members. Open and honest communication is essential to the long-term health of our family's generational relationships.

We also have a responsibility to our community and to those people who are serving the family in an advisory capacity. We will treat all outside people who come in contact with the family with dignity and respect. We must uphold the highest levels of ethics and morals in our dealings with the public. In short, we will be good public citizens and encourage the betterment of the communities we live in.

POLICIES

After the values, vision, and mission have been established, the family must have methods of implementing these items. These methods are referred to as a family's policies. The policies that families establish can be thought of as the ground rules for communication and action about matters of common interest to family members, such as a family business. An example of a vehicle to implement family policies is a family constitution or family charter (FC). While it is outside the scope of this chapter to present a sample of the Incredibles' family constitution, it is important that UAC advisers understand the contents and purpose of the FC. An FC is a document that describes a family's (previously developed) vision, values, and mission and regulates relationships within the family and with the public. Its purpose is to define a code of conduct or a set of rules that apply to issues such as communication, investment objectives, education, and philanthropy.

Establishing these guidelines helps family members interact with one another, especially when they have differing personal views on issues. The FC is a road map which, when put to use, strikes a balance between the rights, obligations, and expectations of family members, facilitating concessions in the interest of the group that ensures long-term survival.

At the minimum, an FC has three components or sections: the preamble, the rules, and a communications section. The preamble is there to recount the family history and the evolution of the family's activities to the present. It identifies the values the family stands for and confirms the family's commitment to continuity. The rules section defines the family's rules of governance and is meant to help members find common ground while recognizing individuals. This section identifies the various constituencies within the family and attempts to address, as far as possible, the expectations and goals of each family member. The communications section addresses the organization of family forums (e.g., family councils or meetings) to ensure that there is a mechanism in place to help members with potentially conflicting views work toward resolution. Like the United States Constitution, a family constitution can evolve over time, adapting to the specific needs of an ever-changing family. Ultimately, a favorable outcome for a family's succession plan over multiple generations relies on the wisdom and vision of the family members it serves.

Practices

Practices support the principles and policies during day-to-day activities of family members. How the family interacts needs to be agreed upon through these practices. Some families hold scheduled meetings organized by their advisers or by family members. Others coordinate their activities and share information through a secure web site or listserv. A family office can also be used to administer the family's nonfinancial affairs, or the family could hire an independent consultant or adviser team. At the end of the day, it doesn't matter what form of communication the family chooses to use, it is only necessary that the chosen interactions best suit the specific family.

STAGES OF DEVELOPMENT

In developing a family governance system, a family typically experiences three phases: chaos, coordination, and cohesion. In the first stage, chaos, the family responds to immediate needs and does not have a firm grasp on their long-term goals. Support structures are set up when the need appears, such as the writing of a will right before the first big family vacation or right

TABLE 17.1 Phases of Development for a Family Governance System

Phase	Characteristics	Actions	Goals
Chaos	Uncoordinated, short-term focus Responds to immediate needs	Create basic estate plans Minimize transfer taxes	"Sleep at night" Cover emergencies
Coordination	Family sees big picture Family meetings Leaders emerge	Define family goals Begin tax planning and education	Create coordinated system Choose leaders Begin succession planning
Cohesion	Act in view of long-term goals Establish regular meetings	Choose family leaders Clarity between joint and individual needs	Sustainability Integration of family members

Source: Family Governance: A Primer for Philanthropic Families.

after the birth of a couple's first child. Family members often act without considering the greater good of the family during this phase. The second stage, coordination, usually begins when a major event occurs in the family, signaling to family members that a more coordinated system is crucial to the family's existence. Family members no longer have a short-term focus in mind; they begin to develop their principles and policies, and they select their leaders and advisers. The last and most rarely achieved stage is cohesion. The family operates under an integrated system, regularly communicates, and looks toward a sustainable future. Once this stage is attained, it is important that the family continues to act in ways that support cohesion.

Table 17.1, adapted from Family Governance: A Primer for Philanthropic Families, summarizes the three phases of development of a family governance system:

CONCLUSION

As I have demonstrated in this chapter, preserving wealth over multiple generations is not a question of having the best estate plan or investment consultant, but rather a question of human behavior choices. Successful multigenerational families need to codify an agreement among its members if each generation is to successfully overcome the natural forces that can dissipate a family's wealth. A system of family governance is the codification of the family's values and a plan to engage members in that system through its stated mission. UAC advisers should now be well-equipped to deal with some of these situations as they arise but at the same time recognize their limitations when expert help is needed. Now that we have covered family governance, we move on to the all-important topic of risk management and asset protection.

CHAPTER 18

Risk Management and Asset Protection

Take calculated risks. That is quite different from being rash.
—General George S. Patton (1885–1945)

Ultra-affluent clients and their advisers are acutely aware that we live in a litigious world and that wealthy families can be the targets of lawsuits (whether or not claims made against the family are real) or even more threatening attacks, such as kidnapping, because of their status. In addition, real world risks exist such as theft, accidents, liability for negligence, and even weather-related disasters. Risk management through insurance and legal asset protection are strategies to combat some of these risks, which can seriously impair intergenerational wealth. In addition, family members may themselves be a potential source of unexpected wealth dissipation, something many advisers and family members may overlook. These family issues can be potentially overcome by many of the topics covered in Chapter 17 but can also be thought of inside the category of asset protection. Although most advisers do not enter this area of the advisory process, they have an opportunity to add value if they can recognize a need.

A recent study by Prince & Associates, Inc. shows that

Many wealthy families lack adequate asset protection plans, with owners saying that the process is just too complicated. In this survey of 242 family-owned businesses with a mean value of $730 million, nearly all expressed concerns about protecting their wealth, even though most had no asset protection plans in place. About a quarter of respondents said the process was too complicated, while others said they lacked sufficient guidance to protect their family fortune. By contrast, nearly 80 percent said they had personal *estate plans. Yet even these plans were likely to be more than six years old and hadn't been updated after a marriage or divorce, the survey found. "Not only do these families need to act on implementing and updating their wealth planning strategies, they need more sophisticated strategies to better protect their wealth," Mindy Rosenthal, the study's co-author, said in a statement.*[1]

Family offices face various risks in their everyday business and could be held legally accountable for services provided to their clients. In addition, family members need to protect their assets from many threats like lawsuits and accidents. Trustees of family trusts also face liability for their acts as trustees and, as such, face fiduciary obligations to beneficiaries. In certain situations, such as gross negligence, a trustee may be legally barred from indemnification by the trust, despite an indemnification provision. In short, risk management and asset protection for UACs is an important subject that is often overlooked by both advisers and clients. We delve in this chapter into three main areas: family office risk management, individual family member risk management, and two key strategies for legal asset protection from creditors. UAC advisers need not be experts in this area, but should be knowledgeable about key risk management and asset protection issues. Knowing this information can help add value to your relationships, especially if you recognize an area of need that the family hasn't thought of. UAC advisers are well-positioned to support clients by delivering trustworthy advice on the risks a family faces and solutions for insurance and risk-management issues, helping to ensure long-term financial security and peace of mind. As has been repeated again and again throughout this book, it is important to bring in the expertise of specialist professionals who understand the unique requirements of UACs—and risk management is no exception.

FAMILY OFFICE RISK MANAGEMENT

Even though family offices are private, owners and professionals who work for these entities are not insulated from liabilities commonly associated with public companies. Legal responsibilities of family office executives fall under the same laws that govern corporate governance. Family offices have directors and officers with the same fiduciary and employment practices obligations as corporations. Insurance can be used to protect family offices and the professionals working in them. There are two primary types of liability insurance for professional organizations. These are general liability

The author gratefully acknowledges Marcy Hall for her review of this section on family office risk management.

insurance and professional liability insurance. Both types of coverage are important to properly indemnify a professional organization such as a family office from financial loss. In this section I discuss six types of insurance to give you a primer on the subject. There is much more to know but this will give you a basic understanding of some of the coverages that family offices are using. These insurance coverages are general commercial liability, professional liability, directors and officers liability (D&O), trustee liability, fiduciary liability, and employment practices liability (EPL).

Insurance and Indemnification

The best way to protect directors and officers against personal liability exposure is to provide indemnification by the family office. Indemnification provisions should be included in the family office's bylaws. To supplement this indemnification protection, the office should establish an insurance program that includes property and general commercial liability, professional liability, directors and officers liability, trustee liability, fiduciary liability, employment practices liability, and workers' compensation. Although we will not cover cyber security, safeguarding computer systems is also an area that family offices need to protect themselves. When the subject turns to family members themselves, mitigating individual risks requires up-to-date professional advice and proper levels of protection. The rest of this section consists of a review of types of family office coverages and individual family member coverages.

General Commercial Liability Insurance　*General liability insurance* pro-
tects the assets of an entity when it is sued for something it is responsible for doing (or, sometimes, isn't responsible for doing!) that causes injury or property damage. This is not a large risk area for family offices, but is needed nonetheless. Under a general liability insurance policy, covered claims include property damage, bodily injury, personal injury, and advertising injury (which is damage from slander or false advertising). General liability insurance policies always state a maximum amount that the insurer will pay during the policy period. These policies usually also list the maximum amount the insurer will pay per occurrence. For example, if a company has a $2 million single occurrence maximum in its liability policy and it loses a suit totaling $2.5 million, the insurer would pay $2 million and the business would be responsible for paying $500,000. Punitive damages aren't covered under general liability insurance policies because they are considered to be punishment for intentional acts.

　　There is additional insurance coverage available for gaps in general liability insurance policies, called an *umbrella* liability insurance policy. This policy picks up where the general liability policy leaves off. Umbrella liability covers payments that exceed the other policy's limits, and provides additional coverage for liabilities not covered in a standard liability insurance policy. General liability insurance can be purchased separately or as part of a business owner's policy (BOP). A BOP bundles property and liability insurance into one policy. Businesses that need more coverage usually purchase liability insurance as a separate policy. The amount of coverage that a family office needs depends on how much risk the family office executives believe they need coverage for, and the state in which the business operates.

Professional Liability Insurance   Professional liability insurance is designed to provide coverage to advisory professionals for claims arising out of professional malpractice while providing services to clients. Professional liability insurance is made up of many segments, and is also called *errors and omissions* (E&O) or *malpractice* insurance. Coverage is typically provided by a professional liability policy and includes coverage for defense costs associated with a claim. In pricing professional liability insurance for a given family office, insurance companies mainly examine the activities the professionals participate in during the delivery of service. Other factors include physical location, office size, education level and training of employees, loss history, and operating characteristics. Because of these variables, professional liability policies come in a wide range of types and are offered by a wide range of insurers. Smaller, niche insurance companies often offer the best price, coverage, and service options compared to the larger, multiline insurers. Professional liability policies typically do not provide coverage for nonfinancial losses or for intentional or dishonest acts. This coverage can be important for family offices, especially if they take on outside clients.

Directors and Officers Insurance   Directors and Officers (D&O) coverage protects those members of corporations and others, such as family offices, against legal judgments and expenses relating thereto that result from allegations of wrongful acts committed in their work. Because directors and officers are fiduciaries, they are responsible for managing the affairs of their organizations. As such, they must act with due diligence in carrying out their responsibilities and can be held personally liable if their neglect results in a loss to the corporation or its shareholders. D&O coverage is typically provided in two parts: direct coverage to the directors and officers, and corporate reimbursement. The direct coverage part is used only when the corporate entity is not permitted to reimburse directors and officers. D&O coverage can become very complex and coverage changes, depending on the type of entity insured. For example, volunteers such as trustees are often covered under D&O policies for nonprofit entities, but rarely under other policies. Some policies include entity coverage, and some include employment practices coverage.

Except for some very specialized policies, D&O coverage does not provide protection to the directors and officers of a professional organization for professional liability claims because there is a separate policy available for professional liability. For D&O coverage, broader policies are not necessarily better policies. For example, employment practices coverage can be purchased for smaller entities for a low price with deductibles lower than most D&O policies. It is often better, however, to purchase a stand-alone employment practices policy for those claims and let the D&O policy cover D&O claims. Employment practices are covered later.

Trustee Liability Insurance   Trustee liability insurance covers trustees for malpractice that occurs while they are carrying out their trustee duties. Trustees can be exposed to a broad range of risks, and laws defining trustees' liability are getting broader. Family trusts are among the most complex because they are the longest-lasting trusts and there is a wide variety of these types of trusts. For example, in some trusts, the predominant assets are securities, such as cash, bonds, and equities, but some trusts hold illiquid assets such as private equity, private real assets, or a family company, which are more difficult to assess and are usually illiquid.

Trustees, service providers, and family offices that provide services to trusts and trust beneficiaries need to be aware of risks they face when executing their duties. Trustee investment and distribution decisions are governed by a combination of the terms of the trust document and trust law. The amount of cash distributions to beneficiaries, however, can have significant implications for the management structure of the trust and ultimately for the liability for trustees. In many cases the trust document gives the trustee wide latitude in making decisions, but can be subject to interpretation and second-guessing by beneficiaries.

Claims against trustees can allege breach of fiduciary oversight, conflict of interest, self-dealing, misrepresentation, negligent supervision and selection and promotion of employees, and professional negligence. Another area of conflict is how investments perform. Trustees have a duty to invest as a prudent investor would, including selecting appropriate investment managers or consultants. As such, trustees have a mandate to oversee and direct investment managers or consultants in accordance with trust guidelines, and to diligently review the performance delivered by the managers. Trustees may need to make investment decisions on assets in the trust that aren't under the control of an investment manager, such as the ownership of a private company—and the trustee must be capable of performing this duty effectively.

The type of trustee insurance coverage one can obtain depends on the insurance company offering coverage and the nature of the trust structure. Typical coverage comes in the form of professional liability insurance, and limits and deductibles vary with the size and type of trust. Standard limits for most small- to medium-sized organizations start at $1 million. The simplest form of coverage protects only the trustee for her duties as trustee of a specific trust or series of trusts. For larger and more complex situations, broader customized coverage can be obtained, although this type of insurance can be more challenging to acquire. Many trust agreements have provisions that permit the trust to pay for insurance coverage, including trustee liability. While the poor performance of investment managers selected by the trustees may be a potential source of litigation by beneficiaries, a more typical dispute arises over whether the investment direction given to a manager by a trustee follows the intent of the trust.

Fiduciary Liability Insurance   Family office executives whose functions are similar to bank trust departments must meet fiduciary standards of care. Furthermore, they must administer their accounts according to the provisions of trust documents and follow prudent investor standards, which require a fiduciary to be proactive and diligently monitor the changing needs of beneficiaries. Fiduciary liability insurance (FLI) pays, on behalf of an insured, the legal liability arising from claims for alleged failure to prudently act within the meaning of the Pension Reform Act of 1974. *Insured* is defined in the Act as a trust or employee benefit plan; any trustee, officer, or employee of the trust or employee benefit plan; employer who is sole sponsor of a plan; or any other individual or organization designated as a fiduciary. Any individual included in the plan document by name or title, or anyone who has discretionary authority over the administration or management of a plan or its assets, is considered a fiduciary and can be exposed to liability.[2]

Under the Employee Retirement Income Security Act (ERISA), fiduciaries may be held personally liable for any breach of their responsibilities. Although FLI is not required by ERISA, it is recommended if personal assets are at risk. Many fiduciaries incorrectly assume that fiduciary insurance is included in a D&O policy; it is not. Most D&O policies exclude fiduciary liability exposures as well as exposures pertaining to ERISA. ERISA also broadly defines the types of employee benefit plans for which fiduciaries are responsible. If a family office has a pension plan, profit-sharing plan, or similar plan, designated fiduciaries (the employer or the plan itself) can be targets of lawsuits. Claims may include allegations of poor advice or lack of transparency, questionable investment manager selection, imprudent investments, or lack of proper diversification of asset classes.

Employee Practices Liability and Workers' Compensation Insurance   Employee relations represent a robust area of liability exposure to family office employers and their directors, officers, and supervisors. The at-will employment canon has numerous exceptions, including breach of contract, breach of good faith or fair dealing, and promissory estoppel (which is defined as the reliance on an employer's promise to the detriment of the employees). There are also various statutes that govern workplace practices, including the Americans with Disabilities Act, the Civil Rights Act of 1964, and the Age Discrimination Act. The best tool for maintaining good employee relations is communication and education by keeping supervisors up on the current state of workplace law and proper workplace procedures through employee meetings or handbooks. Another measure is proper documentation of employee activities, including performance reviews, workplace deficiencies, and disciplinary measures. The greatest loss prevention measure, however, is to treat employees with common decency in return for hard work. Workers' compensation coverage is needed for families who employ household staff. In fact, state law may require it. This insurance indemnifies the family and covers legal expenses associated with a situation in which a domestic worker (regardless of citizenship status) sues for harassment, wrongful discharge, or discrimination.

INDIVIDUAL FAMILY MEMBER RISK MANAGEMENT

UAC advisers need not be insurance experts to help their individual clients but there are concrete things one can do to be of service. First, advisers should be familiar with the client's insurance coverage and the key issues surrounding them. UACs have risk exposures that standard policies don't cover (or don't adequately cover), and you can add value by pointing out these issues to clients. You can help by reviewing the client's situation annually to make sure all insurance risks are managed. But don't go it alone; coordinate oversight of these issues with a well-qualified insurance professional. As with investment advice, UAC advisers should look to independent service providers who have access to multiple insurance companies rather than a broker tied to a single carrier. Whoever the insurance specialists and carriers are, they should be committed to delivering high-touch service. Let's take a look at what risk management services you should be familiar with.

Liability Insurance

For UACs, the risk of a liability loss has catastrophic potential. Lawsuits can easily stray into the multimillion dollar range and the loss of a liability suit is a major exposure of one's assets. Probably the single most important component of an insurance program for the UAC is adequate liability limits. These limits provide protection for unforeseen or unavoidable events associated with accident and negligence claims. Claims of this nature can linger for many years while legal defense costs mount and ultimate settlement amounts remain unknown. A secondary policy may also be needed to cover court-awarded damages, as well as legal fees. A personal excess liability policy (commonly known as a *personal umbrella* policy) is one designed to protect the insured against multimillion dollar settlements resulting from personal injury, bodily injury, or property damage lawsuits. Personal umbrella coverage applies to losses over a large dollar amount, but the terms of coverage are at times broader than those of underlying policies. Coverage extends above and beyond that provided by the primary policies, covering an individual's home, automobile, watercraft, and so on. The amount of insurance is often unique to each client and depends upon how much coverage is available. A typical red flag for an adviser is the addition of a youthful operator to an insurance policy. If your client has a child that has turned 16 and will be operating a family vehicle, a review of the umbrella policy is critical, as well as a discussion about the exposures the family now faces. Teenage drivers need to understand that their actions behind the wheel can have a broad impact on a family's financial security. A full-service agent or broker should have access to insurance companies who offer substantial coverage. The key is getting the maximum coverage for the lowest price. A client should never have to use up his or her assets to pay off a liability judgment; but without proper liability coverage, this type of disaster can occur.

Custom and Multiple Homeowner's and Valuable Possessions Insurance

Whether the coverage needed is for primary or secondary residences, co-op apartments, vacation homes, or rental units, homeowner's insurance is a must. The key issue for homeowners is maintaining sufficient coverage to rebuild in case of a partial or total loss. Those policies that pay based on replacement cost normally cap rebuilding payment at, for example, 130 percent of the face amount of the policy. Another area of concern is clients who have older homes that are grandfathered into current zoning laws. These clients need to know that most homeowner's policies pay only for the materials and workmanship that was lost, even though replacement construction would have to conform to modern, and potentially more expensive, zoning rules. Additional protection, sometimes referred to as building ordinance insurance, is needed to cover the incremental cost of getting a home to meet current building codes and standards. One way to protect oneself against underinsurance in this area is to get an appraisal for the cost to rebuild the home. With a current appraisal, the insurance company will more likely pay the actual cost of a loss if it is significantly higher than anticipated. If the UAC has rental homes, it is imperative to make sure there is a legal contract with the renter, and that the renter has purchased his own insurance policy. Regarding valuables, many UACs are unaware of the modest limitations that homeowner's policies typically pay on losses of furs, jewelry, antiques, and other collectibles. Active collectors should get quarterly or semiannual reviews to ensure all new acquisitions are adequately covered. Insurance is also needed for valuables that are in transit, on exhibit, or on consignment. The larger and more complicated a family's valuables, the greater the need for appropriate insurance coverage. A common misperception is that all policies are the same, so long as the coverage limits are identical. There are insurance companies that are dedicated to the UAC market and generally offer broader internal coverages, more favorable loss settlement provisions, and may provide a heightened level of additional services to the client. At a minimum, the client should have their account remarketed every three to five years to make sure they are receiving the best available coverages.

UAC advisers should also be familiar with auto, watercraft, yacht, and aircraft insurance; coverage for "toys" such as jet skis, snowmobiles, motorcycles, and recreational vehicles; kidnap and ransom insurance; travel insurance; and medical insurance. If the UAC is employing domestic staff, they have an added level of exposure, and should be made aware of the employment practices and workers comp coverages available.

Family Member Risks

Lisa Gray of Graymatter Strategies, LLC reminds us that liability to a family's assets may come not just from creditors, but also from so-called outlier sources—sources which may be overlooked but which suddenly and disruptively appear. It may come from disgruntled family members in the form of lawsuits against family leadership or against other family members. It may come from the irresponsible behavior of family members, either socially or within their involvement in the family business. It is possible for family members to find ways to either sidestep or simply ignore a founder's wishes after his lifetime, regardless of the structures put into place before death. Disgruntled family members may form factions which, over time, attract enough other disgruntled family members to usurp leadership either of the

The author gratefully acknowledges Lisa Gray for her substantial contribution to this section on family member risks.

family, the family business, or both. Family secrets can cause disruption within the family which seeps into the family business, adding unnecessary burdens to management and hampering the productivity of employees. A family member with uncontrollable spending habits may affect other family members' abilities to reach their goals by creating unforeseen liabilities for the family or for a particular branch of the family which suddenly finds itself charged with providing financial life support. Family members are not like non-performing material or investment assets; they cannot simply be discarded or sold!

Health issues can pose risks either to the founder or to other family members who are vital to the family business. The need to cover medical costs related to extreme or long-term illnesses may tax the family's material assets. Family members living abroad or who travel overseas regularly may become ill away from home and may not have access to dependable healthcare. Kidnapping and other personal protection issues can threaten the lives of family members and subject the family's material assets to sizeable and unexpected monetary demands. Imprudent entries by younger family members on social networking web sites may expose them and the family to unanticipated liability or danger.

The root cause of most of these issues is grounded in the generational perspectives and dynamics of the family, according to Gray. These are the core risk factors for the family. They are also the most authentic sources for consummate risk management and asset protection. Notice that they all have to do with issues which lie outside of the traditional management and protection of the material wealth. Gray challenges traditional thinking about risk management and asset protection in the traditional sense by asking us to take two proactive steps. The first is to acknowledge that the intellectual, human, and social capacities of family members are the family's core assets. The original creation of the material wealth, both financial and non-financial, is a byproduct of the realization of these capacities by the founders.

The second step is to understand the critical role of governance in the success of the family (see Chapter 17). Through well-designed family governance, favorable family dynamics foster communication and trust among family members. Family members grow to understand their roles and responsibilities as members of a family unit and as dynamic owners of significant material wealth. By approaching risk management and asset protection through the family governance system, the complicated process of developing an adequate asset protection plan is circumvented. This eliminates the excuse by owners mentioned earlier from the Prince & Associates, Inc. survey that the process is too complicated and takes too much time to develop. Risk management and asset protection actually becomes part of the governance system.

Governance which accurately identifies the family's needs and goals and which enables collective input for the development of strategies to fulfill them automatically prescribes a preventive formula for managing a significant portion of a family's core risks. This allows traditional risk management and asset protection vehicles to do what they do best—to support the family governance structure and mitigate external risks which lie outside the family's control.

Taking these two steps enables families and their advisors to identify the keys to effective risk management and asset protection at the source instead of after a problem has arisen. It enables families to examine the ongoing core risk factors which are at work during the lifetimes of the current generations. Upon these factors rest the endurance of the family legacy and the future regeneration of the family's wealth.

LEGAL ASSET PROTECTION

UACs spend decades accumulating wealth, but one frivolous lawsuit could take it all away. Many UACs are taking steps to protect their assets from lawsuits and illegitimate creditor claims by implementing asset protection strategies. Asset protection (sometimes also referred to as debtor-creditor law) refers to a set of legal techniques for protecting the assets of individuals and business entities from civil money judgments and from creditors such as trusts, partnerships, and international entities. Asset protection is an increasingly important aspect of planning, but since so many planning-related areas have begun to use the phrase, its definition has become less distinct. I define asset protection in this section as the use of legal entities, structures, and strategies to make assets difficult or impossible for a potential creditor to acquire. Asset protection planning often has strong estate planning benefits but does not involve insurance or tax strategies. The goal of planning in this area is to mitigate the risk to family net worth from creditors, and it works best when coordinated with a wealth preservation and transfer strategy. Asset protection is not one technique or one entity; rather, it is the use of combinations of strategies to achieve insulation, tax efficiency, and control. It is imperative that asset protection strategies be implemented before there is a problem. Once a creditor makes a claim or is likely to make a claim, any subsequent transfer may be deemed fraudulent. In keeping with the theme of bringing in experts when needed, I asked Daniel Rubin, a partner with

The author gratefully acknowledges Daniel Rubin for his substantial contribution to this section on asset protection.

the law firm of Moses and Singer in New York City contribute his expertise to the asset protection discussion.

Asset protection planning is not new but has become increasingly sophisticated in the last decade. It has developed largely as a response to what former U.S. Supreme Court Chief Justice Warren Burger described in the late 1970s as a "litigation explosion." Domestic and foreign asset protection trusts, described later in this article, are in many cases the strongest asset protection strategy. However, there are a number of other asset protection tactics, including the following:

> Purchasing an umbrella policy for liability insurance.
>
> Transferring assets to a spouse.
>
> Titling a home as a tenancy by the entireties.
>
> Moving to a state less friendly to creditors (for example, moving from New York to Florida).
>
> Choosing certain investments over others (for example, life insurance and annuities have some level of inherent protection from creditors).
>
> Placing the marital share of an estate in a QTIP trust rather than allowing it to pass outright.
>
> Forming a business as an LLC instead of as a sole proprietorship.

Mr. Rubin notes why wealthy families need asset protection: The legal system no longer links liability to causation. This means that juries often decide cases based on emotion and on whether the defendant has the ability to pay. Judges can be unpredictable as well. Reducing the assets one has available to creditors makes one a less appealing defendant. Rubin describes the most likely candidates for asset protection:

> Professionals—doctors, lawyers, accountants, architects, etc.
>
> Officers and directors of public companies.
>
> Fiduciaries—trustees and executors.
>
> Real estate owners with exposure to environmental claims.
>
> Individuals exposed to lawsuits arising from claims alleging negligent acts, intentional torts (discrimination, harassment, or libel), or contractual claims.
>
> Individuals who desire a prenuptial agreement alterative that doesn't involve negotiations with the future spouse.
>
> Financial services professionals such as hedge fund and private equity fund managers.
>
> Any wealthy person who could be sued for negligence; for instance, if her cleaning lady falls off a stepladder or her child injures another child

The percentage of assets that a client might seek to protect by a transfer to an asset protection trust, for example, can vary significantly. For instance, a billionaire may transfer only $20 million of her assets to a trust—believing this amount to be a sufficient nest egg in case of a financially disastrous judgment—but an attorney with $7 million in assets may transfer 95% of his net worth to a trust. It's important to put these issues before clients regardless of their wealth, Rubin said.

Domestic and Foreign Asset Protection Trusts: The Winning Strategy

A trust is "a contractual relationship between a grantor, a trustee, and a beneficiary for the trustee to hold legal title to property, formerly owned by the grantor, for the benefit of the beneficiary," Rubin said. Since an 1871 U.S. Supreme Court case, the law of the land has been that creditors have no access to assets that a person has merely as a beneficiary of a trust. This case applies, however, only when one person (the grantor or settlor) sets up a trust for someone else. If the trust is self-settled—meaning that the grantor is also a beneficiary of the trust—public policy concerns are often cited as a reason to avoid the creditor protection effect.

Certain foreign jurisdictions have permitted self-settled asset protection trusts (APTs) since 1984—the Cook Islands, for instance. Since 1997, 10 states have enacted domestic APT legislation: Alaska, Delaware, Missouri, Nevada, New Hampshire, Rhode Island, South Dakota, Tennessee, Utah, and Wyoming. An eleventh state, Oklahoma, has enacted a variation on these laws. These state laws indicate that the public policy debate is shifting in favor of APTs, and upwards of 40 states will likely permit APTs within the next 20 years. In the meantime, clients who set up an APT can choose which state's law governs the trust; thus, their particular state of domicile doesn't limit their planning options. Important aspects of APTs include that the grantor can be a discretionary beneficiary, though she should not be the sole beneficiary, if possible, because the interests of the other beneficiaries in the trust may prove key to defeating future creditor claims. Also, the settlor can be the trust's protector, which gives her the right to change the trustee. Furthermore, the settlor can retain a limited testamentary power of appointment to change the disposition of the trust's assets upon her death, thus providing her the flexibility of a will while at the same time negating any gift tax consequences in connection with the funding of the trust.

Foreign APTs are preferable to domestic APTs for a number of reasons, Rubin pointed out. He uses U.S. APTs only when a client doesn't want to go offshore because, for instance, the client is a high-profile executive or the assets (e.g., the client's manufacturing business or real estate) are permanently situated in the U.S. Among the reasons why foreign APTs compare favorably to domestic ones are that statutes of limitation are often shorter in foreign jurisdictions; all litigation costs may be imposed on the loser; attorneys don't work for contingency fees; and courts may favor debtors over creditors. Also, while the U.S. Constitution's Full Faith and Credit Clause obliges states to enforce their sister states' judgments, foreign courts will not necessarily enforce a U.S. judgment against a foreign APT. Foreign APTs are often the optimum form of asset protection because the grantor has continued access to the transferred assets (albeit within the trustee's discretion), without the risk that such assets might be lost to the future creditor's claims. Although the same result is possible with a domestic APT, the constitutional issue raised under the Full Faith and Credit Clause leaves open the question of the trust's ultimate effectiveness as a shield against creditors.

Be aware: APTs and other asset protection methods have potentially important tax implications, depending upon their structure. Although these issues are beyond the scope of this book, readers should explore them thoroughly before embarking upon any asset protection planning and bring in experts where needed.

Furthermore, it's important to note that when these types of asset protection plans are established, it's critical to have a discussion with the insurance adviser as to the possible issues on the liability portion of the policy. If a home is transferred to a FLP, LLC or trust, the name of the entity needs to be added to the policy. Not all insurance companies will readily agree to the additional interest.

CONCLUSION

Risk management is an often overlooked, yet incredibly important facet of the wealth preservation process. What is presented here is only scratching the surface. UAC advisers should now be in a position to discuss some important things with their clients. But UAC advisers should be keenly aware that with risk management, professional help is essential. Not only is it essential, it is readily available. Seek it out!

CHAPTER 19

Philanthropy

*I resolved to stop accumulating and begin the infinitely more
serious and difficult task of wise distribution.*
—Andrew Carnegie

Philanthropy is of considerable interest to wealthy families around the
world. In the United States, philanthropy is a tradition that keeps getting stronger. According to Giving USA Foundation's annual report on
philanthropy, American giving reached a record high in 2006, with donations totaling $295 billion, an increase of 1 percent after inflation from
the previous year. Moreover, according to Boston College's Center on
Wealth and Philanthropy, by the year 2055, some $41 trillion will change
hands as Americans pass on their accumulated assets to the next generation likely creating a multitude of philanthropic endeavors for years
to come.[1]

In addition to multigenerational philanthropic activity, wealth is being
created by first-generation entrepreneurs who want their philanthropy do
something important. For many of these people, philanthropy needs to be
run like any other business. According to Mark Evans, head of philanthropy
and family business at Coutts, the private bank in London, newly affluent
clients "want to get involved, not just write out a cheque. They see the
opportunity to enjoy giving, as much as if not more than making the money
in the first place, and there's a real interest in applying business solutions
to charitable giving. People have a lot more to offer than just money."[2]
And not only are people applying business solutions to charitable giving,
many are beginning to apply the principles of 'venture philanthropy' to their

investments as well. Techniques such as Socially Responsible Investing (SRI), Mission Related Investing (MRI), and Program Related Investing (PRI) are becoming part of the landscape for UAC families.

Given the importance of charitable giving to both first-generation and established wealthy families, UAC advisers need to be well versed in family philanthropy concepts. Having an effective philanthropy strategy can be every bit as important to a family as taxes, investing, and educating family members. For many families, philanthropy is a tool not only for making a difference in the world but also for transferring family values. I discussed earlier in the book the difficulty of raising responsible children in a family with wealth. A highly effective way to battle the negative influences of money is to get young children involved in philanthropy. Doing so creates unique opportunities for real-world educational experiences, builds family ties, and shapes stronger individuals and families. The act of giving to those less fortunate in an organized way can prepare children for the responsibilities of inheriting wealth by helping them understand the value of money as well. By so doing, children can be less prone to becoming spoiled, which often leads to bigger problems later in life.

Another positive aspect of philanthropy is that it can transfer family values throughout the generations. A coordinated giving effort can make a significant difference in helping younger family members carry on family traditions, particularly through family foundations, which I discuss later. These foundations help individual family members learn about rallying to a cause, developing leadership skills, and expressing their feelings and beliefs. Foundations can also be used to teach about corporate governance, budgeting, investing, and much more.

Because the options for creating a philanthropy strategy are many, UA families are often vexed as to how to create and develop one. They need to decide what missions to support, how engaged they want to be in those missions, what region of the world they will give to, and what the best tax strategies for giving are (see Chapter 15 for tax-efficient charitable giving strategies). Acting as a primer on some key philanthropy concepts, I discuss three main subjects in this chapter. First, I review some key questions that can help families explore the fundamental underpinnings of developing an effective philanthropic strategy. Then I discuss implementing a philanthropic strategy through two popular charitable vehicles: a family foundation and a donor-advised fund. Third, I review some key issues with giving large gifts to institutions such as colleges and universities. There are examples in the appendix of how younger-generation family members are building character and making a difference in the world by engaging in philanthropic activity.

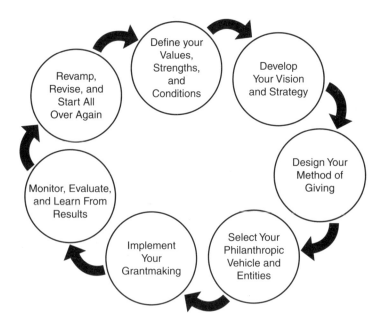

FIGURE 19.1 A Philanthropic Framework: A Cycle of
Engagement and Education
Source: © 2006 Rockefeller Philanthropy Advisors, Inc. All rights reserved.

PHILANTHROPIC STRATEGY DEVELOPMENT
THROUGH ASKING QUESTIONS

There are a number of highly qualified organizations that help families develop philanthropy strategies. One of the most recognized names in this world is Rockefeller Philanthropy Advisers (RPA). RPA has developed a broad framework for helping families with their charitable endeavors, shown in Figure 19.1. UAC advisers should familiarize themselves with these professional organizations and how they help families create a philanthropic strategy. As has been a common theme throughout the book, bringing in specialists to assist in complex advisory strategies such as philanthropy is essential to serving UA families properly. With that said, UAC advisers can help their clients think about the fundamentals of their philanthropic effort.

This type of framework can be used as a big picture guideline for developing a strategy. For UAC advisers, it has the most impact on the first three steps: identifying values and vision, developing a mission, and designing a strategy around giving. It is important to note that when working with a family on their philanthropic strategy, UAC advisers need to be good listeners. Developing philanthropic solutions is a collaborative process that begins with discussions with the donor and family members (if appropriate) to isolate the motivations for designating funds for philanthropic endeavors. Researching areas of concern to the family can be very helpful, as can facilitating workshops to review how philanthropy has been handled historically by the family and identifying the areas or activities of most interest to different family members. What follows are some key questions that advisers can ask to begin the process.

1. What issues are important to you?
2. What do you want to achieve with your philanthropic activities?
3. Do you want to be involved as a donor only or do you want to have direct involvement in the organizations or causes you support?
4. How much of your time do you want to devote to administering the grant requests that fund your giving?
5. How many and what type of organizations would you like to support?
6. Do you want your philanthropic involvement to be in perpetuity or do you anticipate a defined period of time for your giving?
7. Do you wish to leave a legacy of giving for your children or others to continue?
8. Do you wish to leave assets directly to charities at death?
9. What philanthropic endeavors has the family been involved in historically?
10. What values does the family wish to express through its philanthropy?
11. What family members will be involved in developing the philanthropic strategy for the family?
12. What legacy do you want to leave?
13. What approach will work best to effect the mission?
14. How will the philanthropic effort be governed?
15. How do you know if you're succeeding?
16. How will you measure the effectiveness of your giving, track progress, and evaluate outcomes?

MISSION STATEMENT

Once the family has spent time answering the questions in the previous section, the next step is to begin crafting a mission statement for the family's philanthropic effort. When families begin to think about the legacy they want to leave and articulate their values, they often hope that future generations will share the same values and carry on family traditions. This is not always the case. Using a family foundation as a philanthropic vehicle is a great way of communicating family values and giving guidance to younger generations of the family. An excellent resource for advisers learning about developing a mission statement is the Council on Foundations Family Foundation Library Series. The following is excerpted from the Family Foundation series called "Articulating the Foundation's Mission."[3] In this case, the mission statement relates to a family foundation. But the lessons learned here can be applied to other philanthropic efforts.

> *A mission statement gives all who are interested an idea of why the foundation was established and how it defines its own work. The statement is usually broad, worded to reflect the donor's intent and give a flavor of the foundation's values and interests. For family foundation trustees, developing a mission statement is a means of honoring donor intent and giving an identity, set in the context of family and the outside world, to the foundation.*
>
> *The goals of a family foundation are communicated by its mission statement to the family, to the foundation's trustees, staff and grantees, and to other grantmakers, grantseekers and the community at large. The mission statement reflects the intent and wishes of the donor as well as the shared values of the trustees and their aims for the organization. Rooted in the foundation's articles of incorporation and the vision of its trustees, mission statements are living documents that often evolve as new generations assess changing needs and bring their own philanthropic and family objectives to the foundation.*
>
> *For a family foundation, a mission statement serves as a short- and long-range planning tool—a yardstick for measuring the foundation's progress over time. Articulating such a statement is the first step in managing a family foundation.*

After the mission statement is completed, the family then moves on to implementing the philanthropic strategy.

IMPLEMENTATION OF PHILANTHROPIC STRATEGY

Once the family has developed the philanthropic framework, the time comes to implement the strategy. As shown in Figure 19.2, the family must select the charitable vehicle within the context of the overall wealth management plan: a direct gift or a charitable trust. These vehicles were discussed in

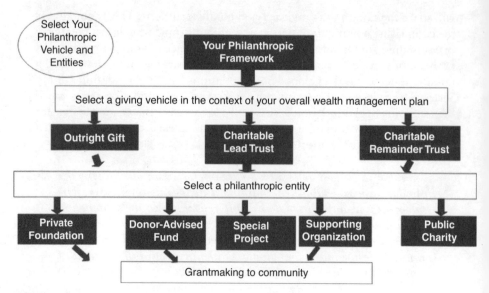

FIGURE 19.2   The Realization of Your Philanthropic Framework

Chapter 15. After that step is completed, the task is to select a philanthropic entity. There are multiple choices that families use for their private philanthropy, with the two most common being the private foundation and the donor-advised fund. These are discuss here.

Private Foundations

Private foundations can be divided into two groups: (1) *private operating foundations* that directly carry out charitable activities and are exempt from certain distribution and other requirements, and (2) *private non-operating foundations,* which do not directly perform any charitable functions; instead they receive charitable gifts, invest the funds, and make grants to other charitable organizations. A nonoperating foundation generally receives its funding from one primary source, such as an individual, a family, or a corporation. The most common type of private foundation is the nonoperating foundation.

A private foundation is established by the creation of a nonprofit entity during life or by a testamentary disposition at death. The most tax-efficient method of creating a foundation is to establish it during the donor's life by obtaining a tax exemption from the IRS. Even if the foundation is not fully funded during life, it can be funded at death. The family foundation is growing in popularity among UACs because it provides more control to the donor than does a donation to a community foundation or other supporting organization. From a private foundation, the donor has the right to distribute funds to the organizations (public charities) he prefers and can stay in control of the foundation's investments. But careful consideration should be given as to whether a foundation structure is appropriate. Often, families overlook or don't know the rules and restrictions placed on private foundations. For example, for gifts of cash and nonappreciated property, a donor's income tax deduction is limited to 30 percent of adjusted gross income (AGI) in the taxable year. Gifts to foundations that qualify as public charities, on the other hand, confer a 50 percent deduction for gifts of cash and other nonappreciated property (any excess can be carried forward for five years). For gifts of appreciated property, a donor's income tax deduction is limited to 20 percent of the AGI, as opposed to 30 percent for gifts of appreciated property to public charities. In addition, gifts of appreciated assets are limited to a deduction of only the donor's basis in the asset, unless the asset is publicly traded stock. Any excess can be carried forward for five years.

Another attractive feature of a foundation is that it can make donations for the family as a whole. This provides a highly efficient way to deliver philanthropic effort by designating one entity to receive all requests for donations and make disbursements. The establishment of procedures for making grants and reviewing grant applications makes the approval process an objective one, which can provide relief from the pressure on family members that can come from grant-seeking organizations or other individuals. In addition, foundations can be organized so that a family can maintain members as directors of the foundation, which provide younger family members with an opportunity to participate in meaningful causes and become familiar with the charitable goals and intentions of the family and other benefits discussed earlier.

UAC advisers should be familiar with some of the restrictions placed on private foundations. Some of these are:

1. A tax of 2 percent of the net investment income of a private foundation for the taxable year (this tax is not applicable to operating foundations).
2. Restrictions on self-dealing.
3. Minimum requirements for income distribution.
4. Restrictions on retention of excess business holdings.
5. Restrictions on investing assets in a manner that jeopardizes carrying out the exempt purposes.
6. Restrictions on expenditures.

7. Tax upon termination of status as a private foundation, unless certain requirements are met. UAC advisers can bring in specialists to help in this area.

Donor-Advised Funds

Understanding the client's philanthropic intentions will help the UAC adviser properly guide the client to the appropriate vehicle for his philanthropic endeavor. I discussed private operating foundations, which are created to directly carry on one or more charitable activities but require substantial administrative support in the previous section. Another option with substantially less administration is a *donor-advised fund*. A donor-advised fund is a charitable giving vehicle administered by a third party (often a community foundation) and created for the purpose of managing charitable donations on behalf of an organization, family, or individual. A donor-advised fund offers the opportunity to create a low-cost, flexible vehicle for charitable giving as an alternative to direct giving or creating a private foundation. With this vehicle, a donor has the ability to recommend the charitable recipients of its fund without the overhead and administrative effort associated with a private foundation. Donor-advised funds are the fastest-growing charitable giving vehicle in the United States, with more than 100,000 donor-advised accounts established, holding over $17.5 billion in assets.[4]

Because the fund is housed in a public charity, donors receive the maximum tax deduction available while avoiding excise taxes and other restrictions imposed on private foundations. Furthermore, donors do not incur the cost of establishing and administering a private foundation, which can be substantial (due to staffing and legal fees). Since the maximum tax deduction is received by the donor in the year the gift is made, the foundation administering the fund gains full control over the contribution, granting the donor advisory status. As such, the foundation is not legally bound to the donor, but makes grants to other public charities upon the donor's recommendation. This is an important distinction between a donor-advised fund and a private foundation. UA families need to consider the pluses and minuses of each of these options.

PHILANTHROPIC INVESTING

As families become more involved and sophisticated in their philanthropic giving, many begin to ask themselves a simple question: The money we give away is working for our cause, but what about the money we invest? Can't we use our investment dollars to support our philanthropy too?

Some families conclude that the answer is yes; others believe the opposite. Nevertheless, a subgroup of financial service firms has begun to emerge in order to support families who wish to invest in a socially responsible manner. This section describes the three basic techniques these families pursue: SRI, MRI, and PRI. Then it briefly addresses a fundamental controversy that surrounds the notion of philanthropic investing.

Socially Responsible Investing (SRI)

Over the past three or four decades, investors have become increasingly worried about making investments that inadvertently support destructive, distasteful, or inhumane corporate activities. Examples abound—South African gold mining companies during the time of Apartheid, The Nike Corporation back when it worked with foreign sub-contractors who employed child labor and sweatshop manufacturing techniques, tobacco companies, gambling companies, defense contractors—you name it. Of course, you invest in order to make money. Many of these companies and industries are highly profitable, and at times, they represent excellent investments. But if you invest in these companies, are you implicitly supporting unintended consequences?

SRI investing exists to counteract this problem by imposing investment screens. There are two types of screen, negative and positive. Most investment managers and many mutual funds will accommodate a small set of negative screens. For example, a family could instruct an equity manager to avoid tobacco and gaming (gambling) companies. It is relatively easy to carve out specific companies or industry sectors, and most people are content to leave it at that.

Positive screens work in the opposite direction. For example, families may wish to invest in companies that are involved in alternative energy production, subsidized food distribution, or medical initiatives in developing countries. Positive screens can be more difficult to implement because they often require additional layers of due diligence. However, negative and positive SRI screens are generally easier to manage than other types of philanthropic investing, because once the screens are in place, ongoing maintenance becomes fairly passive. The tough part involves selecting the screens and weighing the trade-offs. Do you really want to carve out the entire defense industry? How about the auto industry? It feels good, but where do you draw the line, and what impact will this socially responsible influence have upon your bottom line?

The author gratefully acknowledges Brad Fisher for his substantial contribution to this section on philanthropic investing.

Mission Related Investing (MRI)

MRI takes SRI investing to the next level. The MRI process involves actively identifying organizations—for-profit and non-profit alike—whose work directly complements the philanthropic mission of the family.

SRI screens typically apply to large, multinational corporations, but MRI opportunities often involve private investments with small or emerging organizations. For example, if a family's mission focuses upon ecology and climate change, they may wish to dedicate some of their investment dollars to venture capital investments that support groups who are involved in solar or wind power, or they may invest in funds that are dedicated to the green building industry.

MRI investments require a greater commitment than SRI investments for several reasons. First, as the name implies, Mission Related Investing assumes that the family has already adopted a specific philanthropic mission. This assumption is not trivial; it extends much further than simply selecting passive SRI screens. Second, MRI deals require extensive upfront and ongoing due diligence, much more so than typical SRI screens. And finally, since they generally involve small or emerging organizations, the investment risks for MRI opportunities are typically much higher than the risks associated with SRI screens.

In addition to their philanthropic orientation, MRI investments share an important characteristic in common with SRI investments; SRI and MRI investors expect to receive market returns. In other words, SRI and MRI investors want their investment cake, and they want to eat it too. Therein lies the controversy mentioned in the introduction to this chapter. Some people believe that long-term market returns are possible; others believe that the double bottom line of SRI and MRI investments represents a crippling constraint that makes long-term market returns unattainable.

Program Related Investing (PRI)

PRI investments resemble MRIs, but there is one essential difference: PRI investors do not expect to receive market returns. In fact, they fully expect PRI returns to be below market.

PRIs can involve venture capital-like equity investments, but more often, they take the form of low-interest loans or loan guarantees, generally to charitable organizations in order to fund initiatives that correspond with the family's investment mission.

In some ways, PRI investments represent a bridge between grants and investments, because foundations are able to apply the below-market portion of their return to their 5 percent spending requirement. Unfortunately, UACs who invest directly rather than through a foundation are not able to enjoy that additional benefit.

As with MRI investments, PRIs are serious business. They require extensive due diligence and ongoing scrutiny. The underlying organizations are generally small groups attempting to do great things. The risks are high, but the potential rewards are also significant.

The Philanthropic Investing Controversy

As mentioned above, when it comes to SRI, MRI, and PRI investing, there are two opposing schools of thought. Supporters of philanthropic investing assert that UAC investment dollars represent a powerful tool. To them, it stands to reason that if harnessed correctly, investment dollars have the potential to generate a great deal of social value ... along with a great deal of associated profit. They assert that over the long term, various forms of philanthropic investing can generate market returns. In fact, some supporters argue that SRI and MRI investments can actually outperform the broad markets because they often involve macro themes that aim to solve society's greatest problems. These include opportunities such as alternative energy generation, efficient food production, education, and health care—initiatives related to the undeniable progression of climate change, population growth, income disparity, and excess energy consumption.

There is an opposing view, however. Many investors prefer to draw a bright line between their giving and their investing. They argue that commitments to SRI, MRI, and PRI represent constraints, and generally speaking in economics and investing, constraints lead to lower returns. If you limit your universe of investments, it stands to reason that you will miss profitable opportunities that would have otherwise come your way. People in this camp say, "Let me earn as much money as possible on my investments. Then I will have more money to give away."

In the end, it comes down to philosophy and perhaps the intensity of the UAC family's commitment to their philanthropic mission. Philanthropic investing has become compelling and rewarding for many families, but be careful. Plenty of literature and support are available. Be sure to engage support if you decide to become involved.

BEST PRACTICES OF GIVING LARGE GIFTS TO COLLEGES AND UNIVERSITIES

Donations to colleges and universities are substantial. In 2006, the latest year with available data, these institutions received $14.1 billion in donations.[5]

Making this kind of donation—naming a building or endowing a department chair—can be one of the proudest moments in a UAC's life. However, what donors often overlook is that the intent of the gift and what the institution has in mind may be two completely different things. Even restricted gifts can go well beyond the intent of the original donor. Given that these donations can be fraught with peril, UAC advisers should have some familiarity with the issues. A classic case of a "donation gone wrong" is the case of the Robertson family and the Woodrow Wilson School at Princeton University. Several key lessons can be learned from this case that can help advisers with clients who are considering major gifts to colleges or universities.

The following is from the web site robertsonvprinceton.org, which summarizes the lawsuit of the Robertson family against Princeton University, originally filed on July 17, 2002, in the Superior Court of New Jersey.[6] *Robertson v. Princeton University* is perhaps the most important "donor intent" lawsuit in U.S. history.[7]

> *The lawsuit was filed by the descendants of Charles and Marie Robertson and all of the Family-Designated Trustees of the Robertson Foundation, a charitable foundation whose mission was and is to assist the United States Government by preparing graduate students for federal government careers, particularly in foreign and international affairs. The defendants in the case are Princeton University and the University-Designated Trustees of the Robertson Foundation.*
>
> *The Robertson Family Trustees have asked the Court to: (1) Amend the Robertson Foundation's Certificate of Incorporation and By-Laws "so that [the Foundation] will no longer be controlled by Princeton, but will instead be a private foundation with all of its trustees appointed by the Robertson Family and all of its assets dedicated to graduate training for government service, particularly for federal government careers in international affairs." (2) Reverse the university's improper takeover of the Robertson Foundation's investment portfolio. 3) Require Princeton to "account for all of its expenditures of Foundation funds so that the Court can determine whether such expenditures are consistent with the terms of the restricted gift" and order Princeton to reimburse the Robertson Foundation "for all improper expenditures," an amount estimated at nearly $500 million in 2006 dollars.*

From the perspective of Princeton University, the Robertson family was attempting to infringe on the University's academic freedom by dictating the intent of the gift's terms. Its administrators fear that if this case stands they will be inundated with donors' heirs who want to change the terms of gifts many years after they are made.

In December of 2008, the case was settled.[8]

> *Princeton University will have full control of the endowment associated with the Robertson Foundation and will continue to use the endowment to support the graduate program of the Woodrow Wilson School of Public and International Affairs under a settlement agreement that ends the six-year-old lawsuit brought against the University by members of the Robertson family.*
>
> *Under the terms of the agreement, the Robertson Foundation will be dissolved and its assets will be transferred to the University to create an endowed fund that will be controlled solely by the University. The fund will provide the same kind of support for the graduate program of the Woodrow Wilson School as these funds have been providing for the past 47 years. In addition, over a three-year period the foundation will reimburse the Banbury Fund, a Robertson family foundation, for $40 million of legal fees that were paid by that fund during the course of the litigation, and beginning in 2012 the Robertson Foundation will provide $50 million, paid over seven years, to a new charitable foundation designated by the Robertson family that will support the preparation of students for government service.*
>
> *"This settlement achieves the University's highest priorities in this lawsuit, which were to ensure that Marie Robertson's gift will continue to support the graduate program of the Woodrow Wilson School and that the University would have full authority to make academic judgments about how these funds are to be used," said Princeton President Shirley M. Tilghman. "The funds will continue to be managed by our investment managers at PRINCO [the Princeton University Investment Co.], who have significantly increased the value of the Robertson gift since being engaged by the Robertson Foundation in 2004.*
>
> *"It is tragic that this lawsuit required the expenditure of tens of millions of dollars in legal fees that could have and should have been spent on educational and charitable purposes," Tilghman said. "We had every confidence that we would prevail at trial, and looked forward to the opportunity to refute the claims that were made and demonstrate Princeton's diligent stewardship of this gift over almost five decades. We agreed to this settlement so that we could bring the rapidly escalating legal expenses to a halt before a lengthy trial added even more tens of millions of dollars. The settlement also*

allows the Banbury Fund to resume funding the charitable objectives for which it was established, and it restricts the spending of the new foundation to activities that are compatible with the purposes we serve in carrying out the terms of Marie Robertson's gift."

Several lessons can be learned from this situation:

1. Although it might sound obvious, those who are considering making a large gift such as the one described in the Princeton case should clearly delineate their wishes. This is because the recipient may misinterpret a donor's intent or heirs may wish to challenge the intent of the gift based on how the grant was implemented by the recipient.
2. Potential donors should recognize that institutions of higher learning may indeed need some amount of flexibility when administering gifts and they will likely be resistant to having heavy restrictions placed on donated funds. If the family wants to attach many restrictions, they may wish to make a donation in a different way, such as through a family foundation.
3. If a college does agree to restrictions on a gift, the language should be so clear and unambiguous that there can be no equivocation about the restrictions. Otherwise, heirs will have significant problems in the future if they wish to challenge the interpretation of the intent of the owner.
4. An alternative to a single endowment gift is a donation that is given in stages over the course of time. By spending down the gift over time, the donor can ensure that his or her intent is being honored each time money is put to use.

APPENDIX: THE NEXT GENERATION: REDEFINING THE PHILANTHROPIC LANDSCAPE

Author's note: Much has been written about the benefits of young family members getting involved in philanthropy. But many families don't have ideas about what their kids might do. This article provides some vivid examples of what some young people are doing to change the world and develop real-world skills along the way.

This article was originally published by Synergos in *Global Giving Matters* as "The Next Generation: Redefining the Philanthropic Landscape," February-April 2007. www.synergos.org/globalgivingmatters/features/0704nextgeneration.htm. Reprinted with permission.

Global Giving Matters invited five young people of wealth who believe in social change to describe their personal approach to giving. The stories of Philipp Engelhorn, Ben Goldhirsh, Kim Kreiling, Katherine Lorenz and Rebecca Winsor reflect the diverse face of today's "next generation" of philanthropists.

While each generation of philanthropists is shaped by the distinct societal forces of its time, today's 20- and 30-somethings have come of age in an era of unprecedented challenges and opportunities.

More than ever before, the problems and issues that confront today's young donors—poverty, environmental degradation, conflict—are global in scope and impact. In recent years, giving for international purposes has reached record levels, thanks to a heightened focus on global peace and security, climate change and initiatives such as the Millennium Development Goals. Yet global giving still represents a small percentage of all philanthropic dollars.

Today's philanthropists are in a unique position to help fill that resource gap in thoughtful and sustainable ways. With the coming massive intergenerational transfer of wealth in the U.S., Baby Boomers will pass on an estimated $40 trillion to their children over the next 50 years.

These young people will inherit unparalleled amounts of money, along with the responsibility to manage these philanthropic funds wisely. They will also be presented with a wealth of opportunities to apply their resources and talents in creative and effective ways to address global challenges.

Our interviews with five young agents of social change—all of whom are members of Synergos' Global Philanthropists Circle—illustrate a variety of strategies for addressing the complex global realities of their times. In their stories, you will see a fair sampling of the characteristics attributed to next-generation members as a whole.

They are global in outlook and adept at using media and technology as a platform for connection, communication, entertainment and empowerment. Their engagement in the world is linked to pursuing a passion, not fulfilling an obligation. They are creating new models of entrepreneurship. Their aim is to make a difference, not to be considered a philanthropist. They are avid social networkers but not socialites. And they are seriously concerned about climate change and the global environment.

Katherine Lorenz: Nutrition as a Bridge to Community Wellbeing

"I don't consider myself a philanthropist, because I don't give away very much money. What I give is time," said Katherine Lorenz, a self-described "workaholic" and co-founder of a nonprofit organization that partners with rural communities in Mexico to promote better nutrition and health. Puente a la Salud Comunitaria, the organization Lorenz established and now directs, centers on an unusual entry point to community empowerment: the re-introduction of an ancient and highly nutritious grain, amaranth, into the diet of the largely indigenous, rural poor population of Oaxaca.

Lorenz first came to Oaxaca to explore sustainable solutions to rural poverty in Latin America as a volunteer after college. Initially interested in women's reproductive health, she came across research on the nutritional value of amaranth and decided in 2004 to launch a nonprofit using the reintegration of amaranth in the diet as a portal for addressing a range of community needs.

"Getting them to try it is not hard. It's getting them to build it into their lifestyle that's the challenge," said Lorenz, who now serves as executive director of Puente. The organization's work usually begins with the women of the community, who do most of the cooking. They are encouraged to add amaranth to tortillas and start family gardens. Puente also partners with health department doctors and nurses to build trust and credibility.

Sustainable development is also a major focus of her family's philanthropy, and at 28, Lorenz is the first member of her generation to serve as a board member on the Cynthia and George Mitchell Foundation, established by her grandparents. Lorenz is trying to establish a next-generation committee to bring the interests of younger family members to the board.

As a next-generation member of Synergos' Global Philanthropists Circle, Lorenz has had the opportunity to explore the issue of rural poverty with other young people of wealth interested in working for social change. She recently hosted a trip to Oaxaca that gave younger Circle members an opportunity to visit the villages where Puente works. Participants purchased and distributed materials for greenhouses to help Puente's rural constituents extend the growing season for their amaranth crop.

Meanwhile, Puente is one of the few organizations working on the community education aspects of amaranth in the diet, and Lorenz is looking at ways to replicate her organization's model.

While fundraising to sustain Puente's operations continues to be one of Lorenz's biggest challenges, the organization recently received a large and unexpected grant from an anonymous donor. Her vision for Puente includes "having involved donors, people who give their time as well as their money."

As she moves into a position to take a more active role with her own philanthropic resources, Lorenz says, "I'd love to be a more involved donor myself."

Kim Kreiling: Putting Faith into Action through Small-Farmer Finance

"Through being involved in civil society and nonprofits, I've realized how empowering a loan can be," said Kim Kreiling, whose efforts are helping identify and fill the gaps in funding for sustainable rural development.

Kreiling's interest in land access for the poor began on a school trip to Central America where, as a teenager, she witnessed the struggle of peasants to achieve a sustainable quality of life. As an adult, her work as a fundraiser for Agros International, a faith-based nonprofit that promotes land ownership for the rural poor in Latin America, helped hone her thinking about empowering the poor through land tenure initiatives.

To determine how to help, Kreiling mapped what organizations around the world were doing to enable land access for the poor. She discovered that, apart from Agros International, few, if any, nonprofit organizations were lending to the poor for the purpose of purchasing land.

To expand access to rural development financing, Kreiling went to work for Boston-based Ecologic Finance (soon to be called Root Capital) and helped launch the organization's "Loans for Land Initiative." One of the few organizations making loans to low-income farm cooperatives around the world, Ecologic Finance was named a winner of *Fast Company* magazine's 2007 Social Capitalist awards honoring leading social entrepreneurs.

Kreiling is now sharpening the organization's focus on sustainable energy loans for small-to-medium sized enterprises in the developing world. One potential project involves a solar-powered coffee dryer fueled by biowaste from a coffee plant. Kreiling met with representatives of a leading U.S. foundation in March to discuss a possible role for Ecologic Finance in funding the technology.

Still, Kreiling wanted to do more. Sparked by a conversation with her mother, Helen L. Hunt, Kreiling decided to research ways to leverage the family's philanthropic resources to serve the rural poor.

What emerged was a $1 million, donor-advised fund established last August with Calvert Foundation. Calvert Giving Funds allows individuals and families to easily start a "personal foundation," and then recommend socially responsible ways for their funds to be invested.

Through her donor-advised fund, Kreiling is providing low-cost loans and grants to poor communities in the developing world, including a $135,000 guarantee for an Ecologic Finance loan for land to a cooperative of farmers in Nicaragua.

Wishing to share her knowledge of how to invest creatively to make a difference, Kreiling and her family have documented the process in a report they hope can serve as a guide for others interested in creating their own donor-advised funds.

Kreiling is quick to acknowledge the role that her "community of practice" has played in her activities. During her research, Kreiling cultivated a network of peer practitioners—her mother and other family members, friends, work colleagues, advisers and others who provided invaluable insights, encouragement and collaboration.

Her faith has been an important inspiration as well. Kreiling, a divinity school graduate, is now working with graduate students at Harvard through Intervarsity Christian Fellowship. In March, she joined a mission in New Orleans to help with clean-up and construction work, and in May she will travel with a team to visit prisoners in Ecuador.

Kreiling's personal blend of passion and pragmatism defies easy labeling. "I like the term social entrepreneur that Bill Drayton popularized. We're being entrepreneurial in how we want to generate social change through giving and investing. I'm a small part of a global movement to create hope and opportunity, and along the road all of our lives are being changed."

Ben Goldhirsh: Doing Well by Doing GOOD

"I feel like I'm part of a generation engaged in the effort to move our world forward," says Ben Goldhirsh. And with a bold multi-media experiment called GOOD, Goldhirsh is already turning heads—and a profit—while promoting this sensibility among like-minded 18–40 year olds.

Based in Los Angeles, the GOOD venture is reaching out to its media-savvy target audience via a film company, magazine, events division and website. Goldhirsh funded the start-up himself, and recruited GOOD's staff of 25 largely from a group of school friends from Phillips Academy and Brown University.

In his decision to launch a media venture, Goldhirsh, 26, was both inspired and challenged by the legacy of his late father, Bernie Goldhirsh, founder of *Inc.,* the pioneering magazine for entrepreneurs.

"I was impressed by the role he was able to play in entrepreneurship," said the younger Goldhirsh. From his father's example, Goldhirsh said he came to recognize that "media was limitless in the sense that it was a platform. It didn't preclude, in fact, it demanded engagement."

One of the ways Goldhirsh is promoting engagement is through a "Choose GOOD" campaign. Subscribers to *GOOD Magazine,* now in its third issue, get to designate which of 12 partner organizations receive their $20 subscription fee. The campaign seeks to net 50,000 subscribers and $1 million for partners such as Teach for America, Millennium Promise and UNICEF. Simultaneously, it is designed to build the GOOD brand, generate buzz, and stimulate demand. To date, more than 15,000 subscribers have generated around $300,000 in donations for GOOD's nonprofit partners.

To appeal to a generation of avid social networkers, GOOD is also hosting a series of events—parties, concerts and speakers—in cities across the country. "We're creating a really interesting crowd tied together by a shared sensibility. If we can provide content, virtual space and physical spaces in which to meet, we're adding value to this community," said Goldhirsh.

With his film division, Reason Pictures, Goldhirsh is demonstrating the financial potential of the GOOD model. Goldhirsh hit the jackpot at the 2007 Sundance Film Festival, with his sale of *Son of Rambow*, a British coming-of-age feature, to Paramount Vantage. The film sale was the biggest deal of the year at Sundance, and the second largest in the festival's history.

Reason Pictures, which is expecting revenues of more than $5 million this year, currently has four films in production and another 10 in development, a mixture of features and documentaries that set out to entertain as well as provide socially relevant content.

"Hollywood is a hard business, but we didn't hire professionals, we hired friends and others with a sensibility of good and learned the business as we went along," said Goldhirsh.

While GOOD's film projects are earning acclaim and financial rewards, the other divisions are finding success as well, by making altruism fashionable and supporting a range of nonprofit partners. One of the biggest payoffs may come from making GOOD succeed on its own terms. "We get to make what we want and we're doing it for ourselves," said Goldhirsh.

Philipp Engelhorn: Creating Media that Matters

Fresh out of film school, Philipp Engelhorn is wasting no time in translating his passion for cinema into a vehicle for social change.

Although his New York–based nonprofit organization, Cinereach, has been active for less than a year, it has already funded more than a half dozen media projects by independent filmmakers and other organizations. And he's working on his first in-house production, a feature film aimed at bringing a human face to the issue of global warming.

Originally from Germany, Engelhorn's global orientation is evident in the range of projects he has chosen to support. These include Film Aid's participatory video project, which is putting cameras into the hands of refugees in Kenya, so they can tell their own stories.

Chat the Planet's web-based video series centers on four young residents of Baghdad as they decide whether to stay or flee a city under siege. And Project Kashmir, one of four documentaries chosen for the Sundance Lab, chronicles two American women, one Indian, one Pakistani, who travel to Kashmir to understand the human impact of the region's conflict.

Another of Cinereach's major focus areas is global warming. "I've had this long concern with the environment, and Al Gore's film, *An Inconvenient Truth,* further fueled my desire to do something," Engelhorn said. Working with Caroline Baron, producer of *Capote,* Cinereach is currently developing its first in-house feature, yet unnamed, that will "tackle global warming from a non-scientific perspective that people can actually connect with."

While there has always been an expectation that he will use his family's wealth for entrepreneurial purposes, Engelhorn said his first introduction to the possibilities of strategic giving came when he joined Synergos' Global Philanthropists Circle.

Synergos helped in the creation of a mission and vision for Cinereach, and Engelhorn said he has benefited from opportunities to network with other young GPC members, particularly those involved in their own media projects.

Engelhorn said he avoids labels such as *filmanthropist,* which have come into use recently to describe cause-oriented filmmakers. "I'm not comfortable calling myself a philanthropist, either, because I don't yet have the experience and knowledge it takes to be a full-hearted philanthropist, but I'm trying!" he added.

Concerned by the lack of social activism on the part of U.S. youth, Cinereach is starting a new web-based campaign that Engelhorn hopes will stimulate young people to action. "Worldwide, you still see people taking to the streets. We want to foster that activism here, to get young people to do something, even if it's something small."

Rebecca Winsor: Organizing Communities for Change

For Rebecca Winsor, a decision to pursue her calling in India during college proved to be transformative in ways she had never imagined.

What began with a year abroad studying art and music near Calcutta evolved into a commitment to giving in India, and a deepening of her involvement with social change philanthropy.

In India, Winsor encountered a young girl begging in a train station. The child had been seriously injured and required a skin graft. Winsor took the girl in to help her find medical care. In the process, she developed a close relationship with an extraordinary local doctor, and spent time in the rural hospital he ran.

This experience ignited a desire to get more involved. Winsor, who was born with a cleft palate that was corrected after birth, had noticed a high incidence of cleft lip and other facial deformities in India. She decided to reach out to Operation Smile (operationsmile.org), a nonprofit organization that provides medical training and free corrective surgery to individuals with cleft lip, palate, and other facial deformities.

Operation Smile was eager to have a greater presence in India. Winsor established a linkage between the organization and the doctor she knew, making it possible for Operation Smile India to set up operations on a larger scale.

"It was the happiest moment of my life," said Winsor, about launching the multi-year medical initiative. The program trains local health care workers, provides hygiene education and incorporates the healing power of music and art. "It's exciting because the community has taken ownership, and is leveraging its own networks of support. Pretty soon, they're not going to need outside help."

Winsor, 27, an artist, has since become active in the young donor organizing movement, encouraging other young people to give around the world.

She serves on the board of Resource Generation, a social change organization for young people of wealth, and is active in Leverage Alliance, a new organization aimed at young donors who are already in positions of leadership.

"I feel vested in this young donor organizing movement. There's so much potential," said Winsor. "It's such a new field, but this constituency of people is very hard to organize. It's like herding cats! I would like to create a unified movement around the world."

Alison Goldberg: Tools for Transforming Giving for Good

A new book, *Creating Change Through Family Philanthropy: The Next Generation*, aims to give young people of wealth the tools they need not just to participate in giving, but to help transform the field itself.

The book, by Alison Goldberg, Karen Pittelman, and Resource Generation—a social change organization by and for young people of wealth—draws on interviews with more than 40 next-generation members. It includes personal stories, exercises, and an extensive resource guide.

The authors leave no doubt about the need for change, arguing that many institutional practices of family philanthropy actually perpetuate, rather than ameliorate inequalities in society.

Goldberg, 32, has served as a board member of her family foundation for the past 10 years. She joined the program staff of Resource Generation after the organization she created and directed, Foundations for Change, merged with Resource Generation.

In an interview with *Global Giving Matters,* Goldberg outlined some of the trends that emerged from her research for the book and her work with Resource Generation's young constituents.

Although Resource Generation is focused on family philanthropy in the United States, Goldberg noted that "young people who are concerned about change are concerned about how little is being given internationally. It's all happening against a backdrop of a highly unequal society. The top 10 percent of wealth holders in the U.S. have 70 percent of the wealth," she said and the disparity is "even more staggering when looked at through a global lens."

Goldberg said she's "hopeful about changing the paradigm in the face of inequity in family philanthropy. It's really exciting seeing many young people creating a whole new range of models.

"It's not just about where the money is going, but how it's being given, from opening up to include activists in grants decision-making . . . to proactively supporting issues through shareholder activism and creating new partnership models with the organizations they're funding.

"So far, I've been very excited about the response to the book," Goldberg said. "We're finding more young people involved. As a conversation starter, it's serving the purpose."

CHAPTER 20

Multigenerational Asset Allocation Strategies

Our ideals, laws and customs should be based on the proposition that each generation, in turn, becomes the custodian rather than the absolute owner of our resources and each generation has the obligation to pass this inheritance on to the future.
                                        —Charles Lindbergh (1902–1974)

O n the investment advisory side, UAC advisers often encounter questions about multigenerational asset allocation. A question along the lines of "Should I have a single asset allocation for my whole family or have different ones for each generation?" usually pops up at some point in the advisory relationship. This is a tricky question, but UAC advisers need not stress out about it. What advisers need to understand is that there is not one right answer to this question. The appropriate asset allocation for a family will often depend on multiple factors such as:

- Desire or need for complexity.
- Size of the staff or external firm implementing the asset allocation.
- Liquidity needs of the family.
- Types of investments used.
- Sophistication of family members.
- Manner in which wealth is distributed throughout the generations.
- Types of investment vehicles used—and many, many others.

Not to worry. You will get a conceptual handle on how to address this key question. I provide three blueprints for intergenerational asset allocation strategies in this chapter, based on some of my own experiences.

These blueprints can be used on a stand-alone basis or pieces of them can be blended together to form a customized strategy for a client. These scenarios are not intended to be exhaustive. There are myriad ways for an intergenerational asset allocation strategy to be developed and implemented. These three are meant to demonstrate some common strategies that UAC advisers are likely to encounter. I discuss here the factors that go into using each of these strategies, including a section on asset allocation targeting at the end of the chapter. The three asset allocation strategies are:

- Different asset allocations for each generation.
- A single asset allocation for the entire family.
- Multiple customized asset allocations for each generation or family group.

Before we get into the strategies, a few introductory comments are in order. UAC advisers need to understand the importance of flexibility when selecting a multigenerational asset allocation strategy. A 2008 study by the Wharton Global Family Alliance at the Wharton School, University of Pennsylvania, titled "Single Family Offices: Private Wealth Management in the Family Context" by Raphael Amit, Heinrich Liechtenstein, M. Julia Prats, Todd Millay, and Laird P. Pendleton has data that demonstrate this point. As shown in Table 20.1, first-generation UACs have different asset allocations than later generations.[1]

One should not go into the multigenerational asset allocation decision with an inflexible plan that the family needs to follow. An adviser with a flexible approach goes into these types of meetings with suggestions, then,

TABLE 20.1 First-Generation vs. Later Generation Asset Allocation

	First Generation Average	Later Generations Average
Equities	32%	33%
Fixed Income	15%	17%
Hedge Funds	13%	13%
Private Equity	11%	9%
Real Estate	11%	12%
Other Tangible Assets (e.g., Oil, Gas, Timber, and Commodities)	3%	4%
Principal Investment in Companies	14%	9%
Other Stores of Value (e.g., Art Collection, Wine Cellar)	1%	3%

Source: Wharton Global Family Alliance.

based on the reaction to a suggested course of action, adjusts the suggestion and forms a recommendation customized to the family. Again, there is not a single right solution to this issue for every family. Case studies are presented to illustrate each strategy listed here.

DIFFERENT ASSET ALLOCATIONS FOR DIFFERENT GENERATIONS

Suppose a UAC adviser is working with a family that has clearly definable generational lines and that there is a single group of like-minded people at each generational level. For example, at the first generational level there are a patriarch and matriarch who created the wealth. At the next generational level, there are the two children of the first generation. The third generation in this example is the four grandchildren of the matriarch and patriarch, two by each of the two children at the second generational level. We can look at this family has having three family units, one in each generation. Their family tree would look like Figure 20.1.

At G-1, there are the wealth creators. After careful planning, these two people created various trusts for future generations (such as generation-skipping trusts) and are in the process of passing wealth down. This generation is 75 to 80 years old with a substantial portion of the wealth, 40 percent, in their name or in their control—decreasing every year as wealth is passed down. The risk tolerance at G-1 is lower than that of the family as a whole; their objective is to live out their lives comfortably while at the same time preserving and passing the family wealth to future generations.

At G-2, there are the like-minded children of G-1 and their spouses. These four people are 40 to 50 years old, two of whom are working (although

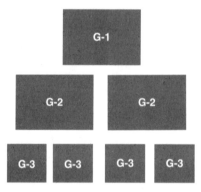

FIGURE 20.1   Sample Family Tree

TABLE 20.2 Asset Allocation Strategies for Generations 1–3

Generation	Risk Tolerance	Percentage of Wealth	Liquidity of Portfolio Allocation	Asset Allocation Strategy
G-1	Low to moderate	40	High	Wealth preservation
G-2	Moderate to high	30	Moderate to high	Growth
G-3	High to very high	30	Low to moderate	Aggressive growth

they don't need to) and two not working. The objectives of the members of G-2 are to grow wealth mainly for the benefit of future generations and to have money for themselves if they need it. They have a moderate to high risk tolerance and control about 30 percent of the family's wealth.

At G-3, there are the four children of the G-2 family members. Decisions are being made for them as a group; they are aged 10 to 20. Since the wealth is multigenerational and the time horizon very long, the risk tolerance of this group is high to very high. The family is targeting many long-dated assets, such as private equity, private real estate, and timber, at this generation. This generation controls about 30 percent of the assets of the family, and the percentage is growing. Table 20.2 describes the asset allocation strategy for each unit in the family. In short, G-1 has a wealth preservation–oriented asset allocation strategy, G-2 has a growth-oriented asset allocation strategy, and G-3 has an aggressive growth-oriented allocation strategy. This is a very typical structure for a multigenerational family.

SINGLE ALLOCATION FOR AN ENTIRE FAMILY

Suppose a UAC adviser encounters a situation in which a single family has two generations: the first generation (the parents) is 50 to 60 years old and the second generation (the children) is 15 to 20 years old, and there are no children after that. The parents were successful entrepreneurs and created substantial wealth through a major liquidity event. G-1 are the sole decision makers with respect to the wealth and own 70 percent of it. Should the family have two asset allocations, one for the parents and one for the children? This really could go either way. In this case, the UAC adviser and the family decide that because the objectives for the wealth are essentially the same for both generations (growth with moderate risk) and also for

TABLE 20.3 Combined Asset Allocation Strategy for Generations 1 and 2

Generation	Risk Tolerance	Asset Allocation Strategy	Percentage of Wealth
G-1	High	Growth	70
G-2	High	Growth	30

TABLE 20.4 Separate Asset Allocation Strategy for Generations 1 and 2

Generation	Risk Tolerance	Asset Allocation Strategy	Percentage of Wealth
G-1	Moderate	Moderate Growth	70
G-2	High	Aggressive Growth	30

simplicity's sake, there will be only one asset allocation strategy for the entire family. There is, in effect, just one family group to be concerned with.

With regard to implementing the asset allocation strategy, the manager selection and asset location of various investments occurs without particular regard to generation, except for long-dated assets, which are skewed toward the children's accounts. Liquidity is managed at the family level and does not disparately concern different generations. The family also has a foundation that is managed separately with a separate asset allocation strategy, but this is a relatively small portion of the wealth. Table 20.3 summarizes this situation.

If the adviser and the family had decided to have distinct asset allocation strategies for each generation, it would probably look like Table 20.4.

The key factors that inform this decision are whether the family wants to administer separate asset allocation strategies, the overall risk tolerance of the family, the types of investments in the portfolio (a strong desire for illiquid assets could make the case for a separate allocation or investment strategy at G-2), and the overall tolerance for complexity. Simplicity would favor the combined allocation strategy.

CUSTOMIZED ASSET ALLOCATION BY GENERATION OR FAMILY UNIT

Suppose the UAC adviser encounters a larger family containing three unique family groups, each with four generations—a total of twelve individual family units. Each family group is a distinct operating entity managed by a large family office. Figure 20.2 illustrates this family.

Each family group has individual asset allocation preferences, as does each individual family unit. Through an extensive evaluation process, the

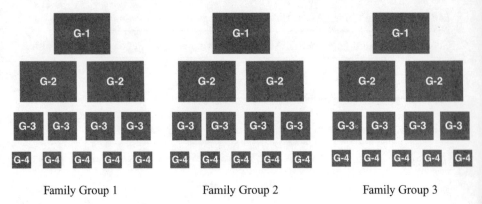

Family Group 1   Family Group 2   Family Group 3

FIGURE 20.2   Illustration of Family Groups

UAC adviser has determined the individual risk tolerances and objectives of each family unit and has decided to suggest the following strategies for each one. For the purpose of these examples, we will assume that the wealth is distributed evenly throughout each generation.

Family Group 1

For Family Group 1, the first generation has a low risk tolerance and a wealth preservation strategy. In this case, the first generation still holds a substantial portion of the wealth, 70 percent, and the remaining generations own about 10 percent each. Since the second, third, and fourth generations expect to receive the remainder of the wealth after a fairly long time, about 10 years, they have all selected an aggressive growth-oriented asset allocation strategy and have agreed on the same risk tolerance and objectives. Table 20.5 summarizes Group 1.

Family Group 2

In Family Group 2, the family has adopted a similar asset allocation framework as in the first example family. The first generation has a low

TABLE 20.5   Asset Allocation Strategy of Family Group 1

Generation	Risk Tolerance	Asset Allocation Strategy
G-1	Low	Wealth Preservation
G-2	High	Aggressive Growth
G-3	High	Aggressive Growth
G-4	High	Aggressive Growth

TABLE 20.6 Asset Allocation Strategy of Family Group 2

Generation	Risk Tolerance	Asset Allocation Strategy
G-1	Low	Wealth preservation
G-2	Moderate	Moderate growth
G-3	High	Growth
G-4	Very high	Aggressive growth

risk tolerance and a wealth preservation strategy. The second generation has a medium risk tolerance and a conservative-to-moderate growth asset allocation strategy. The third generation has a more aggressive strategy of growth and the fourth generation has the most aggressive growth strategy. This is a more classical asset allocation strategy. Table 20.6 summarizes Family Group 2.

Family Group 3

In the case of Family Group 3, each generation has decided to adopt its own asset allocation strategy. The circumstances of each family unit are such that a common asset allocation strategy is not feasible nor is it desired, mainly because family units tend not to communicate with one another even though they are serviced by a family office. The first generation still has a low risk tolerance and a wealth preservation strategy. The second generation has a risk-taking mentality and has adopted an aggressive risk tolerance and an aggressive growth asset allocation strategy. The third generation is actually very conservative and has adopted a modest risk profile and a conservative asset allocation strategy. The fourth generation has an aggressive growth strategy. Table 20.7 summarizes Family Group 3.

As can be seen in these case studies, a myriad of multigenerational asset allocation strategies can be used. Numerous factors come into play before a firm strategy can be adopted. UAC advisers need to be flexible and open-minded when working with families on this issue. It may take many

TABLE 20.7 Asset Allocation Strategy of Family Group 3

Generation	Risk Tolerance	Asset Allocation Strategy
G-1	Low	Wealth preservation
G-2	Very high	Aggressive growth
G-3	Moderate	Conservative
G-4	Very high	Aggressive growth

iterations of work before a strategy is decided upon. The family needs to be very comfortable with the strategy or else problems can arise later in the relationship with the client. Note that these case studies can be blended or various parts can be used together to create a customized strategy for a client.

ASSET ALLOCATION TARGETING

There is an important consideration that UAC advisers need to be aware of when selecting and implementing a multigenerational asset allocation. In my experience, unless there is a single account of cash to begin with (meaning that embedded capital gains taxes need not be considered and there are no restrictions on access to one's own capital [i.e., lock-ups]) and the family makes a decision to invest in long-dated assets such as private equity or private real assets, *it will take many years to reach a target asset allocation.* This is especially true for families with concentrated equity positions that need to be worked down over many years. Therefore, both families and advisers alike need to remember that the selection of an asset allocation need not be a painstaking process of fine-tuning the allocation over many months or even years to arrive at a starting asset allocation decision. The initial asset allocation is going to be a target anyway and will likely change over the course of time well before it is implemented. UAC advisers need to point this out to their clients so as not to waste time during the initial process of deciding upon an initial asset allocation strategy.

THE BEHAVIORAL FINANCE APPROACH
TO ASSET ALLOCATION

Many UA families are in the business of wealth preservation, not wealth accumulation. The leaders of these families' investment functions, however, are accustomed to taking risk and often choose asset allocations that are geared more toward wealth accumulation, taking on more risk than is needed. Taking a behavioral finance or goals-based approach to asset allocation often helps to keep financial goals in mind when creating a portfolio. I have found the following approach, outlined in Figure 20.3, and based on clients' tendency to put money in separate mental accounts, to be of tremendous value in certain cases.

What UAC advisers should aspire to do is get their clients focused on their needs and obligations, and make sure that they have enough of their portfolio carved out in capital preservation assets to meet those needs and obligations. Next, if desired, more risk can be taken to attain one's priorities

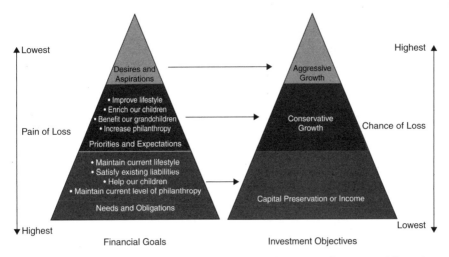

FIGURE 20.3 Behavioral Finance or "Goals-Based" Approach to Asset Allocation
Source: UBS.

and expectations, and even more risk to meet one's desires and aspirations. At the end of the day, advisers will end up with a normal-looking, diversified portfolio using this methodology. The components of the portfolio are individually justified, however, on the basis of how much risk one is willing to take to fulfill those categories beyond needs and obligations. Risk is better appreciated and applied to the portfolio under this methodology and advisers will be better able to handle disruptions in the advisory process brought on by market volatility or dislocations.

CONCLUSION

Creating an asset allocation for a multigenerational family is much more art than it is science. As I demonstrated in this chapter, many factors need to be assessed when deciding which allocation strategy is best. Of utmost importance is communication with family members. They will give UAC advisers clues as to what approach they will be most comfortable with. If for any reason your approach fails, don't be afraid to reassess the situation and restructure your allocation recommendation. The best solution will be the one that simultaneously satisfies the psychological needs of the client and achieves the financial goals established by the family.

Notes

Chapter 1: Who Are the Ultra-Affluent?

1. *Global Private Banking/Wealth Management Survey 2007*, Pricewaterhouse Coopers, January 2008, 7.
2. Capgemini/Merrill Lynch, *World Wealth Report 2007*, Annual Report, 2007, 6.
3. The World Bank, *Spain Data Profile*, 2007, http://devdata.worldbank.org/external/CPProfile.asp?PTYPE=CP&CCODE=ESP.
4. Jeremy Siegel, "The Short- and Long-Term Outlook for Stocks" (Philadelphia: University of Pennsylvania *Knowledge@Wharton*, June 2, 2004).
5. Capgemini/Merrill Lynch, *World Wealth Report 2007*, 6.
6. MSCI Barra, *MSCI BRIC Index*, January 2007, https://www.menafn.com/updates/research_center/Global/Equity_val/MSCIJan07.pdf.
7. Capgemini/Merrill Lynch, *World Wealth Report 2007*, 3.
8. Chinability, *China's Gross Domestic Product*, 2006; http://www.chinability.com/GDP.htm.
9. Capgemini/Merrill Lynch, *World Wealth Report 2007*, 8.
10. Capgemini/Merrill Lynch, *World Wealth Report 2007*, 9.
11. Capgemini/Merrill Lynch, *World Wealth Report 2007*, 9.
12. Capgemini/Merrill Lynch, *World Wealth Report 2007*, 8.
13. Capgemini/Merrill Lynch, *World Wealth Report 2007*, 8–9.
14. Capgemini/Merrill Lynch, *World Wealth Report 2007*, 9.
15. "Ownership Succession Planning for Family Businesses," http://www.familybusinessinstitute.com/succession-planning/ownership-succession-planning-for-family-busin-4.html.
16. Roger Winsby, "Sell-Side Trends: The Business Transition Tidal Wave," *Association for Corporate Growth Hub News*, August 27, 2003, 8; http://www.imakenews.com/acgboston/e_article000178731.cfm.
17. Laird Norton Tyee, *Family to Family: Laird Norton Tyee Family Business Survey 2007*, 2007, 12.
18. *American Family Business Survey 2007*, Mass Mutual, FFI, and Kennesaw State University; http://www.ffi.org/.
19. Rob Slee, "Sell-Out While You Can," *Baby Boomer Business Blog*, 2007, http://babyboomerbusinessblog.blogspot.com/2007/09/sell-you-company-now-to-get-maximum.html.
20. Winsby, "Sell-Side Trends," http://www.imakenews.com/acgboston/e_article000178731.cfm.

21. Austin Family Business Program reports from 1997 and 1999. http://www.familybusinessonline.org/resources/res_collection.htm.
22. Charles Paikert, "American family offices eye Europe," *Investment News,* 2008, http://www.investmentnews.com/apps/pbcs.dll/article?AID=/20080811/REG/60700370.
23. European Commission, *Transfer of Businesses—Continuity through a New Beginning,* MAP 2002 Project, Final Report, 2003, 33.
24. Philip Yea, "Family Businesses Gain Confidence in Private Equity," *In Touch* (London: 3i International, March 2007), http://www.3i.com/publications andevents/family-businesses-gain-confidence-in-private-equity.html.
25. Erkki Liikanen, *Helping the Transfer of Business* (Luxembourg: Office for Official Publications of the European Communities, 2003), 7.
26. Michel Beyet, "Business Transfer in France," presentation to Chamber of Commerce and Industry Rhone Alpes, Stuttgart, Germany, October 25, 2006, 3.
27. European Commission, *Transfer of Businesses,* 41.
28. ibid.
29. "Family business growing steady and strong but face future risks," MassMutual Financial Group press release, 2007; http://www.massmutual.com/mmfg/about/pr_2007/11_1_2007.html.
30. Yea, "Family Businesses Gain Confidence in Private Equity."

Chapter 2: Understanding the Mindset of the Ultra-Affluent Client

1. "Bridging the Trust Divide: The Financial Advisor-Client Relationship," report by Knowledge@Wharton and State Street Global Advisors, 2006; http://knowledge.wharton.upenn.edu/papers/download/ssga_advisor_trust_Report.pdf.
2. *Jerry Maguire,* directed by Cameron Crowe (Sony Pictures, 1996).
3. www.finra.org/Industry/Regulation/Guidance/InterpretiveLetters/ConductRules/index.htm.
4. Charlotte B. Beyer, "Understanding Private Client Characteristics," Investment Counsel for Private Clients, AIMR (now CFA Institute) conference proceedings, 1992.

Chapter 3: Wealth Attitudes, Aspirations, and Investor Behavior of Ultra-Affluent Clients

1. Lisa Gray (managing member, graymatter Strategies, LLC), in discussion with the author, January 2009.
2. William Strauss and Neil Howe, *The Fourth Turning: An American Prophecy* (Broadway Press, New York: 1998); James E. Hughes, Jr., *Family: A Compact Among Generations* (Bloomberg Press, New York: 2008).
3. Karl Mannheim, "The Problem of Generations," *Psychoanalytic Review* 57 (1970): 378–404, 389.

4. Michael Pompian, *Behavioral Finance and Wealth Management* (Hoboken, NJ: John Wiley & Sons, Inc., 2006).
5. Terrance Odean and Brad Barber, "Boys will be Boys: Gender, Overconfidence, and Common Stock Investment," *Quarterly Journal of Economics,* February 2001, vol. 116, no. 1, 261–292.
6. Brad Barber and Terrance Odean, "Trading is Hazardous to Your Wealth," *Journal of Finance,* April 2000, vol. LV, no. 2.
7. Terrance Odean, "Volume, Volatility, Price, and Profit When All Traders Are Above Average," *Journal of Finance,* vol. LIII, 1998, 1887–1934.

Chapter 4: Noninvestment Best Practices

1. Roy Williams and Vic Pressier, *Philanthropy, Heirs and Values* (Bandon, Ore.: Robert D. Reed Publishers, 2005).
2. http://www.tribuneindia.com/2002/20021114/edit.htm#6.
3. Stephane Fitch, "Pritzker v. Pritzker," *Forbes Magazine* online, November 24, 2003.
4. Pramodita Sharma, James J. Chrisman, and Jess H. Chua, "Strategic Management of the Family Business: Past Research and Future Challenges," *Family Business Review,* vol. 10, issue 1, 1–35. (Boston: Family Firm Institute, Inc., 1997).
5. Peter Bernstein, *Against the Gods: The Remarkable Story of Risk,* (New York: John Wiley & Sons, Inc., 1998), 170.
6. James Hughes Jr., *Family: The Compact Among Generations,* (New York: Bloomberg, 2007), 198–200.
7. http://www.nationalcenter.org/MayflowerCompact.html.
8. Patricia Angus, *Family Governance: A Primer for Philanthropic Families* (Washington, D.C.: National Center for Family Philanthropy, 2004), 3.
9. Stephen Covey, *The 7 Habits of Highly Effective Families* (New York: St. Martin's Press, 1997), 120–126.
10. Covey, 15–16.
11. Covey, 16.
12. Covey, 76.

Chapter 5: Practices of the Best Investment Organizations

1. Jay A. Yoder, *Endowment Management: A Practical Guide* (Washington, D.C.: Association of Governing Boards of Colleges and Universities, 1993), 67.
2. Foundation and Endowment Money Management, http://www.foundation endowment.com/LandingPage.aspx.
3. Russell Olson, *The Independent Fiduciary: Investing for Pension Funds and Endowment Funds* (New York: John Wiley & Sons, Inc., 1999), 101–110.
4. Gary P. Brinson, L. Randolph Hood, and Gilbert L. Beebower, "Determinants of Portfolio Performance," *Financial Analysts Journal,* July-August 1986, vol. 42, no. 4, 39–44.

Chapter 6: Asset Allocation Considerations for Ultra-Affluent Clients and Family Offices

1. Gary P. Brinson, L. Randolph Hood, and Gilbert L. Beebower, "Determinants of Portfolio Performance," *Financial Analysts Journal,* July-August 1986, vol. 42, no. 4, 39–44.
2. ibid.
3. ibid.
4. Roger D. Ibbotson and Paul D. Kaplan, "Does Asset Allocation Policy Explain 40, 90, or 100 Percent of Performance," *Financial Analysts Journal,* January-February 2000, vol. 56., no. 1, 26–33.

Chapter 7: Domestic and International Equity

1. Jeremy J. Siegel, *Stocks for the Long Run: The Definitive Guide to Financial Market Returns and Long-Term Investment Strategies,* 3rd ed. (New York: McGraw-Hill, 2002).
2. ibid.
3. Roger D. Ibbotson and William Goetzman, "History and the Equity Risk Premium," working paper, Yale International Center for Finance, 2005, no. 05–04, 1–15.
4. Fahimeh Rezayat, and Burhan F. Yavas, "International Portfolio Diversification: A Study of Linkages among the U.S., European and Japanese Equity Markets," *Journal of Multinational Financial Management,* 2006, vol. 16, no. 4, 440–458.
5. Rex Sinquefield, "Asset Management: Active versus Passive Management," opening statement at the Schwab Institutional Conference, San Francisco, October 12, 1995.
6. http://www.gmo.com/America/About/InvestorInfo.htm.
7. http://www.leggmason.com/individualinvestors/documents/product_fact_card/LMVT-Fact_Card.pdf
8. Thomas Kostigen, "Index Bull, Active Bear," *Marketwatch,* October 3, 2006.
9. "The Impact of Exchange Traded Products on the Financial Advisory Industry," joint study by State Street Global Advisors and Knowledge@Wharton, 2008.

Chapter 8: Domestic and International Bonds

1. Yale Endowment Report, 2007, 7, www.yale.edu.
2. Robert Rubin and Jacob Weisberg, *In an Uncertain World* (New York: Random House, 2003), 124.
3. http://www.pimco.com/LeftNav/Bond+Basics/2007/EM+Basics+8-07.htm.
4. http://www.pimco.com/LeftNav/Bond+Basics/2007/EM+Basics+8-07.htm.
5. http://www.pimco.com/LeftNav/Product+Focus/2008/Product+Focus+Unconstrained+Bond+Strategy+August+2008.htm.
6. http://www.surs.com/pdfs/SMP/funds/PIMCO-ToReFu.pdf.

7. http://quicktake.morningstar.com/FundNet/Fees.aspx?Country=USA&Symbol =PTTRX; https://institutional.vanguard.com/VGApp/iip/site/institutional/home.
8. ibid.

Chapter 9: Private Equity

1. Robert A. Samuelson, "The Private Equity Boom," *Washington Post,* March 15, 2007, A19.
2. http://www.usatoday.com/money/markets/2007-06-22-blackstone-cover-usat_ N.htm.
3. http://money.cnn.com/magazines/fortune/fortune_archive/1986/07/21/67874/ index.htm.
4. http://www.fundinguniverse.com/company-histories/DIGITAL-EQUIPMENT-CORPORATION-Company-History.html.
5. Joseph W. Bartlett, "What Is Venture Capital?," http://vcexperts.com/vce/ library/encyclopedia/documents_view.asp?document_id=15.
6. Brian G. Cartwright, general counsel for the U.S. Securities and Exchange Commission, "The Future of Securities Regulation," speech delivered at the University of Pennsylvania Law School Institute for Law and Economics, Philadelphia, Penn., October 24, 2007.

Chapter 10: Hedge Funds

1. http://www.merriam-webster.com/dictionary/hedge%20fund.
2. http://www.rkco.com/pdflib/on_the_rise_9-30-08.pdf.
3. Family Office Exchange 2008 Fall Forum Presentation Book
4. "Hedge-fund managers, lords of lucre," *The Sunday Times,* Times online, http:// business.timesonline.co.uk/tol/business/movers_and_shakers/article3196956.ece, London, January 20, 2008.
5. John Russell, "Alfred W. Jones, 88, Sociologist and Investment Fund Innovator," *New York Times,* June 3, 1989, Section 1, 11.
6. "The Jones Nobody Keeps Up With," *Fortune Magazine,* April 1966, 237–248.
7. http://www.gabelli.com/news/articles/mario-hedge_102500.html.
8. ibid.
9. "Dow Jones biggest percentage declines," South Florida *Sun-Sentinel,* September 30, 2008, 11; Jennifer Karchmer, *CNN Money,* "Tiger Management closes," March 30, 2000.
10. Alan Greenspan, "Risk Transfer and Financial Stability," remarks delivered at the Federal Reserve Bank of Chicago's Forty-first Annual Conference on Bank Structure, Chicago, Ill. (via satellite) May 5, 2005, http://www. federalreserve.gov/Boarddocs/Speeches/2005/20050505/default.htm.
11. Barry Eichengreen, Donald Mathieson, et al., "Hedge Funds and Financial Market Dynamics," Occasional Paper no. 166, (Washington, D.C.: International Monetary Fund, May 15, 1998); Gordon De Brouwer, *Hedge Funds in Emerging Markets* (Cambridge: Cambridge University Press, 2001).

12. Matthew Goldstein, "Bear Stearns Big Bailout," *Business Week,* March 14, 2008.
13. http://www.investmentnews.com/apps/pbcs.dll/article?AID=/20081121/REG/811219991/1088.
14. Kate Walsh, "Hedge Funds: Sorry Seems to be ...," *Times of London,* November 2, 2008.
15. Yale Endowment Report, 2007; www.yale.edu.
16. *Protecting Investors: A Half Century of Investment Company Regulation,* (Washington, D.C.: United States Securities and Exchange Commission, Division of Investment Management, May 1992).
17. ibid, xvii.
18. http://www.sec.gov/rules/final/ia-2333.htm.
19. http://www.sec.gov/about/laws/ica40.pdf.
20. http://www.cftc.gov/anr/anrabout00.htm.
21. http://www.sec.gov/about/laws/ica40.pdf.
22. Hedge Fund Research, Inc. "Hedge Fund Strategy Classification," January 2008; https://www.hedgefundresearch.com/pdf/new_strategy_classifications.pdf; http://www.hedgefundresearch.com/index.php?fuse=indices-str.

Chapter 11: Real Assets

1. H. Russell Fogler, Michael R. Granito, and Laurence R. Smith, "A theoretical analysis of real estate returns," *Journal of Finance,* 1985, vol. 40, no. 3, 711–719.
2. David Hartzell, John S. Hekman, and Mike E. Miles, "Real Estate Returns and Inflation," *AREUEA Journal,* 1987, vol. 15, no. 1, 617–637.
3. Jack H. Rubens, Michael T. Bond, and James R. Webb, "The Inflation-Hedging Effectiveness of Real Estate," *Journal of Real Estate Research,* 1989, vol. 4, no. 2, 45–56.
4. http://www.reit.com/AllAboutREITs/REITsbyTickerSymbol/tabid/146/Default.aspx. http://www.reit.com/IndustryDataPerformance/USREITIndustryFactSheet/tabid/84/Default.aspx.
5. Barclay's Capital, *The Commodity Refiner,* Summer 2008, 11–12.
6. Changyou Sun and Daowei Zhang, "Assessing the Financial Performance of Forestry-Related Investment Vehicles: Capital Asset Pricing Model vs. Arbitrage Pricing Theory," *American Journal of Agricultural Economics,* August 2001, 617–628.
7. John Hancock Timber Resource Group, "Timberland as a Portfolio Diversifier," Research Notes, 2003.
8. *2008 International Timberlands Ownership and Investment Review,* DANA Limited, www.dana.co.nz/.
9. Jacek Siry and Frederick Cubbage, "World forests: forest area, ownership, and management," in *Forests in a Market Economy,* Erin Sills and Karen Lee Abt, eds. (Norwell, Mass.: Kluwer Academic Publishers, 2003), 9–21.

10. *2008 International Timberlands Ownership and Investment Review,* Dana Limited, www.dana.co.nz/.
11. National Council of Real Estate Investment Fiduciaries, "Timberland Index: Total returns 1987–2008," http://www.ncreif.com/indices/timberland. phtml?type=total.

Chapter 12: Selecting an Adviser

1. "Bridging the Trust Divide: The Financial Advisor-Client Relationship," http://knowledge.wharton.upenn.edu/special_section.cfm?specialID=70.
2. ibid.
3. ibid.
4. ibid.
5. ibid.

Chapter 13: Selecting a Custodian and Investment Vehicle Structure

1. http://www.globalinvestormagazine.com/default.asp?Page=1&hID=141.
2. ibid.

Chapter 14: Considerations for Creating a Family Office

1. Yap Ming Hui, "Business: A family office to manage wealth," *The New Straits Times* online, June 1, 2008, http://www.nst.com.my/Current_News/NST/Sunday/Focus/2253686/Article/index_html.
2. Stephen Martiros and Todd Millay, "A Framework for Understanding Family Office Trends" (Boston: CCC Alliance, 2006).
3. The Merrill Lynch/Campden Research European Single Family Office Survey, 2008.
4. Russ Prince and Hannah Grove, *Inside the Family Office: Managing the Fortunes of the Exceptionally Wealthy* (Overland Park, KS: Wealth Management Press, 2004), 6.
5. Martiros and Millay.
6. The Merrill Lynch/Campden Research European Single Family Office Survey, 2008.
7. ibid.

Chapter 15: Wealth Transfer Planning

1. http://www.irs.gov/businesses/small/article/0,,id=108139,00.html.
2. http://bankofamerica.mediaroom.com/index.php?s=press_releases&item=8187.

3. http://www.hklaw.com/content/whitepapers/JEH-ABA_Sept_2007_Split_Dollar_Outline.pdf.
4. http://foundationcenter.org/getstarted/faqs/html/pfandpc.html.

Chapter 16: Concentrated Equity Risk Management

1. Brendan I. Koerner, "Fat Pipe Dream: Softbank founder Masayoshi Son lost $75 billion in the dotcom crash," *Wired*, 2003, vol. 11, part 8, 84–87.
2. "Jimmy Cayne's Sudden Wealth Loss," *Wall Street Journal*, March 28, 2008.
3. http://www.marketwatch.com/news/story/cayne-sells-over-61-million/story.aspx?guid=%7B4FA56775-C37A-471C-BD36-D32F42AF99CC%7D.
4. "Jimmy Cayne's Sudden Wealth Loss," *Wall Street Journal*.
5. http://www.nytimes.com/2004/10/08/business/08martha.html; http://www.answers.com/topic/martha-stewart.
6. Benjamin Graham, *The Intelligent Investor* (New York: HarperBusiness), 2005.
7. John Y. Campbell, Martin Lettau, Burton G. Malkiel, and Yexiao Xu, "Have Individual Stocks Become More Volatile? An Empirical Exploration of Idiosyncratic Risk," *Journal of Finance*, 2001, vol. 56, no. 1, 43.

Chapter 17: Family Governance

1. James E. Hughes Jr., *Family Wealth—Keeping It in the Family: How Family Members and Their Advisers Preserve Human, Intellectual, and Financial Assets for Generations* (New York: Bloomberg Press, 2004).
2. Gregory T. Rogers with Kelly Costigan, *Spread The Wealth—Seven Realities for Affluent Family Leadership* (Greenwich, Conn.: RayLign Advisory LLC, October 2007).
3. Patricia Angus, *Family Governance: A Primer for Philanthropic Families* (Washington, D.C.: National Center for Family Philanthropy, 2004).
4. Peter M. Senge, Art Kleiner, Charlotte Roberts, Rick Ross, and Bryan Smith, *The Fifth Discipline Fieldbook* (Garden City, N.Y.: Doubleday, 1994).
5. Yogi Berra and Dave Kaplan, *When You Come to a Fork in the Road, Take It!: Inspiration and Wisdom from One of Baseball's Greatest Heroes* (New York: Hyperion, 2001).

Chapter 18: Risk Management and Asset Protection

1. Michael Gadd, "Owners Shirk Estate Planning", Inc.com, June 12, 2008, http://www.inc.com/news/articles/2008/06/estate.html, 1.
2. Mark Larsen, "Fiduciary Liability Basics" expert commentary, International Risk Management Institute, Inc. online, July 2001.

Chapter 19: Philanthropy

1. "National Philanthropic Trust Giving & Volunteering in the United States 2001, Independent Sector," http://www.nptrust.org/philanthropy/philanthropy_stats.asp.
2. Clare Gascoigne, "Family giving" *Financial Times* online, July 8, 2007, http://www.ft.com/cms/s/2/ae4ee5be-2d49-11dc-939b-0000779fd2ac.html.
3. "Articulating the Foundation's Mission," excerpted from the Family Foundation Library Series Council on Foundations, 2008, http://www.cof.org/Council/content.cfm?ItemNumber=927.
4. "Philanthropy Statistics," National Philanthropic Trust, http://www.nptrust.org/.
5. "The Endowment Tax," *Worth*, August/September 2008, 34.
6. *USA Today* editorial, May 28, 2008; http://www.robertsonvprinceton.org/about.php.
7. ibid.
8. "Settlement retains Princeton's control, use of Robertson funds," December 10, 2008, http://www.princeton.edu/robertson/statements/viewstory.xml?storypath=/main/news/archive/S22/81/66C43/index.xml.

Chapter 20: Multigenerational Asset Allocation Strategies

1. Rafael Amit, Heinrich Liechtenstein, M. Julia Prats, Todd Millay, and Laird Pendleton, "Single Family Offices: Private Wealth Management in the Family Context," Wharton Global Family Alliance 2008, http://wgfa.wharton.upenn.edu/WhartonGFA_SFO_Study.pdf.

Index

A

Advisory firm
 open *vs.* closed platform firms,
  229
 potential selection questions,
  234–237
 selection criteria for, 228–234
*Against the Gods: The Remarkable
 Story of Risk*, 65
Alternative investments, 23, 86
Angus, Patricia. *See* National
  Center for Family
  Philanthropy
Asset allocation
 considerations for individuals,
  100
 definition of, 96
 importance of, 99
 investment policy and, 84
 legal environment, 109–110
 liquidity, 103–105
 process, 97
 and taxes, 106–109
Asset protection, *See* risk
  management; legal asset
  protection
Attitudes, client, 43–47

B

Behavioral finance, 47
 approach to asset allocation
  374–375
 and investor biases, 48–60

Beyer, Charlotte. *See* Institute for
  Private Investors
Bias
 ambiguity aversion, 54
 anchoring, 51
 availability, 55
 cognitive dissonance, 54
 confirmation, 57
 conservatism, 55
 endowment bias, 49
 framing, 53
 hindsight, 53
 illusion of control, 58
 loss aversion, 49
 mental accounting, 51
 optimism, 59
 overconfidence, 57
 recency, 52
 regret aversion, 50
 representativeness, 56
 self-attribution (self-serving), 56
 self-control, 59
 status quo, 50
Blackstone group, 160
Bonds
 asset classes, 141–142
  corporate bonds, 145
  foreign bonds, 146–148
  government bonds, 143
  municipal bonds, 141–142
  treasuries, 144
 credit risks, 151
 interest rate risk, 150–151

Bonds (*Continued*)
  interest rates, 139
  introduction to, 137–141
  quality and credit ratings, 138
  redemption, 140
  tax treatment of, 142
  types of, 145
Boston College Center on Wealth
    and Philanthropy, 345
BRIC (Brazil, Russia, India, China)
  growth in, 12
Buyouts 166

C

Campden Research and Merrill
    Lynch. *See* Merrill Lynch
Capgemini/Merrill Lynch survey,
    10, 12, 13
Cayne, James 299
Charitable gift planning, 291
Client segmentation, 231–234
College donations, 355–358
Commodities. *See* natural resources
Commodity Exchange Act of 1974,
    191
Competence, 27
Complexities of managing wealth, 4
Compliance
  rule 2310 NASD, 30
Comprehensiveness of family
    services, 29
Concentrated equity position, 300
  and exchange funds, 314
  and hedging, 308–312
  minimization strategies 304–308
Consultant/adviser questionnaire,
    33–37
Contrarian investment strategies,
    90
Covered call writing, 306–307
Covey, Stephen, 69

Custodial services, description of,
    239–249
  criteria for selection, 249–250
  customization, 25–26
  formation decisions, 255–257
  investment vehicle structure
    (partnerships), 251–257

D

Diversification, need for. *See*
    concentrated equity position

E

Endowment governance, 78
Endowment management, 79, 80
Endowment model of investing, 75
Energy. *See* natural resources
Engelhorn, Philip, 363–364
Equities
  active *vs.* passive management,
    122–126
  five step strategy and selection
    process, 115
  investment vehicles, 128
  manager selection, 126–128
  performance analysis, 129–133
ERISA Act, 336
Estate planning overview, 280–282

F

Family aspirations, 40–42
Family firm institute, 15
Family governance, 340
  generational division, 318
  implementation of, 319
  phases of development of , 70
  policies and practices, 69–70
  principles, 321
  system of, 67–69

three elements of, 69–70
triangle of components, 320
Family limited partnerships,
    294–295
Family office
  administrative considerations,
    268–269
  challenges of, 265–267, 272
  costs and pricing, 269–271
  governance structure of,
    262–264
  private trust company and,
    274–277
  reasons for, 264–265
  services provided by, 267–274
  types of, 261–262
Family Office Exchange, 185, 231
Fiduciary duty, advisory challenges
    of, 25
Fiduciary liability insurance 336
Foundations,
  family foundations, 293
  private types of ,350–351
  restrictions on, 351–353
Fund of funds, 173

G

Gates, Bill, 63
Generational wealth management
  guide for fostering global family
    wealth, 43
Gifts
  annual exclusion, 283
  lifetime gift exclusion, 284
Global Investor magazine, 240
Goldberg, Alison, 365–366
Goldhirsh, Ben, 362–363
Governance. *See* family
    governance
Grantor retained trusts (GRTs)
    285–289

Gray, Lisa, 43–44, 339
Graymatter Strategies. *See* Gray,
    Lisa

H

Harvard University, 75, 92
Hedge funds
  characteristics of, 180–185
  comparison to mutual funds,
    181–183
  history, 187–189
  legal environment, 189–199
  manager selection 202
  Rothstein Kass survey of UAC
    Investors, 185–187
  strategies, 191–201
    equity hedge, 192–195
    event driven, 195197
    macro, 197–199
    relative value, 199–201
High net worth population and
    trends
  Europe, 11, 12
  Latin America, 12
  Middle East, 12
  U.S.A., 10
Hughes, James E., 66, 317

I

Inflation protection, 92
Institute for Private Investors,
    32–33
Insurance and indemnification,
    333–337
Intergenerational wealth
  Hughes Mean Reversion
    Concept, 66
Intermediate wealth, definition
    of, 9

Investment committee, 77
  establishing investment policies,
    77–78
  hiring staff, 79
  responsibilities of, 85–87
Investment Company Act of 1940,
    190
Investment policy statements, 82
Investor biases, 48–60

K

Kreiling, Kim 361–362

L

Legal asset protection planning,
    341
  domestic and foreign trusts,
    343–344
Life insurance planning,
    289–290
Lorenz, Katherine, 359–360

M

Madoff scandal, 225
Marston, Richard, 227
Martiros, Stephen, 260–261
Merrill Lynch-Campden survey of
    family offices, 260, 266,
    269
Mezzanine financing. *See* private
    equity
Middle East, 12
Milken, Michael, 167
Millay, Todd, 260–261
Mission of family, 324–326
Mission related investing, 354
Mission statement, 348–349
Monetization against hedged
    positions, 311–313

Multigenerational wealth
  asset allocation strategies for,
    367–372
  sustaining, 63
Musser, Warren 299

N

National Center for Family
    Philanthropy, 67–68, 70–71
Natural resources investing
  commodities, 213
  energy, 211
  how to invest, 207–210
  portfolio benefits of, 204
  timber, 216–221
  ways to invest, 214–216
Number of UACs, 10–11

O

Olson, Russell, 81

P

Partnerships. *See* custodial services
Permissible investments, 85
Philanthropic investing, 352–354
Philanthropy, Heirs and Values,
    61–62
Philanthropy, 345–353
  framework, 347
  questions for strategy
    implementation, 348–349
  strategy development, 347
  value of, 345–347
  venture philanthropy techniques,
    345
PricewaterhouseCoopers (PWC)
  categorization of affluent
    investors, 5
Private placement memorandum,
    164

Private trust company
  considerations for establishing,
    274–276
Portfolio monitoring. *See* portfolio
  oversight
Portfolio oversight, 88–90
Private annuities, 286
Pritzker *vs.* Pritzker, 65
Private equity
  capital flows, 164
  creating a customized program,
    172–173
  distressed investing, 171
  due diligence, 178
  fees, 165
  manager selection, 176
  mezzanine financing, 167– 170
  program related investing,
    354–355
  types of, 166–170
    buyouts (LBOs), 166
    venture capital, 169–170
Private trust company.*See* family
  office

R

Real assets. *See* natural resources
Real estate investment strategies,
    208–210
Relationship building, 20–22,
    29–33
Relationship management, 21–22
Risk management
  family office, 332–333
  individual family member, 337
Robertson *vs.* Princeton University,
    356–358
Rubin, Daniel, 341–342
Russia
  market capitalization, 12
  UAC population, 12

S

Securities Act of 1933, 1934,
    189–190
Sharpe ratio, 153–157
Siegel, Jeremy, 11, 112
Socially responsible investing,
    353
*Splendid Legacy: The Guide to
  Creating Your Family
  Foundation*, 69
Standards of performance, 86
Succession planning, Europe, 17
Succession plans, trends in. *See*
  business transition
Sustaining wealth, 64
Synergos' Global Philanthropists
  Circle, 358– 360

T

Taxes, 105–109
Transition, business
  in Europe, 16–17
  in U.S.A., 14–15
  trends in, 18
Transition, estate 62
Transparency, importance of,
    230
Trustee liability insurance, 335
Trust, importance of, 226–228
Trusts, domestic and foreign. *See*
  legal asset protection
  planning

U

Ultra-affluent clients,
    needs of, 7–9
  PricewaterhouseCoopers
    definition of, 5
  service model, 9–10

V

Valued qualities in advisers,
    23–29
Values of family, 321–323
Vanderbilt family, 260

W

Wealth
    attitudes, 42
    detrimental effects of, 63
    transfer planning. *See estate
        planning*
Wesray Capital, 166

Wharton Global Family Alliance,
    368
Wharton School and State Street
    Survey, 23, 226
Winsor, Rebecca, 364–365

Y

Yale University
    endowment management , 92,
        135, 189

Z

Zero premium collar, 309